Lamb

What you need to know
about food & cooking for
health

WHAT YOU NEED TO KNOW ABOUT FOOD & COOKING FOR HEALTH

Also by Lawrence E. Lamb, M.D.

YOUR HEART AND HOW TO LIVE WITH IT

WHAT YOU NEED TO KNOW ABOUT FOOD & COOKING FOR HEALTH

Lawrence E. Lamb, M.D.

THE VIKING PRESS
New York

Viking Compass Edition issued in 1976 by The Viking Press, Inc.
625 Madison Avenue, New York, N.Y. 10022
Distributed in Canada by
The Macmillan Company of Canada Limited
LIBRARY OF CONGRESS CATALOGING IN PUBLICATION DATA
Lamb, Lawrence E.
What you need to know about food & cooking for health.
(A Viking compass book; C614)
1. Cookery. 2. Nutrition. I. Title.
TX715.L215 1976 641.1 75-42027
ISBN 0-670-00614-9
Printed in U.S.A.

Foreword

Food has always been a necessary preoccupation of man. Centuries ago he depended upon fruits, berries, roots, wild grains, wild animals, and fish for sustenance. Like the animals of the forest, man was part of the balance of nature. As we have learned to control and modify nature, we have managed also to control and modify our sources of food. But this control has not always been to our benefit, and many authorities think that the vast array of diseases now troubling us are related to our living patterns, such problems as heart attacks, strokes, cancer, and that old bugaboo of "civilized man," constipation.

The body changes very slowly, too slowly to keep pace with the sweeping and sudden changes in our environment and food supply made possible by modern technology. There is abundant evidence that we could enjoy better health if we would eat more of nature's unadulterated foods. After a quarter century of research concerning the influence of the diet in causing heart and vascular disease, for example, the real thrust of the dietary recommendations is to return to more natural ways of eating.

Following World War II it was assumed that cholesterol was the villain in heart disease and the low-cholesterol diet was born. Continued studies proved that the trouble was more than just cholesterol. Too much fat in a diet (even a diet low in cholesterol) causes the body to produce excess amounts of cholesterol, resulting in fatty deposits in the arteries—hence the low-fat diet. But this didn't solve the problem either. The decreased cholesterol levels in individuals on diets devoid of fat were often temporary. Some experiments showed clearly that the addition of polyunsaturated fats to the diet of some people lowered the cholesterol levels to the levels observed in people entirely free of heart and vascular disease. The polyunsaturated fats used were from fish, vegetable, and cereal products such as corn oil. Some investigators reported that in certain cases the cholesterol level even decreased as much as fifty per cent after fish was eaten.

But simply adding polyunsaturated fat in unlimited quantities to the diet also failed to produce the desired biochemical changes in the bodies of many people. It became apparent that the total fat must be limited to practical levels and that part of the fat should be from foods rich in polyunsaturates. A greater appreciation of the necessity to prevent obesity by controlling the total caloric intake has supplanted older concepts. The concept most widely accepted today, which is based on world-wide studies, is that the number of calories eaten should be limited sufficiently to prevent obesity and that the total fat intake should provide less than thirty-five per cent of all the calories eaten. Of these fat calories less than one third should be saturated fat, while one third should be polyunsaturated fat. In addition, the cholesterol intake should be limited to less than three hundred milligrams a day.*

Many factors besides diet can be beneficial to health, of course—such factors as exercise, the cessation of unhealthy habits like smoking, hormones and other medicines. But the simple truth is that within the framework of modern society one of the best and most effective ways to improve health is to learn to eat properly. That is what this book is all about.

In order to eat properly you will need to know some basic facts about food, which are not always easy to obtain. In writing this book I learned a great deal, even though I have been concerned about diet and heart disease for over twenty years. It *does* make a difference which piece of chicken you eat. Whether or not you eat the skin is important. Many so-called low-fat foods aren't low in fat at all. About one third of the calories in "low-fat" milk is from fat. Over 20 per cent of the calories in black raspberries is from fat. Some so-called low-fat foods are simply low-calorie foods, and a large proportion of their calories often come from fat.

There is an abundance of misleading information available. Often a food is called "low-fat" because a small portion of its total weight is from fat. A good example is lean round steak, in which only about 5 per cent of the weight is fat. But most of the weight is water and over 30 per cent of the calories in the meat is from fat. This sounds a great deal different from the misleading statement that only 5 per cent of the meat is fat.

Most available books on food confuse the consumer by providing food values in grams. What you need to know is just how many *calories* of fat, carbohydrate, and protein are in your food. How can you easily

*These recommendations were made in Dec. 1970 by the Inter-Society Commission for Heart Disease, based on a special study sponsored by the United States Government in conjunction with the American Heart Association.

restrict the number of calories of fat in your diet to 35 per cent if you can't find out how many calories of fat your food contains? In an effort to simplify this problem I have in this book converted to calories all the values usually expressed in grams. You need not be confused by the water content of food, the gram values, or other complexities. You can simply look in the tables and find out how many calories in a given food are from fat and from what kind of fat. This will make it possible for you to follow the recommendations that have been made by scientists who have investigated the effects of food on health.

Following more natural food habits doesn't mean you have to stop eating any specific food. You need only to learn how to prepare foods to limit the excess use of fat and how to balance fat foods with other foods containing other essential food elements.

To enable you to use a variety of different foods without giving up your favorites, a special "point system" has been developed for this book. You can choose the food you like as long as it is "balanced" with other foods. This means you can easily design a balanced diet that suits your taste without eating excess amounts of fat or resorting to fad diets. The special recipes will enable you to use more meat in your diet. By using polyunsaturated fat in baking, desserts, and salads rather than saturated fats, you can enjoy more meat and still have a diet low in saturated fat.

A good word for the beleaguered food industry is in order. In doing my research for this book I was favorably impressed by the desire of many segments of the food industry to provide products that are most conducive to good health. The prevalent idea that the food industry is a subversive organization out to destroy the health of the populace is simply not true. A logical mind soon realizes that the food industry exists to make money, and that in order to do this must provide food products its customers demand. The consumers—you and I—have demanded steaks marbled with fat, the richest ice cream that money can buy, chickens tenderized by lack of exercise, and a myriad of food products now available. The food industry has simply given us what we have demanded. If we demand leaner meats, less saturated fat in bakery products, and similar healthier foods, the food industry can and will be glad to serve our needs.

It is not possible to provide the whole vast array of more natural methods of preparing food in a single volume, but this book does include basic principles and examples to enable anyone to alter his eating habits and food preparations along more healthful lines. It is not intended to provide a method for gourmet cookery—although it is full of delicious dishes which are good for you. Nor is it designed to tell you what you *shouldn't* eat. It has been my intention in this book to offer advice and practical assistance so that you can learn how to eat most of the things you like and at the same time have a healthier, more natural diet than you have now.

A Word about Using This Book

This book has been arranged so that each chapter builds on the information that has preceded it. To illustrate: when you reach the salad chapter you will already have covered the chapters on vegetables, fruits, and salad dressings. The chapters with recipes all follow chapters which provide special instructions applicable to low-fat cooking.

The caloric value of many of the recipes has been specially calculated. In some recipes the food values for one or more ingredients were not available, and these had to be omitted. In other instances when the recipe is a general one the food values are often omitted, as when I do not specify the cut of beef used, or when the recipe consists of a single ingredient, such as a turkey to be roasted. In these instances the values can be obtained directly from the food tables, which start on page 285.

In addition to the total number of calories, we have also given the values for carbohydrates, proteins, and types of fat in terms of calories rather than grams. This will enable you to know how many calories in a given recipe are from fat or other food elements. In each instance the values listed after each recipe are for the entire recipe. The abbreviations used for the recipes are the same as those used for the food-value tables and are as follows:

TC	Total calories for recipe
P	Protein in calories
C	Carbohydrate in calories
F	Fat in calories
S	Saturated fat in calories with per cent of total calories
M	Monounsaturated fat in calories with per cent of total calories
PU	Polyunsaturated fat in calories with per cent of total calories
CHOL	Cholesterol in milligrams

The values for fat are based on the use of corn oil, unless otherwise specified. Food values for the recipes are calculated in the same way as those in the food tables, and this is explained in greater detail on pages 281–284.

The individual food tables provide information on the caloric value of the food elements for each food category; for example, dairy products, cereals and grains, meats, fish, desserts, and others. A master table for menu-planning is also included. A complete explanation of its use in meeting various dietary objectives is given in the final chapter, page 260.

Contents

	Foreword	*v*
	A Word about Using This Book	*ix*
1	*Food Does Make a Difference*	3
2	*Calories Do Count*	10
3	*Ingredients of Food*	17
4	*Hints for Successful Low-Fat Cooking*	35
5	*Cereals and Grains*	42
6	*Dairy Products*	46
7	*Breads, Biscuits, and Pancakes*	55
8	*Gravies, Sauces, and Salad Dressings*	78
9	*Bouillon, Consommé, Chowder, and Soup*	99
10	*Vegetables*	113
11	*Fruits*	126
12	*Salads*	134
13	*Fish and Shellfish*	145
14	*Poultry*	160
15	*Meat*	177
16	*Desserts*	207
17	*Appetizers and Hors d'Oeuvres*	241
18	*Sandwiches*	248
19	*Beverages*	252
20	*Planning Your Diet*	259

TABLES

	Using the Food-Value Tables	281
I	*Water Content and Caloric Value of Different Types of Foods*	285
II	*Calories Used in Walking at Three Miles per Hour*	285
III	*Composition of Sugars, Sirups, Jellies, and Jams*	286
IV	*Composition of Fats and Oils*	287
V	*Cholesterol Content of Edible Foods*	288
VI	*Vitamin A Content of Common Foods*	289
VII	*Calcium Content of Common Foods*	290
VIII	*Spices for All Occasions*	291
IX	*Composition of Miscellaneous Common Ingredients*	293
X	*Composition of Cereal Products*	294
XI	*Composition of Prepared Breakfast Cereals*	296
XII	*Composition of Dairy Products*	297
XIII	*Composition of Bread, Rolls, and Pastas*	299
XIV	*Composition of Commercial Sauces and Salad Dressings*	301
XV	*Composition of Soups*	302
XVI	*Composition of Vegetables*	304
XVII	*Composition of Berries, Fruit, and Melons*	312
XVIII	*Composition of Fish and Shellfish*	319
XIX	*Composition of Poultry*	324
XX	*Composition of Beef*	326
XXI	*Composition of Veal*	330
XXII	*Composition of Pork*	331
XXIII	*Composition of Lamb*	332
XXIV	*Composition of Luncheon Meats and Sausages*	333
XXV	*Composition of Organ Meats*	334
XXVI	*Composition of Desserts*	336

XXVII *Composition of Nut Products* 339
XXVIII *Composition of Beverages* 341
XXIX *Master Food-Exchange List* 342

APPENDIX: *How to Calculate Points* 395
INDEX 403

WHAT YOU NEED TO KNOW ABOUT FOOD & COOKING FOR HEALTH

CHAPTER

I

Food Does Make a Difference

The human body is a wonderful machine and a complex chemical plant, which developed gradually over thousands of years through the process of adaptation. Early man did not know the joys of fat-marbled beef, an infinite variety of cheeses, and a galaxy of desserts. Life was more famine than feast, and obesity, along with many other modern ailments, was quite unknown.

Man's success in controlling his environment, for better or worse, has provided an abundance of new foods. But our body chemistry has not yet developed a capacity to process all of these foods without difficulty. The crux of the problem is that the body changes slowly, while modern technology brings about swift changes.

Man has no ability, by taste or appetite, to select only those specific food elements his body needs. He tends to eat what is put before him, and more often than not this is lacking in the essential nutrients and contains food elements that are actually detrimental to his health.

It is generally recognized that modern civilization has polluted the air, the waterways, and the soil. It is less generally known that it has also adulterated man's natural food. The complex food industry because of consumer demands has taken out essential food nutrients and added a vast array of chemicals to available food. Marketing practices have affected vegetables, meat, and even peanut butter. It is not too surprising that world-wide studies have shown that those people who have eating habits not so far removed from the original scheme of nature are essentially free of the major diseases of the industrialized nations. The most important of these diseases is heart and vascular disease, but such conditions as diabetes, constipation, diarrhea, cancer of the rectum or colon, the various ailments brought about because of obesity, and perhaps even senility are all directly influenced by dietary patterns.

In the United States over half of all deaths from accidents and disease combined are caused by heart and vascular disease. Heart disease is the most common cause of sudden death in young men. Most of these deaths are caused by a deposit of fatty substances in the walls of the arteries to the heart, brain, and kidney (atherosclerosis). This fatty material is a mushy combination of fat particles (triglycerides) and cholesterol, which is transported in the blood stream, combined loosely with naturally occurring blood proteins called lipoproteins (lipo for fat). The more fat particles (cholesterol, triglycerides, and lipoproteins) there are in the blood, the more there are deposited in the walls of the arteries.

The buildup of fat particles in an artery can gradually decrease the amount of blood that flows through it. Sometimes a small deposit of fat particles will rupture, causing a sudden blockage of the arterial opening. Whenever the blood flow to any part of the body is limited, the function of that part is impaired. When the artery affected is in the heart, a heart attack may occur. If the artery involved is in the brain, the stoppage causes a stroke.

Atherosclerosis is often a silent killer. The fat particles gradually accumulate in the arteries without anyone being the wiser. Then, the victim suddenly has a heart attack or stroke. Half the individuals with a heart attack do not live long enough to be admitted to the hospital units designed to care for them. Many more die in the hospital or within the first year after their initial attack. The picture for strokes is equally dismal.

Men are especially prone to heart disease. Heart attacks are common in men under fifty years of age, and they are not rare before the age of thirty. Over 70 per cent of the young men killed in the Korean war at an average age of twenty-two years already had deposits of fat particles in the arteries to their hearts. Women have just as many heart attacks as men after age sixty-five, but they seem to get some protection from their female hormones until that time. Nevertheless, there is some evidence that heart disease is increasing in women.

Deaths from atherosclerosis represent only part of the problem. Many people are disabled by strokes, and countless numbers of older people have lost the normal function of their minds because of diseased arteries in the brain. What is often brushed off as "senility" or "old age" is often caused by fatty deposits in the arteries with small occlusions (little strokes) and generalized inadequate circulation to all or part of the brain. Atherosclerosis not only causes heart disease and brain disease, it can also affect the function of any of the muscles, including those in the legs, seriously impairing a person's ability to walk. Atherosclerosis induces gangrene and high blood pressure; it can also affect the kidneys and there is evidence that it even causes impotence. All of this serves to point up the fact that atherosclerosis not only causes sudden death, but is also responsible for a vast amount of human misery.

The influence of civilization in causing atherosclerosis is evident from the fact that heart attacks from this cause were essentially unknown before the twentieth century. They remain rare in parts of Asia, Africa, Latin America, and those areas where food is neither overly abundant nor excessively rich in calories.

History has provided a number of examples of the influence of "soft living" on the development of fat particles in the arteries. During World War II the German occupation of the lowlands and Scandinavian countries was accompanied by a sharp reduction in the number of heart attacks, presumably because there was less to eat for the populace and many of the fat-rich cholesterol-laden foods were in short supply. The same was true of Germans imprisoned in Russia. The final months of war in Germany and the long painful aftermath reduced the evidence of atherosclerosis to such a low level that medical students had few if any patients to study. Americans imprisoned by the Japanese and Germans also experienced a sharp decrease in cases of atherosclerosis. These are important observations since they enable us to disregard inherited tendencies and racial factors as primary causes for the high rate of atherosclerosis in the industrialized world, and point the finger at the soft, abundant life of modern civilization.

Studies of people living in different ways have proved that the accumulation of fat particles in the arteries can be reversed. Actual damage to an artery that causes scarring or results in calcification cannot be fully corrected, but much of the simple fat deposits can be eliminated from the artery just as they can be elsewhere in the body. In short, it is usually not too late to get some benefit from improving one's patterns of life.

The factors in modern civilization most clearly implicated in the high rate of atherosclerosis are improper diet, inadequate physical activity, and the use of cigarettes. It is tempting to blame stress, strain, and heredity as the main factors in causing heart and circulatory disease. But man has always been under stress. A population occupied by a foreign country and subjected to police oppression certainly cannot be devoid of stress. Aggressive goal-oriented personalities cannot be blamed for the problem. Certainly, the men who led the American Revolution and wrote the Constitution can hardly be thought of as lacking in ambition or drive. Yet heart attacks were unknown in their time.

No doubt heredity does influence one's susceptibility to atherosclerosis, and most of us have genes that enable us to develop fatty deposits in the arteries with the attendant complications. This is all the more reason we should develop living patterns to minimize the problem. We know that a tendency for diabetes can be inherited, but that is no reason why a potential diabetic shouldn't avoid obesity, any more than it is a valid reason for failing to treat a diabetic with both medicine and diet. The more undesirable a family history the more important preventive measures become.

It is a mistake to assume that because one's parents and grandparents did not have heart attacks or strokes one will also be spared. Very often the previous generations had better living habits; they exercised instead of watching TV, ate fewer calories and less fat, were less obese, and smoked few if any cigarettes. Their life was more in tune with their natural environment.

Despite all that is known about disease there is very little that modern medicine can really do to improve an individual's health unless he understands the facts and has the ability to use them. The cook who does not alter food preparation for the family's benefit is a saboteur of the family's health just as surely as if the food were loaded with dangerous bacteria or more obvious poisons. Too often the modern housewife is an unwitting Lucrezia Borgia in disguise, aided and abetted by modern food-marketing methods.

Particularly in Western Europe and America, where heart and vascular disease is a major medical problem, the culinary art has been based on the use of copious amounts of butter, lard, and animal fats. These have been the mainstay for imparting flavor to otherwise tastelessly prepared foods. By contrast, in many parts of Asia, where heart disease is less common, some of the most flavorful and delicious dishes in the world are produced without the use of fat to prepare them. Although one can point out that herbs and spices were in short supply in Europe, it is clear to us today that the imaginative cook need not rely solely on fats to impart flavor to food.

Basic to almost all valid commentaries on man and his food is the simple observation that obesity is a real enemy of mankind. Excessive fat accumulations tend to increase blood pressure, which increases the possibility of heart attacks and strokes. Fat people are prone to diabetes and its complications. Almost any surgical procedure, such as a gallbladder operation, is more difficult in fat people, and obese individuals are more prone to have complications after the operation. And, aside from the medical implications, obesity is considered unattractive in much of the world. Perhaps most important, however, is the observation that obesity is associated with a high level of fat particles and cholesterol in the arteries, and a high rate of atherosclerosis. In a recent diet-heart study, individuals who lost the most body weight had the greatest persistent decrease in the amount of cholesterol in their blood stream.

There are many cases on record of individuals who are capable of maintaining a low level of cholesterol while obtaining a large amount of their calories from food rich in fat and cholesterol. These people, however, are usually very lean, and most of them exercise very heavily, some of them walking as much as sixty miles a day. Studies of young athletes in peak physical condition have shown that in over half of them only 11 per cent or less of their bodies was fat, as compared to the usual 17 to 20 per cent for other men of their age. These individuals have no evidence of fat accumulation around the waist, over the back, or around the navel. The commonly observed fat pads in these areas, which are often accepted as normal, particularly in men, indicate an excessive intake of calories, and suggest evidence of high levels of cholesterol and fatty particles in the blood, more damage to the arteries, and a greater risk of heart attack, stroke, disability, and sudden death.

The diet principle that enables one to prevent disease of the arteries to the heart and elsewhere in the body also enables one to prevent obesity. In fact, prevention of obesity should be one of the primary goals of such a diet. There are limits to what the human organism can bear. This is true in terms of the purity of the air we breathe, the presence or absence of atmospheric pressure, radiation, and other environmental factors. It is equally true of the types and quantity of food that we eat. In the space program, for example, recognition of the limits of man's biological capacity dictates the design of the space capsules. A similar approach is necessary to man's life on Planet Earth, a giant space vehicle. While many environmental factors are currently within acceptable limits, others, such as pollutants in the air and the food we eat, are in danger of becoming unacceptable. By careful selection and balance of the proper foods and diet, it is possible to stay within the limits for optimal health.

The importance of environment and living habits as a factor in health cannot be overstressed. Not only are heart and vascular diseases related to these factors but man's second most common group of diseases, the cancers, are also often the outgrowth of improper living. Cancer of the skin (23 per cent of all cancer in men and 13 per cent in women) is frequently activated by excess harmful radiation from the sun and constant irritation from the elements. The practice of removing our natural facial protection by shaving has made the male of the species a frequent victim of skin cancer of the face. The relationship of smoking to lung cancer (18 per cent of cancer in man) has been well established.

It is becoming evident now that cancer of the colon and rectum (11 per cent of all cancers in men and 13 per cent in women) is related to the diet. This form of cancer is more frequent in the United States and Canada than anywhere else in the world. The rate in Connecticut is eight times the rate in Cali, Colombia, on an age-matched basis. The highly refined diet, devoid in bulk, of the industrialized world affects the digestion. The refined foods move more slowly through the digestive tract, causing constipation and being associated with a higher rate of cancer. Many of the diet factors implicated in the high rate of heart disease are the same as those associated with cancer of the colon and rectum.

The physical stature of an individual can be significantly affected by his diet. Some studies suggest that mental health and intelligence can be influenced by the type of food one eats. Many of the health problems we call old age are really illnesses. Often senility is a disease of the arteries, the atrophy of bone and muscle from disuse combined with other changes in the body.

The truth is that we have no real concept of what old age is. Many of the things that we classify as old age today are really failures in man's adaptation to his environment or to the events of modern living. The United States' longest-living man, Sylvester Magee, was healthy at one hundred and twenty-nine. He fought on both sides of the Civil War and fathered a child at the age of one hundred and nine. His history does not suggest the debility or senility which we commonly observe in much younger men today. There are many other parts of the world where man's life span appears to be much longer than that of our own culture, and where the late years are good years, often associated with a full capacity for the enjoyment of living.

There are marked differences in longevity which are not totally explained by racial or ethnic factors in the world today. A man who is fifty years old in the United States can expect to live to be seventy. In Sweden, a man of the same age can expect to live to be seventy-eight, while on the island of Cyprus the average life expectancy of a fifty-year-old man is eighty-three.

Of course, there are many factors that influence long life and the health to enjoy it, but what you eat is one of the most important. Optimal eating habits are necessary ingredients for an optimal life span in optimal health. This objective can be achieved if you know enough about food and how to prepare it. The practical information and the recipes in this book will enable any cook to deal with any diet, no matter how relaxed or strict that diet may be. Although the book will be useful in meeting special dietary requirements recommended by physicians for improving or reversing particular conditions, its main purpose is to instill healthy eating patterns in healthy people.

CHAPTER 2

Calories Do Count

It is possible to eat as much as any reasonable person would wish to eat and still not get fat or increase the fat particles in your blood. It is more important to consider *what* you eat than *how much* you eat. To illustrate the point, there are nearly eight times as many calories in a pound of raw cured bacon as there are in a pound of uncreamed cottage cheese. Bacon has ten times as many calories as whole milk, and more than twenty-five times as many calories as asparagus tips. Raw pork fat has nearly twelve times as many calories as whole milk, and nearly eight times as many calories as the light meat of fryer chicken without its skin.

All those calories in bacon and pork fat do not mean these foods contain more nutrients. In fact, there are more healthy nutrients and more than twice the protein in the chicken. Many of the calories in fatty foods "don't count"—meaning that they don't count in terms of essential vitamins, minerals, and nutrients. They do count in causing obesity, fat-particle deposits in the arteries, and other health problems. Separable animal fat is almost devoid of everything *except* calories. Most people know that fat contains over twice as many calories as protein or carbohydrates. But that just refers to the actual digestible fat, carbohydrate, and protein. This simple fact doesn't even begin to explain the difference in the calorie content of different foods. The food we eat is composed of much more, including water and fibrous material, or cellulose. One of the major factors determining the amount of calories in a food is its water content. Raw pork fat contains only eleven per cent water. Raw cured bacon is 19.3 per cent water, while uncreamed cottage cheese is 79 per cent and the light meat of fryer chicken without the skin is 77 per cent.

Muscle tissue, like lean round steak, contains a lot of water. It takes three-fourths of a pound of lean round steak to yield 620 calories and the amount of protein usually considered as a daily minimum for health. On the other hand, less than one-fourth of a pound of bacon yields nearly 700 calories and about as much fat as should be allowed from all sources in any one day.

If you want to know how many calories you are really eating there is no substitute for knowing the caloric content of the different foods you eat. For the most part, lean meat, fish, vegetables, and fruit permit a person to eat a fairly large quantity of food without eating too many calories—*unless* they are soaked in fat, butter, or sauces made with fat.

Sugar is a problem in controlling the number of calories because it, too, contains little water. It also contains very little except calories for the body's nutritional needs. There is less than 1 per cent water in sugar, and a quarter of a pound contains nearly 400 calories—about four times as many calories as a comparable amount of light meat of fryer chicken without the skin.

Lard is a good example of how little other than calories some fat contributes to nutrition. It is essentially devoid of any vitamins or minerals; it doesn't even contain any water. Lard is one of the richest foods available. The influence of water content on the calories of some common types of food is clearly pictured in Figure 1 and Table I, page 285.

It seems as if everyone talks about calories—but just what is a calorie? It is a way of measuring energy by the actual heat it produces. The metabolism of food generates energy in the form of heat, and this heat energy is the fuel for the body. This is why physical work makes a person hot, and why, after death, when food metabolism stops, the body begins to cool. The heat energy in food is released as the complex organic material composed of carbon and hydrogen is broken down into the simple elements of carbon dioxide and water. Just as the destruction of an atom generates heat, the breakdown of a food molecule releases heat, though in lesser amounts.

If the food is not fully metabolized into its end products of carbon dioxide and water, the intermediate products will still contain potential

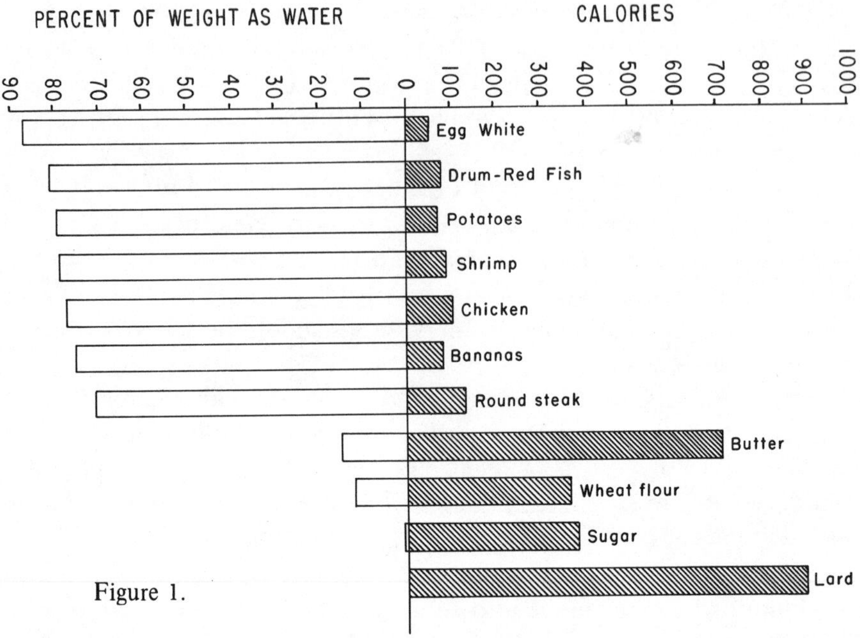

Figure 1.

heat energy, or calories. Food stored as fat really represents a fuel storage that can be used for energy if needed. In some animals, such food storage is desirable since there are only certain times during the year when they can obtain food. The bear is an excellent example, eating everything in sight in summer, and storing much of the food energy in fat deposits for use while hibernating.

Calories can be obtained from carbohydrates, proteins, fats, and even alcohol. The caloric content of the food has little or nothing to do with its content of essential vitamins, minerals, or other nutrients. It is just an expression of available heat energy. A proper diet cannot be defined in terms of calories alone, since the body needs iron, calcium, other minerals, and a host of vitamins.

Measuring the calorie content is useful in evaluating food energy intake and expenditure. The active person needs energy, and this means food. The physically inactive person needs less energy, and he should eat less food. If more food energy is eaten than expended on a daily basis, the excess food is stored as fat deposits. Here, then, is the only way to determine if you are getting too many calories, regardless of how little or how much you eat: if you are gaining fat deposits, you are storing excess calories and eating too many calories for your level of activity. This doesn't always mean you are eating too much food. It can mean that you are eating the wrong kind of food, such as fat containing a large number of calories in a very small portion. Or it can mean that your level of physical activity is too low.

It is important to appreciate that even though the body weight is a useful guide in detecting overeating, the only good test is to feel for the accumulation of fat around the waist, hips, and other locations. This is the real indication of excess food storage. A tall person may not appear to weigh too much for his height according to the scales, but if there is an accumulation of fat, or the familiar spare tire, he is too fat regardless of what the scales read.

Because of our ritualistic fixation on the pounds registered by the scales, we often do not realize that our goal in dieting should be to eliminate excess fat storage, not to reduce the number of pounds. It is important to understand this concept. A physically inactive person may weigh the "normal" amount, but his muscle mass may be relatively small and the rest of his body weight may be made up of dangerous fat deposits. With physical activity the calories stored in fat tissue will be gradually mobilized and used to provide food and energy for the body, and the muscle mass will actually increase. In this way physical activity will convert much of the fat tissue in the body to muscle tissue. Since one pound of fat tissue contains as many calories as five pounds of lean muscle tissue, there may be no evidence whatever of weight reduction according to the scales. The significant evidence of improved health is in the disappearance of fat deposits underneath the skin and the development of better-formed, firmer muscles.

Slavish adherence to the numerical reading on the scales has occasionally contributed to the ineffectiveness of recent studies. Instead of determining the influence of obesity on body chemistry and how it is related to heart disease, diabetes, high blood pressure, and other health problems, most studies are based on body weight. Men of the same age and body weight will have quite different amounts of obesity if some are inactive office workers and others are laborers in a lumber camp. A greater portion of the body weight of the office worker will be fat and the amount of fatty particles in his blood will be greater than in the lumberjack.

A growing child, especially during rapid growth periods, can consume lots of calories without getting fat. In addition to providing energy for physical activity, the calories are used in building new muscles, bones, organs, and even increasing the amount of blood in the body. Even so, the level of physical activity is still important. Growing muscles and strong bones need to be used, and this means physical activity. The child in front of the television set needs fewer calories than the active child.

It is important that children not get too fat. There is some evidence that the number of fat cells in the body increase if a child gets too much food and is allowed to be fat during the growth phase. The number of fat cells in an adult is permanent. When weight is lost the amount of fat in the cells decreases, but the number of cells do not. This makes it easy to regain fat. Childhood obesity creates a lifetime problem.

The body never really is at rest. Respiration, circulation, metabolism, and other body functions are constantly occurring. We speak of being at rest when we are quiet or not performing any apparent task. The energy used by the body in this quiet state is called the basal metabolism. An average one-hundred-and-fifty-pound man will use about 68 calories an hour under basal conditions, although the amount of energy needed during rest may vary a great deal according to height and age as well as weight. Most short people have more body fat and less muscle or other active tissues than taller people of the same weight. They require less energy because fat tissue does not require a lot of energy to maintain. The circulation through fat deposits is small compared to the amount through muscles. A fat deposit is an inactive food pouch. The muscles are much more active chemically even at rest. The cells are busy manufacturing energy compounds and making adjustments for previous activity. As a person converts fat tissue to muscle the basal metabolism increases. This means that the muscular person can eat more calories than the fat person with less muscle and still not develop fat deposits. As people get older and are less active, they lose muscle mass, which contributes to obesity and causes their energy requirements at rest to decrease.

In general, however, body weight is the most useful guide in determining basal metabolism. Light individuals require less energy at rest than heavy people. An average hundred-pound individual needs only 55 calories an hour at rest, while a two-hundred-pound individual needs 81 calories. Lying quietly at rest, the hundred-pound person needs 1320 calories a day and the two-hundred-pound person 1944 calories.

The number of calories required for simple physical tasks also varies according to a person's body weight. A one-hundred-and-fifty-pound person walking on a level surface at a speed of three miles per hour uses about 84 calories a mile. Since he would need 23 calories for the twenty-minute period at rest, the work of walking a mile requires an additional 61 calories above his resting needs. A hundred-pound person would require 63 total calories per mile and about 45 calories for the exercise. A two-hundred-pound person needs more than 100 calories per mile and about 78 calories for the exercise. These are all approximations; clothing, shoes, the smooth or rough characteristics of the surface all affect the number of calories expended. For purposes of relating food to exercise we have simplified the value to an arbitrary figure of 60 calories per mile—using a one-hundred-and-fifty-pound person as a basis for calculations. Food values in this book will include an *exercise equivalent* (EE) which will relate food energy to the amount of energy used for exercise. The unit, one EE, will equal 60 calories, or about the amount of additional energy used by a one-hundred-and-fifty-pound person walking one mile at a speed of three miles per hour on a level surface as opposed to resting. The EE unit is in miles. A food containing one EE unit provides enough energy to walk one mile.

Since people of different weights use different amounts of energy at rest and during walking, you may wish to convert the EE to values for different weights. You can do this using Table II, page 285. Use the "mile-equivalent factor." A hundred-pound individual must walk 1.38 miles to use the same energy used by a one-hundred-and-fifty-pound person, while a two-hundred-and-thirty-pound individual must walk only 0.70 miles.

What does all this mean in terms of diet and fat prevention? If our standard individual of one hundred and fifty pounds walks an hour a day he will increase his calorie needs 180 calories a day. Since a pound of fat contains 3500 calories, that won't eliminate much fat. The key is regularity. In a year's time an hour of walking each day will expend 65,700 calories, equivalent to the number of calories present in about nineteen pounds of fat tissue. A hundred-pound person would use less and a two-hundred-pound person more. Thus, if our standard person walked only thirty minutes a day for a year he would use the calories present in over nine pounds of fat tissue.

This does not mean that he would lose nine pounds in body weight, however, even by keeping his caloric intake the same, since he will be converting fat tissue into heavier muscle tissue. If two pounds of fat are converted into ten pounds of muscle, the body weight at the end of the year will be unchanged. But the important health benefit is that much less of the body weight is fat and more is muscle. This in turn affects the amount of fat particles in the blood, the blood cholesterol, and factors related to heart and vascular disease caused by atherosclerosis.

Of course all the benefits of exercise in terms of eliminating fat storages can be negated by eating a little bit of the wrong thing. Only four level teaspoons of sugar (15 calories per teaspoon) each day will negate the caloric benefit of walking a mile a day. The person who starts exercising and also increases his calorie intake may not lose any fat stores but may increase his muscle mass and actually gain weight. Choosing the right food can make an exercise program work. The energy in a 3½-ounce apple can be used by walking one mile (one EE), but the energy in the same amount of raw cured bacon would require the same person to walk eleven miles to use its calories. The same amount of butter contains the energy needed to walk twelve miles.

If you assume that the average person needs 1500 calories a day for the basal needs of the body, you mean that the body at rest uses as much energy as would be expended in walking twenty-five miles a day. Every calorie over 1500 must be used up by some kind of activity if you want to prevent obesity. If a sedentary individual uses 2500 calories a day, 1000 calories are used for his daily activities. His activities are equivalent to walking sixteen miles. By choosing foods that have fewer calories per unit of bulk the body can be satisfied without requiring impractical levels of daily exercise. This means avoiding fats and sugars and placing more emphasis on vegetables, fruit, cereals, and low-fat or nonfat dairy products. By using a sensible exercise program combined with a sensible diet *consistently*, dangerous fat deposits can be prevented and good health promoted.

CHAPTER 3

Ingredients of Food

Food that has caloric value is of organic origin and contains carbon atoms. Inorganic material, such as salt, does not contain carbon atoms and has no caloric value. To provide the body with all its needs foods must contain both organic material for calories, vitamins, and other essential nutrients, as well as inorganic material to supply such essential minerals as iron, calcium, and phosphorus. Most calories are produced by the breaking down of carbohydrate, protein, fat, and alcohol.

Carbohydrates

There are many kinds of carbohydrates, but those that the human digestive system is capable of breaking down are starches and sugars. They are made up of carbon, hydrogen, and a small amount of oxygen. The starches and sugars are readily absorbed into the digestive system and converted to glucose (a type of sugar). The glucose is easily broken down into carbon dioxide and water, and in the process yields energy in the form of calories. Even proteins and fats (from either the body stores or food) are converted to glucose and then used as energy. Glucose itself is a common carbohydrate in some foods, such as fruit. It and the sugars readily converted to glucose are immediately available for the body's use for quick energy. Carbohydrates are processed by the stomach much more quickly than either proteins or fats.

Carbohydrates occur as starches in grains, cereals, and vegetables, and as sugars in fruit and some vegetables. Milk also contains appreciable amounts of carbohydrates, as well as protein and fat. Meat, whether it is of animal, fowl, or fish origin, does not contain significant amounts of carbohydrates. An exception is shellfish; about 8 per cent of the calories in shrimp are from carbohydrates. Much of the world's population, the rice-eating countries for example, still gets 70 per cent or more of their calories from carbohydrates. Interestingly, these people are essentially free of the problems of atherosclerosis and are less likely to be obese. They get their carbohydrates from natural foods such as vegetables, fruits, and cereals, which means that they can eat considerable bulk without eating too many calories. They also get the natural vitamins and minerals abundant in these foods.

Processed carbohydrates are a different story. Sugar is a good example. After man has extracted the sugar from the beet or cane, the end product has almost no water and even small amounts contain many calories. This refinement of nature's food supply has not been entirely beneficial to our health. You can appreciate the effects of sugar by realizing that one level teaspoon (that does not mean rounded) has an EE of one-quarter of a mile, and just that much sugar a day for a year means adding the calories in one and a half pounds of fat tissue. Just adding four level teaspoons of sugar a day to your diet will mean you will need to walk a mile a day more to use the added calories, or within a year you can gain six pounds of fat. Because fruit, vegetables, and grain contain cellulose and water in addition to sugar, they have far fewer calories than the same amount of refined sugar. A pound of sugar has over six times as many calories as a pound of apples.

A few scientists believe that an excess intake of granulated sugar is a major factor in developing heart and vascular disease. Certainly there has been an enormous increase in consumption of sugar. At one time man had to satisfy his sweet tooth with honey, which was available only in limited amounts. In Elizabethan times sugar was almost unknown to the common man. In 1750 the average Englishman ate only four pounds of sugar a year; in 1850 he consumed about twenty-five pounds and now he uses one hundred and twenty pounds a year, or 2.3 pounds a week. Naturally, the more affluent populations eat the most sugar, but the United States is not first among them. The average consumption of sugar per person in the United States is ninety-nine pounds, a little less than two pounds each week. The amounts used in some other countries are: Ireland, one hundred and twenty-seven pounds; Holland, one hundred and twenty pounds; Australia, one hundred and fifteen pounds; and Denmark, one hundred and ten pounds.

Because of the well-established relationship between excess sugar intake and obesity many sugar substitutes have been developed. No doubt there will be others. For those who have an unrelenting sweet tooth they are useful. Some sugar substitutes can be exchanged spoonful for spoonful with sugar, although often the flavor is not as pleasant as real sugar. A good way to cut down calories and still have the sweet taste is to use half sugar and half artificial sweetener in recipes calling for sugar or in beverages. For the average American consuming about one hundred pounds of sugar a year, that substitution would represent a decrease of about 80,000 calories a year with an EE of 1,333 miles per person.

Some natural sweets contain fewer calories than sugar because they contain more water (the calorie content and EE value of sugars and sirups are listed in Table III, page 286). Molasses, particularly blackstrap molasses, contains appreciable amounts of calcium and iron as well as small amounts of vitamins.

If you prefer to use honey in cooking rather than sugar simply decrease the amount of water in the recipe by ½ cup for each cup of honey used. Better results are often obtained by using half honey and half sugar; for each cup of sugar in a recipe, use ½ cup of honey, ½ cup of sugar, and decrease the water by ¼ cup. The same principle can be used for sirups and molasses. Since these contain more water than honey you may need to decrease the water in the recipe by more than ½ cup per cup of sirup or molasses used.

In the industrialized nations of the world, such as the United States, eating patterns have gradually changed so that less of the average diet is composed of carbohydrates and more calories come from fat. The kind of carbohydrate used has also changed, so that there is a greater consumption of calories from sugar or sirups in the form of desserts and beverages.

There is no exact number of carbohydrate calories that a person should eat daily. While there is a basic minimal amount of protein that is considered essential for good health, the same is not true of carbohydrates, except that you must eat enough of these foods to provide the essential vitamins and minerals. A person eating a diet fairly high in protein (and, we hope, low in fat) may need fewer calories from carbohydrates than a person who is not. Within reasonable limits, proteins, carbohydrates, and fats can be substituted for each other to achieve the total number of calories that a person can eat. An individual eating a minimal number of calories from fat of any type and the minimal number of calories from protein will obviously need to eat lots of food with carbohydrates just to provide a sufficient number of total calories. If you are gaining weight or accumulating excess fat deposits, you would be wise to cut down on your calories, and the easiest way to do this is to cut down carbohydrate calories. Since sugars and some refined flours or cereals are not rich in vitamins and do not contribute essential nutrients, these are good items to eliminate.

As a general rule of thumb, a normal adult eating 300 calories of protein a day, restricting his fat to 35 per cent of the total calories, and consuming 2500 calories a day, would need 1220 calories of carbohydrate.

Proteins

Proteins are the building blocks of the body. Muscle, bone, blood, skin, and in fact almost all parts of the body except fat tissue are developed in part from protein. This is why growing bodies need lots of protein. Even in adults, old tissues are constantly being destroyed and replaced, and this rebuilding requires a small amount of daily protein intake.

Proteins contain not only carbon and hydrogen, but also oxygen and nitrogen. There are many kinds of proteins and they can be broken down into organic compounds known as amino acids, which the body must have for building tissue and constructing enzymes, hormones, and other substances necessary for life. Fortunately, the body can manufacture most of the different amino acids it needs from sugar or fat combined with nitrogen. There are a few, called the essential amino acids, which the body cannot make, and these proteins must be included in the diet. Proteins differ from one another because of the different amino acids they contain. To ensure a variety of amino acids it is best to have several different types of proteins in the diet.

Proteins can also be used for heat energy or calories. Unused nitrogen is discarded in the urine, and the remaining carbon and hydrogen are converted to energy or stored as fat. When the body does not get enough calories it uses its protein as well as its stored fat for energy. In starvation man loses not only fat stores but gradually his muscle mass as well.

Proteins are found in a variety of foods. The foods containing the most protein are fish, shellfish, meat, fowl, milk and milk products, certain cereals, and some nuts and vegetables. The problem is that many of the foods that are high in protein content also contain lots of fat. Whole milk (3.7 per cent fat) has twice as many calories from fat as from protein. Raw lean round steak, with all the visible fat removed, contains enough fat to account for one third of its calories. Cheddar cheese has a lot of protein, but nearly three fourths of its calories come from fat. It is clear that many of the so-called high-protein foods are really high-fat foods.

You can increase the protein in the diet without increasing the fat by using nonfat dry milk powder, uncreamed cottage cheese, gelatin, and certain vegetables such as beans. The percentage of calories from proteins is rather high in asparagus, spinach, and broccoli. Egg whites are an excellent nonfat protein source. Most fish have lots of protein and little fat (but not all fish are low-fat). The light meat of a fryer chicken, without the skin, is a good low-fat protein source, while dark meat, skin, and more mature birds are all higher in fat content.

It is an interesting fact that people using vegetables, cereals, and seafoods for their protein source are usually not fat and have small amounts of fat and cholesterol in the blood with very little evidence of atherosclerosis. Societies obtaining their protein from foods also rich in fat are afflicted with obesity, heart disease, strokes, and other signs of widespread atherosclerosis.

How much protein do you need a day? Opinion differs on this point, but most authorities agree that 280 calories from protein, per day, is usually sufficient, even for growing boys. A common misconception is that you need a lot of protein in order to get essential nutrients. There is *no* advantage in eating more protein than the body needs. The excess protein is stripped of its nitrogen, converted to fat, and stored as fat deposits. *You can get fat eating protein.* There are no essential nutrients in meat that you cannot also get in other food sources. However, you will need to learn how to include all the essential amino acids in your diet without eating too much meat, poultry, and fish. Over 20 per cent of the calories in mature beans, for instance, are from protein (the figure is even higher in soybeans). Over 10 per cent of the calories in all-purpose wheat flour and almost half the calories in gluten flour are from protein. These foods, combined with protein from egg white, uncreamed cottage cheese, skim milk, and similar low-fat or nonfat milk products provide a sufficient variety of proteins to enable one to get all the essential amino acids without meat. All too often the meats we choose for a "high-protein diet" really provide a *high-fat* diet.

Fats

A lot has been said about fat since investigators began studying the effects of diet in causing atherosclerosis, and most of it has been bad. Fats, unlike protein, contain no nitrogen, and unlike most carbohydrates, cannot be dissolved in water (they are soluble in alcohol). Because most foods containing fat have very little water fat foods are a much richer source for calories than an equal amount of almost any other kind of food. In fact digestible fat contains over twice as many calories as the same amount of protein or carbohydrates. Look at the difference between beef fat and raw round beefsteak without visible fat. The beef fat contains five times as many calories as the lean beefsteak, despite the fact that the calories from the fat remaining within the lean beefsteak still represent almost one third of all its calories. The simple fact is that if you eat much fat you are getting a lot of calories in your diet. It doesn't matter which kind of fat you eat. Animal fat, vegetable fat, saturated fat, unsaturated fat, monounsaturated fat, and polyunsaturated fat all have about the same number of calories, and that is usually too many.

Fats require more time to be digested, and a fatty meal will stay in the stomach for a much longer time than either carbohydrates or proteins. This is one reason a person feels full for a long time after a meal high in fat content. A meal of carbohydrates is normally processed rather rapidly by the stomach, absorbed from the intestine, and either used for energy or stored as fat. The satisfying fullness from fat plus the fact that a large number of calories are available in a small amount of fat make it a very popular economical food for people who must do a great deal of physical labor.

A small amount of fat is necessary for the absorption of the fat-soluble vitamins, which are A, D, and E. (All other important vitamins are water-soluble.) And, as we know, fat also aids in the absorption of cholesterol from the digestive tract. Although the Inter-Society Commission for Heart Disease recommends that *no more than* 35 per cent of the calories in your daily diet come from fat, you can still have a healthy balanced diet on as little as 15 per cent fat.

You have often heard it said that saturated fats are considered worse for the health than the unsaturated fats. The word "saturated" is a chemical term, and can be demonstrated by dissolving sugar in a cup of coffee. When you add too much sugar, some of it does not dissolve and settles in the bottom of the cup. The coffee is "saturated" with sugar. If you add less sugar than the amount the coffee can dissolve, the coffee is "unsaturated." Applying these terms to fat, a saturated fat is one that holds as much hydrogen as it can, while an unsaturated fat is one that could hold more hydrogen.

In forming organic compounds, carbon atoms are often joined to each other like a long chain of people holding hands. Each carbon atom in the chain can also hold two hydrogen atoms. When all of the carbon atoms in a fat molecule do so, that fat is holding as much hydrogen as it can and is a saturated fat. If one or more carbon atoms are not holding two hydrogen atoms, it is an unsaturated fat.

A distinction is made between fats that are short only two hydrogen atoms (indicated by one double bond between two carbon atoms), and those that are short four or more additional hydrogen atoms (indicated by the presence of more than one double bond between carbon atoms). If only two hydrogen atoms are missing it is called a monosaturated fat. The most common monounsaturated fat in food is oleic acid. If more than two hydrogen atoms are missing from the chain, it is called polyunsaturated fat; the most common example in food is linoleic acid (see figures 2, 3, 4, 5).

In general, unsaturated fats are liquid at room temperature; corn and safflower oil are composed mostly of polyunsaturated fat, for example. Some saturated fats (such as coconut oil), which have short carbon chains instead of the usual long carbon chains, are also liquid at room temperature. Butter is soft at room temperature because it is made up mostly of butyric acid, a saturated fatty acid with only four carbon atoms in its chain. Some fish oils have very long carbon chains with lots of missing hydrogen atoms and are highly unsaturated. Liquid vegetable oils, such as corn oil, can be hydrogenated (by having hydrogen atoms added to the carbon chain) and made into a solid. The food industry does this in making margarine, for example, in order to improve the creamy texture and to lengthen the shelf life of the food product. When you read "hydrogenated" or "partially hydrogenated" on a label, you know that at least part of the unsaturated fat has been artificially converted to saturated fat. When natural unsaturated fats are converted by hydrogenation, they become saturated fats and have no advantage whatever over natural saturated fats. Unfortunately, unless the food is labeled properly, it is not possible to tell how much fat of the unsaturated type and how much of the saturated type it contains.*

What is "bad" about saturated fats? Diet studies in the United States

* For years, in the United States, the Food and Drug Administration prohibited simple labeling of the contents of food according to type of fat. In May 1965 the American Diabetic Association and the American Heart Association both recommended the labeling of foods according to their actual fat content. However, in February 1966 the FDA rejected their recommendations and asked that the problem be studied by the Council on Foods and Nutrition of the American Medical Association. The Council recommended to the FDA that foods be so labeled and again the FDA took no action. Thus the FDA and the food industry prevented the consumer from knowing what he was eating. This is in sharp contrast to the attitude demonstrated by the Scandinavian governments when they made it a policy in 1968 to recommend dietary alterations and other measures designed to reduce heart and vascular disease. In short, the FDA knowingly or unknowingly has adopted a policy that, in the opinion of many leading scientists in the field, is deleterious to the public health.

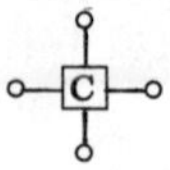

Figure 2: Carbon atom with four hands

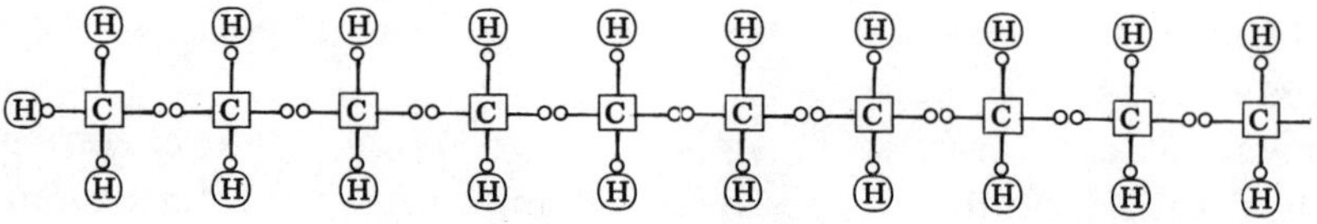

Figure 3: Saturated fat carbon chain

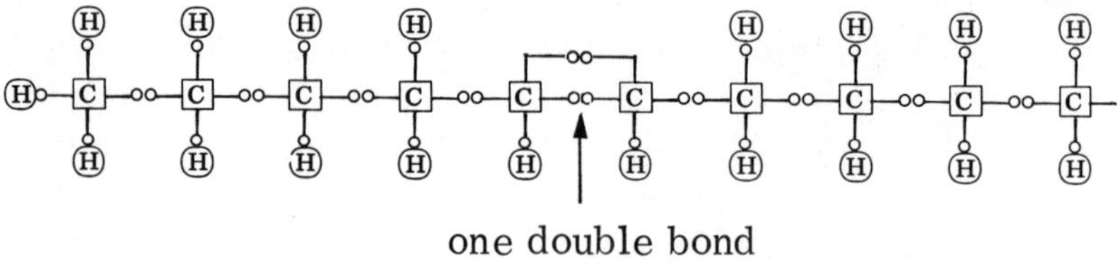

Figure 4: Monounsaturated fat carbon chain

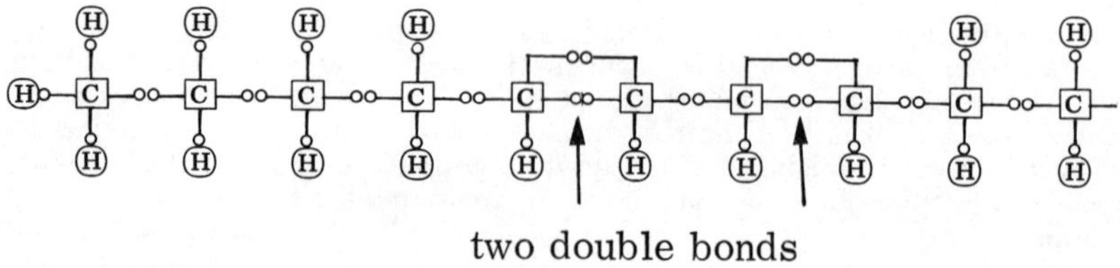

Figure 5: Polyunsaturated fat carbon chain

and other countries have demonstrated a decrease in heart attacks when part of the saturated fat in the diet is replaced with polyunsaturated fat. The exact mechanisms involved are not clear. Some doctors strongly favor a reduction in all fats in the diet and others place more emphasis on using polyunsaturated fats rather than saturated fats. It is clear, however, that people who have no evidence of atherosclerosis usually eat more polyunsaturated fats since these are found in cereals, vegetables, and seafoods. People who eat such saturated fats as animal fats, butter, and coconut oil often have high rates of heart disease, but they are also usually fatter, less active physically, and are heavy cigarette smokers. After reviewing all facets of the problem, the Inter-Society Commission for Heart Disease recommended in December 1970 that the fat from all food sources be limited to less than 35 per cent of the total calories. Saturated fat should be limited to 10 per cent or less of the total calories, monounsaturated fat to 10 per cent, and polyunsaturated fat to 10 per cent. The tables in this book and the tabulations with each recipe specify the different types of fat, so that it will be possible for you to restrict the fat intake or alter the ratio of saturated to polyunsaturated fat as desired or as recommended by your physician. You will also be able to control the amount of cholesterol in your diet at different levels, or you can ignore it. In other words, the food-preparation methods described in this book can be adjusted to the individual need.

Alcohol

There is a popular misconception that alcohol has no calories—*rubbish!* It does, and nearly as many as fat. There are 693 calories in 3½ ounces (100 grams) of alcohol. It is rapidly absorbed from the digestive tract. Most alcoholic beverages also contain other food elements, such as carbohydrates. The EE for 3½ ounces of eighty-proof alcoholic drinks is about four miles.

Of course, alcohol does not count if used during cooking. The heat causes the alcohol to evaporate and what is left are the flavor elements of the wine or other beverage. Wines are an excellent source of flavor in cooking.

Cholesterol

Cholesterol is not a fat and does not provide calories. It is an alcohol made up of a very long chain of carbon atoms. The alcohol (ethyl alcohol) in alcoholic beverages has only two carbon atoms and is a liquid just as short-carbon-chain saturated fats are liquid. The long-carbon-chain cholesterol is a waxy solid, like long-carbon-chain fats. Cholesterol is normally produced in the body. It is abundant in bile formed by the liver ("Chole" in Greek means bile and "steros" means solid; hence bile solids), and it enters the small intestine with the bile flow. Here it is added to whatever amount of cholesterol has been absorbed in the diet. Part of this combined pool of body-produced cholesterol and dietary cholesterol is absorbed along with fats from the small intestine and in this way enters the circulation.

The amount of cholesterol in the blood is not dependent solely upon the amount eaten. The presence of large amounts of fat (particularly saturated fat and particularly in the male) results in an increased production of cholesterol in the body. This is why simply limiting the amount of cholesterol in the diet is not enough to prevent atherosclerosis. Remember that both protein and carbohydrates in excess amounts can be converted to fat for storage, and the generation of this fat results in an increased production of cholesterol.

The measurement of cholesterol in man related to heart and vascular disease is made by examining the blood and it is expressed in the number of milligrams present in about one-half cup of the liquid part of the blood (or serum) remaining after the red blood cells and other solid elements are separated from the whole blood. A milligram is a very small amount; there are 454,000 of them in a pound. Individuals with readings below 200 milligrams are less likely to have vascular disease than those with higher levels. Those individuals with readings over 240 milligrams have a significantly greater likelihood of having a heart attack. In general, for each 100 milligrams of cholesterol in the diet the cholesterol value in the blood will be increased by 3 milligrams. A person eating 500 milligrams of cholesterol daily (equivalent to two egg yolks) would have a cholesterol value 15 milligrams higher than he would if he ate no cholesterol.

The amount of cholesterol, as well as the type and amount of fat particles in the blood, is also affected by female hormones (which is one reason why women in the childbearing age seldom have heart attacks), thyroid function, stress, and differences in intestinal absorption (although the latter is a minor factor in healthy people). Cholesterol is found throughout the body in both men and animals. It is necessary for the formation of important hormones such as those from the adrenal gland, and it is found in very large amounts in the nerve tissue; hence, there is a lot in the brain. Cholesterol is an animal product, and is not found in vegetables, vegetable oils, or fruit, although carotenoid pigments, or related substances, are. This means that a strictly vegetarian diet would be essentially cholesterol-free.

One should not be misled into thinking that because cholesterol is a natural substance, the amount in the body or in the diet is not important. The fallacy of this type of thinking is pointed up in diabetes. It is an accepted fact that having sugar (glucose) in the blood is essential and, further, that marked elevations in blood sugar are abnormal. Moreover, it is generally accepted that a person with an elevated blood sugar from diabetes would do well to limit the ingestion of additional sugar, even though the body can and does manufacture glucose sugar from fats and proteins. Similarly, a person with an elevated cholesterol value would do well to limit the ingestion of additional cholesterol even though the body can and does manufacture cholesterol.

Cholesterol occurs in greatest abundance in organ meats, such as the brain and liver, and in egg yolks. Some shellfish, such as shrimp, contain a moderate amount of cholesterol. The average diet of Americans contains more than 600 milligrams of cholesterol a day, and many people eat much more than this. The person who regularly eats two eggs for breakfast ingests approximately 500 milligrams of cholesterol a day from that source alone. To this you can add the cholesterol in meat, shellfish, and that in egg yolks used in making desserts, bakery products, and sauces.

How much cholesterol should you eat a day? There are many different opinions, but most doctors who have studied the problem agree that the amount should be limited. The Intersociety-Commission for Heart Disease recommends no more than 300 milligrams a day and the American Heart Association recommends no more than three egg yolks a week, including those used in cooking. Individuals with medical problems or with very high cholesterol values will need a strict limit; those with very low cholesterol values can be less concerned.

The amount of cholesterol found in common foods adapted from the *U.S. Department of Agriculture Handbook Number 8*, Composition of Foods, is listed in Table V, page 288.

Vitamin A

It is generally agreed that vitamin A is essential to maintain the normal ability of the human eye to see in the darkness—night vision. It appears to be important in the normal function of membranes of the eyes and possibly the skin. Dry scaly skin and perhaps secondary infections can be caused by abnormal function of the skin cells resulting from inadequate amounts of vitamin A. Many more abnormalities have been identified in animals deficient in vitamin A, but most of these are not seen in man. Curiously enough, vitamin-A toxicity is more common nowadays than vitamin-A deficiency. This problem is usually observed in babies who are fed too much fish-oil concentrate. Vitamin-A deficiency can also cause skin problems, scales, loss of hair, bone pain, cracked lips, and irritability. Acute severe illness, even death, can occur in adults eating polar-bear liver, which is naturally toxic because of large amounts of stored vitamin A.

Five thousand units of vitamin A a day is usually sufficient for adults, and even less is needed for children. The vitamin can be manufactured by the body from the pigment found in many vegetables and fruit. Disorders of the digestive tract such as diarrhea conditions can sometimes, though rarely, prevent absorption of the pigment, and even more rarely the body may not be able to convert the pigment to vitamin A. The manufactured vitamin A is stored in the liver, hence the liver of animals and fish commonly contains lots of vitamin A.

Egg yolks, butter, and cheese all contain large amounts of vitamin A. However since many vegetables and fruit, as well as fish, contain adequate amounts of vitamin A, or the pigments the body uses to manufacture vitamin A, it is not necessary to eat foods loaded with saturated fats or cholesterol to obtain a sufficient amount. Some meats contain very little vitamin A. In general pigmented vegetables, such as carrots, spinach, squash, and sweet potatoes, contain vitamin A. Three-and-a-half ounces of cooked carrots provides about twice the daily requirement for vitamin A. The values for vitamin A content in common foods are listed in Table VI, page 289. Since vitamin A is soluble in fat and not in water some fat in the diet (minimal) is needed to facilitate absorption from the digestive tract.

Vitamin D

If you live in a sunny climate and get enough exposure to the sun you may not need any vitamin D in your diet. This is the anti-rickets vitamin. Bone deformities and loss of bone structure occur when vitamin D is not sufficient. Excess amounts are also harmful, causing softening of the bones, calcification of the kidneys, and eventually kidney failure, among other problems. About 400 units a day is adequate, and 10,000 units a day is toxic.

Sunlight activates certain skin oils, converting them to vitamin D. In cities with long periods of little sunshine and major air-pollution problems there is not enough sunshine, and vitamin D must be obtained from food. Only a few foods naturally contain vitamin D. Fish is an important source, particularly salmon, sardines, herring, and oily fish. Cod, halibut, and tuna liver oil are very rich in vitamin D. Modern milk products often are fortified with vitamin D. You must consult the label to evaluate them.

Vitamin E

Vitamin E is sometimes called the fertility vitamin. It was observed that rats on a milk diet receiving other vitamins and fats but no vitamin E were sterile. Adding lettuce, alfalfa, and wheat-germ oil corrected the problem. Lack of vitamin E can cause many abnormalities in animals, but their counterpart has not been conclusively observed in man. One possible reason is that large amounts of vitamin E may not be necessary and it occurs naturally in a wide variety of foods. Cereals and vegetable oils are rich sources of vitamin E, for example. Should there be any merit in taking lots of vitamin E, the proper diet would be one rich in polyunsaturated fats.

Vitamin K

One of the fat-soluble vitamins affects blood coagulation and is called K (Koagulation). Its natural sources include green leaf vegetables such as cabbage, spinach, and tomatoes. Deficiencies in man occur usually because of liver disease, disease of the digestive tract, or overdosage with certain medicines used to prevent blood coagulation.

Vitamin B_1 (Thiamine)

Lack of sufficient thiamine causes neuritis, muscle atrophy, and heart failure, and it may also play a role in certain liver diseases. Thiamine deficiency as a cause of disease was unknown until man started refining his foods. The removal of the germ and husk from wheat, the polishing of rice, and the refining of other natural foods caused certain symptoms which were described as beriberi. People depending mostly on refined cereals were the ones most affected. Thiamine is widespread in natural foods, and whole cereals, vegetables (especially dried beans), dried yeast, and lean pork are all excellent sources. Commercially baked breads are enriched to provide abundant amounts of vitamin B_1; low-fat milk and other fortified or enriched food products often have thiamine added. The daily requirement is less than 1.4 milligrams, and it is nearly impossible to have a thiamine-deficient diet if whole cereals such as oatmeal, mixed vegetables, and modern bread are included in the diet. Fish contains more thiamine than beef as a rule. There are apparently no toxic effects from ingesting large amounts of thiamine. It is not stored long, necessitating a regular intake.

Vitamin B_2 (Riboflavin)

Riboflavin deficiency is much more apt to occur in animals than in man. Although it is believed to be essential for all the cells of the human body, insufficient amounts in the diet have only been proved to affect the eyes and skin in man. Deficiency of vitamin B_2 has been linked with cracked lips and seborrheic dermatitis. Its most serious effects are in the eyes. Blood vessels develop in the cornea; intolerance to light and marked loss of vision can occur. Riboflavin deficiency is very rare in man, unless combined with general vitamin and nutritional deficiency, because it is so widespread in our food source, including commercially enriched and fortified food products.

The daily requirement of riboflavin is met if the diet contains 2.0 milligrams. Important food sources are leafy vegetables, eggs, egg whites, organ meats (especially liver), meats, vegetables, and both whole and nonfat milk. Any diet containing nonfat milk, low-fat milk, uncreamed cottage cheese, enriched white bread, and vegetables will likely satisfy the riboflavin needs. There should be no riboflavin deficiency in a low-fat, low-cholesterol diet.

Niacin (Nicotinic Acid)

Niacin is plentiful in fish, meat, yeast (a very rich source), legumes, and many vegetables and cereals. Enriched bread and fortified milk are good sources. Neither ordinary whole milk nor eggs provide an adequate source. An excellent low-fat, low-cholesterol diet can be served without danger of niacin deficiency, especially if fish and chicken are eaten often. A 3½ ounce serving of white fish contains three milligrams of niacin. An equal portion of raw fryer chicken light meat without the skin contains 6.7 milligrams and with the skin 11.9 milligrams; a slice of enriched white bread contains 0.7 milligrams, and 3½ ounces of raw lean round steak 5.2 milligrams. The daily requirement from all sources is around 22 milligrams.

Niacin deficiency inducing such conditions as pellagra causes skin changes, a swollen red tongue, and mental changes ranging from slight aberrations to dementia and death.

Vitamin B_6 (Pyridoxine)

Although insufficient vitamin B_6 causes a variety of changes in animals, the same conditions have not been observed in adult man. Babies have been known to have convulsions if their diet does not contain pyridoxine. The daily requirements are not known since no disorder in mature man can be produced because of pyridoxine deficiency. It is plentiful in the same foods containing Vitamin B_1, B_2, and niacin.

Vitamin C (Ascorbic Acid)

For centuries man suffered from scurvy, the disease caused by a vitamin C deficiency. The teeth were weakened, the gums swollen and bleeding, and there was a generalized tendency toward bleeding and death. The availability of fresh fruits and vegetables throughout the years rid mankind of this dreaded problem.

Vitamin C is abundant in fresh fruits and vegetables and in lesser amounts in canned preparations. Milk is also a good source of vitamin C.

The minimal daily requirement is 70 milligrams, but since it cannot be stored in the body the intake must be fairly regular. Some investigators have suggested that smoking destroys large amounts of vitamin C and may contribute to a low level of available ascorbic acid in the body. In reasonable amounts vitamin C causes no harm, since the excess is excreted by the body.

Considering the widespread distribution of vitamin C in fresh fruits and vegetables there is no reason for the ascorbic acid intake to be deficient in low-fat or low-cholesterol diets.

Miscellaneous Vitamins

There are other vitamin substances—some of doubtful importance to man. It suffices to say that if the foods necessary to provide sufficient amounts of the previously discussed vitamins are included in the diet there should be no vitamin deficiencies. Thus vitamin deficiencies are not a hazard to a healthy low-fat, low-cholesterol, or low-calorie diet. In truth fresh fruits, vegetables, fish, and cereals are some of the richest sources of needed vitamins. The fact is that animal fat is seldom a significant source of any needed vitamins or minerals. Saturated fats are essentially just calories and nothing else.

Minerals

There are many minerals essential to health. These include sodium from ordinary salt, potassium (abundant in fruits), copper, zinc, magnesium, iron, and calcium. They are essential in many of the enzyme systems and metabolic functions. Even the ability to taste is dependent upon small amounts of some of these. Fortunately small amounts of minerals are plentiful in a vast number of foods.

Calcium is not abundant in many foods. Any diet should give special attention to the calcium requirement. To ensure an adequate intake the diet should include 1.5 grams of calcium a day; some authorities think it should be more. Calcium is particularly important in developing and maintaining the skeleton. Degeneration of the spine, leading to curving of the spine between the shoulder blades and loss of height (osteoporosis), occurs in one out of every four women in the United States, and it is five times as common in women eating diets marginal or deficient in calcium. The bones in the spine soften and literally dissolve. The process usually begins right after the menopause. Every woman should include in her diet the amount of calcium found in one quart of milk (nonfat milk and low-fat fortified milk are fine) each day. This does not mean that a person must drink a quart of milk. Using the amount of nonfat dry milk powder used for one quart of milk in cooking will be adequate —or part can be used for cooking and part for drinking.

Dairy products and fish (particularly if the bone is included, as in sardines) are two rich sources of calcium. Foods rich in calcium are listed in Table VII, page 290. Amounts of nonfat dry milk powder in excess of the amount used to mix milk for drinking can be used in cooking to increase the calcium intake.

Fish flour, usually called fish protein or some similar name, can be obtained in most health-food stores. This is very rich in calcium and can be added to other foods or drinks like tomato juice. It contains lots of protein as well as calcium.

Many foods have been "fortified" or "enriched." Low-fat milk and even nonfat dry milk powder usually contain added amounts of vitamins and minerals. One popular low-fat milk, for instance, has been fortified with one thousand units of vitamin A in each cupful. It is necessary to look at the label of all purchased foods to determine their vitamin content. If you use a particular product labeled simply "fortified with vitamins," write the manufacturer and request more complete information. If you can't get a reply stop using the product. Excess amounts of some vitamins and minerals can be just as harmful as not enough.

Sufficient amounts of iron are present in enough foods that a mixed diet can hardly avoid supplying the daily requirements of most people. In general, children, men, and nonmenstruating women need only 4 to 10 milligrams a day from food sources. Adolescents and menstruating women need between 10 and 20 milligrams a day. Pregnant women and infants need even more, and the amount should be determined individually by their doctors. If a person needs more than these amounts there is a reason for the need, and all too often the reason is unrecognized bleeding. Thus if an iron deficiency problem persists a medical examination is advisable.

The body tends to store iron. Too much iron in the body can be harmful, particularly to people with certain types of liver disease. With an increasing tendency to fortify natural foods, there is some danger of getting too much iron.

There are many and varied food sources for iron. The following list of milligrams of iron found in a 3½-ounce portion of food provides a guide to the source of iron for daily needs:

Baby-food cereals with added nutrients	50.0 milligrams
Beans, dry seeds, raw	6.5–7.8
Fish	1.0
Sardines, canned with liquid	10.7

Shrimps, oysters, clams	5.008.0
Meat, separable lean only	3.2
Chicken	1.5
Spleen, hog	29.4
Spleen, beef or calf	10.6
Liver, hog	19.2
Liver, beef, lamb, chicken	7.0–10.0
Flour, all-purpose enriched	2.9
Wheat flakes, added nutrients	4.4
Oatmeal, dry	4.5
Blackstrap molasses	16.1
Sorghum	12.5
Cocoa	10.7
Egg yolks (6)	4.0
Prunes	4.4
Spinach	3.1

Obviously, if you need 4 to 10 milligrams of iron a day, 7 ounces of lean beef should provide sufficient. Beans, dry mature seeds, cereals, and organ meats are excellent sources of iron.

CHAPTER

4

Hints for Successful Low-Fat Cooking

Give the same recipe to two cooks and one may produce a superb flavorful dish and the other a disaster. That is the difference between a good cook and one not so good. Experience helps. The first attempt at a new recipe is not always as successful as later efforts. The same applies to cooking with limited amounts of fat. There are some tricks to it. The experienced cook will have no trouble converting to low-fat cooking, but the less experienced, who depends on frozen food packages and prepared foods and who compensates for a lack of skill with copious amounts of butter, will need some help in order to achieve satisfactory results. None of the principles involved is difficult; it is just a matter of knowing a few secrets and then applying them.

The basic elements of good cooking apply equally well to low-fat cooking. Rules of measuring, timing, and temperature should be observed carefully, and all ingredients should be of good quality if you want to be sure of achieving good results. Tastes vary, of course, especially in the use of herbs and spices, but I suggest that you follow the exact measurements given in the following recipes the first time you try them; the second time, you can adjust the measurements or ingredients to suit yourself. Unless otherwise noted, all teaspoon, tablespoon, and cup measurements are to be level, not heaping. Timing is also a matter of exact measurement, and it often makes the difference between a perfect dish and a disaster. I recommend the use of a kitchen timer, but I also suggest that you learn how to adjust the timing and temperature of the recipes to the particular behavior of your stove. The wise cook will use a variety of thermometers to tell the actual temperature inside the oven (which is often much different from the gauge outside the door and a frequent cause of improper roasting or baking) and to tell the temperature inside the meat, fish, or poultry.

In addition to these common-sense rules, which apply to all kinds of cookery, there are a number of special low-fat cooking techniques that you can adapt to your own methods. There are also certain ingredients that can be substituted for the fat-rich foods commonly used in thickening sauces and gravies or in flavoring bland dishes.

You will find that nonfat milk powder, for instance, is an essential part of low-fat cooking and an invaluable aid to almost every kind of dish you will want to make. The powder can be used to thicken sauce or gravy, although in adding milk to a hot liquid, it is often better to mix the powder first in a little cold water and to add the milk to the hot liquid slowly, stirring constantly. Even so, it may be necessary for you to use a rotary beater to eliminate the lumps. See the recipes in the dairy chapter also for other uses of nonfat milk powder.

Gelatin is often neglected as an aid in cooking. Not only can it be used in making desserts and salads, it can also be employed as a thickener because of its ability to cause jelling. It is an excellent fat-free source of protein coming from the tendons and bones of animals. It can be used in making nonfat mayonnaise (see recipe 83), and in making ice cream and other frozen desserts, as well as foods that are served at room temperature.

In many standard recipes, egg white can be substituted for whole eggs. It improves the texture of baked products and has many other uses in nonfat cooking. As a general rule, use two egg whites for every whole egg listed in a recipe. If stiffly beaten whites are called for, the other ingredients must be folded gently into the egg whites without further beating if the light texture is to be maintained.

The usual hiding places for calories, and fat calories especially, are the sauces and gravies used to dress up meats, vegetables, and salads. It is therefore a good idea to study your methods of preparing sauces and to adjust them to the techniques for low-fat cooking. It is important to know, for instance, that excellent sauces can be made without any fat at all, and that it is care and skill that guarantee the success of a sauce rather than the use of butter or other fats. Natural starch, such as that found in cereals and vegetables, or in flour and cornstarch, is not easily digested and has an unappetizing flavor when raw. Starch cooked with moisture softens, as the inside of a potato softens. When cooked in dry heat, starch will break down into dextrine, which has a sweeter flavor. The crust of bread, for instance, tastes different from the inner loaf because the moisture on the outside has evaporated and the starch there has been converted to dextrine. Inadequately cooked starches—in sauces, vegetables, or breads—are usually what causes failure, either in texture or in flavor.

The use of fat is an aid in cooking starches, since the fat helps to separate the small starch granules to make a smoother sauce. But there is a way of obtaining the same results without the fat; simply add about a fourth of the water called for in the recipe to the starch, stirring constantly. Be sure you add the water, which should be cold, very gradually so that lumps do not form. Then add the cold solution to the rest of the ingredients in the recipe, a little at a time. If lumps do result, just strain the sauce. In cooking sauces, it is a good idea to use a double boiler, because the temperature will remain constant, just below boiling, and there is much less chance of burning or lumping. Allow about ten minutes for cooking flour sauces, and longer for cornstarch sauces. An additional five minutes will be necessary if a glass double boiler is used.

When starch is converted to dextrine, it loses its thickening power. For this reason, a larger quantity of browned flour is needed for thickening than white flour. Acid mixtures such as fruit juice or vinegar, which tend to convert starch to dextrine, decrease its thickening ability. Gelatin is a good thickener when acid liquids are used (with the exception of raw pineapple). Pectin is another useful thickening agent, and egg whites can also be used for this purpose.

Flavorings, Herbs, and Spices

The key to flavorful dishes in low-fat cooking is often the skillful use of flavorings, herbs, and spices. It is no accident that the spice world has fewer problems with atherosclerosis, heart attacks, and other ills characteristic of the fat-eating world. Since many of these flavorful agents common in Asia, South America, and the Mediterranean region were not natural products of northern Europe, people in these countries learned to depend upon butter and meat fats for seasoning. But vegetables need not be flavored by butter to be tasty, and the flavor of meat can be perked up with spices rather than thick gravies. A basic white sauce is an excellent vehicle for flavoring agents, be they spices, herbs, vegetable flavorings, seafood, or sweet sirups. If the sauce is flat, don't blame it on the absence of fat. The more he learns about spices, herbs, and flavoring agents the greater the cook's versatility. A list of the principal herbs and spices and their use is given in Table VIII, page 291.

Herbs and spices are not the only flavoring agents. Many vegetables are useful for this purpose. Meat, fowl, fish, other vegetables or salads, and sauces can take on new flavors with the addition of garlic, chives, leeks, parsley, pepper cress, mustard leaves, onion, pimento, horseradish, or tomato sauce. There are many uses for pickles and relishes. Nonfat mayonnaise can be turned into any variety of flavorful sauces; tartare sauce is just one example. Add chives to uncreamed cottage cheese for a vegetable salad or fruits for a sweeter salad.

In addition to vegetables as flavoring agents, there are many ways of using low-fat or nonfat meat drippings (drippings that have been cooled and the fat skimmed off the top). Bouillon cubes are excellent for gravies, sauces, and vegetables, and of course there are fruit juices and wines.

Keep the following hints in mind when using flavoring agents. Spices and herbs should be as fresh as possible; those that have been on the shelf for a long time lose their flavor. Flavorings, herbs, and spices should not be overcooked, since the volatile oils will be lost. Vanilla, for example, should be added at the end of cooking (except in baking).

As every experienced cook knows, these agents are used to enhance the flavor of a dish, not to overpower it. Use them singly or in combination, but don't overdo it. A case in point is garlic, which in limited amounts can enhance the flavor of meat, but in larger amounts can overwhelm it.

Prepared Cooking Utensils

If you wish to avoid fat in foods it is self-defeating to cook foods in pans that have been greased or oiled. There are a number of ways this can be avoided. There is a whole line of utensils that have been coated with Teflon or similar substances. With care, you can use these to fry foods successfully without grease or oil. They must not be overheated and must be washed carefully to retain the Teflon coating. Some cooks are happy with these products and find they can bake without grease or use them to grill such foods as hot cakes or to sauté meats. Other cooks find that they are soon overheated and with the loss of the protective coating become more troublesome than ordinary kitchenware.

A good choice is to use one of the products that can be sprayed into an ordinary utensil before using it. These are available in supermarkets.

A product made of lecithin is excellent. It does not contain grease or oil in any form and acts like Teflon to prevent sticking. It has the advantage of providing a temporary coating for ordinary utensils. It can be used to pan-broil, sauté, or bake.

If neither of these methods are available to you, rub the utensil very lightly with cooking oil before using it. There is no way one can avoid absorbing fat into the food, but if very little oil is used, little harm is done. In this book, "prepared pan," "prepared bake dish," or other "prepared" utensil will mean that one of the above three methods has been used (Teflon, spraying, or lightly oiling). Calculations of food values will be based on the assumption that no fat is absorbed from the cooking utensil.

Breading, Crumbling, and Dredging

Meat, poultry, and fish are often rolled in flour, meal, crushed cereals, or bread crumbs before cooking. Some recipes call for a special batter. In low-fat cooking such batter should not include oil, fats, or egg yolk, but you can dip food in nonfat milk, egg white, or water before "dredging" in flour or crumbs and then place it on a piece of aluminum foil until the flour has dried.

In general it is better to avoid this means of preparation. The outside crust from the batter or flour tends to soak up fat that would otherwise drip out of the meat or poultry. A lean fish can be breaded, as can shrimp, if no additional fat is used in the process. Commercial products that are already breaded should be avoided unless the ingredients are known and do not conflict with the basic diet.

Browning

If the cooking process you use does not impart a brown color to a food and such is desired, then paprika can be used to advantage. Sprinkle paprika on fish, for example, and a nice brown crust will develop as the fish cooks.

Cooking Methods

BASTING is usually defined as pouring melted fat over a roast or barbecue, and of course this should never be done in low-fat cooking. The same result can be accomplished by pouring nonfat meat drippings over the roast or barbecue. A solution of bouillon or some other nonfat sauce can be used instead of fat or drippings with fat.

BOILING is an excellent low-fat method of cooking. You need not lose any of the nutrients if you cool the liquid and remove the fat from the top, serving the remaining liquid or using it to make gravy, sauce, or basting liquid. It is particularly useful in preparing fat-rich meats or poultry.

BRAISING means to sear food in fat, then simmer it in a closed container with a little moisture. The process is meant to brown the food, and it must be modified for low-fat cooking. In this book it means to sear food in a specially prepared utensil rather than in fat. The browned meat can then be steamed or stewed as desired.

BROILING is well suited to low-fat cooking. Whatever fat drips from the food helps decrease the remaining fat content. If you cool the drippings and remove the fat from the top, the remainder can be used as nonfat drippings. This method is not as good as boiling simply because the temperature for proper broiling is rather low and tends to allow more fat to remain between the tissues of meat, poultry, and fish.

FRICASSEEING means to cook by stewing in a gravy. The gravy should be made without fat for this purpose.

FRYING commonly means to fry in fat. You can still fry, but it must be in a prepared pan, which means without fat. Vegetables, meat, fish, poultry can all be fried in this manner. The disadvantage is in cooking fat foods because the food can soak up the accumulated fat rendered by the frying. If the food is lifted off the frying surface so that the fat runs away then it is called pan-broiling.

PAN-BROILING is accomplished by cooking on a hot surface, such as a grill or skillet, in such a way that the fat runs off. A perfectly flat surface with a depressed rim to collect fat will serve for this purpose, as will a wire grill or a ridged pan placed over a heated surface.

ROASTING is quite acceptable for low-fat cooking, but one must avoid placing the meat so that fat drips into it during the cooking process. Remove all excess fat from the meat and if the drippings are to be used, remove the fat before doing so.

SAUTÉING usually means to cook quickly in a small amount of fat by shifting and turning the food. This can be done easily without the fat.

STEAMING by cooking directly over boiling water is a fine way to cook. It poses no special problems in low-fat cooking, and is a particularly good way of preparing fish.

STEWING is really the same as boiling except that the quantity of liquid used is generally smaller. The principles mentioned in boiling apply equally well to stewing.

Cooking at High Altitude

Almost all recipes are designed for sea-level cooking. At increased altitudes, modifications are sometimes necessary. At sea level the boiling point is 212°, but the boiling point decreases about one degree for each increase of five hundred feet in altitude. Boiling or stewing meat, fowl, and fish can still be accomplished at high altitudes since these foods are cooked when their internal temperatures are still below 200° F. It may be necessary, however, to cook food a little longer. At very high altitudes it may be desirable to use pressure cooking for vegetables.

Baking at altitudes above three thousand feet affects quick breads and cakes, although yeast breads are not affected. It is usually necessary to decrease the amounts of baking powder, sugar, and fat (if any is included) for best results. In this regard the decreased fat content given for the recipes in this book will be a plus factor, but it may still be necessary to decrease the amount of baking powder and sugar. If you use half sugar and half artificial sweetener, only the baking powder will need to be decreased.

Cooking candy and frostings may also be a problem since they cannot be tested at the soft-ball stage. You may need a saccharometer to judge consistency correctly.

CHAPTER 5

Cereals and Grains

Cereals are one of the oldest of man's natural foods. Primitive man stripped the grass of its seeds and chewed them for nourishment. Eventually he learned to cultivate barley and related grasses, which was a necessary forerunner to the domestication of animals and the beginning of man's change from a nomadic wild animal into a creature of civilization.

For centuries cereals provided a major source of food for man. Bread was truly the staff of life. *Since cereals are mostly carbohydrate, it is plain that man's diet was a high-carbohydrate diet. In their natural form cereals provided much of man's nutritional needs.* The husk and germ of the cereals contained many important vitamins, such as the vitamin-B group. They were rich in minerals extracted from the soil and of course they were low in fat content. What fat they did contain was of the polyunsaturated type. Thus diets containing a large portion of their fat in the polyunsaturated form are not new, but as old as man. This does not mean that early man's diet was rich in polyunsaturated fat, but only that what fat was in the diet was usually of the polyunsaturated type—a great difference from a high-polyunsaturated-fat diet. As a general rule about half of the fat in cereals is polyunsaturated fat.

It did not take long for man to tamper with his natural food supply. Rice was polished in order to provide nice white rice. Wheat was husked so that the flour would be white. As in many other instances, the importance of natural foods was not apparent until after the food was altered. The value of the husk and germ of cereals as a source of essential vitamins had to be discovered through their absence. People with diets largely based on these "refined" products began having a lot of curious diseases. The loss of an adequate source of vitamin B_1, or thiamine, for example, caused skin disorders, disorders of the nerves with pain in the legs and feet, and even heart failure. Man discovered that there were hidden substances in his food necessary for life (hence the term VITAMIN), but though the effects of nutritional deficiencies were noted, it was not until the twentieth century that vitamins were officially recognized. Sir Frederick Hopkins of England published experimental proof of their existence as late as 1912.

It had been learned as early as 1720 that fresh fruits and vegetables prevented the dreaded scurvy, and at the end of the nineteenth century Admiral Takaki, Director General of the Medical Service of the Japanese navy, discovered that he could prevent the sickness of muscle pain and heart failure common to sailors by adding to their supply of "polished rice" a sufficient amount of fish and meat. Many people thought the cause of the sailors' illnesses was contamination of the rice supply with an unknown microbe.

When the importance of the husk of cereals was demonstrated, there arose a wave of food additives and "refined" products which are still with us today. White flour became "enriched" with the various members of the vitamin-B group. Rice was enriched to replace, partially at least, nature's supply of vitamins, and today we have enriched breakfast foods, enriched bread, enriched milk, and enriched flour. Some of these products contain much more of the vitamin substances than were present in the natural foods, sometimes causing a dangerous oversupply. Too much iron, for instance, can cause disease just as too little iron can lead to anemia. The refinement of enriched products has eliminated a lot of the bulk and fiber natural to foods which, though it has satisfied the palate of modern man, has been a frequent factor in constipation and other ills. In general, however, the fortified, enriched foods of today have made an important contribution to man's health, and his food supply today is better than at any time in his long history as an inhabitant of the planet.

Cereals are rather rich in calories compared to a number of other foods. An average value for a 3½-ounce portion of dry cereal is 360 calories. This is equivalent to twice the number of calories found in the same amount of lean round steak, and over three times the quantity found in a similar weight of fryer chicken, lean fish, shrimp, egg whites, and vegetables. It is more than five times as many calories as are found in most fresh fruits. Only the concentrated carbohydrates, such as sugar, honey, and sirups, and such fats as margarine, butter, and lard contain more calories than the cereal group. The reason for this is that cereals contain very little water. Less than 15 per cent of whole-grain wheat is water, while over 70 per cent of lean round steak is water.

Many cereals compare favorably with foods normally classed as "high-protein" foods in terms of the percentage of their calories that come from protein. Whole-wheat flour contains enough protein to account for 16 per cent of all its calories, and gluten flour 41 per cent. Compare this to choice ribs of beef (eleventh and twelfth ribs) with 16 per cent of their calories from protein, or whole milk including 3.7 per cent butterfat with 23 per cent of its calories from protein. The protein supply is comparable but the significant difference is that meat and milk contain a lot of calories from fat and the cereals contain a lot of calories from carbohydrate. (The food composition of cereals is listed in Table X, page 294, and the composition for prepared breakfast foods is listed in Table XI, page 296. In a low-fat, low-cholesterol diet, these differences can be crucial.)

Is it really true that commercial breakfast cereals have little food value? The answer depends on what standards you are using. The simple truth is that commercial cereals contain about as many or more nutrients for a given weight as natural cereals. Puffing up a grain of rice or wheat does not change its nutrient value, but it does increase the bulk by adding a lot of hot air to the situation. Rice provides a classic example. A 3½-ounce portion of uncooked enriched white rice contains 363 calories, while the same weight of puffed rice contains 399 calories. There is not much difference in the protein content and in both instances the rice is enriched. If you wish to talk about calories per cupful, however, that is another matter, since the puffed rice is full of air. A 3½-ounce portion of puffed rice would fill up about four cups where the uncooked rice would fill up less than half a cup. The same principle applies to flakes and popcorn. A given weight of flakes contains about the same amount of nutrients as the original grain. The practical difference in your diet is that, of course, you are likely to eat less because of the increased bulk, which explains why popcorn is relatively low in calories compared to other snacks such as potato chips or nuts.

A common myth is that home-cooked cereals are more nutritious than commercial dry cereals. The truth is they contain less food for a given weight. The reason is simple. Cooked oatmeal, cooked rice, or similar cooked preparations contain a lot of water, which contributes to the weight in exactly the same manner as it contributes to the weight of fresh vegetables, fresh fruits, or lean meat. As an example, look at rice again: a 3½-ounce portion of cooked rice contains only 109 calories, only about a fourth as many calories as a similar weight of puffed rice, and it has a similar decrease in proteins, minerals, and vitamins because its entire food value is diluted with water. This does not mean that home-cooked cereals are not good for you, but it does mean that a lot of propaganda on the relative merits of home-cooked cereals and commercially prepared cereals is just that—propaganda.

What should you eat on breakfast cereals? That depends a lot on the goal of your diet. If you really need to restrict calories you should probably use an artificial sweetener. If you need to limit only your fat intake you can eat cereals with low-fat milk or reconstituted nonfat milk; you might even try it with a fruit juice.

A major source of calories for breakfast cereals is sugar. If limiting calories is your goal, you may wish to use an artificial sweetener or simply some fresh fruit. For those people who don't like the taste of artificial flavorings, use half sugar and half artificial sweetener.

In addition to the usual breakfast cereals, there are many excellent grains which, because of their low-fat nature, are acceptable in a low-fat, low-calorie diet as long as they are not coated with butter or rich sauces, and as long as they are taken into account in adding up total calories. Unrefined, unhusked grains are to be preferred to refined varieties, not only because their taste and texture are superior but also because they contain many valuable vitamins and some proteins. Converted rice, brown rice, wild rice, barley, bulgar wheat, buckwheat groats (kasha), and millet are all widely available, and they are delicious accompaniments to meat, poultry, or fish dishes.

There are several methods of cooking grains, but the simplest is to sauté the grain gently in a prepared no-fat pan (or a very small quantity of corn oil if your calorie allowance can spare it) for two or three minutes to remove the starchy coating. Then add 2 or 2½ cups of hot water or bouillon to each cup of raw grain and simmer very slowly, covered, until all the liquid is absorbed and each grain is tender but not mushy (anywhere from twenty to thirty-five minutes, depending on the grain used). Cooked mushrooms or onions, peppers, pimientos, and even raisins or nuts are interesting and flavorful additions, but you should calculate their calories, of course, in planning your menu. Two excellent additions to cooked grain are nonfat dry milk and wheat germ, each of which is low in fat, high in protein and vitamins, and distinctly pleasant in flavor. Table X, page 294, gives the food values of individual grains.

CHAPTER 6

Dairy Products

If a little is good more is not necessarily better. This certainly applies to the dairy products: eggs, butter (and margarine), milk, cream, and cheese. If you must restrict your intake of fat, cholesterol, or calories you will need to pay special attention to the use of dairy products in your diet. They are essential in building a healthy diet, but you must know which products can be used and in what amounts to meet your nutritional objectives. The composition of dairy products is listed in Table XII, p. 297.

Eggs

It is not known when man first began eating eggs, though we know that he had discovered the egg long before the birth of Christ. When animal experiments early in the twentieth century showed that much of the fatty deposits in arteries was cholesterol and, worse, that feeding animals lots of egg yolk increased the amount, the reaction of true egg-lovers and those in the egg business was akin to shock. But it has been only in recent years that the egg consumption in the United States (in 1969 the average was 314 eggs a year per person) began to decline.

The egg yolk is the most common source of cholesterol in the diet of industrialized nations, as we have already discussed. One yolk contains about 225 to 250 milligrams of cholesterol, nearly the entire daily amount recommended by the Inter-Society Commission on Heart Disease. But egg yolks contain a lot more than just cholesterol. One yolk has 58 calories and 46 of these are from fat. Only 3 of the calories are polyunsaturated fat, while 15 are saturated fat (the rest are monounsaturated). These are approximate values since the quality of the yolk is affected by the food the hen eats. You must walk one mile to use the calories in one egg yolk.

The egg white is an excellent source of animal protein, and unlike the yolk it is essentially fat- and cholesterol-free. You can use as many of these as you wish limited only by your total calorie allowance. The white of one egg contains only 17 calories, almost all protein.

There are some low-fat, low-cholesterol egg products on the market now and there will be others. One product available in powdered form contains only one fifth as much cholesterol and fat as an average egg. This product can be used to make fried or scrambled eggs, and it may also be substituted for eggs in standard cookbook recipes.

Such commercially prepared foods as bakery products often contain eggs or egg yolks. If you want to limit your egg-yolk intake, you must exercise care in purchasing prepared foods. Many standard recipes calling for eggs can often be prepared without them. Ordinary pancakes are an excellent example; you can use the standard recipe or commercial mix, eliminating both the egg and fat, and still have good pancakes. Of course, there are some recipes that are not satisfactory without the egg, but in that case you can try using egg whites alone (usually twice as many as the number of whole eggs suggested) or one of the powdered low-fat, low-cholesterol products.

It is worth pointing out that while the egg is rich in vitamins and minerals, it contains no nutrients that cannot be obtained from other food sources compatible with a low-fat, low-cholesterol diet.

Butter and Margarine

Neither butter nor margarine is commonly used in most of the world. This may sound strange to the cook schooled in the use of butter for seasoning, frying, and baking. Even the idea of using butter sounds strange to most cooks of Asia, Africa, and the Mediterranean region, where olive oil is used. Oriental cooks rely on spices for flavor, shunning the use of either butter or animal fats for this purpose. Much of the world simply does not use much fat for cooking purposes. In fact, butter is a relative newcomer to man's diet, but once it was introduced into the cuisine of Western Europe butter or its substitute, margarine, remained entrenched. The French have placed a high value on the "buttery flavor" in a vast array of dishes from vegetables to desserts. Interestingly enough, it was the French who gave birth to margarine when, in 1867, Napoleon III encouraged the development of a cheap butter substitute. The first margarines were made of solid animal fats, but most margarines today are made from vegetable oils. Despite its French origin, margarine is poorly regarded by the *cordon bleu* and France still uses five pounds of butter for every pound of margarine.

What are the disadvantages of butter and margarine? First, they each contain a large number of calories. A level tablespoon of either one contains about 100 calories. Eight tablespoons of butter (nearly a ¼-pound stick, or 100 grams) contain 250 milligrams of cholesterol or about the same amount as found in one egg yolk. Over half of the calories in butter are from saturated fat; hardly any are from polyunsaturated fat. Since cholesterol is not found in vegetables, the margarines made of vegetable oil do not contain it, an important consideration if there is a need to limit the cholesterol intake.

Most margarine products contain less saturated fat and more polyunsaturated fat than butter. Because new products are constantly appearing on the market it is not possible to give any exact figure applicable to all margarines. If you want a margarine low in saturated fat and high in polyunsaturates, the best rule is to look for one made from a liquid oil containing lots of polyunsaturated fat, such as safflower oil or corn oil. The softer of these margarines (usually tub margarine) contains the least amount of hydrogenated or hardened oil (polyunsaturated fat that has been converted to saturated fat). The first item on the label will usually read liquid corn oil or another liquid oil. If the first item is hydrogenated or hardened fat, the product will contain less polyunsaturated fat than the one using liquid oil.

You can replace ordinary butter with margarine for toast, pancakes, or anything else that you are accustomed to eating with butter. In most recipes calling for butter you can substitute a polyunsaturated oil and achieve good results. It is often better to use a little less oil than the amount of butter suggested. Sometimes the butter can simply be omitted without substitution. Polyunsaturated margarines may be used to season vegetables within the limits of your fat allowance.

Butter is often an ingredient in bakery products. Some breads are enriched with it, and rolls, cakes, pies, cookies, and pastries are usually loaded with butter. Some frozen vegetables are packaged in "butter sauces." If you really wish to eliminate butter from your diet you must be constantly on the alert for its presence in commercially prepared foods.

Milk and Cream

Man was not originally a milk drinker. For thousands and thousands of years he hunted or gathered his food from the forest. Milk was consumed only during infancy, and most babies were weaned by two years of age. Eventually man domesticated animals and ceased to depend solely on hunting. As herds of milk-producing animals were developed, some groups learned how to milk them, and the art of dairying was born.

In much of the world, even today, adults cannot drink milk without developing disagreeable symptoms. Even a small amount of milk can cause bloating, abdominal discomfort, and diarrhea. People who have this difficulty cannot digest lactose, the sugar in milk. Lactose is a double-sugar compound and before it can be absorbed from the intestine it must be converted to its simple one-sugar compounds (lactose is converted to glucose and galactose). This conversion of a complex sugar to simple sugars is made possible by an enzyme, lactase. Lactase is normally present in all babies, but after weaning it can disappear. If a person does not have lactase in his digestive tract he cannot tolerate milk. Most people of the milk-drinking world do have lactase, but its absence is common elsewhere. Although there are some exceptions, it is the milk-drinking world that develops fatty deposits in the arteries causing heart and vascular disease.

Although the people of Cyprus are dairy people, they cannot drink milk. They can use cheese, however. When milk is soured or fermented, the lactose sugar is broken down and lactase is no longer necessary for digestion. Thus a person who cannot tolerate milk may be able to tolerate cheese. Incidentally, the cheese-eating, milk-abstaining Cypriots have the longest life expectancy of any people in the world. This is not necessarily an endorsement for cheese, however, since they, like the Bantus, are affected by many other factors, such as exercise and freedom from obesity.

Apart from the problem of lactose intolerance, milk is an excellent food. The only question is the amount of butterfat it contains. The desirable features of milk as a protein and calcium source have nothing to do with the butterfat it contains. *Whole milk is actually a high-fat food, not a high-protein food.* Over half of the calories in whole milk (which is 3.7 per cent fat) are from its fat content; many of its calories are from the lactose sugar, and the rest are from protein. A third of the calories in the 2-per-cent-fortified milk products are from its fat content—and over half of that is saturated fat.

Because of some dishonest practices within the dairy industry—such as watering down the milk—standards of quality for milk have traditionally been based upon its fat content, which is unaffected by added water. Some consumers and consequently dairymen began to turn to breeds of cattle that produced milk rich in fat. Some Jersey cows produce milk containing 6 per cent butterfat; other breeds such as the Holstein produce milk with much less butterfat. This demonstrates that the breeding of animals does make a difference in the food source. Incidentally, the camel naturally produces fat-free milk, in case you have ready access to camel's milk.

One of the most important reasons for milk in the diet is its calcium content. There are only a few good food sources for calcium, and milk is one of the best. A cup of milk contains about 300 milligrams of calcium. Some of the low-fat fortified products contain even more. During the adolescent years both boys and girls need nearly 1.5 grams of calcium a day. Pregnant and lactating women need about the same amount. In the middle forties and beyond the calcium intake again needs to be about 1.5 grams a day to help prevent degeneration of the skeleton. A quart of milk a day will satisfy those requirements. Uncreamed cottage cheese can also be used to meet the calcium requirements.

You might well ask what primitive man did for calcium before milk was used. Recent paleontological studies suggest that the squat stature of the Neanderthal man was actually caused by rickets caused by a secondary vitamin D deficiency and lack of sunshine. It is likely that calcium deficiency also was a factor. Dietary intake is not the only factor to affect the strength and calcification of bones. Physical activity seems to favor the absorption and deposition of calcium. Bedrest (and the weightlessness of space flight, incidentally) causes calcium to be withdrawn from the bones and lost through the urine.

Most low-fat milks are fortified with milk solids and vitamins. Some contain in a single quart about half of the total daily requirements of many vitamins and iron and all the vitamin D and calcium needed every day.

One of the most useful products of the dairy industry is nonfat dry milk powder, which is usually fortified with vitamins A and D. You can obtain from it all the nutritious benefits of milk without adding to your fat consumption. By increasing the ratio of dry powder to water, the amount of calcium and protein can be increased.

In mixing your own milk from dry milk powder you can avoid lumping by shaking the powder through a wire strainer or sieve as you stir it into cold water and by using a rotary beater, a wire whisk, or an electric mixer to blend it. You may prefer to mix half 2-per-cent-fortified milk with half reconstituted nonfat milk. Some people object to the distinctive flavor of reconstituted milk. A good way to cut the flavor is to add a small amount of honey, which will impart a more natural flavor to the milk. Only a little honey is needed, a teaspoon or so being sufficient for a quart of milk. A small amount of salt will also serve this purpose very well.

Reconstituted milk can be used in standard recipes that call for milk, and I have done so throughout this book. You may choose to mix the dry power with a little cold water before adding it to the recipe, or you can shake the powder through a wire sieve as you add it.

Natural buttermilk is what is left when sour cream is churned into butter. Buttermilk purchased at the store is usually made from skim milk and is essentially fat-free, though it contains the same amount of calcium as sweet milk. If it is packaged with flakes of butter in it these can be strained out. You can make your own buttermilk from nonfat dry milk powder.

#1 Buttermilk

1. To

    1 quart reconstituted milk

    add

    ½ cup buttermilk.

2. Allow to curdle at room temperature. A small amount of this can then be used to make more buttermilk.

Cream is just milk with a high butterfat content. The old-fashioned cream separator could be adjusted to produce thick cream with a high butterfat content or a thinner cream with a lower butterfat content. Since the farmer was paid for the butterfat and not the amount of milk that diluted it, the thickness of the cream was unimportant from that standpoint. The various creams available on the market today are categorized according to their fat content (see Table XII, page 297).

Many housewives have turned to artificial cream to avoid butterfat. There is no reason for this other than convenience of storage. The truth is most of these have far more saturated fat than cream. The innocent label stating the product is made from vegetable oil is a not-so-innocent deception—the vegetable oil is coconut oil, almost all saturated fat. People who use coconut oil as a main source of food have a high incidence of heart and vascular disease caused by fatty deposits. There is little or no difference in calorie content either. If you are going to use cream you might as well enjoy the real thing. If you want a cream substitute you can make your own.

#2 Sweet-Cream Substitute

1. Mix together

    1 cup sifted nonfat milk powder
    ½ cup cold water.

2. Add

    1 teaspoon of honey.

3. Mix thoroughly.

TC*	P	C	F	S	M	PU	CHOL
267	105	158	4(1%)	—	—	—	11

You can also make your own whipped-cream substitute from nonfat dry milk powder. Beware of commercial artificial whipped cream and toppings if you want to avoid saturated fats. These are usually packaged in pressurized cans—and, yes, you guessed it—the vegetable oil is coconut oil again. You'd better make your own.

#3 Whipped-Cream Substitute

1. Gradually mix

    1 cup nonfat milk powder

    into

    1 cup cold water.

2. Add

    1 tablespoon lemon juice
    ½ cup sugar or honey
    ½ teaspoon vanilla.

* Total Calories in the recipe (TC), Calories of Protein (P); Calories of Carbohydrate (C); Calories of fat (F); Calories of Saturated fat (S); Calories of Monounsaturated fat (M); Calories of Polyunsaturated fat (PU); Cholesterol (Chol).

3. Whip until stiff. Chill and if desired whip again before using. Mixture will stiffen further on cooling.

TC	P	C	F	S	M	PU	CHOL
632	105	523	4 (0.6%)	—	—	—	22

#4 Sour-Cream Substitute

1. Mix together
   ¼ cup nonfat milk powder
   ½ cup cold water.
2. Blend well with
   8 ounces uncreamed cottage cheese
   2 teaspoons lemon juice
   ¼ teaspoon salt.
3. Refrigerate until used.

TC	P	C	F	S	M	PU	CHOL
256	191	58	7 (2.7%)	—	—	—	40

Cheese

Man has been eating cheese for at least four thousand years. No one knows where cheese first originated, but obviously it was unknown before man domesticated animals and started dairying. Legend has it that cheese was discovered by an Arab transporting his milk in a pouch made of a sheep's stomach. The rennet of the stomach lining and the hot sun fermented the milk into curds and whey—so they say. Cheese was a common food in Biblical times and was known throughout the Roman Empire. It was the Romans who introduced it to England. Cheese came to North America aboard the Mayflower in 1620. For years it was a local farm product, but in 1851 the first cheese factory was built in the United States. Now almost all cheese is factory-made.

Americans do not eat as much cheese as the people of many other countries, but consumption has been steadily increasing. Americans now eat about 14 pounds per person a year, approximately twice the amount eaten twenty years ago.

The simplest cheese is cottage cheese, sometimes called country-style or farm-style cheese. It is also known as Dutch cheese or pot cheese. It is an uncured cheese made from skim milk or nonfat dry milk solids to which rennet is added. In the process of fermentation the lactose is converted to glucose and galactose. For this reason cottage cheese and all other cheeses can be digested without difficulty by people who cannot digest milk because of its lactose content. When cream is added to the cottage cheese curds it is called "creamed cottage cheese." To qualify for this label it must have 4 per cent fat or more, which makes it a high-fat food since one third of its calories is from fat. It offers no nutritional advantages over low-fat or uncreamed cottage cheese, which is nearly fat-free and does not contain cholesterol. This is an ideal food for low-fat, low-cholesterol diets. It is truly a high protein, essentially no-fat food. If you can't find uncreamed cottage cheese you can make your own by simply washing the curds of creamed cottage cheese in a colander. Uncreamed cottage cheese can be used in salads, for making substitute sour cream, or for flavoring. It can also be eaten by itself, plain or seasoned with chives, pimentoes, or other ingredients. It is an excellent source of calcium. Use as much uncreamed cottage cheese as you like.

The other cheeses, natural or processed, are very high-fat foods. In general over half the calories in cheese are from fat. They also contain about half as much cholesterol as butter. Clearly, if fat intake is limited the amount of cured cheese eaten must also be limited. The cured cheese is, however, a good source of calcium. (See Table XII, page 297, for the comparative food values of cheese.)

Yogurt has long been a common food in many parts of the world and its consumption in the United States is increasing. There are many varieties of yogurt. Bulgarian yogurt is made from a mixture of water-buffalo milk and goat's milk. The end product is rather high in fat content. Yogurt made from ordinary whole milk gets about half its calories from its fat content. Yogurt made from partially skimmed milk contains less fat. New yogurt products, some classified as low-fat, are appearing on the market. Yogurt is really a form of cheese and like all soured or fermented milk products contains less lactose.

CHAPTER

7

Breads, Biscuits, and Pancakes

Bread has been one of the basic foods of man since cultivation began. Bread and wine often were the basis for a meal or a repast with a friend. Time and different cultures have spawned an infinite variety of breads. Ground meal with nothing more than salt and water added before baking was an early bread. It was hard and tough, bearing little resemblance to the soft fluffy commercial breads of today's supermarket. The addition of yeast to breadmaking provided a new dimension to breads. Bread can be made from flour, salt, water, and yeast alone. The ancient Egyptians were the earliest accomplished breadmakers. They learned that the sour dough used by the Hebrews contained yeast, and developed the art of making yeast bread. By 4000 B.C. the Egyptian bakers were enriching their bread with honey, fruits, spices, and herbs.

The quality of bread is affected by the flour used in its preparation. The protein content is increased when the darker flour is used. Thus rye bread and whole-wheat bread contain more protein than white bread. The dark flour is also richer in the vitamin B group. Wheat flour with the grain husk removed loses some of its nutritive value, and in order to offset undesirable features of white bread, I recommend the use of enriched flour to which vitamins have been added. Yeast adds to the vitamin content of bread.

In order to produce a smoother texture and a bread that keeps longer, fat and sugar are often added. These added ingredients increase the caloric value of the bread, and the breads enriched with butter or lard make matters worse if you want to restrict your saturated-fat intake. Eggs are often used as an additive to impart a yellow color to bread. This adds to the cholesterol in the diet, which may not be desirable. The addition of sugar, fruits, and nuts all increase the calorie content of bread. Sugar has no essential nutrients other than carbohydrates, since it is devoid of vitamins and minerals.

How much bread you should eat in your diet depends upon the kind of bread, the number of calories you utilize, your body-fat stores, and what you want to do about them. Limiting the amount of bread you eat is one good way of limiting calories, but sufficient vitamin B, calcium, and protein for daily needs must be obtained from other foods if bread is eliminated.

Bread is often a good source of calcium if it is made with milk rather than water. To avoid unwanted amounts of saturated animal fat a nonfat dry milk preparation should be used. By increasing the amount of nonfat dry milk in proportion to water the calcium and protein content of the bread can be significantly increased.

There is a wide variety of commercial breads available, and their contents are constantly changing. You can get a general idea of their composition by consulting Table XIII, page 299.

How Yeast Works

It is the growth of yeast plants that causes bread to rise. The process gives off tiny bubbles of carbon dioxide gas within the dough. The gas is trapped in the gluten fibers of the dough. The temperature must be right for the yeast action. This is why yeast must be dissolved in lukewarm water (80°–90°F for compressed yeast cakes and 110°F for dry yeast). If the temperature is too hot the tiny yeast plants will be killed, and if it is too cold the fermentation process will be slowed or stopped.

When the bread is baked the tiny gas bubbles expand—causing the bread to rise even more and resulting in the light bread texture. The rising time can be shortened by increasing the amount of yeast used.

The following recipes provide a simple way of making low-fat bread. The expert breadmaker will have no trouble with the recipes, and the beginner can become an expert with a little practice. Making bread is actually very simple. Some people find a significant difference in taste when they use moist yeast cakes as opposed to dry cakes or powdered yeast, with the moist yeast cakes providing a more delicate flavor.

#5 Low-Fat White Bread

1. Dissolve

    2 cakes yeast

    in

    ¼ cup warm water (80°–90°).*

2. Add

    2 tablespoons sugar
    2 teaspoons salt.

3. In a large container bring to a boil

    1 cup water.

4. In a bowl mix

    1 cup nonfat milk powder
    1 cup cold water.

5. Remove boiling water from the heat and add the milk.
6. If the temperature of the water and milk is suitable (80°–90°), add the yeast, sugar, and salt mixture.
7. Add to the liquid gradually

    6 cups sifted all-purpose enriched flour

    or enough to produce dough of the desired consistency.

8. Place the dough on a lightly floured board and knead thoroughly, until the dough has a satinlike appearance (about 15 minutes).
9. Replace the dough in the large container and cover with a damp towel. The container should be kept in a warm place or set in a larger container of warm water. Let dough set until it has risen to twice its volume (about 1½ hours).
10. Place the dough on the molding board again and knead thoroughly. Then divide into equal parts. Shape into loaves and place in two prepared loaf pans. Press the dough gently into the corners. Let rise to double its volume, or more if a lighter bread is desired (about 2 hours).
11. Place the pans in a preheated oven of 400° for 15 minutes. Reduce temperature to 350° and bake until done (about 40 minutes). The loaves will be evenly browned and will shrink slightly from the edges of the pan.
12. Remove the finished loaves. Brush the tops with roll glaze if desired (Recipe #12). Place on a wire rack to cool.

TC	P	C	F	S	M	PU	CHOL
2965	392	2400	64(2.2%)	12(0.4%)	18(0.6%)	30(1.0%)	22

* For packaged yeast use a temperature of 110°–115° or as indicated on the package.

#6 High-Protein Low-Fat White Bread

Follow the directions for Recipe #5 but add

3 egg whites

to the yeast and sugar mixture. You may need to increase the flour for desired thickness.

TC	P	C	F	S	M	PU	CHOL
3016	440	2403	64(2.1%)	12(0.4%)	18(0.6%)	30(1.0%)	22

#7 Sugar-Free White Bread

Follow directions for Recipe #5 for white bread, omitting sugar.

TC	P	C	F	S	M	PU	CHOL
2869	392	2304	64(2.2%)	12(0.4%)	18(0.6%)	30(1.0%)	22

#8 Whole-Wheat Bread

Follow directions for white bread, Recipe #5, substituting

6 cups whole-wheat flour (stone-ground, if you can get it)

for white flour and using

¼ cup molasses

instead of sugar.

TC	P	C	F	S	M	PU	CHOL
2847	452	2270	124(4.4%)	80(2.8%)	120(4.2%)	60(2.1%)	22

#9 Rye Bread

1. Follow directions in Recipe #5 for white bread, substituting

   6 cups rye flour

   1½ cups whole-wheat flour (stone-ground, if you can get it)

   for white flour.
2. Bake at 350° about 55 minutes.

TC	P	C	F	S	M	PU	CHOL
3085	347	2733	46(1.5%)	6(0.2%)	9(0.3%)	15(0.5%)	22

For people who need to increase the protein in their diet and cannot utilize any more fat intake the gluten breads are made to order. Well over half of the calories in gluten flour come from protein.

#10 High-Protein Gluten Bread

1. Mix together
   ¼ cup lukewarm water (80°–90°)
   2 yeast cakes.
2. In separate container mix
   2 cups cold water
   1 cup nonfat milk powder.
3. Add
   1 teaspoon salt
   2 egg whites, lightly beaten.
4. Gradually stir in, mixing thoroughly,
   4 cups gluten flour.

The mixture should have a consistency that can be dropped from a spoon.

5. Fill prepared bake pan ⅓ full. Cover top with damp cloth and let dough rise to over twice its volume.
6. Bake at 350° until done (about 1 hour.)

TC	P	C	F	S	M	PU	CHOL
2173	920	1072	84(3.9%)	16(0.7%)	20(0.9%)	40(1.8%)	22

#11 Kneaded Gluten Bread

1. Dissolve
   1 cake yeast
   in
   ¼ cup warm water (80°–90°).
2. Dissolve
   ½ cup nonfat milk powder
   1 teaspoon salt
   in
   1 cup cold water
   and warm over low heat to 80°–90°.

3. Remove from heat and add dissolved yeast.
4. Gradually mix in

2 cups gluten flour

until the dough is satiny.

5. Knead and let rise to about double volume in a warm room (about 1 hour).
6. Knead again, fill prepared bake pan about ⅓ full, and let rise to well over double volume.
7. Bake at 400° for 15 minutes, then reduce heat and bake at 350° until done (about 40 minutes).

TC	P	C	F	S	M	PU	CHOL
1070	444	535	42(3.9%)	8(0.7%)	10(0.9%)	20(1.9%)	11

Dinner Rolls

If you eat many rolls you would be wise to make your own. Most commercial rolls contain more fat than ordinary bread, and unless the package is clearly labeled it is impossible to tell if saturated or unsaturated fats have been used. Of course you should especially avoid rolls enriched with butter or eggs or both if you are on a low-fat low-cholesterol diet.

You can use the dough from any one of the bread recipes to make dinner rolls. The calories and contents of the recipe of course will be the same for rolls as for bread. To determine the calories and food composition for each roll divide the values given for the total recipe by the number of rolls it makes.

If you wish to give the rolls a glaze, brush the tops lightly before baking with

#12 Roll Glaze

Mix together

1 egg white, lightly beaten
1 tablespoon water.

#13 Plain Rolls

1. Roll dough ¾ inch thick.
2. Cut with floured biscuit cutter or open can into 2-inch rounds.
3. Roll up each round into a smooth ball.
4. Place rolls 1 to 1½ inches apart in a prepared pan or on a baking sheet.
5. Cover and let rise until volume doubles.
6. Bake at 425° 15–20 minutes.

For clover-leaf rolls, substitute the following direction for stage 4: Place three balls into each cup of a prepared muffin pan. Parker-House rolls can be made according to the same general directions as plain rolls except that instead of rolling the 2-inch round into a ball, simply crease the round with a knife and fold one half over the other.

#14 Crescents

1. Roll yeast-bread dough into a round, ¼ inch thick.
2. Cut the round into pieces as you would cut a pie.
3. Take a section and begin rolling it up from the outer edge to the point so the point is on the outside of the roll.
4. Bend the tips of each roll to form a crescent.
5. Place on a prepared baking sheet or pan over 1 inch apart so rolls won't touch as they rise.
6. Allow to rise to double volume.
7. Bake at 400° 15–20 minutes.

#15 English Muffins

1. Prepare yeast by softening

    1 cake yeast

    in

    ¼ cup water—lukewarm.

2. In a separate large container add

    1¼ teaspoons salt
    2 tablespoons sugar
    ½ cup nonfat milk powder

    to

    1 cup cold water.

3. Mix in

   1 egg white, beaten.

4. Add yeast mixture.
5. Blend in gradually

   4 cups sifted flour.

6. Knead dough until smooth, then let rise to double volume (usually 1 hour).
7. Roll to ¼ inch thick on lightly floured board.
8. Cut into 4-inch rounds.
9. Cover and let rise to double volume.
10. Bake slowly in an oven or cook on a hot ungreased griddle—browning slowly—about 7 minutes for each side.

TC	P	C	F	S	M	PU	CHOL
1985	260	1610	42(2.1%)	8(0.4%)	12(0.6%)	20(1.0%)	11

Sweet Rolls

Many commercial sweet rolls are made with large amounts of saturated fats and with egg yolks. If you wish to avoid excess intake of these you must make your own sweet rolls. Commercial preparations are not a satisfactory substitute. The dough used for making yeast bread is exceptionally good for making your own sweet rolls. With a little innovation you can adapt the following recipes to make a wide variety of rolls for home use. You can put fruit and jellies in the center of your rolls if you can afford the extra calories in your diet.

#16 Cinnamon Rolls

1. Use half of dough from Recipe #5 for white bread.
2. Roll dough into an oblong ¼ inch thick.
3. Mix

   ½ cup sugar
   2 teaspoons cinnamon.

4. Spread sugar and cinnamon mixture evenly over oblong of dough.
5. Roll up the oblong of dough from one end into a single roll.
6. Cut roll crosswise into 1-inch segments.
7. Place segments on cut surface on prepared baking sheet or pan.
8. Cover and let rise to double volume.

9. Bake at 350° for 25 to 30 minutes.

TC	P	C	F	S	M	PU	CHOL
3350	392	2785	64(1.9%)	12(0.4%)	18(0.5%)	30(0.9%)	22

#17 Brown-Sugar Rolls

Follow directions for Recipe #16, but substitute

½ cup brown sugar

for sugar and cinnamon.

TC	P	C	F	S	M	PU	CHOL
3761	392	3196	64(1.7%)	12(0.3%)	18(0.5%)	30(0.8%)	22

Quick Breads

A wide variety of quick breads can be made suitable to the most discriminating palates. These rely on the chemical release of carbon dioxide gas from baking powder to accomplish the same effect as yeast. Most of the quick breads can be made with or without polyunsaturated fat.

#18 Banana Bread

1. Beat until stiff

   2 egg whites.
2. Add

   1 cup sugar.
3. Press through a sieve and add

   1 cup mashed ripe bananas.
4. Add and mix thoroughly

   1 teaspoon lemon juice.
5. Sift together

   2 cups sifted flour
   5 teaspoons baking powder
   ½ teaspoon salt.
6. Mix dry ingredients into banana mixture.
7. Bake in a prepared loaf pan at 375° about 1 hour.

TC	P	C	F	S	M	PU	CHOL
1937	139	1734	25(1.3%)	4(0.2%)	6(0.3%)	10(0.5%)	—

#19 Banana-Nut Bread

Follow directions for banana bread, Recipe #18, adding
1 cup chopped English walnuts at Stage 6.

TC	P	C	F	S	M	PU	CHOL
2737	203	1815	699(25.5%)	47(1.7%)	112(4.1%)	432(15.7%)	—

#20 Banana-Date Bread

Follow recipe for banana bread, Recipe #18, adding
1 cup chopped dates at Stage 6.

TC	P	C	F	S	M	PU	CHOL
2425	151	2200	32(1.3%)	4(0.2%)	6(0.2%)	10(0.4%)	—

#21 Boston Brown Bread

1. Sift together
   1 cup yellow corn meal
   1 cup rye meal
   1 teaspoon salt
   1 teaspoon baking soda
   1 cup graham flour
   ½ cup nonfat milk powder.
2. Mix in thoroughly
   ¾ cup molasses
   1½ cups cold water.
3. Use prepared baking-powder cans or similar containers that can be covered and fill each can about ⅔ full.
4. Place covered cans on a rack in a kettle of boiling water. The water should be at a level to cover the bottom of the cans.
5. Cover kettle and boil for 3 hours. Replenish boiling water as needed.
6. Remove from kettle, uncover cans, and place them in a 400° oven for a few minutes to dry the top.
7. Unmold from cans immediately. Serve hot.

Variation: Add 1 cup seedless raisins to mixed dry ingredients at Stage 2.

#22 Date Bread

1. Sift together
   2½ cups sifted flour
   ½ cup sugar
   ½ cup nonfat milk powder
   ½ teaspoon salt
   5 teaspoons baking powder.
2. Add
   1¼ cups chopped dates
   3 egg whites—beaten stiff.
3. Stir in
   1¼ cups cold water.
4. Stir only until all the flour is damp.
5. Bake in lightly oiled loaf pan at 350° for 1 hour.

TC	P	C	F	S	M	PU	CHOL
2292	225	1967	36(1.6%)	5(0.2%)	8(0.3%)	12(0.5%)	11

#23 Date-Nut Bread

Follow instructions in Recipe #22, adding
1 cup pecan pieces at Stage 2.

TC	P	C	F	S	M	PU	CHOL
3158	265	2041	787(24.9%)	58(1.8%)	482(15.3%)	159(5.0%)	11

#24 Corn Bread

1. Sift together 3 times
   1½ cups yellow corn meal
   ¾ cup sifted flour
   3 teaspoons baking powder
   2 tablespoons sugar
   1 teaspoon salt
   ½ cup nonfat milk powder.

2. Stir in

1¼ cups water.

3. Fold in

2 egg whites stiffly beaten.

4. Pour into prepared pan and bake at 400° 20–25 minutes. When finished the bread will shrink from the sides of the pan.

TC	P	C	F	S	M	PU	CHOL
1250	167	1000	70(5.6%)	2(0.2%)	17(1.4%)	36(2.9%)	11

Biscuits

Biscuits are a form of quick bread, and are easy to make. The commercial dough mixes often contain large amounts of saturated fat, but you can make polyunsaturated biscuits or nonfat biscuits to suit your own needs. Biscuit dough can be stored in the refrigerator and used to make a variety of hot biscuits over a period of days.

#25 Baking-Powder Biscuits

1. Sift together

2 cups sifted flour
3 teaspoons baking powder
½ teaspoon salt
⅓ cup nonfat milk powder.

2. While mixing add

¼ cup oil.

3. Then add

¾ cups water and mix.

4. Place mixture on lightly floured board and knead lightly until dough is smooth.
5. Roll dough ½ inch thick.
6. Cut with floured biscuit cutter.
7. Place rounds on prepared bake sheet.
8. Bake at 450° about 12 minutes. Makes 12 biscuits.

TC	P	C	F	S	M	PU	CHOL
1460	131	784	506(34.6%)	53(3.6%)	142(9.7%)	268(18.4%)	7

#26 Drop Biscuits

1. Follow instructions for
   baking-powder biscuits, Recipe #25
   and increase water sufficiently to make dough soft enough to drop from spoon.
2. Do not knead or roll dough, but drop it by the spoonful onto prepared bake sheet.

TC	P	C	F	S	M	PU	CHOL
1460	131	784	506(34.6%)	53(3.6%)	136(9.3%)	268(18.4%)	7

#27 Orange Biscuits

Follow directions for

baking-powder biscuits, Recipe #25,

adding

1 tablespoon sugar
1 tablespoon grated orange rind.

TC	P	C	F	S	M	PU	CHOL
1508	131	832	506(33.6%)	53(3.5%)	136(9.0%)	268(17.8%)	7

#28 Whole-Wheat Biscuits

Follow recipe for

baking-powder biscuits, Recipe #25,

but substitute

fine whole-wheat flour

for white flour.

TC	P	C	F	S	M	PU	CHOL
1386	151	706	526(38.0%)	57(4.1%)	148(10.7%)	278(20.0%)	7

#29 Nonfat Baking-Powder Biscuits

Prepare without oil

baking-powder biscuits, Recipe #25

using

5 teaspoons baking powder

instead of 3 teaspoons.

TC	P	C	F	S	M	PU	CHOL
986	131	793	20(2.0%)	4(0.4%)	6(0.6%)	10(1.0%)	7

#30 Nonfat Drop Biscuits

1. Follow instructions for

   nonfat baking-powder biscuits, Recipe #29,

   but increase the water enough to make dough sufficiently soft to drop from spoon.
2. Do not knead or roll but drop dough by the spoonful onto prepared bake sheet, oiled lightly.

TC	P	C	F	S	M	PU	CHOL
986	131	793	20(2.0%)	4(0.4%)	6(0.6%)	10(1.0%)	7

#31 Nonfat Orange Biscuits

Follow directions for

nonfat baking-powder biscuits, Recipe #29,

adding

1 tablespoon sugar
1 tablespoon grated orange rind.

TC	P	C	F	S	M	PU	CHOL
1034	131	841	20(1.9%)	4(0.4%)	6(0.6%)	10(1.0%)	7

#32 Maple-Sugar Biscuits

Follow directions for

nonfat baking-powder biscuits, Recipe #29,

and fold into dough

½ cup crushed maple sugar.

TC	P	C	F	S	M	PU	CHOL
1843	131	1167	506(27.4%)	53(2.9%)	142(7.7%)	268(14.5%)	7

#33 Nonfat Maple-Sugar Biscuits

Follow recipe for

nonfat baking-powder biscuits, Recipe #29,

and fold into dough

½ cup crushed maple sugar.

TC	P	C	F	S	M	PU	CHOL
1369	131	1176	20(1.5%)	4(0.3%)	6(0.4%)	10(0.7%)	7

#34 Nonfat Whole-Wheat Biscuits

Follow recipe for

nonfat baking-powder biscuits, Recipe #29,

substituting

fine whole-wheat flour

for white flour.

TC	P	C	F	S	M	PU	CHOL
912	151	715	41(4.5%)	8(0.9%)	12(1.3%)	20(2.2%)	7

Muffins

Muffins are another form of quick bread. They can be made with polyunsaturated oil or without fat.

#35 Plain Muffins

1. Sift together

 2 cups sifted flour
 ¼ cup sugar
 ½ teaspoon salt
 4 teaspoons baking powder
 ½ cup nonfat milk powder.

2. In a separate bowl mix

 1 egg white, beaten
 ¼ cup oil
 1 cup water.

3. Stir liquid ingredients into dry ingredients. Mix only enough to dampen all the flour. The batter should be lumpy. Overstirring results in poor texture.
4. Pour batter into prepared muffin pans. Fill cups ⅔ full.
5. Bake at 400° for 25 minutes. Makes 12 to 15 muffins.

TC	P	C	F	S	M	PU	CHOL
1717	164	1004	508(29.6%)	53(3.1%)	142(8.3%)	268(15.6%)	11

Variations: You may add any of the following chopped dried fruits to Recipes #34 and #35: prunes, figs, dates, peaches, currants, or apricots. Be sure to add the necessary calories in calculating total amount.

#36 Blueberry Muffins

To

 Recipe #35 at Stage 3

add

 1 cup blueberries or 2/3 cup chopped, drained cherries.

Based on blueberries:

TC	P	C	F	S	M	PU	CHOL
1806	167	1083	514(28.5%)	53(2.9%)	136(7.5%)	268(14.8%)	11

#37 Nonfat Muffins

Follow directions for

plain muffins, Recipe #35

but omit the oil and use

5 teaspoons baking powder

instead of 4 teaspoons.

TC	P	C	F	S	M	PU	CHOL
1237	164	1009	22(1.8%)	4(0.3%)	6(0.5%)	10(0.8%)	11

#38 Nonfat Blueberry Muffins

To

Recipe #37

add

1 cup blueberries, or 2/3 cup chopped, drained cherries.

Based on blueberries:

TC	P	C	F	S	M	PU	CHOL
1326	167	1088	28(2.1%)	4(0.3%)	6(0.4%)	10(0.8%)	11

#39 Pecan Muffins

To batter for

plain or nonfat muffins, Recipe #35 or #37

add

⅓ cup chopped pecans.

Using Recipe #35:

TC	P	C	F	S	M	PU	CHOL
2006	177	1029	758(37.8%)	71(3.5%)	300(15.0%)	317(15.8%)	11

Using Recipe #37:

TC	P	C	F	S	M	PU	CHOL
1526	177	1034	272(17.8%)	22(1.4%)	164(10.7%)	59(3.9%)	11

#40 Raisin Muffins

Add to either plain or nonfat muffins, Recipe #35 or #37,

1/3 cup raisins.

Using Recipe #35:

TC	P	C	F	S	M	PU	CHOL
1876	168	1157	509(27.1%)	53(2.8%)	136(7.2%)	268(14.3%)	11

Using Recipe #37:

TC	P	C	F	S	M	PU	CHOL
1396	168	1162	23(1.6%)	4(0.3%)	6(0.4%)	10(0.7%)	11

#41 Whole-Wheat Muffins

Follow directions for either

plain or nonfat muffins, Recipes #35 or #37,

using

1 cup whole-wheat flour

and

1 cup white flour.

Using Recipe # 35:

TC	P	C	F	S	M	PU	CHOL
1680	174	965	518(30.8%)	55(3.3%)	145(8.6%)	273(16.2%)	11

Using Recipe #37:

TC	P	C	F	S	M	PU	CHOL
1200	174	970	32(2.7%)	6(0.5%)	9(0.8%)	15(1.2%)	11

Pancakes and Waffles

Hot cakes or waffles are always a treat for breakfast and sometimes for other meals as well. Best of all, they do not require any fat or eggs. You can use most commercial pancake mixes and simply change the directions by omitting the egg and shortening. If you use nonfat milk powder mixed with water to replace the milk in the recipe, the end result will be nonfat pancakes. But pancakes are so easy to mix that you can do it yourself with very little trouble, and much more cheaply, too.

Pancakes can be made quite thin with a thin batter and used in a variety of dishes. You can spread them with jellies or jams and fold them into a roll for serving.

The temperature of the griddle should be hot enough so that a drop of water will bounce on it. If the water disappears immediately it is too hot. A prepared (Teflon, sprayed, or lightly oiled) griddle should be used. Pour batter into cakes three inches in diameter and cook until the top surface is completely covered with bubbles. Turn the cakes once and brown on the other side. Serve immediately while hot. If you plan to use them in another recipe (such as crepes), stack them and keep warm until used.

Toppings for Pancakes and Waffles

If you like butter on your cakes but must restrict your intake of saturated fat, you should switch to one of the polyunsaturated margarines. You will still get an appreciable amount of fat in your diet, but most of it will be of the unsaturated type.

Various sirups are fine and may be mixed with melted margarine, thereby decreasing the amount of margarine used. There are a number of diet sirups in most supermarkets which can be used to restrict the total number of calories. Preserves, jams, and jellies of lower caloric value can also be found in the diet section of your market.

Sweet-cream substitute (Recipe #2) can be used for pancake or waffle toppings. You may wish to add a teaspoon of vanilla and a little sugar, or perhaps ½ teaspoon of cinnamon if you like it.

#42 Plain Wheat Cakes

1. Sift together

   1 cup flour
   ½ teaspoon salt
   1 teaspoon sugar
   2 teaspoons baking powder
   ⅓ cup nonfat milk powder.

2. Mix in thoroughly for desired batter thickness

   ⅔ to 1 cup water.

   (For thin cakes use more water.)

3. Pour on griddle in cakes 3 inches in diameter. Turn only once.

TC	P	C	F	S	M	PU	CHOL
547	83	433	11(2.0%)	2(0.4%)	3(0.5%)	5(0.9%)	7

#43 Blueberry Griddle Cakes

Follow directions for

plain wheat cakes, Recipe #42

but use

2 teaspoons sugar
⅔ cup blueberries.

If berries are frozen thaw slightly.

TC	P	C	F	S	M	PU	CHOL
638	85	518	15(2.4%)	2(0.3%)	3(0.5%)	5(0.8%)	7

#44 Banana Griddle Cakes

Follow directions for

plain wheat cakes, Recipe #42

but use

2 teaspoons sugar

and

1 large ripe banana, thinly sliced.

TC	P	C	F	S	M	PU	CHOL
707	89	585	14(2.0%)	2(0.3%)	3(0.4%)	5(0.7%)	7

#45 Apple Griddle Cakes

Follow directions for

plain wheat cakes, Recipe #42

but use

2 teaspoons sugar

and

1 juicy apple, thinly sliced.

TC	P	C	F	S	M	PU	CHOL
674	85	550	19(2.8%)	2(0.3%)	3(0.4%)	5(0.7%)	7

#46 Buckwheat Cakes

1. Sift together

    1½ cups buckwheat flour
    ½ cup white flour
    1 cup nonfat milk powder
    ½ teaspoon salt
    5 teaspoons baking powder.

2. Mix in

    2 cups water (or more for desired batter thickness)
    1 tablespoon blackstrap molasses.

3. Beat with egg beater until batter is smooth.
4. Pour into cakes 3 inches in diameter and cook on a hot griddle. Then serve at once.

TC	P	C	F	S	M	PU	CHOL
1038	187	794	41(3.9%)	1(0.1%)	2(0.2%)	2(0.2%)	22

#47 Plain Waffles

1. To prepare batter follow directions for

    wheat cakes, Recipe #42

2. Into a prepared waffle iron (an electric iron, set at the temperature indicated for the individual iron is preferable), pour

    ⅓ cup waffle batter.

3. Close and wait until steam no longer escapes. The waffle should be brown and crisp, ready to remove with a fork and serve.

TC	P	C	F	S	M	PU	CHOL
547	83	433	11(2.0%)	2(0.4%)	3(0.5%)	5(0.9%)	7

Toast

Toast has the same food value as the slice of bread it is made from. You can calculate the calories from the values given for breads. If you can afford the calories and the fat intake, you may use polyunsaturated margarine on toast.

#48 Cinnamon Toast

1. Prepare 8 slices toast.
2. Spread with mixture of

2 tablespoons sugar
1 egg white
¾ teaspoon cinnamon.

3. Set under broiler of oven with the spread surface up for less than 2 minutes.

TC	P	C	F	S	M	PU	CHOL
721	96	553	64(8.9%)	16(2.2%)	40(5.5%)	8(1.1%)	8

#49 Creamed Cinnamon Toast

1. Spread toast with

cream substitute, Recipe #2.

2. Add to taste sugar and cinnamon, mixed.

Calculate calories in topping and sugar to determine calories. You can also use brown sugar or maple sugar instead of cinnamon.

#50 Toast Sticks and Croutons

1. Cut bread slices into ½-inch sticks.
2. Bake at 300° until crisp and brown—usually 20 minutes. Turn once while baking. These are excellent for soup and contain less calories and fat than most crackers. For croutons, cut the bread slices into cubes.

#51 Milk Toast

1. Brown in hot skillet
   2 teaspoons margarine (polyunsaturated).
2. Add and bring to boil
   1½ cups water.
3. Remove from heat. Stir in gradually mixture of
   1 cup nonfat milk powder
   ½ cup cold water.
4. Add
   ½ teaspoon salt.
5. Pour milk mixture in bowl over
   4 slices toast.

TC	P	C	F	S	M	PU	CHOL
618	144	366	103(16.7%)	22(3.6%)	60(9.7%)	16(2.6%)	26

CHAPTER

8

Gravies, Sauces, and Salad Dressings

A relatively tasteless food can be made into a variety of delicious dishes by the use of sauces and dressings. A plain lettuce salad with few other vegetables is always more interesting topped with a tasty salad dressing. Meat takes on a new flavor with mushroom gravy. Vegetables can be served in a vast number of ways if you use different sauces. A versatile cook will know just how to convert a simple white sauce into a tasty seasoned sauce in order to bring out the best in vegetables or meat dishes. Sauces are also important in desserts, adding variety and flavor to fruits, puddings, and unfrosted cakes.

But sauces, gravies, and salad dressings can also be sources of many additional calories in your diet. Most often the excess calories come from fat. In gravies it is often animal or chicken fat, and in salad dressings it may be cheese fat or oil. Salad dressings are a good place to include polyunsaturated fat (safflower or corn oil) if you need to balance out the intake of saturated fat, but they can also be made without fat. A simple fat-free mayonnaise can be made from the recipe included in this chapter, and it can be used as a base for many other salad dressings and tartare sauce. Gravies can be made from meat drippings with the fat removed. White sauce can be made without the inclusion of fat. By applying the principles used in the recipes in this chapter you can make a variety of sauces, gravies, and salad dressings and not overload your fat intake.

The composition of commercial sauces and dressings is given in Table XIV, page 301.

Meat Sauces and Gravies

#52 Fish Sauce

1. Heat

    2 tablespoons corn oil.

2. Add

    1 cup white wine
    ½ minced clove garlic
    1 clove
    ½ teaspoon minced parsley
    Small piece bay leaf
    Dash powdered thyme
    ⅛ teaspoon chopped tarragon
    Salt and pepper to taste.

3. Simmer fish in the sauce over low heat and serve.

Variation: for a meat sauce, substitute red wine for the white wine. (NOTE: the values for this sauce cannot be calculated because heat causes the alcohol, a major source of the calories in wine, to evaporate.)

#53 Fish Relish

1. Mix

    ½ cup tomato catchup
    3 tablespoons any finely chopped pickle relish.

2. Pour over baked fish.

#54 Pan Gravy

1. In pan or skillet heat

    4 tablespoons fat-free stock (see Chapter 9).

2. Mix and blend in thoroughly, heating until brown,

    4 tablespoons flour.

3. Remove from heat and add

    2 cups water.

4. Stir over direct heat to full boil. Keep scraping the sides and bottom

of pan to prevent sticking. Heat until desired thickness is obtained. If too thick a little more water can be added.

5. Season with salt and pepper.

Add a 4-ounce can of mushrooms (with liquid) and a tablespoon of sherry for variation.

#55 Milk Gravy

1. In a pan or skillet heat

   4 tablespoons fat-free stock.

2. Mix and blend in thoroughly, and heat until brown

   4 tablespoons flour.

3. Remove from heat and gradually stir in

   1½ cups water.

4. In a separate container mix well

   ½ cup cold water
   1 cup nonfat milk powder.

   and add gradually to gravy.

5. Stir over direct heat to full boil. Keep scraping the sides and bottom of pan to prevent sticking. Heat until desired thickness is obtained. If too thick a little water can be added.

6. Season with salt and pepper to taste.

Without stock values:

TC	P	C	F	S	M	PU	CHOL
355	114	228	6(1.7%)	T	T	2(0.6%)	22

Add a 4-ounce can of mushrooms (with liquid) and a tablespoon of sherry for a variation.

#56 Wine Gravy

(for baked fowl or ham)

1. Mix

   1 cup pineapple juice
   1 cup orange juice
   ¼ cup white or rosé wine.

2. Baste ham or fowl with wine-and-fruit-juice mixture while baking.

3. When meat is done, remove it from oven and put cooking juices or

stock in refrigerator to cool. Remove congealed fat from top of chilled stock.

4. Replace meat in remaining nonfat stock and warm to desired temperature for serving, basting meat again.

5. Remove meat and add to stock a paste made of

¼ cup cold water
1½ tablespoons flour.

6. Cook directly over heat, stirring constantly, until thickened.

7. Add salt and pepper to season to taste and add another

¼ cup wine.

NOTE: If you are in a rush you can skim the fat off the meat stock by running a paper cup of ice (made by freezing the cup full of water) over the surface of the stock. Most of the fat will congeal on the ice.

#57 Newburg Sauce

1. Cook in double boiler until reduced

¼ cup sherry.

2. Mix smoothly, add to sherry, and heat until slightly reduced

⅔ cup nonfat milk powder
⅔ cup water with
½ blade mace (or ¼ teaspoon powdered mace).

3. Mix together and beat

*2 eggs in powder form**
⅓ cup water.

4. If ½ blade mace was used, remove from concentrated milk mixture. Then gradually stir in egg mixture. Blend with wire whisk.

5. Stir in cooked shellfish or chicken and heat until sauce thickens slightly.

6. Remove from heat and season with

¼ teaspoon salt
Pepper to taste.

TC	P	C	F	S	M	PU	CHOL
290	93	117	14(4.8%)	4(1.4%)	5(1.7%)	T	72

* These are available with ½ the usual content of cholesterol and fat found in whole eggs (Eggstra, a Tillie Lewis Product).

#58 White Sauce

1. Stir into

    1 cup cold water

    and mix until smooth (sift through a wire strainer if necessary or beat with an egg beater or wire whisk)

    2 tablespoons flour
    ½ cup nonfat milk powder.

2. Heat at least 3 minutes or longer to achieve desired thickness over low heat or in double boiler. Stir constantly.
3. Add

    ¼ teaspoon salt
    ⅛ teaspoon pepper
    or other seasoning as desired.

TC	P	C	F	S	M	PU	CHOL
178	58	114	3(1.7%)	T	T	1(0.6%)	11

The medium white sauce above may be used for gravies, sauces, creamed and scalloped dishes, with vegetables, fish, fowl, or meat. A thin sauce can be prepared by using only 1 tablespoon of flour for soups and thin gravy or lightly creamed foods. A thick sauce for croquettes, cutlets, and soufflés can be made using 4 tablespoons of flour. Remember, the sauce will thicken if it sits on the stove before it is served.

NOTE: For seasoning don't forget the use of bouillon cubes or nonfat drippings. A chicken bouillon cube makes a white sauce that goes well with green peas or other vegetables.

#59 Cheese Sauce

1. Add

    ½ cup uncreamed cottage cheese

    to

    white sauce, Recipe #58.

2. Heat over boiling water. You may wish to season with Tabasco, minced onion, dry mustard, or paprika, depending on your taste.

TC	P	C	F	S	M	PU	CHOL
264	130	124	6(2.3%)	T	T	1(0.4%)	26

#60 Tomato Cream Sauce

1. Cook together for 20 minutes
   1 cup canned tomatoes
   1 stalk celery
   1 sliced onion
   dash of cayenne.
2. Rub vegetables through sieve and add while stirring constantly to
   white sauce, Recipe #58.

The mixture may be put into a blender for a smooth texture, if desired.

TC	P	C	F	S	M	PU	CHOL
278	68	192	9(3.2%)	T	T	3(1.1%)	11

#61 Tomato Cheese Sauce

1. Add
   ½ cup uncreamed cottage cheese
   to
   tomato cream sauce, Recipe #60.
2. Heat over boiling water.

TC	P	C	F	S	M	PU	CHOL
364	140	202	12(3.3%)	T	T	3(0.8%)	26

#62 Soubise Sauce

1. Boil until soft
   4 onions, medium size
   with
   2 sprigs of parsley.
2. Rub onions through sieve.
3. Add to
   white sauce, Recipe #58.

TC	P	C	F	S	M	PU	CHOL
346	74	258	7(2.0%)	T	T	1(0.3%)	11

#63 Oyster Sauce

1. Heat to boiling

   1 pint oysters in their liquor

   and simmer for 5 minutes.
2. Stir into

   white sauce, Recipe #58,

   or rub through sieve before adding to sauce.

TC	P	C	F	S	M	PU	CHOL
524	229	213	79(15.1%)	23(4.4%)	34(6.5%)	39(7.4%)	152

#64 Mushroom Sauce

1. Add

   ½ cup mushrooms, chopped

   to

   white sauce, Recipe #58.
2. Season to taste.

TC	P	C	F	S	M	PU	CHOL
188	61	120	4(2.1%)	T	T	2(1.1%)	11

#65 Shrimp Sauce

1. Stir

   ⅓ cup cooked shrimp, finely chopped

   into

   white sauce, Recipe #58.
2. Season to taste.

TC	P	C	F	S	M	PU	CHOL
222	97	115	7(3.1%)	2(0.9%)	—	2(0.9%)	68

#66 Lobster Sauce

1. Stir

    ½ cup cooked lobster, diced

    into

    white sauce, Recipe #58.

2. Season to taste.

TC	P	C	F	S	M	PU	CHOL
232	84	115	13(15.6%)	2(0.9%)	T	2(0.9%)	125

#67 Celery Sauce

1. Stir

    ½ cup cooked celery, chopped

    into

    white sauce, Recipe #58.

2. Season to taste.

TC	P	C	F	S	M	PU	CHOL
190	40	123	4(2.1%)	T	T	1(0.5%)	11

#68 Asparagus Cheese Sauce

1. Stir

    1 10-ounce can asparagus tips, chopped
    ½ cup uncreamed cottage cheese

    into

    white sauce, Recipe #58.

2. Season to taste and heat over water to desired thickness.

TC	P	C	F	S	M	PU	CHOL
306	142	148	12(3.9%)	2(0.6%)	2(0.6%)	5(1.6%)	26

#69 Curry Sauce

1. To

white sauce, Recipe #58,

add

1 teaspoon lemon juice
1 teaspoon minced onion
1 teaspoon curry powder.

2. Heat over water to proper thickness. Or if the white sauce has been previously prepared, to desired temperature.

TC	P	C	F	S	M	PU	CHOL
179	58	115	3(1.7%)	T	T	1(0.6%)	11

#70 Spanish Creole Sauce

1. Cook together until tender

2 green peppers
2 medium onions, finely chopped
3 tablespoons water.

2. Stir in

1 cup cooked tomatoes
¼ teaspoon salt
½ teaspoon paprika.

3. Simmer together for 2 minutes or as much longer as necessary until all the vegetables are tender. Makes 1½ cups.

TC	P	C	F	S	M	PU	CHOL
168	17	133	10(6.0%)	T	T	3(1.8%)	—

#71 Barbecue Sauce

Mix together and simmer 30 minutes

2 medium onions, chopped
2 tablespoons vinegar
2 tablespoons brown sugar
⅓ cup lemon juice
1 cup tomato catchup

¼ cup Worcestershire sauce
½ cup chopped celery
½ teaspoon prepared mustard
½ cup water
¾ teaspoon salt
⅓ teaspoon black pepper
1 teaspoon paprika
1 teaspoon chili powder.

TC	P	C	F	S	M	PU	CHOL
491	24	443	13(2.5%)	2(0.4%)	1(0.2%)	5(1.0%)	—

#72 Spaghetti Sauce

1. Stew
2 medium onions, chopped
2 cloves garlic, mashed
in
1 cup water.
2. Remove all visible fat before grinding; then add
1½ pounds finely ground separable lean round steak.
3. Brown meat in stew mixture slowly.
4. Heat in a large kettle
1 6-ounce can Italian tomato paste
2½ cups tomato juice
2 cups tomato purée
4 hot chili peppers
1 teaspoon sugar
⅔ teaspoon salt
¼ teaspoon pepper
½ cup dry cottage cheese.
5. Simmer 3 hours or as much longer as necessary to thicken.
6. Remove chili peppers.
7. Add
16 stuffed green olives, sliced.
8. Simmer 15 minutes longer. Makes sufficient sauce for 1 pound of spaghetti.

TC	P	C	F	S	M	PU	CHOL
1647	758	478	373(22.7%)	156(9.6%)	185(11.2%)	22(1.4%)	492

Glazes

These do add calories to the meat. Since they can be prepared without fat or cholesterol you can use them without affecting a low-fat, low-cholesterol diet, if your diet plan does not have calorie restriction. If you need to restrict calories omit them, or stick to Recipe #75.

#73 Ham Glaze

Currant: Melt one glass currant jelly and spread over ham 45 minutes before baking is finished.

Orange: Use ½ cup orange marmalade.

Pineapple: Use puréed pineapple and cover ham with pineapple slices.

#74 Lamb Glaze

Grape: Melt ½ cup grape jelly in ½ cup of hot water. Baste meat frequently during last 30 minutes of cooking.

Pineapple: Baste meat with puréed pineapple for a few minutes until well covered; then cover meat with slices of pineapple for the last 30 minutes of cooking.

#75 Transparent Glaze

1. Soften

   2 tablespoons unflavored gelatin

   in

   ¼ cup cold water.
2. Dissolve gelatin in

   1 cup boiling water.
3. Add

   1 tablespoon lemon juice
   ¼ teaspoon salt
   Dash of pepper (preferably white).
4. Remove from heat and add

   1 cup cold water (or ice) to hasten gelling process.
5. As mixture begins to thicken spread over nearly baked meat.

Variation: A pink color can be obtained by using a cup of cranberry juice instead of cold water.

Salad Dressings

You should avoid buying prepared salad dressings unless the contents of the bottle are clearly and completely identified and you can tell that they are satisfactory for your diet goals. Remember olive and coconut oils are not ideal for diets limiting saturated fats. Safflower oil, corn oil, and soy bean oil are all rich in polyunsaturated fat and are excellent as salad oil. Eggs, egg yolks, and cheese are part of many commercial salad dressings and mayonnaise. So if you want to buy your salad dressing you had best look with a sharp critical eye at the label. If you find dehydrated salad dressing mixes that meet your criteria as to fat content you can mix them into a low-fat, low-cholesterol dressing.

#76 Low-Calorie Commercial Dehydrated Salad Dressing

1. Mix together

   1 package dehydrated salad dressing
   ¾ cup water
   ¾ cup lemon juice
   2 tablespoons powdered pectin.

2. Put in bottle or jar and shake well. Calories will be close to value given on the package.

#77 Nonfat French Dressing

1. Blend together

   ½ teaspoon salt
   ⅛ teaspoon pepper
   ⅛ teaspoon dry mustard
   1 tablespoon chives, chopped (*optional*)
   ½ teaspoon sugar
   ¼ cup tarragon or red wine vinegar
   ¼ cup cold water.

2. Add

   2 cloves garlic, peeled (*may be omitted if desired*).

3. Let stand 30 minutes; then remove garlic.

Without chives:

TC	P	C	F	S	M	PU	CHOL
16	—	16	—	—	—	—	—

#78 Polyunsaturated-Fat French Dressing

1. To

   nonfat French dressing, Recipe #77

   add

   2 tablespoons polyunsaturated oil.
2. Blend together and chill.

TC	P	C	F	S	M	PU	CHOL
259	—	16	243(93.8%)	24(9.3%)	68(26.2%)	129(49.8%)	—

#79 French Dressing with Cheese

1. To

   nonfat French dressing, Recipe #77

   add

   ¼ cup low-fat uncreamed cottage cheese.

TC	P	C	F	S	M	PU	CHOL
59	36	21	2(3.4%)	—	—	—	8

#80 French Dressing with Horseradish

1. To

   nonfat French dressing, Recipe #77

   add

   1 teaspoon prepared horseradish.

TC	P	C	F	S	M	PU	CHOL
18	—	18	—	—	—	—	—

#81 French Dressing with Mustard

1. To

nonfat French dressing, Recipe #77

add

2 teaspoons prepared mustard.

TC	P	C	F	S	M	PU	CHOL
23	1	18	3(13.0%)	1(4.3%)	1(4.3%)	1(4.3%)	—

#82 French Dressing with Lemon

To

nonfat French dressing, Recipe #77

add

¼ cup lemon juice.

TC	P	C	F	S	M	PU	CHOL
31	1	30	—	—	—	—	—

#83 Nonfat Mayonnaise

1. In top of double boiler dissolve
   1 teaspoon gelatin
   in
   1½ cups cold water.
2. In separate bowl mix together lightly with rotary beater
   2 egg whites
   2 tablespoons sugar
   1½ teaspoons dry mustard
   1 teaspoon salt
   ¼ cup mild vinegar.
3. Sift into the water and gelatin mixture while stirring
   1 cup nonfat milk powder.
4. Add egg-white mixture to milk and gelatin and stir until well mixed.
5. Heat over boiling water, stirring all the while, until thickened ade-

quately, about 15 minutes. It will be about the thickness of a medium batter.

6. Set aside to cool and stir once more when cooled. Store in refrigerator. Makes about 2 cups.

For a red-mayonnaise variation, add a little beet juice if you are using it with vegetables or cranberry or raspberry juice for fruit. Spinach juice or purée will make green mayonnaise.

TC	P	C	F	S	M	PU	CHOL
395	146	244	4(1.0%)	T	T	T	22

#84 Russian Dressing

1. Mix thoroughly

   2 tablespoons thick tomato chili sauce
   2 tablespoons lemon juice
   1 tablespoon Worcestershire sauce.

2. Add

   ½ cup nonfat mayonnaise, Recipe #83.

TC	P	C	F	S	M	PU	CHOL
150	39	106	12(8.0%)	T	T	4(2.7%)	6

#85 Shrimp-Salad Dressing

1. Mix together

   ½ cup nonfat milk powder
   ½ cup cold water.

2. Blend in

   ½ cup nonfat mayonnaise, Recipe #83.

3. Add

   ¼ cup tomato chili sauce
   2 teaspoons prepared horseradish
   1 teaspoon Worcestershire sauce
   1 tablespoon lemon juice
   ½ teaspoon salt
   ¼ teaspoon paprika.

TC	P	C	F	S	M	PU	CHOL
305	93	200	5(1.6%)	T	T	1(0.3%)	6

#86 Chiffonade Salad Dressing

To

nonfat mayonnaise, Recipe #83

add

1 tablespoon green peppers, chopped
1 tablespoon red peppers, chopped
½ tablespoon sweet pickles, chopped
½ tablespoon stuffed green olives, chopped
½ teaspoon horseradish.

TC	P	C	F	S	M	PU	CHOL
413	146	254	9(2.2%)	1(0.2%)	4(1.0%)	T	22

#87 Sherry Mayonnaise

To

nonfat mayonnaise, Recipe #83

add

1 tablespoon sherry.

TC	P	C	F	S	M	PU	CHOL
416	146	248	4(1.0%)	T	T	T	—

#88 Thousand Island Dressing

To

nonfat mayonnaise, Recipe #83

add

⅓ cup tomato chili sauce
1 tablespoon chives
4 tablespoons catchup
1½ teaspoons tarragon vinegar
2 tablespoons green pepper, chopped
3 tablespoons red pepper, chopped
1½ teaspoon paprika.

TC	P	C	F	S	M	PU	CHOL
572	156	395	9(1.6%)	1(0.2%)	T	2(0.3%)	22

#89 Tartare Sauce

1. To

   ¾ cup nonfat mayonnaise, Recipe #83

   add

   1 tablespoon minced parsley
   1 teaspoon chopped green olives
   2 teaspoons chopped sweet pickle
   1 teaspoon minced onion
   ½ tablespoon minced capers.
2. Mix thoroughly.

TC	P	C	F	S	M	PU	CHOL
165	55	103	6(3.6%)	1(0.6%)	3(1.8%)	T	8

#90 Horseradish Creamy Dressing

1. Whip together until stiff

   1 cup cold water
   1 cup nonfat milk powder
   1 egg white.
2. Add

   1 tablespoon lemon juice
   1 tablespoon tarragon vinegar
   1 tablespoon red wine vinegar
   ¼ cup grated horseradish
   ¼ teaspoon prepared mustard
   dash salt
   dash sugar.
3. Beat again.

TC	P	C	F	S	M	PU	CHOL
286	121	159	6(2.1%)	T	T	T	22

There are numerous kinds of cocktail sauces. Many of them are variations with catchup, horseradish, and other spicy sauces or seasoning. You can improvise to suit your own palate. Try chili sauce, lemon juice, Tabasco sauce, salt, pepper, Worcestershire, cayenne pepper, vinegar, or any combination of these ingredients. None of them has any significant amount of fat or cholesterol and all are low in calories. If you want to include mayonnaise, use the nonfat mayonnaise, Recipe #83, and add the caloric values.

A typical seafood cocktail sauce is given below.

#91 Seafood Cocktail Sauce

Mix together

¼ cup tomato catchup
1 tablespoon prepared horseradish
2 tablespoons vinegar
¼ cup lemon juice
1 teaspoon salt
¼ teaspoon Tabasco sauce.

TC	P	C	F	S	M	PU	CHOL
89	6	79	2(2.2%)	1(1.1%)	—	1(1.1%)	—

Dessert Sauces

A wide variety of fruit cocktail sauces can be made without using any fat or cholesterol. Wine and liquors poured over a fresh fruit cocktail are delicious. Combinations of fruit juices and honey are tasty. You can use nonfat sour cream, Recipe #4, for a topping or a mayonnaise topping, Recipe #83. The following all-purpose fruit cocktail sauce is excellent over all kinds of fresh fruit.

#92 Fruit Cocktail Sauce

Mix together

½ cup grapefruit juice
½ cup grenadine sirup
1 cup pineapple sirup.

#93 Maple Sauce

1. Boil together until desired thickness is obtained

1 cup water
4 cups maple sugar (or brown sugar if preferred).

2. Add

1 cup English walnut meats, chopped.

TC	P	C	F	S	M	PU	CHOL
3884	64	3145	674(17.4%)	43(1.1%)	106(2.7%)	422(10.9%)	—

#94 Cornstarch Sauce

1. Mix together

2 teaspoons cornstarch
3 tablespoons sugar
¼ teaspoon salt
2 cups cold water.

2. Cook in double boiler, stirring constantly, until thickened and smooth.
3. Stir in gradually

1 cup nonfat milk powder.

4. Cover and cook another 25 minutes; stir occasionally. If too thick add a little more water, and if too thin heat a little longer. Remember, it will thicken further after removal from the stove.
5. As a final step when cooking is complete add

1 teaspoon vanilla.

This sauce can be used on cakes or puddings. Since it is relatively low in calories, it is often preferable to frostings for a low-calorie dessert.

TC	P	C	F	S	M	PU	CHOL
410	104	300	4(1.0%)	T	T	T	22

Variations on cornstarch sauce: Add drained canned cooked fruit or fresh fruit after cooking (don't forget to add the calories also). Or use other flavors in addition to or in place of vanilla. A caramel flavor can be obtained by adding ¼ cup caramelized sugar sirup (add calories for additional sugar).

#95 Marshmallow Sauce

1. Boil together for 5 minutes
   ½ cup water
   1 cup sugar.
2. Cut into small pieces and put in sirup
   16 marshmallows.
3. Stir until marshmallow pieces are dissolved.
4. Beat until stiff
   2 egg whites.
5. Gradually pour marshmallow sirup over egg whites and beat until smooth.
6. Before serving cut and add 6 marshmallows.

Variation: Add 2 drops oil of peppermint before final beating of sauce.

#96 Caramel Sauce

1. Caramelize
   1 cup sugar
   by heating sugar in a thin layer in frying pan over very low heat until a light-brown liquid is formed.
2. Stir caramelized sugar cautiously and slowly into
   1 cup water.
   Continue stirring until sugar is dissolved.
3. Continue heating until a rich sirup is formed.
4. Remove from heat and add
   ½ teaspoon vanilla.

TC	P	C	F	S	M	PU	CHOL
770	—	770	—	—	—	—	—

#97 Brandy or Liquor Sauce

1. Boil together until desired thickness of sirup is obtained
   ½ cup water
   1 cup sugar.
2. Remove from heat and add
   2 tablespoons brandy or liquor
   ½ cup lemon juice
   grated rind of 1 lemon.
3. Food coloring or wine may be added.

#98 Fruit Sauce

1. Drain fruit and reserve sirup from
   1 can fruit packed in heavy sirup.
2. Rub fruit through a sieve.
3. Measure heavy sirup and gradually stir in equal measure of nonfat skim-milk powder.
4. Add
   ½ teaspoon vanilla.
5. Whip until stiff; then add fruit pulp and beat a little longer.
6. Cool in refrigerator and if desired whip again before serving.

CHAPTER 9

Bouillon, Consommé, Chowder, and Soup

For the calorie-watcher it is hard to beat soups, bouillon, or consommé. They are a wonderful way to cut the appetite for calorie-rich dishes that follow the soup course. They can be low in fat or they may contain mostly the polyunsaturated type of fat. They can also be a rich source of vitamins or minerals.

Bouillon is an especially good way to avoid calories if you enjoy drinking lots of beverages. Commercial bouillon cubes often contain as few as 6 or 7 calories per cube. One cube dissolved in a cup of hot water is far better for the health than a cup of caffein-rich coffee, and it contains far fewer calories than most soft drinks do. Actually a bouillon cube contains fewer calories than a half teaspoon of sugar (level, not rounded). Bouillon can be used as a base for many clear soups. Although homemade bouillon may be preferred, the commercial bouillon cubes are satisfactory for the busy cook.

There are a variety of commercial soups available. Their food composition is given in Table XV, page 302. Many of the canned commercial soups qualify as low-fat foods, but except for consommé and bouillon, over 20 per cent of the calories in most canned soups comes from fat. You can significantly reduce this source of fat by making your own soup. Some of the creamed soups are actually high-fat foods. One soup rich in fat is cream of mushroom soup, with 60 per cent of its total calories from fat. Fortunately, for those who want a polyunsaturated-fat diet, over half the fat is from polyunsaturated fat and less than 8 per cent from saturated fat. The source of the fat is the corn oil used in making the emulsion.

The high percentage of fat in commercial soups can be reduced by the addition of nonfat milk to condensed soups. The principle can be illustrated with commercial tomato soup. The condensed can contains

TC	P	C	F
72	3.6	50.8	17.6 (24.5%).

After a half cup of nonfat milk powder mixed with enough water to make the liquid volume directed by the label is added, the composition is as follows:

TC	P	C	F
113	20.6	73.8	18.6 (16.5%)

Thus the percentage of calories from fat is significantly reduced, which would not occur if you simply added water. With water the calories would be the same as those for the can of condensed soup; only the volume of liquid and the total weight of the diluted soup would be increased. If your goal is to limit the percentage of calories from fat in your diet, you can achieve this by adding calories that are not from fat. If your goal is to limit the total amount of calories rather than to reduce the percentage of fat, add water rather than nonfat milk. Remember that you cannot reduce the percentage of calories from fat by adding regular whole milk, since whole milk is a high-fat food.

A number of the dehydrated soup preparations are reasonably low in fat content (less than 20 per cent of calories from fat). Many people prefer frozen soups. Like canned soups, they can be diluted with nonfat milk to decrease the percentage of fat calories. Whenever the package suggests the option of using milk or water, remember that nonfat milk will help provide protein and such minerals as calcium while reducing the percentage of calories in the total diet from fat, though it will, of course, add to the total calories.

Chowder is an exceptionally fine dish, and by adding cooked meat or poultry of your choice to the recipes in this section, you can make a well-balanced meal in one dish. All that is lacking is the green salad. (See also Chapter 13 for some fish chowders.)

The composition of commercial bouillon and soups is given in Table XV, page 302.

#99 Beef or Ham Bouillon

1. Prepare by removing all visible fat and cutting into small pieces
2 pounds beef (1/3 may be bone) or 2-pound ham and bone.

If a dark bouillon is desired, brown 1/3 of the meat in a prepared skillet, searing the meat and then moving it and turning it to prevent sticking or burning. If you do not want a dark stock, this step can be omitted.

2. Soak meat and bone for 30 minutes or more in
1 1/4 quarts cold water.
3. Gradually heat to a temperature just below boiling. Do not boil or some of the flavor will be lost. Simmer covered for 3 or 4 hours.
4. One hour before the meat is tender, add
1 tablespoon turnips, diced
1 tablespoon carrots, diced
1 tablespoon onion, diced
1 tablespoon celery, diced
1 tablespoon turnips, diced
1 teaspoon sweet herbs
5 peppercorns
2 cloves
1 blade mace
1 bay leaf
sprig parsley.
5. Simmer an hour longer and add salt to taste.
6. Strain through several thicknesses of cheesecloth.
7. Cool quickly in the refrigerator.
8. Fat will rise to the top of container. Leave fat there as a sealer until the bouillon is to be used. Keep in cold storage. If a proper container has been used the bouillon can be stored in a freezer until used.
9. At time of use remove fat from the surface. The remainder will be essentially fat-free. Reheat bouillon and serve hot or use for other recipes. For instructions on clearing or jellying bouillon, see Recipes #102 or 103.

#100 Chicken Stock

1. Soak for 30 minutes
2 pounds chicken or turkey meat, cut in small pieces and trimmed of skin and fat

in

1 1/4 quarts cold water.

2. Gradually heat and simmer for 2 hours just below the boiling point. (Do not boil.)
3. Add

1 tablespoon diced onion
1 tablespoon celery, diced
2 peppercorns
1 clove
½ teaspoon sweet herbs
1 teaspoon salt.

4. Simmer for 30 minutes.
5. Remove from heat and strain through several layers of cheesecloth.
6. Cool quickly. Store with fat layer on top of container until ready to use. Then remove fat and heat stock. Serve hot.

#101 Fish Stock

1. Simmer for 90 minutes (do not boil)

2 pounds white fish, cut in small pieces

in

1¼ quarts water.

2. Add

1 tablespoon onion, diced
1 tablespoon celery, diced
1 tablespoon carrots, diced
2 peppercorns
1 clove
sprig parsley
1 bay leaf.

3. Simmer 30 minutes more (do not boil).
4. Strain through several layers of cheesecloth.
5. Reheat for serving or use in other recipes.

#102 To Clear Stock

1. Remove fat layer from stock.
2. Wash an egg carefully; then separate. Beat the egg white and add the broken shell. Add this to

1 quart stock.

3. Boil for 5 minutes.

4. Remove and add ½ cup cold water. Let stand 15 minutes.
5. Strain through several layers of cheesecloth. It is well to use stock above any layer of sediment that may have settled at the bottom of the container. This sediment is excellent for sauces and gravies.

#103 Jellied Stock

1. Soak for 5 minutes
   2 tablespoons unflavored gelatin*

   in

   ½ cup cold water.
2. Add to
   1 quart clear stock (bouillon or consommé).
3. Boil for 10 minutes.
4. Let stand for 5 minutes; then strain. Pour into container for serving and chill until firm.
5. Whip with a fork into small pieces and serve.

TC	P	C	F	S	M	PU	CHOL
84	69	5	T	—	—	—	—

#104 Vegetable Variety Soup

1. To
   3 cups beef bouillon, Recipe #99†

   add

   ½ potato, diced
   1 carrot, diced
   ½ turnip, diced
   ½ cup shelled green peas
   ½ leek, chopped
   ⅓ cup shredded cabbage
   1 teaspoon minced parsley.
2. Simmer 40 minutes; then add
   salt to taste.

TC	P	C	F	S	M	PU	CHOL
178	36	132	5(2.8%)	1(0.6%)	T	4(2.2%)	—

* Or 2 packets Knox unflavored gelatine U.S.P.
† Substitute 3 beef bouillon cubes dissolved in water if desired.

#105 Green Pea Soup

1. To

    2 cups beef bouillon, Recipe 99*

    3½ cups water

    add

    3½ cups green peas

    ¼ cup celery, diced

    1 turnip, diced

    1 onion, diced.
2. Cook until vegetables are tender.
3. Rub peas, water, and stock mixture through sieve.
4. To

    ½ cup cold water

    add

    1 tablespoon flour.
5. Blend flour and water until smooth; then add

    1 teaspoon salt

    ⅛ teaspoon pepper

    ½ teaspoon sugar

    2 sprigs mint.
6. Combine vegetable purée with flour and seasoning.
7. Heat to boiling, stirring constantly.
8. Add

    ½ cup green peas

    and cook until tender.

TC	P	C	F	S	M	PU	CHOL
581	137	416	20(3.4%)	4(0.7%)	T	13(2.2%)	—

#106 Tomato Chowder

1. To

    1 cup water

    2 cups ham stock

    add

    1 medium onion, minced

    1 cup potatoes, diced

* Or 2 beef bouillon cubes dissolved in 2 cups water.

1 cup carrots, diced
1 cup celery diced.

2. Heat to boiling and cook until vegetables are tender.
3. To

½ cup cold water

add and stir until smooth

¼ cup flour.

4. Add flour mixture to chowder mixture.
5. Add to mixture

2 cups canned tomatoes
½ teaspoon salt
¼ teaspoon pepper.

6. Heat to boiling.
7. Remove from heat and stir in gradually mixture made of

1 cup cold water
2 cups nonfat milk powder.

8. Heat over low flame, stirring constantly to avoid scorching, or heat 2 minutes in double boiler.

TC	P	C	F	S	M	PU	CHOL
963	259	656	27(2.8%)	T	1(0.1%)	6(0.6%)	44

Variation: Use ½ cup flaked dried beef and 4 cups water, omitting ham stock.

TC	P	C	F	S	M	PU	CHOL
1093	357	654	67(6.1%)	20(1.8%)	19(2.0%)	7(0.6%)	94

#107 Corn Chowder

1. To

2 cups ham stock

add

1 onion, sliced
3 cups boiled potatoes, diced
1 cup cooked corn, fresh or canned
½ teaspoon salt
3 cups water
dash pepper
½ teaspoon minced parsley.

2. Gradually heat to boiling and cook 5 minutes more.

3. Remove from heat and add gradually a mixture of

   1 cup cold water
   1 cup nonfat milk powder.

4. Heat 2 minutes longer just below the boiling point. Do not boil.

TC	P	C	F	S	M	PU	CHOL
790	162	610	20(2.5%)	T	2(0.2%)	3(0.4%)	22

Variation: Use ½ cup flaked dried beef and 6 cups water, omitting ham stock.

TC	P	C	F	S	M	PU	CHOL
1088	260	608	60(5.5%)	20(1.8%)	20(1.8%)	4(0.4%)	72

#108 Corn and Tomato Chowder

1. To

   2 cups ham stock
   5 cups water

   add

   2½ cups corn
   2 cups potatoes, diced
   1½ cups tomatoes
   1 medium onion, sliced
   1 teaspoon salt
   1 tablespoon sugar
   dash pepper.

2. Cook slowly until vegetables are tender.
3. Remove from heat and stir in gradually mixture of

   1 cup cold water
   1 cup nonfat milk powder.

4. Simmer (do not boil) for 2 minutes, stirring constantly or in a double boiler. Remove and serve.

TC	P	C	F	S	M	PU	CHOL
958	171	741	40(4.2%)	T	5(0.5%)	10(1.0%)	22

Variation: Use ½ cup flaked dried beef and 2 quarts water, omitting ham stock.

TC	P	C	F	S	M	PU	CHOL
1088	269	739	80(7.4%)	20(1.8%)	23(2.1%)	11(1.0%)	72

#109 Corn and Potato Chowder

1. To

    2½ cups water

    add

    2½ cups cooked corn
    2 cups potatoes, diced
    ¼ cup dried onion
    ½ teaspoon salt
    ⅛ teaspoon pepper.
2. Gradually bring to a boil and cook until potatoes are tender.
3. To

    ½ cup cold water

    add, stirring in until smooth

    1 tablespoon flour.
4. Add to chowder and heat gradually to boiling. Stir frequently.

TC	P	C	F	S	M	PU	CHOL
625	67	568	37(5.9%)	5(0.8%)	8(1.3%)	15(2.4%)	—

#110 Mixed Vegetable Chowder

1. To

    2 cups ham stock
    2 cups water

    add

    3 cups potatoes, diced
    2 cups carrots, diced
    ½ cup onion, sliced
    1 green pepper, diced.
2. Boil until vegetables are tender. Remove from heat.
3. To

    ½ cup water

    add and stir until smooth

    2 tablespoons flour.
4. Add to chowder mix the flour mixture and

    2 cups canned tomatoes
    1 teaspoon salt
    ⅛ teaspoon pepper
    1 cup nonfat milk powder.

5. Cook in double boiler 5 minutes or simmer (do not boil), stirring constantly.

TC	P	C	F	S	M	PU	CHOL
949	177	733	29(3.0%)	T	T	8(0.8%)	22

Variation: Use ½ cup flaked dried beef and 4 cups water, omitting ham stock.

TC	P	C	F	S	M	PU	CHOL
1079	275	731	69(6.4%)	20(1.8%)	18(1.7%)	9(0.8%)	72

#111 Fish and Potato Chowder

1. To

    3 cups water

    add

    3 cups potatoes, diced
    1 onion, sliced.

2. Boil until potatoes are fully cooked.
3. Add

    1 pound haddock, diced.

4. Simmer until fish is cooked—usually 10 to 15 minutes.
5. Remove from heat and stir in gradually mixture of

    1 cup cold water
    1 cup nonfat milk powder
    salt to taste
    pepper to taste.

6. Simmer over low heat or in double boiler for 2 minutes, or longer if a thicker chowder is desired.

TC	P	C	F	S	M	PU	CHOL
1025	503	513	16(1.6%)	T	T	T	136

Variation: Other fish can be used as a substitute for haddock. Change calorie composition according to differences in fish used.

#112 Oyster Stew

1. In saucepan heat to boiling (do not boil)
   5 cups water
   1 tablespoon polyunsaturated margarine
   1 quart oysters with liquor
   1 tablespoon minced parsley.
2. Simmer until oysters puff and crinkle at the edges.
3. Remove from heat and stir in gradually mixture of
   1 cup cold water
   2 cups nonfat dry milk powder
   salt and pepper to taste.
4. Simmer but do not boil for 2 more minutes. Serve at once.

TC	P	C	F	S	M	PU	CHOL
1289	550	475	260(20.2%)	67(5.2%)	128(10.0%)	94(7.3%)	326

Variation: Substitute a quart of clams with their liquor for the oysters.

#113 Salmon and Pea Chowder

1. To
   4 cups boiling water

   add
   ¼ cup flaked dried beef
   3 cups potatoes, diced
   1 medium onion, diced
   2 teaspoons salt.
2. Cook until potatoes are tender.
3. Remove from heat and add
   2 cups flaked canned salmon
   2½ cups cooked peas.
4. Stir in gradually mixture of
   1 cup cold water
   1 cup nonfat milk powder.
5. Simmer just below the boiling point for 3 minutes, stirring constantly.

TC	P	C	F	S	M	PU	CHOL
1344	491	708	189(14.1%)	41(3.0%)	54(4.0%)	70(5.2%)	243

#114 Cream of Salmon Soup

1. Prepare a salmon purée by rubbing through sieve
   1 cup canned salmon (drained).
2. In top of double boiler heat to boiling
   5 cups water
   1 onion slice.
3. Remove onion.
4. Add slowly, stirring constantly, mixture of
   1 cup cold water
   2 cups nonfat milk powder.
5. In a separate container mix together until smooth
   2 tablespoons flour
   2 tablespoons cold water.
6. Stir in gradually flour mixture and add salmon purée.
7. Heat over water, stirring occasionally to desired thickness.
8. Salt to taste and serve.

TC	P	C	F	S	M	PU	CHOL
750	330	324	85(11.3%)	16(2.1%)	23(3.1%)	19(2.5%)	45

#115 Creamed Vegetable Soup

Use carrots, celery, mushrooms, tomatoes, corn, potatoes, onions, or other vegetables.

1. Boil until tender
   2 cups chopped vegetable
   in
   3 cups water.
2. Drain cooked vegetable and save liquid.
3. Add sufficient water to liquid to make 3 cups fluid.
4. In separate container mix together until smooth
   2 tablespoons flour
   2 tablespoons water.
5. Gradually add and mix together the vegetable juice and flour mixture, stirring until smooth.
6. Add and stir or beat until smooth mixture of
   1 cup cold water
   2 cups nonfat milk powder.

7. Stir cooked vegetable into white sauce and heat in double boiler to desired thickness.
8. Add

   salt and pepper to taste.

   Add more water if too thick.

Calculation, using canned tomatoes:

TC	P	C	F	S	M	PU	CHOL
650	224	393	19(2.9%)	T	T	5(0.8%)	44

Variations:

Use 2 cups drained canned vegetables and save juice to add to water.

If a purée is desired, rub cooked vegetables through sieve before adding to white sauce.

Other seasonings can be added, such as cayenne to tomato soup.

#116 Cheese Variation of Vegetable Soup

Rub through sieve

¼ cup uncreamed cottage cheese curds

and add to white sauce at the time the vegetable is added.

TC	P	C	F	S	M	PU	CHOL
693	260	398	21(3.0%)	—	—	5(0.7%)	52

#117 Cream of Chicken Soup

1. Simmer just below boiling until soft

   ½ cup celery, diced

   in

   3 cups chicken stock.*
2. Mix together until smooth

   3 tablespoons flour

   3 tablespoons water.
3. Add flour mixture slowly to chicken stock.
4. Add gradually mixture of

   2 cups cold water

   1 cup nonfat milk powder.

* Or 3 chicken bouillon cubes in 3 cups water, or stock from stewed chicken, Recipe #202, or use chicken stock, Recipe #100.

5. Heat soup to desired thickness. Do not boil.
6. Add

   salt and pepper to taste.

TC	P	C	F	S	M	PU	CHOL
359	123	226	7(1.9%)	—	1(0.3%)	1(0.3%)	22

#118 Navy- or Black-Bean Soup

1. Soak overnight

   2 cups navy beans (*or* ***black beans***)

   in

   6 cups water.
2. Drain and add beans to

   3 quarts water
   1 tablespoon minced onion
   ½ teaspoon celery salt.
3. Cook until beans are quite soft.
4. Rub beans and liquid through coarse sieve.
5. Add

   ¼ teaspoon mustard
   ⅛ teaspoon pepper
   2 teaspoons salt.
6. Heat to boiling and cook for 5 minutes. Stir constantly.

TC	P	C	F	S	M	PU	CHOL
1368	312	1001	54(3.9%)	8(0.6%)	25(1.8%)	29(2.1%)	—

Variation: Add ½ cup catchup with mustard and seasoning. Other sauces may be added to give a variation in flavor.

#119 Lima-Bean Soup

Follow directions for navy-bean soup but substitute

2 cups lima beans

for navy beans.

TC	P	C	F	S	M	PU	CHOL
1098	224	827	43(3.9%)	6(0.5%)	11(1.0%)	23(2.1%)	—

CHAPTER

10

Vegetables

Vegetables are excellent for diets that must restrict fat and cholesterol. Since cholesterol is not manufactured by plants, all vegetables are cholesterol-free, and most of them contain very little fat. They provide considerable bulk because they contain a lot of water and a large amount of indigestible cellulose. For volume and weight vegetables have fewer calories than most other foods. There are exceptions. The dried bean is rich in calories for any given weight or volume, but when it is cooked the absorption of water dilutes its components so that a portion weighing the same as dried beans has only about a third as many calories. In spite of the calories, beans are actually a high-protein, low-fat food, since approximately 23 per cent of their calories is from protein while less than 4 per cent of their calories is from fat. The rest, of course, is carbohydrate.

Sweet corn is another example of a vegetable food with some protein value. About 12 per cent of its calories is from protein and 8 per cent from fat; which is mostly polyunsaturated fat.

Vegetables are important sources of vitamins and minerals. Before the means existed to preserve fresh vegetables and fruits, man often had severe malnutrition in the cold winter months caused by vitamin and mineral deficiencies. A good balanced meal should always include green and yellow vegetables.

Many vegetables are best eaten raw because their natural vitamins are preserved this way. Or they can be baked, broiled, pan-broiled, or fried in a prepared skillet. Such vegetables as sliced cucumbers and eggplant may be dipped in nonfat milk and then in flour and pan-broiled in a prepared skillet. Since vegetables contain little or no fat, the breading material will not soak up grease from the food as it will from meats with fat between the meat fibers.

See Table XVI, page 304, for the composition of vegetables.

Boiled Vegetables

Boiling is the most common way of cooking vegetables, yet it can rob them of vitamins and minerals if done improperly. To save as many nutrients as possible, boil the vegetables in very little water and take care not to overcook them. It is best to apply a lot of heat at first to destroy enzymes that can cause the loss of vitamins during slower cooking. After the initial high heat the vegetables can be simmered until tender. It is important not to boil vegetables for a long time because both taste and nutrients will be lost. Steaming vegetables in a collander or strainer over boiling water is another successful method for cooking vegetables.

Waterless cooking and the double-boiler method are two other ways of boiling vegetables without destroying their goodness. Consult one of your standard cookbooks for details or follow directions for your particular utensil.

White vegetables such as cauliflower and red vegetables such as beets retain their color if a drop or two of white vinegar or lemon juice is added to the water. Salt and seasoning should be added only after the vegetables are cooked because salt draws out the nutrients. Be sure to save the water or juices from cooking to pour over the vegetables or to use in making sauces and soups.

The following general approach is recommended for boiling vegetables.

#120 Boiled Vegetables

1. Place a small amount of water in utensil and bring to full boil.
2. Add prepared vegetables and bring to second boil over high heat. Do not cover pan.
3. Simmer over low heat until cooked—do not overcook.

A list of vegetables commonly boiled and their approximate cooking time is given below:

Artichokes	25–40 minutes
Asparagus	15–30
Green or wax beans	20–35
Lima beans	25–35
Beets	25–45
Broccoli	15–25
Brussels sprouts	15–20
Cabbage	10–20
Carrots	20–30
Cauliflower	20–30
Chayote	20–30
Chicory	15–25
Collards	15
Corn on the cob	5–8
Eggplant	15–20
Green peas	30–40
Kale	25–30
Mushrooms	10–15
New potatoes	15–20
Okra	15–30
Onions	15–30
Parsnips	30–40
Potatoes	30–40
Rutabagas	20–35
Spinach (cover, add no water)	5–10
Summer squash	15–20
Sweet potatoes	20–30
Tomatoes	15–20
Turnips	20–35

Most cookbooks call for butter and salt to be added after the vegetables are cooked. To avoid the addition of fat to your diet use other seasonings or add one of the nonfat cream sauces (see Chapter 8). If a vegetable is to be creamed with a white sauce or one of its variations, the sauce should be prepared separately and added to the cooked vegetables. You can substitute the juice from the vegetables for water in the preparation of white sauce.

One or more bouillon cubes may be added to cooking vegetables to improve flavor. Corn is especially good with curry powder. Such commercial sauces as Worcestershire sauce and A-1 sauce add just the right touch to some vegetables. Green peas and boiled (or baked) potatoes are good with Worcestershire sauce.

Nonfat mayonnaise, Recipe #83, can be used to dress up vegetables.

If calories or amount of fat are no object, you can use one of the polyunsaturated margarines in place of butter for seasoning. But remember, it is fat and does have calories.

A variety of seasoning, limited only by the imagination and experience of the cook, can be used to replace the traditional butter-and-salt approach.

You can preserve the nutrients in vegetables by cooking them in nonfat milk. The vegetables should be well coated with milk so that its protein can act to protect the vegetable.

#121 Milk-Simmered Vegetables

1. Prepare skim milk by mixing together
   ½ cup nonfat milk powder
   1 cup cold water.
2. Place desired amount of skim milk in the top of double boiler, using only enough milk to coat vegetables.
3. Cover vegetables tightly and cook over boiling water until tender.
4. Drain and serve vegetables with desired sauce or seasoning. The milk can be used in making a sauce or in preparing soups, if you don't wish to serve it with the vegetables.

#122 Asparagus Casserole

1. Boil or steam for just 5 minutes enough for
   3 cups cooked asparagus.
2. Place asparagus in casserole.
3. Pour over asparagus
   2 cups cheese sauce, Recipe #59.
4. Sprinkle with
   ¼ teaspoon salt.
5. Cover with ¾ cup dry bread crumbs.

6. Bake at 325° for 30 minutes.

TC	P	C	F	S	M	PU	CHOL
587	186	352	44(7.5%)	8(1.4%)	15(2.6%)	11(1.9%)	28

#123 Lima-Bean Casserole

1. Mix together
   2 cups cooked fresh Lima beans
   ½ cup pimentos, chopped
   2 cups cheese sauce, Recipe #59
   2 tablespoons tomato catchup.
2. Pour into lightly greased or treated casserole.
3. Cover with
   ½ cup dried bread crumbs.
4. Bake at 350° for 30 minutes.

TC	P	C	F	S	M	PU	CHOL
817	222	550	36(4.4%)	9(1.1%)	9(1.1%)	11(1.3%)	28

#124 Boston Baked Beans

1. Soak overnight in cold water
   1 quart dried navy beans.
2. Drain beans, cover with water, and simmer until skins break.
3. Put beans in bean pot.
4. Pour over beans mixture of
   1 cup boiling water
   ½ teaspoon dry mustard
   ¼ cup molasses
   1½ tablespoons brown sugar
   2 teaspoons salt.
5. Cover and bake at 275° for 8 hours.

TC	P	C	F	S	M	PU	CHOL
2997	624	2269	104(3.5%)	16(0.5%)	48(1.6%)	56(1.9%)	—

#125 Harvard Beets

1. Mix together until smooth
   1/3 cup water
   2 teaspoons cornstarch
   1/3 cup vinegar
   3/4 cup sugar.
2. Boil for 5 minutes.
3. Add
   4 cups cooked beets, diced or sliced.
4. Simmer ½ hour or cook in double boiler.
5. Season to taste before serving with
   salt and pepper.

TC	P	C	F	S	M	PU	CHOL
859	20	839	8(0.9%)	T	T	T	—

#126 Beets in Orange Sauce

1. Mix together until smooth
   3/4 cup water
   2 tablespoons cornstarch.
2. Add
   1 1/2 teaspoons grated orange rind
   1 cup orange juice
   1/4 teaspoon salt
   1/4 teaspoon pepper
   2 teaspoons sugar.
3. Cook to desired thickness, stirring constantly.
4. Add
   3 1/2 cups cooked beets, diced
   and heat.

TC	P	C	F	S	M	PU	CHOL
422	23	394	12(2.8%)	T	T	T	—

#127 Spiced Beets

1. Simmer together for 10 minutes
   1 cup water
   ⅔ cup vinegar
   ¼ teaspoon salt
   3 tablespoons sugar
   10 cloves
   1 cinnamon stick.
2. Add
   4 cups cooked beets, sliced
   2 small onions.
3. Simmer until vegetables have been heated thoroughly.

TC	P	C	F	S	M	PU	CHOL
460	24	434	9(2.0%)	T	T	T	—

#128 Broccoli Casserole

1. Place in a prepared casserole
   3 cups cooked broccoli.
2. Pour over broccoli
   2 cups cheese sauce, Recipe #59.
3. Sprinkle with
   ¼ teaspoon salt.
4. Cover with ¾ cup dried bread crumbs.
5. Bake at 325° approximately 30 minutes.

TC	P	C	F	S	M	PU	CHOL
677	205	418	49(7.2%)	7(1.0%)	14(2.1%)	14(2.1%)	28

Variation, using 5 cups cooked cabbage instead of broccoli:

TC	P	C	F	S	M	PU	CHOL
616	207	353	52(8.4%)	7(1.1%)	14(2.3%)	13(2.1%)	13

Variation, using 3 cups cooked cauliflower instead of broccoli:

TC	P	C	F	S	M	PU	CHOL
635	190	397	46(7.2%)	7(1.1%)	14(2.2%)	11(1.7%)	28

Variation, using 3 cups sliced cooked eggplant instead of broccoli:

TC	P	C	F	S	M	PU	CHOL
749	193	496	55(7.3%)	7(0.9%)	14(1.9%)	17(2.3%)	28

#129 Stuffed Eggplant

1. Cut in half
   1 eggplant.
2. Scoop out all pulp, leaving a thin shell for each half.
3. Chop pulp fine.
4. Mix
   ½ cup cold water
   ¼ cup nonfat milk powder.
5. Add chopped pulp and milk to
   2 cups dried bread crumbs
   salt and pepper to taste
   sage (a small amount if desired, optional).
6. Fill eggplant shells with stuffing and cover with dried bread crumbs.
7. Bake at 375° for 45 minutes.

TC	P	C	F	S	M	PU	CHOL
971	145	721	101(10.4%)	18(1.8%)	36(3.7%)	23(2.4%)	12

#130 Broiled Eggplant

1. Peel and cut lengthwise into long slender pieces
   1 eggplant.
2. Dip eggplant strips in
   egg white, lightly beaten.
3. Roll dipped eggplant in cracker crumbs.
4. Place on a bake sheet and put under broiler. Turn to brown other side. Cook until tender. Salt to taste.

TC	P	C	F	S	M	PU	CHOL
146	31	104	10(6.8%)	T	T	5(3.4%)	—

#131 Mushrooms au Gratin

1. Brush thoroughly with damp cloth, separate caps and stems, and peel caps of

   12 ounces fresh mushrooms.
2. Place mushroom caps, cap side down, in baking dish.
3. Chop stems and mix with

   white sauce, Recipe #58.
4. Pour over mushroom caps.
5. Bake at 325° for 30 minutes.

TC	P	C	F	S	M	PU	CHOL
274	82	168	10(3.6%)	T	T	4(1.4%)	11

#132 Okra and Tomatoes

1. Put in a saucepan

   2 cups cooked okra

   2 cups cooked tomatoes, boiled.
2. Simmer for 5 minutes.
3. Season to taste with basil, salt, and pepper.

TC	P	C	F	S	M	PU	CHOL
174	22	126	14(8.0%)	2(1.1%)	T	6(3.4%)	—

#133 Baked Stuffed Onions

1. Boil for 15 minutes

   6 large onions, peeled.
2. Take onions from heat and remove centers, leaving only two or three layers of onion shell.
3. Chop centers and combine them with

   white sauce, Recipe #58, or variation.
4. Fill onion shells with above mixture, and put in baking pan.
5. Cover top of onions with

   dried bread crumbs.

6. Bake at 350° for 25 minutes.

TC	P	C	F	S	M	PU	CHOL
430	82	330	9(2.1%)	T	T	1(0.2%)	11

Baked white or sweet potatoes may be served with a variety of low-fat sauces. Nonfat sour-cream substitute, Recipe #4, may be used. Some people like the flavor of Worcestershire sauce. If calories or fat are not limited, one of the polyunsaturated margarines may be utilized in place of butter.

#134 Mashed Potatoes

1. Take desired amount of freshly cooked boiled potatoes and drain them if any water is present.
2. Mash and whip the potatoes, adding to them cream substitute made from nonfat milk, Recipe #2.
3. Salt and pepper to taste.

Variation: If calories or fat are not limited, polyunsaturated margarine may be utilized as a substitute for butter. Otherwise, it may be omitted. Low-fat sour cream, Recipe #4, is good with chives mixed in, for a variation.

#135 Scalloped Potatoes

1. In baking dish place one layer of
   sliced raw potatoes.
2. Cover with layer of
   sliced raw onions.
3. Place another layer of sliced potatoes covered with a second layer of sliced onions in the dish.
4. Pour over all
   white sauce, Recipe #58, or any white-sauce variation desired.
5. Cover with
   dried bread crumbs.
6. Bake at 350° one hour.

#136 Grilled Sweet Potatoes

1. Peel and cut in half boiled sweet potatoes.
2. Dip halves in egg white, lightly whipped.
3. Sprinkle lightly with salt and cover generously with brown sugar.
4. Place on broiler rack 3 inches below heat. Cook until brown.

#137 Sweet Potatoes in Honey

1. Pare and cut into quarter-inch slices
   6 boiled sweet potatoes.
2. Place potato slices in bottom of prepared casserole.
3. Cover with mixture of
   ¼ cup honey
   juice of one orange
   salt to taste.

TC	P	C	F	S	M	PU	CHOL
1306	80	1194	38(2.9%)	6(0.4%)	6(0.4%)	18(1.4%)	—

#138 Marshmallow Sweet Potatoes

1. Remove the skins from
   8 baked sweet potatoes.
2. Mix together until smooth
   1 cup cold water
   ½ cup nonfat milk powder.
3. Add milk to sweet potatoes and also beat in
   ½ teaspoon salt
   1 teaspoon cinnamon or nutmeg
   ¼ teaspoon paprika.
4. Whip potatoes thoroughly until light and fluffy, and place them in prepared casserole.
5. Cover with
   ½ pound marshmallows.
6. Bake at 350° until potatoes are heated throughout and marshmallows are brown.

#139 Mashed Sweet Potatoes

1. Peel and mash
   6 medium boiled sweet potatoes.
2. Mix together, then add to potatoes
   ¾ cup cold water
   ½ cup nonfat milk powder.
3. Whip until fluffy. If needed, additional hot water may be added.
4. Season to taste.

TC	P	C	F	S	M	PU	CHOL
1132	94	1005	38(3.4%)	6(0.5%)	6(0.5%)	18(1.6%)	11

#140 Baked Tomatoes

1. Cut the tops and remove the pulp from
   6 tomatoes.
2. Mix tomato pulp with
   ¼ cup green pepper, chopped
   ¾ cup cooked corn
   1 teaspoon salt
   ¼ teaspoon pepper
   6 tablespoons dried bread crumbs
   2 tablespoons nonfat cream substitute, Recipe #2.
3. Fill tomato shells with pepper-corn mixture.
4. Cover with dried bread crumbs.
5. Bake at 375° 25 minutes.

TC	P	C	F	S	M	PU	CHOL
567	86	442	53(9.3%)	5(0.9%)	9(1.6%)	20(3.5%)	3

#141 Cooked Dried Beans

1. Wash and soak overnight
   1 cup dried beans

   in

   3 or 4 cups water.

2. Drain beans and again cover with water.
3. Simmer over low heat until beans are tender and their skins have popped. The liquid should be simmered to a paste.
4. Beans may be seasoned with

   tomato catchup
   mustard
   Worcestershire sauce
   minced onions
   salt
   pepper

   or

   other seasonings, as desired.

The beans should be cooked until the fluid has cooked down. If the beans are not tender and the juices are becoming too pasty, additional water may be added.

CHAPTER II

Fruits

Fruits and melons are ideal foods for individuals restricting their fat and cholesterol intake. They are carbohydrate foods, being essentially free of fat and cholesterol (with the exception of avocados and olives, which are often classed as fruits. Unless they are dried, like raisins or prunes, they contain few calories compared to their bulk. There are only 100 calories in the average banana, a large orange, or a large apple. These foods are very low in sodium and rich in potassium, and for this reason they are often used in diets when the sodium must be restricted.

There is no truth to the idea that watermelons have more calories than other kinds of melon. A 3½-ounce (100-gram) portion of watermelon has only 26 calories, while cantaloupes, casabas, and honeydews have 30, 27, and 33 calories respectively.

Fruits and melons are wonderful for desserts or salads. They can be used in a great number of dishes but are at their best when they are raw. It is hard to beat fresh peaches topped with nonfat whipped-cream substitute, Recipe #3 or, for that matter, any kind of fruit or berries served in the same way.

One of the fad diets recommends using only fruits for food. This idea should be firmly denounced since such a diet is unhealthy and can lead to a severe case of malnutrition. Berries, fruit, and melons, wonderful as they are, cannot provide the body with all its needed food elements. The body needs proteins, and fruit contains essentially none. It is true that one can lose weight on such a diet, but the loss in weight is caused by malnutrition, which will lead to problems more serious than obesity.

In buying fruit and berries you should keep in mind that the frozen products usually already contain added sugar, which increases the calories. Another point often missed is that bananas and pears both taste better if bought before they are fully ripe. A tree-ripened banana or pear is not as sweet and flavorful as one that ripens off the tree. This rule does not apply to any other berries, fruits, or melons.

For the composition of berries, fruits, and melons see Table XVII, page 312. Please note that the values for some of the recipes that follow cannot be calculated, because they involve the use of drained canned fruits and only the calories for fruit and liquid together are available.

#142 Applesauce

1. Pare, quarter, and remove core from
   4 medium apples.
2. Put apples in deep saucepan and add
   ½ cup water.
3. Cover and simmer for 20 to 30 minutes. When apples are cooked, they can be mashed against the side of the pan with a wooden spoon.
4. Add
   2 tablespoons sugar.
5. Beat until sauce is smooth.

If the apples used are not juicy and flavorful enough, lemon juice may be added at Stage 4, a teaspoonful at a time. Cloves, cinnamon, nutmeg, and other spices may be added if desired. The applesauce can be made smoother by rubbing it through a strainer or coarse sieve.

TC	P	C	F	S	M	PU	CHOL
475	8	436	32 (6.7%)	—	—	—	—

#143 Baked Apples

1. Clean and core
   6 apples.
2. In each apple cavity, put
   1 teaspoon sugar.

3. Place apples in baking dish with enough water to cover its bottom.
4. Bake at 350° until tender.

The centers may be filled with other ingredients for variety, such as brown sugar, red cinnamon candies, raisins, jelly, honey, nuts, other fruits, or marshmallows.

TC	P	C	F	S	M	PU	CHOL
612	12	558	48(7.8%)	T	T	T	—

#144 Baked Stuffed Apples

1. Remove stems and core, but do not peel
   6 large tart red apples.
2. Remove enough of the pulp from apples to leave a shell about ½ inch thick.
3. Mix together
   1 cup chopped bananas
   1 cup brown or maple sugar
   1 cup cranberries, chopped
   1 cup pecans, chopped.
4. Fill apples with fruit and nut mixture and cover them.
5. Bake at 350° until tender.
6. Chill and serve covered with a spoonful of
   nonfat whipped-cream substitute, Recipe #3.

TC	P	C	F	S	M	PU	CHOL
2450	60	1588	809(33.0%)	53(2.2%)	474(19.3%)	147(6.0%)	—

#145 Fruit Snow

1. Prepare
   1 cup fruit purée (apple, peach, plum, other)
   by simmering or steaming sufficient prepared fruit in a little water in a saucepan, then pressing through a sieve.
2. Fold in
   2 stiffly beaten egg whites.
3. Add to desired taste
   ¼ cup sugar
   1 tablespoon lemon juice.

4. Chill until served. Fruit snow may be topped with nonfat whipped-cream substitute, Recipe #3, or another sauce of your choice. This dish can also be baked (in a 275° oven for 30–45 minutes.)

#146 Maple Bananas

1. Peel and place in prepared baking dish
   6 firm bananas.
2. Mix together and pour over bananas
   ¾ cup maple syrup
   2 tablespoons lemon juice.
3. Sprinkle with
   chopped English walnuts.
4. Bake at 375° 15–20 minutes.

Variation: Sirup may be omitted and the bananas sprinkled with brown sugar or powdered sugar.

TC	P	C	F	S	M	PU	CHOL
1463	40	1369	60(4.1%)	3(0.2%)	7(0.5%)	26(1.8%)	—

#147 Apple Meringue Pudding

1. Cover bottom and sides of baking pan with
   toast.
2. Prepare skim milk by mixing together
   1 cup water
   ½ cup nonfat milk powder
   and heat. Soften toast adequately with hot milk.
3. Cook separately
   6 apples, whole, with cores removed.
4. Place cooked apples on toast in baking pan and sweeten with
   sugar seasoned with nutmeg.
5. Cover entire apple dish with
   3 egg whites, beaten stiff.
6. Bake at 325° approximately 15 minutes.

#148 Stewed Rhubarb

1. Wash and cut into ½-inch cubes
   1 pound rhubarb.
2. Place rhubarb in saucepan and add
   ¼ cup water.
3. Cover tightly and simmer until rhubarb is soft, about 45 minutes.
4. Add
   ½ cup sugar.
5. Cover and cook a little longer.

May be served hot or cold, as a sauce or with roast meats.

TC	P	C	F	S	M	PU	CHOL
458	5	454	5(1.1%)	T	T	T	—

#149 Baked Rhubarb

1. In casserole place
   ¾ cup sugar
   ½ cup water.
2. Heat casserole in oven at 350° while preparing rhubarb.
3. Cut into 1-inch lengths
   1 pound rhubarb.
4. Remove casserole from oven, stir to make sure sugar is dissolved, and add rhubarb.
5. Cover and cook for 20 minutes, or until rhubarb is tender.

TC	P	C	F	S	M	PU	CHOL
651	5	637	5(0.8%)	T	T	T	—

#150 Hot Fruit Compote

1. Drain
   1 cup canned apricots
   in colander over bowl.
2. Place drained apricots in a layer in baking dish. Save fruit juice.
3. Drain
   1 cup canned sliced peaches.
   Save juice, and place peaches in a layer on top of apricots.

4. Drain

   1 cup pineapple chunks.

   Save juice, and place pineapple in a layer over peaches.
5. Drain

   2 cups pitted Bing cherries.

   Save juice, and place the cherries in a layer over pineapples.
6. Sprinkle over top of fruit

   grated rind of 1 lemon and 1 orange
   ½ cup light brown sugar
   ½ teaspoon nutmeg.
7. Mix reserved juices and add to a depth of half the fruit.
8. Cover dish with

   3 egg whites, beaten stiffly.
9. Bake at 350° about 20 minutes.

#151 PINEAPPLE-PEACH PYRAMID

1. Drain separately, and reserve the peach juice from

   1 No. 2½ can sliced pineapple
   1 No. 2½ can peach halves.
2. Place peach halves, hollow side up, in center of each pineapple ring in baking dish.
3. Place

   1 marshmallow

   in center of each peach half.
4. Pour peach juice into baking dish.
5. Bake at 375° 20–30 minutes. Baste occasionally.

#152 PEACHES IN MERINGUE

1. Place in baking dish, hollow side up,

   6 cooked peach halves.
2. Place in center of each peach half

   1 teaspoon tart jelly.
3. Prepare meringue by whipping together until stiff

   3 egg whites
   6 tablespoons sugar
   ½ teaspoon vanilla.
4. Cover peaches with meringue.
5. Bake at 275° for 1 hour.

#153 Strawberry Gelatin Supreme

1. Dissolve in top of double boiler
   1 package strawberry gelatin
   in
   1 cup boiling water.
2. Remove from heat, and add
   ½ cup red wine
   1 tablespoon lemon juice.
3. When gelatin becomes the consistency of egg white, fold in
   1 thawed 10-ounce package frozen strawberries.
4. Mold and chill.

TC	P	C	F	S	M	PU	CHOL
394	28	275	6(1.5%)	T	T	T	—

#154 Black-Cherry Wine Gelatin

1. Place in top of double boiler
   1 tablespoon gelatin
   ⅓ cup cold water.
2. Let soak about 10 minutes; then heat over water until gelatin is completely dissolved.
3. Add
   ⅓ cup sugar
   and stir.
4. Remove from heat and add
   1 cup juice drained from can of black cherries
   1 cup dry wine (red or white)
   ⅓ cup lemon juice.
5. Stir well and let set until mixture has the consistency of unbeaten egg white.
6. Put in
   1 cup pitted canned black cherries
   and place in mold to cool.

TC	P	C	F	S	M	PU	CHOL
656	35	454	4(0.6%)	T	T	T	—

#155 Fruit Sponge

1. In top of double boiler put
   2 teaspoons gelatin
   ½ cup cold water.
2. Let stand at room temperature for 10 minutes.
3. Stir over boiling water until gelatin has dissolved.
4. Add
   ½ cup sugar
   and stir until dissolved.
5. Remove from heat and add
   1 cup fruit juice
   or
   ⅓ cup fresh crushed or chopped fruit
   and
   ⅓ cup lemon juice.
6. Let gelatin chill until it has the consistency of unbeaten egg white.
7. Beat gelatin until light.
8. Add
   2 egg whites, beaten stiff.
9. Combine egg white and gelatin and beat mixture until it will hold its shape.
10. Place in mold and chill.

NOTE: When lemon sponge is being made, use ¾ cup of water instead of 1 cup fruit juice. Remember that fresh or frozen pineapple must be heated.

#156 Apple-Nut Salad

1. Mix together
   4 raw apples, cored and diced
   2 tablespoons lemon juice
   ¾ cup nonfat mayonnaise, Recipe #83.
2. Arrange mixture on leaves of lettuce.
3. Sprinkle with
   ¾ cup English walnuts, chopped.

TC	P	C	F	S	M	PU	CHOL
1147	111	501	540(47.1%)	32(2.8%)	80(7.0%)	317(27.6%)	8

C H A P T E R

12

Salads

A well-prepared salad can either help with a program to control weight and reduce fat intake or be a hidden source of additional fat, calories, and cholesterol. There are many ways in which salads can be prepared, and some cookbooks include recipes for five hundred or more salads. Actually one does not need many specific recipes to make salads. A cook with imagination can follow general principles and create a wide variety of salads. The salad can be a good place to add polyunsaturated fat to your diet if you have neglected to include it elsewhere.

Cottage-Cheese Salads

One of the simplest salads to prepare is the uncreamed cottage-cheese combination salad. A variety of fruits and vegetables may be combined with a serving of uncreamed cottage cheese and served on lettuce or other greens. Since it is desirable in terms of calorie control to eliminate fat in the diet, uncreamed cottage cheese, which is relatively low in saturated fats, is preferred. These fruits and vegetables are particularly good with uncreamed cottage cheese: pears, tomatoes, tomato aspic, pineapples, peaches, pimientos, and onions. Salt, pepper, and other seasonings may be used as desired. When low-fat or nonfat uncreamed cottage cheese is used in combination with vegetables or fruits, the salad is low in both fat and cholesterol. The uncreamed cottage cheese provides both protein and calcium.

Mayonnaise Salads

Many salads are based on a combination of fruits and vegetables. Many commercial mayonnaises are unsatisfactory if you want to eliminate cholesterol and saturated fats, since they include egg yolks and some include saturated vegetable oils such as coconut oil. For a low-fat, low-cholesterol diet, use the nonfat mayonnaise in Recipe #83.

Although there are many different fruits that are good with mayonnaise, the following are especially recommended: pears, pineapples, and peaches. The fruit may be arranged on lettuce, and a spoonful of mayonnaise placed in the center or at the side of the fruit as desired.

Vegetables that are particularly good in a salad with mayonnaise include: tomatoes, tomato aspic, lettuce, and assorted greens (and various combinations).

Tossed Salads

Tossed salads can add bulk to a meal without stretching the calorie limit. The secret is in the dressing. An infinite variety of tossed salads can be prepared with different combinations of vegetables and different dressings. The following recipes can be found in Chapter 8:

- Nonfat French Dressing
  - cheese variation
  - horseradish variation
  - mustard variation
  - chive variation
  - lemon variation
- Mayonnaise
  - red mayonnaise
  - green mayonnaise
  - sherry mayonnaise
- Russian Dressing
- Chiffonade Salad Dressing
- Thousand Island Dressing
- Horseradish Creamy Dressing

It is possible to use oil-and-vinegar salad dressings safely as long as you use very little oil. Actually, a single tablespoon of oil is sufficient to prepare enough tossed salad for a family of four. If the salad is extremely well tossed so that all of the leaves are covered with a small amount of oil, a little goes a long way. For individuals limiting their saturated-fat intake, a polyunsaturated oil should be used, which means safflower oil or corn oil. One-fourth tablespoon oil per person for a meal will not do much harm.

Using polyunsaturated oil in salads is one way to increase the ratio of polyunsaturated fat in the diet to saturated fat. If the main course is beef containing saturated fat and very little polyunsaturated fat, the fat in the other dishes should be polyunsaturated. By adding vegetables, fruit, and nonfat bread to the meal, the percentage of calories from fat can be limited to desirable levels.

The tossed salad or combination salad can include several different ingredients. The most commonly used are:

Lettuce (all types)
Spinach (uncooked)
Cabbage, red and green
Tomatoes
Radishes
Green onions
Spanish or Bermuda onions
Chives
Pickled beets
Green peppers
Green olives stuffed with pimientos
Ripe olives
Pimientos, green and red
Avocado
Cooked green beans
Celery
Carrots
Cucumber slices
Jalapeño peppers
Various spices and relishes

Of these, olives and avocados contain a large amount of fat, and they should be used sparingly or rarely in the preparation of salads. Olives contain mostly monounsaturated fat and very little polyunsaturated fat, and though they are not desirable for individuals restricting fat, they are better than animal fat because less than 15 per cent of their fat content is saturated fat.

Tossed salads can be seasoned according to the taste of the individual. Salt, pepper, garlic, and other spices should be added after the salad has been mixed with its dressing. Some salads are garnished with such ingredients as anchovies and sliced hard-boiled eggs. Anchovies are rich in fat content, and hard-boiled egg yolks contain large amounts of cholesterol, so these garnishes should be avoided for the low-fat, low-cholesterol diet. Hard-boiled egg whites, however, are permissible since they are a good source of protein and are essentially fat-free.

There are a few basic principles that you need to follow in preparation of tossed and combination salads. Observe all the standard recommendations for the storage and cleaning of vegetables, and prepare the salad and add the dressing when the salad is to be served, rather than ahead of time. Tear rather than cut the leaves of the greens.

To utilize an oil-and-vinegar dressing properly, the greens should be free of water, vinegar, or any other liquids. The lettuce alone should be tossed with the oil until each leaf has a thin coating and then added to the other vegetables prepared for the salad. Finally, the entire salad is tossed together and seasoned with vinegar and other herbs and spices. The oil protects the vegetables from losing their valuable vitamins and minerals. It also maintains their freshness, preventing the salad from becoming wilted or soggy when other ingredients are added. The more thoroughly and effectively a salad is tossed, the less oil will be required.

Use your imagination in preparing an attractive tossed or combination salad. Green and red pimientos cut in halves with the seeds removed can serve for shells to hold individual salads. Radishes may be cut into decorative forms, and shoestring carrot strips may be used to lace the top of a salad. Chopped red cabbage can add color to the salad, and even cooked and pickled vegetables such as beets may be used. As long as the basic principles for salad preparation are followed, it is possible to create an impressive array of salads and avoid adding large amounts of fat and cholesterol in the diet.

Fruit and Melon Salads

A pleasant change from vegetable salads is the use of fruit and melon salads. This is an excellent way to include the important vitamins of fruit in the diet, and unless one uses a commercial mayonnaise or some commercial dressing containing fat, there is essentially no fat or cholesterol in these foods. Delicious fruit cocktails made of fresh fruit cut into small pieces, mixed together, and covered with their own juices, wine sauces, or specially prepared fruit sauce are a habit in many countries of the world. Raw fruits and melons are best for salads, but canned peaches and pears and cooked seedless grapes are often very satisfactory. Nonfat mayonnaise or any of the nonfat dressings is good in combination with different fruits, and gelatin can be used with fruit for a molded salad. (Be sure to avoid raw pineapple in making gelatin molds.) Some fruits can be mixed with chopped nuts, but it should be remembered that nuts contain large amounts of fat. If the proper nuts are chosen, a good portion of the fat is polyunsaturated in type, although this is not true of all of them (see Chapter 17). A list of some of the more commonly used fruits, either singly or in combination in making fruit salads, is as follows:

Seedless grapes
Tangerines
Oranges
Nectarines
Peaches
Pears
Apples
Cherries
Plums
Pineapple
Cantaloupe
Honeydew
Watermelon
Bananas
Apricots
Grapefruit

Fish Salads

Various combinations of cooked fish and shellfish can be used to prepare appetizing salads. When served in large quantities, these can constitute the main course and are particularly pleasing during hot weather. Fish is a valuable source of protein, and many fish (though not all) contain only limited amounts of fat, and that is chiefly of the polyunsaturated type. As such, it is highly recommended. Shellfish, however, frequently contain moderate amounts of cholesterol, and if one must eat a low-cholesterol diet, salads made from shellfish should be limited.

Canned tuna and salmon, poached or baked white fish, and shellfish can be combined with a variety of different vegetables, such as finely chopped cabbage, lettuce, or pimientos, and served with nonfat mayonnaise or French dressing. Tuna and salmon can be moistened with mayonnaise and added to cooked green peas, cooked bean sprouts, and other vegetables with highly satisfactory results.

Salmon contains large amounts of fat. Atlantic and Chinook (king) salmon contain about twice as much fat as chum, silver, and pink (humpback) salmon. Tuna (unless packed in oil) contains less fat than salmon.

Most of the fat in fish is polyunsaturated. Some studies show that limited amounts of these highly unsaturated fats act to lower cholesterol levels significantly in some people.

#157 Salmon Salad

1. Mix

   1 cup flaked salmon
   1 cup celery, diced.
2. Moisten with

   ***1 cup nonfat French dressing, Recipe** #77*

   and chill for ½ hour.
3. Mound chilled salad on lettuce leaf.
4. Garnish with nonfat mayonnaise, Recipe #83.

This salad is good served in hollowed-out tomatoes. Variations may be prepared by substituting other fish for salmon and following the same recipe. Shellfish should be chopped into small pieces. Other fish or shellfish commonly used are:

Crabmeat
Tuna (packed in water)
Shrimp
Lobster
Halibut.

For salmon:

TC	P	C	F	S	M	PU	CHOL
247	124	46	77(31.2%)	16(6.5%)	23(9.3%)	32(13.0%)	98

#158 Crab-Flake Salad

1. Mix together
   2 cups crab flakes
   2 tablespoons lemon juice
   2 teaspoons grated onion
   1 cup nonfat mayonnaise, Recipe #83
   ¼ teaspoon salt.
2. Chill and serve on
   lettuce leaf or other greenery.

A substitution can be made using chopped shrimp, lobster, baked fish flakes, salmon, or tuna.

#159 Seafood-Pineapple Salad

1. Flake or chop
   1 cup shrimp, lobster, or crabmeat.
2. Combine with
   1 cup pineapple, diced
   ¼ teaspoon salt
   ⅛ teaspoon paprika.
3. Chill until ready to serve.
4. Mix with
   4 tablespoons nonfat French dressing, Recipe #77.
5. Serve on
   lettuce leaf.

For shrimp:

TC	P	C	F	S	M	PU	CHOL
213	118	80	13(6.1%)	5(2.3%)	—	2(0.9%)	171

Non-Leafy Vegetable Salads

Vegetable salads may be prepared with both cooked and raw vegetables. Whenever cooked peas, beans, or potatoes are used, one should remember that these contain fairly large amounts of calories compared to green leafy vegetables.

#160 Tomato-Boat Salad

1. Mix together and chill
   ½ cup cooked green beans
   ½ cup cooked carrots, diced
   ½ cup cooked peas
   ½ cup cooked cauliflower bits
   nonfat French dressing to moisten, Recipe #77.
2. Quarter, leaving intact at stem
   3 large tomatoes, chilled.
3. Spread out quartered tomatoes, fill with salad mixture, and place on
   lettuce leaf.
4. Top each tomato with
   nonfat mayonnaise, Recipe #83.

Variation: Hollowed-out green bell peppers, or even ripe bell peppers, may be used instead of tomatoes.

#161 Potato Salad

1. Mix together
   3 cups boiled potatoes, diced
   ¾ cup hard-boiled egg whites, chopped
   ¾ cup radishes, thinly sliced
   ½ tablespoon onion, finely chopped.
2. Add to moisten about
   1 cup nonfat mayonnaise, Recipe #83.
3. Season with
   salt
   pepper
   to taste.
4. Chill until served.
5. Serve on lettuce leaf.
   This salad may be served in green or red ripe bell peppers.

TC	P	C	F	S	M	PU	CHOL
656	175	481	9(1.4%)	T	T	T	11

#162 Tomato Aspic

1. Prepare gelatin by soaking
   2 tablespoons gelatin
   for 5 minutes in
   ½ cup cold tomato juice.
2. Dissolve gelatin over low heat.
3. Add dissolved gelatin to
   3½ cups tomato juice.
4. Season to taste.

TC	P	C	F	S	M	PU	CHOL
240	76	144	8(3.3%)	T	T	T	—

Variations: Add Worcestershire sauce, Tabasco, horseradish, chili sauce, mustard, or minced fresh basil.

As tomato aspic begins to thicken, chopped vegetables may be added; for example green bell peppers, green onions, radishes, or cooked asparagus tips.

#163 Cole Slaw

1. Let stand for 30 minutes in cold water
   2 cups shredded cabbage.
2. Prepare dressing by mixing together
   ¼ cup sour-cream substitute, Recipe #4
   ¼ cup sweet-cream substitute, Recipe #2
   ¼ cup vinegar
   3 tablespoons sugar
   1 teaspoon salt
   ⅛ teaspoon pepper
   ½ teaspoon celery seed
   ¼ teaspoon dry mustard
   and chill.
3. Drain shredded cabbage and dry between paper towels.
4. Mix dressing and cabbage.

Cole slaw may also be made using shredded cabbage with nonfat French dressing, Recipe #77, and seasoning.

TC	P	C	F	S	M	PU	CHOL
317	68	244	4(1.3%)	T	T	2(0.6%)	10

#164 Chicken Salad

1. Mix

   2 cups cooked chicken (or turkey), chopped
   1 cup celery, diced.

2. Moisten with

   1 cup nonfat French dressing, Recipe #77

   and chill for ½ hour.
3. Mound chilled salad on lettuce leaf.
4. Garnish with nonfat mayonnaise, Recipe #83.

TC	P	C	F	S	M	PU	CHOL
509	330	78	97(19.0%)	32(6.3%)	36(7.1%)	20(3.9%)	240

Variation: Add 1 chopped and seeded green pepper, and serve on pineapple slices.

TC	P	C	F	S	M	PU	CHOL
781	354	322	103(13.2%)	32(4.1%)	36(4.6%)	21(2.7%)	243

#165 Chicken and Asparagus Salad

1. Mix together

   1 cup asparagus tips
   1½ cups cooked chicken, diced
   2 tablespoons minced green pepper
   ¼ cup shredded cabbage
   ¾ cup nonfat mayonnaise, Recipe #83.

2. Chill until served on

   lettuce leaf.

TC	P	C	F	S	M	PU	CHOL
455	270	117	79(17.4%)	21(4.6%)	24(5.3%)	16(3.5%)	233

#166 Ham and Chicken Salad

1. Blend together

   1 cup cooked ham, diced
   1 cup cooked chicken, diced
   ½ cup chopped celery
   ½ cup nonfat mayonnaise, Recipe #83.

2. Serve on

   leaf of lettuce

   or in

   tomato shell.

TC	P	C	F	S	M	PU	CHOL
598	314	68	209(34.9%)	73(12.2%)	85(14.2%)	24(4.0%)	126

CHAPTER 13

Fish and Shellfish

Early man lived close to the water. Lack of transportation limited his distance from a suitable water source, and it is not surprising that fish was one of his sources of food. The fish and the sea gave early man salt, iodine, and protein, all necessary for his well-being. Fish has remained an important part of the diet of man through centuries.

Fish and shellfish are both unique in that they are relatively low-calorie foods that contain limited amounts of saturated fat. Shrimp is the only commonly used seafood that contains a significant amount of carbohydrate. Most of the weight in seafood is water. It is often assumed that fish are low in fat content. This is true in terms of weight, but the percentage of calories from fat in some fish is rather high. It takes only a little fat for a fish containing few total calories to have over 35 per cent of its calories from fat. It makes a great deal of difference which fish you eat if you want to restrict your fat calories. To illustrate the point, the calories from fat in white sea bass are 4.5 per cent, in black sea bass 12 per cent, and in the small-mouth bass, striped bass, and white bass over 20 per cent of the total calories. Codfish (fat calories 3.4 per cent), drum or redfish (fat calories 4.5 per cent), and haddock (fat calories 1.1 per cent) are truly low-fat fish. Lake trout (fat calories 53 per cent), rainbow trout (fat calories 52 per cent), and herring (fat calories 58 per cent) are all examples of high-fat rather than low-fat food, relatively speaking. Consult Table XVIII, page 319, for the difference in fat content for various fishes if you plan to use fish as a low-fat food.

As pointed out in the previous chapter, it also makes a difference which kind of salmon you eat. In raw king salmon 63 per cent of the calories are from fat while only 20 per cent of the calories are from fat in raw pink (humpback) salmon.

Despite the large amounts of fat in some varieties of fish the amount of saturated fat is usually low. As a general rule, only about a third of the fat in fish is of the saturated type. Not all fish have been analyzed for their content of polyunsaturated fat, although they are believed to contain very long carbon-chain fats, which are highly unsaturated. You can assume, however, that about a third of the fat in fish is polyunsaturated.

Early studies of the effects of polyunsaturated fat on cholesterol levels in man reported that fish oil was about twice as effective in lowering cholesterol as corn oil. In some reports cholesterol levels were lowered over 50 per cent. Fish oils with their long carbon chains may have numerous carbon atoms not combined with hydrogen atoms. Although no deficiency in polyunsaturated fats has yet been proved in man, this dramatic change in body chemistry suggests that polyunsaturated fats should play an essential role in man's diet if abnormal chemistry and high cholesterol levels are to be avoided. Certain other high fat levels (triglycerides) have also been lowered with fish oils.

Low-fat fish provide an excellent source of protein and they are also low in cholesterol. All fish with less than 35 per cent of their calories from fat can be used in any amounts for individuals restricting their fat-calorie intake. If you serve fish containing larger amounts of fat, you should see that the meal includes additional food items with a fat content well below 35 per cent of their calories. This can easily be achieved with vegetables, salads, and fruit. Most shellfish are low in fat content. The percentage of fat calories in some of them is as follows: clams, 17 per cent; crab, 18 per cent; crayfish, 6 per cent; lobster, 18 per cent; oysters, 24 per cent; scallops, 2.2 per cent; and shrimp, 8 per cent.

Shellfish cannot be eaten in unlimited quantities if one must restrict cholesterol intake. The cholesterol content is not available for all shellfish, but it is known that a 3½-ounce (100-gram) serving of shrimp contains approximately half as much as found in one egg yolk. If you limit your cholesterol intake from any other food sources, you can eat 7 ounces (200 grams) of shrimp a day and still be within the 300 milligrams of cholesterol intake a day recommended by the Inter-Society

Commission on Heart Disease. A recent analysis shows that some shellfish contain much less cholesterol than previously reported.

It is common practice to add butter to fish or shellfish, which converts even low-fat fish into moderate- or high-fat dishes. Take the drum (redfish) as an example. A serving of 10½ ounces (300 grams) contains only 240 calories, with 10.8 calories (4.5 per cent) from fat. By adding one level tablespoon of butter or margarine in the preparation of the fish its calories will be increased to 340 calories, and 110.8 (33 per cent) of these will be from fat. To use fish and shellfish successfully as low-fat food one must avoid using butter, margarine, oils, commercial mayonnaise, or other sauces that contain lots of fat. You can use any of the sauces described in this book, including nonfat mayonnaise, nonfat tartare sauce, or the special Newburg sauce. Some of the tastiest dishes are made with sauces using only tomatoes and seasonings. It is not necessary to drown fish or shellfish in buttery sauces to have a delicious meal.

If you must dip lobster or steamed clams in butter or a butter substitute and need to limit your calorie or saturated-fat content, you can get some help by using melted low-calorie margarine.

#167 Baked Whole Fish

1. Wash rapidly in cool water but do not remove head, tail, fins, or otherwise cut through the skin (of course if scales are present they must be removed, and the body cavity must be emptied)

    1 whole fish.

2. Insert meat thermometer in the back behind gills deep into meat. Do not let thermometer touch bone.
3. Place fish upright on towel or cloth with back fin up in preheated oven at 250°–300°.
4. When internal temperature registers 150°–160°, remove fish. Do not overcook.

Serve whole if desired. (The soft portion of the fish belly is not always tasty and may be discarded.) To fillet the fish cut skin along the back (it will be fairly dry, like paper). Pull back the skin and cut the meat away from the bone so that each side of the fish comes off in one piece. The juices that run out of the fish can be poured over the baked meat. Season and garnish with lemon. Serve with nonfat tartare sauce, Recipe #89, or other sauce, as desired.

#168 Whole Baked Fish with Sauce

1. Prepare

   baked fish, Recipe #167.

2. To boned fish add

   sauce of choice.

3. Cook in preheated oven at no more than 200° for 5 minutes; then serve. (Be certain sauce is not too hot—preferably not more than 160° or fish will be overcooked.)

For sauces that may be used see section on sauces (fish sauce, white sauce, and variation of white sauce, Spanish Creole sauce).

#169 Baked Fish Steaks with Sauce

1. Place in prepared baking dish

   fish steaks (¾ inch thick).

2. Pour over steaks

   nonfat mushroom sauce, Recipe #64.

3. Bake in oven at 300° until internal temperature of steaks is 150°–160° (approximately 35 minutes).

Variation: Choice of different kinds of fish steaks or fillets with choice of sauces (nonfat cheese sauce, soubise sauce, Creole sauce, fish sauce, others).

#170 Fish Fillets Florentine

1. Cook until barely tender without water in top of tightly covered double boiler

   1½ pounds spinach.

2. Drain spinach, chop coarsely, and spread in bottom of baking dish.
3. Pour over spinach

   nonfat cheese sauce, Recipe #59.

4. Cover with

   1 pound fish fillets.

5. Bake at 300° approximately 30 minutes.

#171 Baked Fillets

1. Cut into serving size
fish fillets.
2. Dip fillets in water and cover with
nonfat milk powder.
3. Place in prepared baking dish.
4. Bake at 250°–300° until done, approximately 20–30 minutes for 1-inch thickness; 30–40 minutes for 2-inch thickness; 40–50 minutes for 3-inch thickness.

#172 Fish Loaf

1. Combine
2 cups cooked fish flakes
3 egg whites, stiffly beaten
1 cup medium white sauce, Recipe #58
salt and seasoning, if desired.
2. Pour into prepared baking dish and bake at 300° 30–40 minutes.

Variations: Add chopped pimiento, tomato, onions, or mushrooms. Serve fish loaf with variety of sauces.

#173 Broiled Whole Fish

1. Wash fish quickly in cold water—do not remove the skin, and leave head, tail, and fins intact.
2. Sprinkle generously with paprika.
3. Place fish in pan under broiler 1 inch from low gas flame, 5 inches from electric heat (leave oven door completely open for electric broiler), or on rack 1 or 2 inches above bed of coals. (A piece of screen wire under the fish is often helpful in preventing fish from falling apart.)
4. After about 10 minutes, turn fish, using pancake-turner, and heat other side until internal temperature is 150°–160°.
5. Serve plain, with lemon wedges or a vegetable garnish, or serve with a sauce. Whole fish may be split after broiling and separated into serving-size pieces. Pour the delicious cooking juices over the fish and season to taste.

#174 Broiled Fillets or Fish Steaks

1. Sprinkle fish with paprika.
2. Place in broiler pan 1 inch from low gas flame, 5 inches below electric grill (leave oven door open), or on wire screen on grill 1 or 2 inches above bed of coals.
3. After about 10 minutes turn with pancake-turner and continue cooking until internal temperature is 150°–160°.
4. Season and serve with lemon wedges, garnish, vegetables, or sauce of choice. For browner crust dip fillets or steaks in skim milk or egg whites, lightly beaten; then roll them in flour, bread crumbs, or corn meal.

#175 Pan-Broiled Fish

1. Sprinkle small whole fish, fillets, or fish steaks with paprika.
2. Place fish in prepared cold skillet.
3. Cook over low heat until nearly done, then turn.
4. Salt and season to taste—serve with lemon wedges, garnish, vegetables, or sauce of choice.

#176 Sole Amandine

1. Roll in flour
   9 fillets of sole.
2. Brown each side in prepared skillet over low heat.
3. Brown in oven (this step may be omitted)
   ¾ cup blanched almonds.
4. Cook in hot prepared skillet and stir constantly
   5 tomatoes, skinned and chopped
   2 teaspoons garlic, chopped.
5. Remove tomatoes from heat and add
   1 teaspoon chopped tarragon
   salt and pepper to taste.
6. Arrange cooked tomatoes on platter and place cooked fillets of sole on top.
7. Put almonds in skillet in which sole was cooked. Toss for one minute; then sprinkle over sole.

#177 Fillets of Fish Poached in White-Wine Sauce

1. In baking dish sprinkle
   1 tablespoon minced green onions.
2. Cut into serving pieces and lay in baking dish
   fillets of fish.
3. Sprinkle over fish another
   tablespoon minced green onions.
4. Pour over fish
   ¾ cup dry white wine.
5. Add enough water to cover fish.
6. Bring almost to simmer over low heat.
7. Remove from burner and cover with oiled brown paper.
8. Place in preheated oven at 350° and cook just below simmer point until done (approximately 8–13 minutes).
9. Drain fish, season, and serve with desired sauce or garnish.

#178 Fish Croquettes

1. Mix and shape into croquettes
   2 cups cooked flaked fish (or salmon without skin or bones)
   1 cup medium nonfat white sauce, Recipe #58
   1 teaspoon onion juice
   salt and pepper to taste.
2. Dip each croquette into lightly beaten egg white and roll it in crumbs or flour.
3. Pan-broil in prepared cold pan over low heat.

#179 Steamed Fish

1. Use fish or fish fillets less than 2 inches thick.
2. Insert meat thermometer in one fillet.
3. Place fish in colander or on rack, or hang it in cheesecloth over boiling water in a closed container.
4. When internal temperature is 150°–160°, remove. Sprinkle with paprika and serve with sauce of choice.

For fish at room temperature allow 3–4 minutes for 1-inch thickness, 6–8 minutes for 2-inch thickness, and longer for chilled fish.

Steamed fish may be flaked and used in appetizers, salads, creamed dishes, or casseroles.

#180 Sautéed Fish

1. Sift together

    ⅔ cup flour
    ⅔ cup nonfat milk powder
    1 teaspoon salt.

2. Add and mix well

    2 egg whites
    ½ cup cold water.

3. Dip in prepared batter

    fish fillets or steaks.

4. Let fish dry at least 10 minutes on aluminum foil.
5. Insert thermometer in one piece of fish.
6. Place fish in cold prepared pan over low heat and heat until surface is brown; turn fish and brown other side. When thermometer reads 150°–160°, remove fish (about 10–15 minutes).

#181 Fish in Parchment

1. Spread out flat one sheet of dampened parchment paper and oil it lightly.
2. Spread out on parchment

    1 pound of fillets (cut to serving size).

3. Spread evenly over fillets

    1 tablespoon minced onion
    ½ tablespoon minced parsley
    ½ tablespoon lemon juice
    salt and pepper to taste.

4. Gather parchment into a bag and tie securely. Cook fish in parchment in gently boiling water for 15 minutes.
5. Remove fish with all its juices to a platter for serving.

#182 Scalloped Fish

1. In prepared baking dish place

    2 cups flaked cooked fish

2 cups nonfat white sauce, Recipe #58.
2 boiled egg whites, finely chopped.

2. Add
salt and pepper to taste.

3. Cover with
bread crumbs or crushed corn flakes.

4. Bake at 350° for 20 minutes, or until crumbs are browned.

#183 Tuna Roll

1. Mix together
1½ cups cold water
½ cup nonfat milk powder.

2. Add
1 cup bread crumbs
3 egg whites, lightly beaten.

3. Combine with
2 7-ounce cans drained water-packed tuna
2 tablespoons lemon juice.

4. Season with
salt and pepper to taste.

5. Place mixture in prepared mold. Put mold in pan of water and bake until firm in oven preheated to 350°.
6. Unmold and serve with or without center filled with cooked vegetables.

TC	P	C	F	S	M	PU	CHOL
1081	628	412	75(6.9%)	17(1.6%)	26(2.4%)	17(1.6%)	222

Variation: Substitute salmon for tuna.

TC	P	C	F	S	M	PU	CHOL
1137	500	412	263(23.1%)	53(4.7%)	82(7.2%)	101(8.9%)	294

#184 Scalloped Tuna and Peas

1. In prepared baking dish alternate layers of
2 cups cooked peas
2 cups flaked cooked tuna (or water-packed tuna).

2. Pour over peas and tuna
   ½ cup medium nonfat white sauce, Recipe #58.
3. Add
   ½ teaspoon salt.
4. Cover with
   ½ cup bread crumbs or crushed corn flakes.
5. Bake at 350° about 20 minutes or until crumbs are brown.

TC	P	C	F	S	M	PU	CHOL
779	559	340	58(7.4%)	13(1.7%)	17(2.2%)	16(2.0%)	214

Variations: White sauce variations, such as mushroom sauce, may be used. Salmon may be used in place of tuna.

#185 Salmon Stew

1. Sift together
   ¼ cup flour
   1 cup nonfat milk powder
   1½ teaspoons salt
   ⅛ teaspoon pepper.
2. Mix well with 3 cups cold water.
3. Heat in top of double boiler over boiling water 3 minutes or more to desired thickness.
4. Simmer 20 minutes in a separate pan
   1 1-pound can salmon, flaked
   1 cup cooked tomatoes
   1 small onion, sliced
   2 cups water.
5. Combine white sauce and salmon and serve at once.

TC	P	C	F	S	M	PU	CHOL
1089	520	300	257(23.6%)	50(4.6%)	73(6.7%)	106(9.7%)	340

#186 Clam Chowder

1. Cook
   1 cup celery, chopped
   2 large onions, chopped

1 green pepper, diced
1 carrot, diced

in

4 cups water.

2. Add

2 cups cooked tomatoes
thyme
salt and pepper to taste

and cook 10 minutes more.

3. Add

2 dozen large clams, shucked and minced

and simmer until clams are tender.

4. Add sufficient

crackers, crushed,

to thicken desired amount.

TC	P	C	F	S	M	PU	CHOL
650	324	215	100(15.4%)	30(4.6%)	20(3.1%)	34(5.2%)	410

#187 Clam-Corn-Pimiento Casserole

1. Drain liquid from

1 7-ounce can clams.

2. To the liquid add

½ cup cold water
¼ cup nonfat dry milk.

3. Then add

4 egg whites, lightly beaten
1 cup cream-style corn
½ cup cracker crumbs
2 tablespoons pimientos, chopped
1 tablespoon onions, minced
½ teaspoon salt
dash cayenne.

4. Pour into prepared casserole and bake at 375° about 45 minutes. When done it will be firm.

TC	P	C	F	S	M	PU	CHOL
532	233	243	72(13.5%)	19(3.6%)	26(4.9%)	22(4.1%)	171

#188 Broiled Oysters

1. Beat lightly

   3 egg whites

   with

   ½ teaspoon salt
   ⅛ teaspoon pepper
   2 tablespoons cold water.

2. Drain

   24 large shucked oysters.

3. Dip oysters in egg-white mix and then roll them in fine dry bread crumbs.
4. Let oysters stand for 5 minutes.
5. Put oysters on prepared broiling pan and place under broiler until browned on one side; then brown other side and serve with nonfat tartare sauce, Recipe #89.

TC	P	C	F	S	M	PU	CHOL
370	64	94	70(18.9%)	21(5.7%)	32(8.6%)	35(9.4%)	130

#189 Oysters à la King

1. To rather thick

   double mushroom sauce, Recipe #64

   add

   2 tablespoons pimiento, minced.

2. Simmer in their own liquid 5 minutes

   1 pint oysters.

3. Add cooked oysters and liquor to mushroom sauce and season to taste with

   salt and pepper.

4. Serve on toast.

TC	P	C	F	S	M	PU	CHOL
722	293	339	84(11.6%)	23(3.2%)	34(4.7%)	42(5.8%)	163

#190 Shrimp à la King

1. Prepare
   2 mushroom-sauce recipes, Recipe #64.
2. Add
   1 tablespoon minced pimiento
   ½ teaspoon celery salt
   1½ pounds boiled shrimp.
3. Serve on toast.

TC	P	C	F	S	M	PU	CHOL
1172	829	261	77(6.6%)	27(2.3%)	T	18(1.5%)	1051

#191 Shrimp Curry

1. Prepare
   2 curry-sauce recipes, Recipe #69.
2. Add
   1½ pounds boiled shrimp.
3. Serve on
   cooked rice.

TC	P	C	F	S	M	PU	CHOL
1154	823	251	75(6.5%)	27(2.3%)	T	16(1.4%)	1051

#192 Shrimp Creole

1. Prepare
   Spanish Creole sauce, Recipe #70.
2. Add
   1 pound boiled shrimp.
3. Serve on
   cooked rice.

TC	P	C	F	S	M	PU	CHOL
698	488	147	56(8.0%)	18(2.6%)	T	12(1.7%)	686

#193 Broiled Breaded Shrimp

1. Mix together
   2 cups cold water
   1 cup nonfat milk powder
   2 egg whites.
2. Add and let stand for 5 minutes
   1½ pounds boiled shrimp.
3. Coat shrimp well with
   bread crumbs
   and let stand 5 minutes.
4. Place under broiler and cook until brown. Turn and brown other side.

TC	P	C	F	S	M	PU	CHOL
1077	843	161	73(6.8%)	27(2.5%)	T	14(1.3%)	1051

#194 Pan-Broiled Scallops

1. Mix together
   2 egg whites
   2 tablespoons water
   1 teaspoon salt
   ½ teaspoon celery salt.
2. Roll
   1 pound scallops
   in
   1 cup bread crumbs.
3. Dip scallops in egg-white mixture and then roll in crumbs again.
4. Let stand on foil for 10 minutes.
5. Pan-broil over low heat until well browned.

TC	P	C	F	S	M	PU	CHOL
792	390	358	54(6.8%)	9(1.1%)	18(2.2%)	14(1.8%)	275

#195 Broiled Scallops

1. Dip

    1 pound scallops

    in

    nonfat French dressing, Recipe #77.

2. Roll scallops thoroughly in

    1 cup bread crumbs.

3. Let stand 5 minutes; then place on a prepared bake sheet and cook under broiler until browned—about 15 minutes.

TC	P	C	F	S	M	PU	CHOL
758	343	356	54(7.1%)	9(1.2%)	18(2.4%)	14(1.8%)	275

CHAPTER

14

Poultry

Wild fowl was part of early man's environment and an early food source. At least 3000 years before Christ wild fowl were domesticated in China. In the past two centuries poultry has become an important food source. Special breeds have been developed for specific purposes. Whereas the wild fowl produced very few eggs a year, specially developed breeds of hens are veritable egg machines. Other breeds, raised for their meat, grow into large marketable birds in a relatively short time.

The two main types of poultry available widely today are chickens and turkeys, and raising them is a big mechanized business. The domesticated mass-produced bird is often much fatter than the barnyard bird of yesterday, and the meat has lost some of its flavor, but mechanization in the poultry industry has made it possible to feed millions of people at economical rates. The price of chicken in the United States would be much higher if mass-production methods had not been developed. In fact, chicken and turkey are two of the cheapest sources of animal protein for the diet and may one day be man's major source of animal protein.

The effects of domestication can be seen in a comparison of the fat content of a wild duck and that of a domestic duck. The calories in the latter are almost all from fat—a whopping 79 per cent. Only 61 per cent of the calories in wild duck are from fat. About half of the fat in all poultry comes from the skin and the layer of fat just beneath the skin. If this is removed from a wild bird, the duck becomes a low-fat food with only 34 per cent of its calories from fat, but the domestic duck without the skin still has 44 per cent of its calories from fat.

Fortunately for those wishing to restrict the amount of saturated fat in their diet, only about one third of the fat in fowl is of the saturated type, and over 20 per cent of the fat is of the polyunsaturated type. In this sense it is almost as good as fish.

Just as there can be fat fish, there can be fat birds. It does make a difference what kind of chicken you buy and which pieces you eat. In general the best bird for low-fat meat is a young bird. For low-fat diets you should concentrate on using fryer chickens, since only 13 per cent of the calories in the light meat of the fryer without the skin is from fat (with only 4.3 per cent from saturated fat). Even with the skin, less than 30 per cent of the calories in the light meat of fryer chicken is from fat (less than 10 per cent saturated fat).

The dark meat has more fat than the light meat. About 30 per cent of the calories in the dark meat (without the skin) is from fat, over twice that seen in light meat. The back has more fat than any other piece of chicken, with 55 per cent of its calories from fat. The percentages of calories from fat in chicken meat with skin is as follows: fryer, 36 per cent; roaster, 58 per cent; hens and cocks, 67 per cent; and capon, 68 per cent. The composition of chicken is given in Table XIX, page 324.

Turkey compares very favorably with chicken. Young turkeys (twenty-four weeks old or under) are only a little fatter than fryer chickens, with 44 per cent of their calories from fat. The light meat, however, contains only 3 per cent fat calories. The medium-fat birds (twenty-six to thirty-two weeks old) have 53 per cent of their calories from fat, and the fat mature birds (over thirty-two weeks old) have 76 per cent. The latter are comparable to the domestic goose, which has over 80 per cent of its calories from fat.

Dry-Roasted Poultry

There are many different ways to roast poultry. Dry roasting means that the bird is cooked in dry heat. Although a shield of aluminum foil may be placed loosely above the bird, the bird must not be cooked in a covered roasting pan. Covering produces moist heat in which the bird is steamed, not dry-roasted.

The prepared bird (stuffed or unstuffed) is placed on the oven rack over a drip pan or on a rack in the bottom of a roasting pan, so that it does not sit in the accumulated pan juices. Water conducts heat rapidly and overcooks part of the bird before the rest of it is cooked.

The moist stuffing used in most roasted birds serves to keep the meat from becoming too dry.

The time required for dry roasting depends upon oven temperature, size of bird, stuffing, and whether the bird is chilled or at room temperature. Chilled birds require 15 to 30 minutes longer at moderate oven temperature.

The most common error in dry roasting is using too hot an oven. The larger the bird the more moderate the temperature (300° or below) should be. The dry heat slowly penetrates the meat to cook the inner portions. If the oven is too hot the outer areas will overcook and lose natural juices. The bird will become dry and tough, and there will be a lot of shrinkage. The more juice that drips into the pan the more likely it is that the meat has been overheated.

A convenient method of dry roasting is to put the prepared bird in an oven preheated to 300°. Small birds of 3 pounds or less can be completely cooked at this temperature until the desired internal meat temperature is reached. For larger birds, after one hour the oven temperature may be reduced to 200° for a slow bake. When the internal temperature of the meat is 185°, the bird is cooked. One of the few exceptions is wild duck, which should be served at an internal temperature of 140°.

Some cooks feel that you can use the temperature of the stuffing to tell when the bird is done and that when that temperature is 165° the bird is cooked. If the meat temperature is used, care must be taken to be sure the thermometer is in the meat, either in the thigh next to the body or in the thickest part of the breast. The thermometer must not touch the bone.

If aluminum foil or a damp cloth is placed over the bird, it should be removed toward the end of the roasting period so that the bird will brown.

Because there is always variation in roasting time, caused by different internal temperatures of the bird and by the presence or absence of stuffing, the most accurate results are obtained by the use of an internal thermometer. The following general guide is based on the weight of the stuffed bird at room temperature and gives the time required to roast most birds to an internal temperature of 185° with an oven temperature of 300°:

Less than 3 lbs.	¾–2 hrs.
3–6 lbs.	2–3 hrs.

6–8 lbs.	2½–3½ hrs.
8–10 lbs.	3–4 hrs.
10–16 lbs.	3½–5½ hrs.
18–25 lbs.	5½–6½ hrs.

Don't forget to add 15 to 30 minutes for a chilled bird (chilled, not partially frozen). If a slow bake is used the time will be longer. The oven can be set at 185° and the bird left for hours without danger of overcooking and without any further attention. In fact, the bird can be left in the oven overnight and the roasting finished the next day.

Although the slow-roast method eliminates the need for basting, many people like to be sure that the meat remains moist by basting it every 30 minutes or so, more often during the last hour of roasting. Non-fat chicken broth, wine gravy (Recipe #56), or barbecue sauce (Recipe #71) are best for this—not butter or the fatty cooking liquid that collects in the roasting pan.

The drippings in the pan should be chilled and the fat skimmed off. The remaining juices can be used to make low-fat gravy. A very slow bake may result in very little drippings. The bird should not be seasoned until the end of baking. Particularly, it should not be salted, since salt tends to draw out the natural juices. Sprinkling the surface lightly with paprika enhances a brown color.

The slow-bake method *is not satisfactory* for any birds except very lean ones if you are trying to restrict the calories in your diet. This method can be used for fryer chickens, guinea hens, pheasants, and young turkeys. (Although the exact fat content is not known, Rock Cornish game hens seem to be lean, and some game birds, such as quail, are also relatively free of fat.) The slow bake retains not only juices but also fat. Note that three fourths of the calories in a hen or cock are from fat and only one fourth from protein. If a fat bird is roasted it is desirable to cook it long enough and at hot enough temperature for the fat to run out of the meat. This will cause shrinkage, but after all one sixth of the total weight (¾ of the calories) of fat birds is fat.

Although eating fat birds is not recommended for a low-fat diet, if they must be used the following method of roasting is recommended:

#196 Roasting Method for Fatty Poultry

1. Prepare bird in the usual manner, but do not stuff it (stuffing soaks up rendered fat).
2. Dry roast at 325° until done (internal temperature 185°–190°).

During roasting, if skin over back is pierced in a few places and bird placed back down, more rendered fat will run out.

3. Remove drippings from pan and chill (they may be placed in metal pan immersed in ice water or set on ice).
4. Skim all fat from drippings.
5. Take desired amount of fat-free drippings to use for gravy.
6. Use portion of fat-free drippings to moisten stuffing.
7. Bake stuffing in covered baking dish at 425° for about 25 minutes.

Some people say you lose valuable nutrients with this method, but if you save the fat-free drippings and use them the only thing you will lose is fat and that is the whole object. Do not eat the skin since that is where a lot of the residual fat will be.

In all birds the breast meat has the lowest fat content. Less than one fifth of the calories in chicken fryer breasts is fat. Breasts from fryers, young turkeys, and other low-fat birds are a particularly good source of protein.

#197 ROASTED POULTRY BREAST

1. Place breasts skin down on a rack and roast at 300° until done (internal temperature of 185°).
2. Remove skin and serve with desired accompaniments.

Breast may be covered with a wine sauce or other low-fat sauce, and served with wild rice or vegetables of choice on the side.

Broiled Poultry

Whether broiling is done over coals or under a gas or electric burner, it is a dry-heat method. The proper temperature is low. As in dry roasting, the key to a low-fat serving lies in selecting the bird. Use only fryer or broiler chicken, young turkeys, or other low-fat birds. Properly broiled breast is an excellent choice for a low-fat entree.

Broiled vegetables served with broiled chicken provide an appetizing combination.

Barbecued Poultry

Simply pour barbecue sauce over the meat. If the bird is on a spit, baste it constantly for 15 minutes until done.

Pan-Broiled Poultry

Place cut pieces of bird in an uncovered skillet or on a flat grill. Use low heat. The pieces should be cut or bones broken or deboned to make them as flat as possible. Cook only low-fat birds this way.

Sautéed Poultry

This variation of pan-broiling is very useful in cooking lean birds, particularly since the pieces are not flat. The method can be used for fryer chicken and young turkey. The batter forms a crust enclosing the moisture; thus much of the cooking is actually done by moist heat.

#198 Sautéed Chicken or Young Turkey

1. Sift together
   2/3 cup flour
   2/3 cup nonfat milk powder
   1 teaspoon salt.
2. Add and mix well
   2 egg whites
   1/2 cup cold water.
3. Dip in prepared batter
   cut pieces of fryer chicken (or young turkey).
4. Let chicken dry at least 10 minutes on piece of aluminum foil.
5. Dip and dry again.
6. Place chicken in cold prepared pan over low heat and cook until surface is brown. Turn and brown other side. Cook until done (internal temperature 185°).

For this recipe use only pieces of chicken which are low in fat. This means lean, young fryer chicken.

#199 Smothered Chicken

1. Prepare in usual manner and remove the skin from

    5-pound young fryer.

2. Place chicken in roasting pan with small amount of water. Cover pan tightly.
3. Roast at 325°–350° 2½–3 hours.
4. Remove cooked chicken from roasting pan. Drain off juices and cool them rapidly over ice. Skim off all surface fat.
5. Return nonfat drippings to roasting pan and add

    2 tablespoons flour

    mixed in

    enough cold water to form a smooth paste.

6. Add

    sufficient water for gravy

    and cook to boiling point.

7. Remove gravy from heat and add the cooked chicken.
8. Simmer 5 minutes over low heat and then remove from heat and let stand covered for about 10 minutes before serving.
9. Salt, pepper, and season to taste.

TC	P	C	F	S	M	PU	CHOL
1707	1273	45	372(21.8%)	124(7.3%)	139(8.1%)	78(4.6%)	927

Variation with 1 4-ounce can mushrooms:

TC	P	C	F	S	M	PU	CHOL
1726	1279	55	373(21.6%)	124(7.2%)	139(8.0%)	78(4.5%)	927

#200 Chicken Smothered with Sweet Potatoes

1. Cook either by baking or boiling

    3 pounds sweet potatoes.

2. Peel cooked sweet potatoes and place in the bottom of the bake dish.
3. Make

    smothered chicken, Recipe #199,

    and put cooked chicken on top of sweet potatoes.

4. Pour the cooked gravy over chicken and sweet potatoes.
5. Set in oven preheated to 300° for 15 minutes before serving.

TC	P	C	F	S	M	PU	CHOL
4295	1377	2451	463(10.8%)	147(3.4%)	162(3.8%)	123(2.9%)	927

#201 Chicken-Mushroom Casserole

1. Skin and remove all visible fat from
   4-pound lean fryer chicken.
2. Dredge chicken in
   flour
   seasoned with
   salt and pepper.
3. Dry at least 10 minutes on aluminum-foil sheet.
4. Dredge and dry again.
5. Brown chicken by pan-broiling or sautéeing.
6. Place browned chicken in deep baking dish and add
   2 cans (4 ounces) sliced mushrooms.
7. Cover chicken and mushrooms with
   2 cups nonfat cream substitute, Recipe #2.
8. Bake in 350° oven until tender (1–2 hours).

TC	P	C	F	S	M	PU	CHOL
1788	1194	273	305(17.0%)	99(5.5%)	111(6.2%)	62(3.5%)	758

Variation: Add one cup of cooked vegetables to the baking dish before adding the nonfat cream substitute. Cooked peas, carrots, or a mixture are good choices. Small pieces of green pimiento or canned red ripe pimiento add interesting color and flavor to the dish.

Stewed Chicken

Included under the general classification of cooking with moist heat are stewing, fricasseeing, steaming, braising, and boiling. Although a chicken may be steamed, it is likely to retain more fat than chicken prepared by special stewing methods. If a chicken is steamed by placing it over hot water in a closed container it should be a lean chicken fryer. Fatter birds should be stewed or boiled.

#202 Boiled or Stewed Chicken

This recipe should be used in preparing chicken for salads, chicken à la king, chicken pies, and other dishes calling for cooked chicken. Since the object is to eliminate fat, the bird should be skinned and all visible fat should be removed. Preferably, the bird should be a young fryer.

1. Prepare, skin and disjoint into pieces
   3-pound chicken.
2. Put chicken into stewing pot and cover with
   water.
3. Add
   1 onion, peeled and chopped
   1 carrot, sliced
   salt and pepper.
4. Simmer until tender (chicken should be tender enough to begin to fall loose from the bone).
5. Remove chicken and strip all meat from bone.
6. Save the water and juices from the boiled chicken and cool. Skim the fat from the surface of the cooled liquid and discard the fat. The liquid may be saved for the preparation of gravies, chicken soup, or other purposes. The chicken stock may be used as the fluid in white sauce for chicken à la king. The chicken and fat-free chicken stock may be packaged and frozen for subsequent use.

#203 Boiled Chicken Dinner

For this recipe use only lean young fryer chicken.

1. Prepare and cover with water
   1 3-pound fryer chicken.
2. Simmer until tender (1 hour).
3. Remove chicken and skim off any fat which may be on the surface of the cooking water.
4. To the cooking water add
   3 medium potatoes
   6 small onions
   1 head cauliflower
   12 small carrots
   1 pint brussels sprouts.

Cook vegetables until tender (about 20 minutes).
5. Serve boiled chicken with boiled vegetables.

TC	P	C	F	S	M	PU	CHOL
2134	930	941	271(12.7%)	77(3.6%)	86(4.0%)	58(2.7%)	565

#204 Chicken Espagnole

1. Clean and skin
 5-pound fryer chicken.
2. Roll chicken thoroughly in
 flour
 and let dry on aluminum foil for about 10 minutes.
3. Roll chicken again in
 flour
 and dry thoroughly.
4. Brown chicken under broiler.
5. Cook in as little water as possible
 2 medium onions, sliced
 1 green pepper, chopped
 2 cups tomatoes, chopped
 for about 10 minutes.
6. Stir in
 1 teaspoon sugar.
7. Add chicken to the cooked vegetable sauce and cover with water. Simmer in tightly covered pan approximately 1–1½ hours, or until tender.
8. Add
 2 cups peas
 1 4-ounce can sliced mushrooms
 2 teaspoons salt.
9. Mix
 2 tablespoons flour
 in sufficient cold water for mixing.
10. Add flour mixture to hot stew.
11. Cover tightly and simmer for approximately 20 minutes.

TC	P	C	F	S	M	PU	CHOL
2090	1337	372	388(18.6%)	124(5.9%)	139(6.6%)	87(4.2%)	927

#205 Chicken with Rice

1. Cut into serving pieces and remove skin from
   3-pound fryer chicken.
2. Combine chicken with
   1 small onion, sliced
   2 cloves garlic, mashed
   2 bay leaves
   ½ teaspoon salt
   water to cover.
3. Simmer until tender.
4. Cook over low heat
   1 cup raw rice
   in 2½ cups chicken stock with
   2 ripe red pimientos, mashed
   1 green pepper, finely chopped
   ½ cup cooked tomatoes
   1 clove garlic, mashed
   1 small onion, minced.
5. Serve cooked chicken with rice mixture.

TC	P	C	F	S	M	PU	CHOL
1854	831	761	237(12.8%)	74(4.0%)	83(4.5%)	49(2.6%)	556

#206 Chicken and Spaghetti

1. Cook in boiling
   salted water
   until tender
   1 8-ounce package spaghetti.
2. Place drained spaghetti in prepared casserole.
3. Cook in as little water as possible until tender
   1 onion, chopped fine
   1 small clove garlic.
4. To the onion-garlic mixture add
   2½ cup cooked tomatoes
   1 tablespoon sugar
   dash of cayenne
   salt and pepper to taste.

5. Heat to boiling.
6. Add

   ½ cup cooked chicken, diced
   1 4-ounce can sliced mushrooms, drained.
7. Pour mixture over sphaghetti and mix thoroughly.
8. Sprinkle surface lightly with paprika and bake at 350° until heated through.

TC	P	C	F	S	M	PU	CHOL
1189	794	299	64(5.4%)	8(0.7%)	9(0.8%)	10(0.8%)	60

#207 Baked Chicken Orleans

1. Cook together for 10 minutes, over low heat

   1 cup cooked rice
   1½ cups cooked chicken, diced
   1½ cups cooked tomatoes.
2. Transfer to baking dish and add

   ½ green pepper, chopped
   1 large onion, chopped
   ½ cup celery, chopped
   salt and pepper to taste

   mix thoroughly.
3. Cover with dry bread crumbs or cracker crumbs.
4. Bake at 350° for 1 hour.

TC	P	C	F	S	M	PU	CHOL
465	261	110	83(17.8%)	24(5.1%)	27(5.8%)	19(4.1%)	180

#208 Chicken in Wine

1. Prepare by skinning and removing all excess fat and cutting into serving pieces

   2-pound fryer chicken.
2. Put pieces of chicken in a pan of

   wine vinegar

   to marinate. After 30 minutes turn the pieces over and marinate 30 minutes longer.
3. Remove marinated chicken and place in baking dish.

4. Pour over chicken

    ½ cup dry white wine.

5. Cover tightly and bake at 350° until tender.
6. Remove chicken and pour sauce over pieces for serving. This chicken in wine goes well with wild rice.

TC	P	C	F	S	M	PU	CHOL
760	507	18	148(19.5%)	49(6.4%)	56(7.4%)	31(4.1%)	371

Variation: Use a dry red wine in place of white wine.

#209 Chicken Newburg

1. Combine

    Newburg sauce, Recipe #57

    with

    1 cup cooked chicken, diced.

2. Heat to desired temperature for serving.

TC	P	C	F	S	M	PU	CHOL
504	257	117	62(12.3%)	20(4.0%)	23(4.6%)	10(2.0%)	192

#210 Chicken and Sauce

1. Combine

    1 cup cooked chicken, diced

    with

    1 cup white sauce, Recipe #58

    or

    1 cup white sauce variation

    or

    1 cup Spanish Creole sauce, Recipe #70.

2. Heat to desired temperature and serve.

With white sauce:

TC	P	C	F	S	M	PU	CHOL
333	203	76	50(15.0%)	16(4.8%)	18(5.4%)	11(3.3%)	27

With Creole sauce:

TC	P	C	F	S	M	PU	CHOL
298	173	67	53(17.8%)	16(5.3%)	18(6.0%)	12(4.0%)	20

#211 Chicken à la King

1. Mix until smooth

   1 tablespoon flour
   ½ cup nonfat dry milk powder
   ½ teaspoon paprika
   ¼ teaspoon salt
   dash white pepper

   with

   small amount cold water.
2. Add flour mixture to

   1 cup chicken stock, Recipe #100

   or

   1 cup water.
3. Cook in top of double boiler until thickened (at least 2 minutes).
4. Add to white sauce

   1 cup cooked chicken, diced

   and

   1 pimiento, chopped.
5. Cook for 15 minutes in top of double boiler.
   Chicken à la king may be served on toast, biscuits, or in various shells.

TC	P	C	F	S	M	PU	CHOL
372	222	92	51(13.7%)	16(4.3%)	18(4.8%)	10(2.7%)	31

Variations: During last 15 minutes of cooking in double boiler, other cooked vegetables may be added as desired—green peas, carrots, mushrooms, asparagus, or cooked corn.

#212 Chicken Pot Pie

1. Prepare

   chicken and sauce, Recipe #210

   or

   chicken à la king, Recipe #211.

2. Place in deep bake dish and top with
   baking-powder biscuits, Recipe #25.
3. Bake in oven at 425° for 20 minutes.

TC	P	C	F	S	M	PU	CHOL
1793	334	860	556(31.0%)	69(3.8%)	106(5.9%)	279(15.6%)	34

#213 Quick Chicken Curry

1. Mix
   1 tablespoon flour
   with sufficient
   cold water
   to make a smooth paste.
2. Add flour mixture to
   2 cups chicken stock
   2 tablespoons curry powder
   and beat until smooth.
3. Cook over low heat in top of double boiler until sauce is thickened.
4. To sauce add
   2 cups cooked chicken, diced.
   Cook a little longer.
5. Serve over cooked rice.

With rice:

TC	P	C	F	S	M	PU	CHOL
469	337	24	97(20.7%)	32(6.8%)	36(7.7%)	20(4.3%)	240

Variation: Add 1 cup diced cooked chicken to curry sauce, Recipe #69, and heat.

Without rice:

TC	P	C	F	S	M	PU	CHOL
392	222	114	51(13.0%)	16(4.1%)	18(4.6%)	11(2.8%)	31

Stuffings

#214 Wild-Rice Stuffing

1. Cook in boiling water until tender (about 25 minutes)
    ½ cup wild rice.
2. Drain and rinse rice.
3. Add
    1 4-ounce can sliced mushrooms
    ½ teaspoon sage
    dash thyme
    salt and pepper to taste.

TC	P	C	F	S	M	PU	CHOL
302	46	248	6(2.0%)	T	T	T	—

In addition to using rice, stuffings or dressings for all occasions can be made using bread as the basic vehicle. The stuffing need not be placed inside a bird, meat, or a fish, but can be baked in a separate pan, so that it does not become soaked in grease rendered from the baking meat. Commercial dressings often contain unspecified vegetable fat of unspecified amounts. The fat cannot be removed, so if you wish to limit your fat intake you should avoid these. Plain bread crumbs may be used in place of bread. You can adjust the amounts of the ingredients in the all-purpose stuffing to suit your needs.

#215 All-Purpose Bread Stuffing

1. Tear into small pieces
    ½ loaf bread.
    It need not be fresh; in fact dry bread is preferable.
2. Add
    2 egg whites.
3. Moisten with sufficient reconstituted nonfat milk made of
    1 part nonfat milk powder
    2 parts cold water
    to soak the bread completely.

The above mixture can serve as a vehicle to make a variety of stuffings which can be seasoned to taste with salt and pepper. Among the various ingredients and seasoning that can be added alone or in combination are:

Garlic or garlic salt
Curry
Sage (sage dressing)
Onions
Celery, chopped
Mushrooms, canned
Savoy
Green pepper, chopped
Tomato, chopped
Oysters (for oyster dressing, use the liquor from the oysters in moistening the bread)
Clams
Shrimp
Nuts (walnuts, chestnuts, pecans, others)
Olives, chopped
Apples, chopped (good with pork)
Prunes, chopped (good with pork)
Raisins, seedless
Giblets, cooked and chopped

A sage dressing, for instance, can include sage, salt, pepper, garlic, onion, celery, and even chopped green pepper. Similar combinations may be prepared from these and other ingredients. You can also use stock or bouillon as a moistening agent.

CHAPTER

15

Meat

Beef

There is no better example of how man's eating habits have been changed than the modern consumption of beef. Primitive man got his meat from the wild creatures about him. These animals were strong in limb with little fat, and rather tough by modern standards. In his earliest stage man was no match for many of these animals and relied more on fruits and vegetables than meat, at least in warm regions. As he moved to colder climates, however, it was necessary that he have meat. The long, cold winter season was no place for tropical abundance, so man the vegetarian became a hunter and fisherman. Soon he learned to domesticate animals for meat, and eventually the cattle industry was born.

In North America Indians followed the herds of bison and hunted deer, until the Spaniards and later the English introduced cattle to the continent. These range cattle were also lean and tough, but during the past few decades, the grass-fed animal has been replaced by the feedlot product—a far cry from nature's original meat source for man. Concentrated foods and supplements including even female hormones are fed to these animals whose flesh graces today's table.

While the beef animal has gotten fatter and fatter through breeding and feeding methods, the consumption of beef has increased, particularly in the United States. The average consumption of beef per person in the United States increased from 62 pounds a year in 1952 to 114 pounds a year in 1970—the highest consumption rate in the world. Cooking techniques generally demand the use of fat meats rather than leaner meats, since fatty beef is more tender with less cooking. And, of course, the fatter the beef, the higher the price.

The fat content of the meat is used to grade its quality. The carcass of a prime-grade animal is 46 per cent fat by weight; the choice grade, 40 per cent fat; good grade, 34 per cent fat; and standard grade, only 27 per cent fat. Individual retail cuts contain far less fat, fortunately, but the general principle of grading by fat content remains true.

If you do not have to limit your calories or your fat intake there is no reason why you shouldn't eat as much as you like of the fattest beef you can find. Those who wish to limit either their fat consumption or calories can still eat beef, but must be selective. The main principle is to buy "good" grade when you can and trim away every bit of visible fat before cooking by any method. What difference does it make? An untrimmed choice round steak has 52 per cent of its calories in the form of fat while only 31 per cent of the calories are from fat in a trimmed cut (separable lean). If you wish to keep your total fat intake below the level of 35 per cent of your total calorie intake, trimming the meat should be an important first step for you.

Among the various cuts of beef none is leaner than the separable lean of round steak, which is a good choice for low-fat cooking. You can use other cuts, of course, but you will have to exercise more care in their preparation. The flank steak deserves special mention since it is all lean meat as purchased and only one third of its calories is from fat (good grade). It is an economical choice if you want lean beef, and it can be used for roasting, broiling, boiling, or to make corned beef. The selection of the cut and trimming are important. Take for example the hipbone sirloin; this choice cut has 85 per cent of its calories as fat and when trimmed 50 per cent of its calories is fat. The composition of various cuts of beef is listed in Table XX, page 326.

That all-American favorite, hamburger, deserves a word. About two thirds of the calories in commercial regular ground beef are from fat, and half the calories in so-called lean ground beef are also from fat. If you like ground beef and want to limit your calories and fat intake, particularly saturated fat, you should make your own from separable lean beef. Nearly half of beef fat is saturated, and almost none of it qualifies as polyunsaturated fat. In this regard it is inferior to pork. The cholesterol content of beef (excluding organ meats) is fairly low.

Do not be misled by statements about beef being a "low-fat" food. Many such statements are based on the percentage of the weight of the meat that is fat. The truth is that the muscle is approximately 70 per cent water by weight. Thus, separable lean meat is often low in total calories, which is good for diets limiting total calories. The 30 per cent of its weight that is calories includes protein and fat. Since the fat has over twice as many calories as the protein, even separable lean round steak (only 4.7 per cent fat by weight) is over 30 per cent fat in terms of calories. Over 50 per cent of the fat in beef is saturated and a little less is monounsaturated, and beef contains no significant amounts of polyunsaturated fat.

Another misleading statement is that nearly half of beef fat is unsaturated fat. This statement is often accompanied by comments on the value of unsaturated fat in the diet. There is *no* evidence that monounsaturated fat of the type found in beef has any cholesterol-lowering effect of the type noted in studies reported for fish oil and vegetable oil, both of which contain polyunsaturated fat. Therefore, when someone tells you that beef is low in fat and contains unsaturated fat, watch out. Pay attention to the difference in percentage of total calories (not weight) and the type of fat. Remember that lean meat contains lots of water, just as fish, vegetables and fruit do, so that percentages based on weight don't mean much. These comments are not intended to discourage you from using meat but to keep you from being misled about what you are eating.

Steaks

Steaks can be broiled on a rack under a broiler or over coals and the fat can be removed after cooking. Pan-broiling, or any method that allows the steaks to cook in their melted fat, should be avoided except for meat from which all fat has been removed before cooking. Steaks that can be broiled on a rack are the good grade of porterhouse, T-bone, wedge or round-bone sirloin, and the double-bone sirloin (not the hipbone sirloin). Round steaks and flank steaks can be pan-broiled, and sautéed or fried in a prepared skillet. Table XX, page 326, gives the composition of beefsteaks and the reason why the fat must be removed.

A common practice is to cook filet mignon with a strip of bacon wrapped around it. This must not be done, since the bacon fat will be partially absorbed into the meat. If the meat is too dry for your taste without the bacon, baste it with a nonfat sauce such as Worcestershire or a special sauce of your own (see Chapter 8). Filet mignon and the rest of the tenderloin are taken from the wholesale sirloin cut. You can use separable lean of sirloin as a comparable measure of fat content.

#216 Broiled Round Steak

1. Remove all fat from amount sufficient to provide
   1 pound round steak, lean and boned.
2. Tenderize by pounding with hammer.
3. Place on sheet of aluminum foil.
4. Pour
   Worcestershire sauce
   on top of steaks—sufficient to fill the dents from pounding.
5. Season to taste with
   salt and pepper.
6. Broil under grill and turn only once.

Variation: Substitute a variety of sauces for Worcestershire sauce or use a red wine.

#217 Swiss Steak

1. Remove all visible fat, leaving
   1½ pounds lean round steak (1½ inches thick).
2. Mix
   ½ cup flour
   ½ teaspoon pepper
   1½ teaspoon salt.
3. Spread half of mixture on board.
4. Place steak on top of flour mixture on board and spread remainder of mixture on top of steak.
5. Pound steak until all flour mixture is taken up.
6. Fry steak in prepared frying pan.
7. When steak is browned on both sides, add
   1½ cups canned tomatoes
   1 small onion, chopped
   1 tablespoon Worcestershire sauce.
8. Simmer until steak is tender or bake (350°) 1½ hours.

TC	P	C	F	S	M	PU	CHOL
1276	664	286	300(23.5%)	144(11.3%)	131(10.3%)	12(0.9%)	477

Roast Beef

There are only a few basic principles to follow in roasting beef for low-fat cooking. It is important to select a cut that yields the least amount of fat from its separable lean. This means that the good grade should be selected, if available, rather than choice. Preferable cuts are arm, flank steak, hind shank, round, and rump.

All visible fat must be removed before cooking. Since it often provides or retains moisture, it is a common practice to roast meat with the fat side up, allowing the melted fat to permeate the meat. This introduces fat into the lean and is not recommended for low-fat cooking. If the meat tends to be too dry for your taste when roasted without fat you can baste with nonfat sauces or wine, or roast over a small amount of water to provide steam heat (a tightly covered roasting pan is desirable for this method). Some cooks wrap roast beef tightly in foil to seal in moisture, but this method is not recommended since it prevents the drippings from accumulating as the meat roasts. The flow of drippings means that melted fat is draining from the roast. The drippings should be placed in the refrigerator and, when cool, the fat should be skimmed from the top. The remaining drippings can be used for the gravy or sauce.

The slow-bake method of dry roasting is fine for taste but can be overdone if you are preparing a low-fat menu. You can cook beef slowly at an oven temperature of 170°–200°, but at these low temperatures there will be no drippings and the hidden internal fat will still be in the meat. It is true that one should avoid overcooking. This can be done simply by dry roasting at 275°–300° oven temperature until the internal temperature of the meat is 150°–170°, depending upon how well done one wishes his meat to be. In general well-done meat contains less residual fat. You should use both an oven thermometer and internal meat thermometer for best results. Avoid using very high temperatures as they will overcook the outer portions of the roast and cause excessive shrinkage and toughness. A suitable temperature of 300° or slightly less will gradually soften the tougher gelatinous fibers.

The time required to roast beef depends a lot on the cut, but as an average figure you can allow 25 minutes per pound at an oven temperature of 300°.

A good way to prepare lean beef and ensure tender meat is to make a pot roast, which is technically a beef stew since the meat is cooked by moist heat. If only a little water is to be used, the cut selected must be as lean as possible with all visible fat removed. The lean round or the lean of an arm roast (good grade) or hind shank is good. The lean of rump (good grade) is acceptable.

#218 Pot Roast

1. Remove every bit of visible fat from quantity sufficient to provide
   4 pounds beef.
2. Dredge in
   ¼ cup flour.
3. Brown in prepared pot by turning rapidly.
4. Season to taste with
   salt and pepper.
5. Add
   ½ cup water.
6. Cover and cook slowly until meat is tender. Add more water if needed.

Cut-up raw vegetables, such as carrots or potatoes, may be added in time for them to cook and be served with the pot roast. Use tomato juice in place of water for a variation.

#219 Beef Stew with Red Wine

1. Remove all visible fat and cut into 1-inch cubes quantity sufficient to make
   1½ pounds round steak.
2. Pan-broil in a skillet until brown on all sides.
3. Transfer browned meat to covered kettle.
4. Rinse skillet with
   2½ cups boiling water
   and add rinse to meat.
5. Add to meat
   ½ cup red wine
   1 teaspoon salt
   ¼ teaspoon pepper
   dash ground cloves.
6. Cover kettle and simmer until meat is tender—usually 2 hours.
7. Add to stew
   6 onions, small

1½ cups carrots, diced
1½ cups string beans, cut

and cook 30 minutes more.

TC	P	C	F	S	M	PU	CHOL
1408	664	280	298(21.2%)	143(10.1%)	129(9.2%)	11(0.8%)	477

Boiled Beef

Boiling beef is often overlooked as a method of cooking beef, although many so-called roasting procedures using water are actually based on the same moist-heat principle. It is just a question of how much water. The moisture penetrates the meat more rapidly than dry heat to soften the tough fibrous material. Unlike the dry-roasting method, which often causes the meat to be too hot at the surface and not hot enough in the center, boiling creates a more uniform heat. Boiling also helps to free the meat of hidden small amounts of fat, which makes it a particularly useful method for a low-fat menu, and the meat does not lose any of its essential nutrients.

#220 Boiled Beef and Vegetables

1. Remove all visible fat from quantity sufficient to provide a
   5-pound chuck, rump, or round (good grade).
2. Place in roasting pan with cover and cover with water. Cook in oven or place on rack in large, covered kettle over burner (do not let roast rest on bottom of kettle directly over burner). Add
   water to cover
   salt and pepper to taste.
3. Cook until meat is tender.
4. Remove meat and place liquid in the refrigerator. When thoroughly cooled remove layer of solid fat from top.
5. If a lesser volume of liquid is desired, boil away some of the liquid first; otherwise add meat directly to the now fat-free liquid and add
   5 potatoes, sectioned
   5 carrots, sectioned.
6. Cook until potatoes and carrots are tender and serve. The liquid with all its nutrients can be served with the meat and vegetables.

When the liquid from boiled beef is fat-free it can be boiled down and a variety of vegetables added, including tomatoes, corn, onions, potatoes, carrots, rice, and also macaroni. Seasonings can be added, including vinegar and wine.

#221 Corned-Beef Boil

1. Select a container large enough to allow
   4 pounds flank steak
   to lie flat in brine made of
   2 quarts boiling water
   1½ cups salt
   ½ cup sugar.
2. Submerge the meat in the brine and cover with a weighted plate.
3. Keep meat covered with brine for 2 days to make it sufficiently corned.
4. Wash meat under running water to remove brine.
5. Simmer meat in water (covered) for 3½ hours.
6. Then add
   8 turnips, small
   8 onions, medium size.
7. After 15 minutes add
   8 carrots
   8 potatoes, medium.
8. After 15 minutes more add
   1 cabbage head, sectioned.
9. When meat and vegetables are tender, remove, drain, and serve.

TC	P	C	F	S	M	PU	CHOL
4777	1881	2019	902(18.9%)	400(8.4%)	363(7.6%)	39(0.8%)	1271

#222 Corned Beef and Cabbage

1. Wash under running water to remove brine from
   4 pounds corned beef, Recipe #221.
2. Simmer meat in water 3½ hours (covered).
3. Add to meat
   1 cabbage head, large-sectioned.
4. Cook until tender and serve.

TC	P	C	F	S	M	PU	CHOL
3236	1730	644	862(26.6%)	400(12.4%)	363(11.2%)	32(1.0%)	1271

#223 Beef Brisket with Sauerkraut

1. Cover
   4 pounds beef brisket
   with
   water.
2. Season with
   1 tablespoon salt
   pepper to taste.
3. Simmer for 1½ hours, adding water if needed to keep brisket covered.
4. Add
   1 cup vinegar
   1 quart sauerkraut
   3 tablespoons brown sugar.
5. Cook until tender, usually about 1 hour, and serve.

TC	P	C	F	S	M	PU	CHOL
2878	1708	327	854(29.7%)	400(13.9%)	363(12.6%)	18(0.6%)	1271

Miscellaneous Beef Dishes

#223a Chili con Carne

1. Remove all visible fat and cut into 1-inch cubes quantity sufficient for
   1 pound lean round steak.
2. Cook in prepared skillet over medium heat
   1 medium onion, sliced.
3. Mix meat with
   3 tablespoons flour
   1 teaspoon salt
   1 tablespoon chili powder (or more)
   and add mixture to skillet and brown.
4. Gradually add to mixture
   2 cups water
   1 No. 1 can tomato purée.
5. Simmer until meat is tender, usually about 45 minutes.
6. Add
   1 cup cooked or drained canned beans (kidney or pinto).
7. Heat as desired and serve.

TC	P	C	F	S	M	PU	CHOL
1236	517	290	214(17.3%)	95(7.7%)	91(7.4%)	18(1.5%)	318

#224 Beef Burger

1. Prepare by removing all visible fat from
   round steak
   and grinding desired amount.
2. Mix into the special ground round for desired seasoning
   Worcestershire sauce
   or
   other meat sauce as desired
   salt
   garlic (optional).
3. Shape into burger patties and either pan-broil or place under a broiler until cooked to taste. Do not overcook or cook at too high a temperature. Serve with one of the sauces described in Chapter 8.

#225 Beef Meat Loaf

1. Remove all visible fat from quantity sufficient to make
   1½ pounds ground round beef.
2. Mix meat with
   1 cup dry bread crumbs
   2 egg whites
   ¾ cup tomato juice
   ¼ teaspoon pepper
   2 teaspoons salt
   2 tablespoons parsley, minced
   ¼ cup chopped onions
   ¼ cup green pepper, minced.
3. Mold into a loaf and place in prepared bake pan.
4. Bake 1½ hours at 350°.

TC	P	C	F	S	M	PU	CHOL
1402	717	342	335(23.9%)	152(10.8%)	147(10.5%)	17(1.2%)	480

#226 Arroz con Carne Español

1. Remove fat from quantity sufficient to make
   1 pound ground round.
2. Boil in as little water as necessary until cooked.
3. Drain fluid from cooked beef and reserve both.
4. Chill fluid in refrigerator and remove fat.
5. Combine cooked beef and nearly fat-free fluid. Then add
   2 cups onions, chopped
   2 green peppers, chopped
   4 cups tomatoes, canned
   2 teaspoons salt
   ½ teaspoon pepper
   ½ teaspoon chili powder
   1 cup raw enriched white or brown rice.

6. Mix well; then cook over high heat in covered pan until steaming starts. Then steam over low heat about 35 minutes.

TC	P	C	F	S	M	PU	CHOL
2476	563	1628	243(9.8%)	95(3.8%)	86(3.5%)	19(0.8%)	318

#227 Stuffed Green Peppers

1. Clean and prepare
   3 green-pepper shells.
2. Steam shells 3 minutes. Drain and fill with mixture of
   ¼ pound ground round beef with fat removed
   1 cup cooked rice
   ¼ cup tomatoes
   1 tablespoon onion, grated
   ½ teaspoon salt
   ⅛ teaspoon pepper.

3. Set stuffed peppers in baking dish containing small amount of water. Bake at 350° 45 minutes.

TC	P	C	F	S	M	PU	CHOL
443	128	259	54(12.2%)	24(5.4%)	22(5.0%)	5(1.1%)	80

#228 Beef Curry Deluxe

1. Remove visible fat from sufficient amount to make
   ½ pound round steak (cubed ½ inch).
2. Add
   3 medium onions, sliced
   ¼ teaspoon black pepper
   pinch thyme
   sprig parsley
   water to cover.
3. Simmer until tender and drain, reserving the liquid.
4. Chill liquid and remove fat.
5. Use liquid with additional water if needed to make
   1 quart curry sauce, Recipe #69.
6. Add
   cooked meat
   ½ cup celery, chopped
   ¾ cup carrots, chopped
   1 cup peas.
7. Cook until vegetables are done.
   Serve over rice.

Without rice or condiments:

TC	P	C	F	S	M	PU	CHOL
959	371	465	112(11.7%)	49(5.1%)	43(4.5%)	8(0.8%)	170

#229 Steak and Green Peppers

1. Remove all visible fat and cut into thin ribbons quantity sufficient for
   1 pound tender round steak.
2. Prepare
   3 large green peppers, sliced.
3. Fry together in prepared skillet until meat is tender—do not overcook.
4. Season to taste and serve.

TC	P	C	F	S	M	PU	CHOL
661	424	39	194(29.3%)	95(14.4%)	86(13.0%)	8(1.2%)	318

#230 Beef Stroganoff

1. Remove all visible fat and cut into thin ribbons quantity sufficient for

1 pound round steak.

2. Brown steak in prepared skillet.
3. Remove any accumulated fat.
4. Add

1 cup nonfat yogurt
1 can Italian tomato paste
1 pound mushrooms, sectioned
2 onions, small, finely chopped.

5. Add water as needed. Cover and simmer 30 minutes.
6. Season with

salt to taste.

Serve over cooked rice.

#231 Beef Shish Kebab

1. Remove all visible fat and cut into 1½-inch cubes quantity sufficient for

1 pound round beef steak.

2. Let beef stand 2 hours (or overnight in refrigerator) in marinade made of

1 cup red wine
1 cup pineapple juice

or

1 cup sherry
1 cup orange juice
2 tablespoons vinegar.

3. Skewer beef, alternating with slices from

3 tomatoes, large
3 green peppers
3 onions, large.

4. Broil in oven or over coals, turning frequently.
5. Season to taste.

TC	P	C	F	S	M	PU	CHOL
871	80	210	206(23.6%)	95(10.9%)	86(9.9%)	11(1.3%)	318

NOTE: You can use other marinades to tenderize the beef and can add seasoning such as garlic to the marinade if desired. Do not add any fats.

Veal

If it's baby beef it's not veal. Calves from four to fourteen weeks old are veal, and they should have been raised on their mother's milk. True veal is a very tender meat and usually pale in color. Although veal is common in Europe, it is not a favorite form of meat in the United States. Americans eat only about four pounds of veal per person a year.

Veal is not graded as beef is. A fat-class veal chuck, trimmed, will be 17 per cent fat; the medium class, 14 per cent; and the thin class 10 per cent. You will find a greater amount of fat if the retail cut has not been well trimmed. The composition of different retail cuts of veal is listed in Table XXI, page 330.

Just as with beef, all visible fat should be removed from veal before cooking by any method. About half the fat is saturated fat.

#232 WIENER SCHNITZEL

1. Remove all visible fat from
   6 veal steaks or cutlets.
2. Season with
   salt and pepper.
3. Dip into
   4 egg whites, slightly beaten
   and dredge in
   flour
   until well breaded.
4. Brown on both sides in prepared skillet.
5. Cover and cook slowly until steaks are tender (usually an hour).

TC	P	C	F	S	M	PU	CHOL
1178	652	4	486(41.3%)	228(19.4%)	216(18.3%)	12(1.0%)	540

After removing steaks you may make pan gravy from the drippings (there will be very little) or melt currant jelly to serve with wiener schnitzel. You can also serve them with a tomato cream sauce, Recipe #60; Creole sauce, Recipe #70; or curry sauce, Recipe #69.

#233 Braised Veal Steak with Mushrooms

1. Remove all visible fat from
   2 pounds veal steak, 1 inch thick.
2. Dredge alternately until well coated in
   2 egg whites, slightly beaten
   and
   2 cups crushed cereal flakes.
3. Brown on both sides in prepared skillet.
4. Add
   1 4-ounce can mushrooms with liquid.
5. Cover tightly and cook slowly until tender, usually 45 minutes.
6. Thicken liquid for gravy.

TC	P	C	F	S	M	PU	CHOL
1728	802	178	738(42.7%)	345(20.0%)	327(18.9%)	18(1.0%)	817

#234 Veal Fricassee Jardinière

1. Cut into 1-inch cubes
   2 pounds lean veal rump.
2. Dredge in flour and sear in prepared skillet.
3. Add
   1 teaspoon parsley, minced
   2 bay leaves, minced
   2 carrots, sliced
   ½ cup celery, sliced
   2 onions, sliced
   1 cup water.
4. Cover tightly and bake at 350° until meat is tender, about an hour.
5. Remove veal.
6. To remaining mixture add
   1 cup cooked peas
   or
   1 cup mushrooms.
7. Thicken liquid with flour paste made of
   flour
   and
   cold water.

8. Cook until liquid is thickened; then pour over veal.
9. Season to taste with

   salt and pepper

   and serve.

Variations: Use different combinations of vegetables.

TC	P	C	F	S	M	PU	CHOL
1644	767	128	741(45.1%)	345(21.0%)	327(19.9%)	20(1.2%)	817

#235 Veal Birds

1. Cut into fillets

   2 pounds lean veal steak

   and pound until thin.
2. Place in center of fillets

   stuffing of choice (see page 175).
3. Fold fillets over stuffing and fasten with toothpicks.
4. Roll fillets in

   flour

   and season with

   salt.
5. Sauté until browned in prepared skillet.
6. Add mixture of

   1 cup water
   ½ cup nonfat milk powder.
7. Cover, then bake or simmer.

Without stuffing:

TC	P	C	F	S	M	PU	CHOL
1613	806	69	737(45.7%)	345(21.4%)	327(20.3%)	18(1.1%)	828

#236 Roast Veal

1. Prepare for roasting by removing all visible fat and place on rack in uncovered roaster

   veal roast.
2. Roast at 300° until internal temperature is 170°. Requires about 35 minutes per pound.

Fat can be separated from drippings and then used for gravy or stock.

#237 Veal Steak with Wine Sauce

1. Prepare
   3 pounds lean veal steak (1 inch thick).
2. Sauté in prepared skillet until brown.
3. Add
   3 medium onions, sliced
   1 green pepper, diced
   1 cup celery, diced
   ¾ cup red wine.
4. Cover and bake at 400° for 30 minutes.
5. Add
   another ¾ cup red wine
   1 cup tomato juice.
6. Bake 60 minutes longer.

TC	P	C	F	S	M	PU	CHOL
2737	1151	223	1110(40.6%)	518(18.9%)	490(17.9%)	28(1.0%)	1225

#238 Veal Scallopine Napoli

1. Cut into 4-inch squares
   2 pounds lean veal steak, ½ inch thick.
2. Mix together and pound into meat squares
   2 teaspoons salt
   1 teaspoon pepper
   ¾ cup enriched flour.
3. Sauté meat in prepared skillet until brown on both sides.
4. Remove meat and add to skillet
   1 pound mushrooms, sliced.
   Cover and sauté until tender (about 10 minutes).
5. Return sautéed meat to skillet.
6. Add
   1 cup dry white wine
   1 cup hot water
   dash nutmeg.

7. Cover and simmer until meat is tender (about 20 minutes).
8. Add

    ½ cup tomato paste
    1 teaspoon sugar

    and mixture of

    ½ cup cold water
    ½ cup nonfat milk powder.

9. Simmer 5 to 10 minutes and serve.

TC	P	C	F	S	M	PU	CHOL
2282	915	423	754(33.0%)	347(15.2%)	329(14.4%)	27(1.2%)	828

Pork

The first pork that man ate was the wild ancestor of today's domestic pig. The Chinese domesticated the wild pig about five thousand years ago. These animals were lean and accustomed to foraging for food. Only in recent times has there been an effort to use the pig chiefly as a lard producer, a practice that has led naturally to the development of breeds with a large amount of fat. Some of the best lard-producing breeds have been developed in the United States. The penned pig who gets little exercise and is fed to maximum weight is the sloppy, out-of-shape city cousin of the wild boar.

Although a low-fat diet requires restraint in the use of pork, one need not omit it entirely. Pork does contain more fat than beef, but it contains a higher ratio of unsaturated fat. The amount and type of fat in the pig varies widely according to the way the animal is fed; it is quite possible to raise pork which is rather lean and has a lesser proportion of saturated fat.

As with other meats, all visible fat should be removed before cooking. The importance of this with pork cannot be overstressed. For example, over three fourths of the calories in a fresh ham are from fat, but less than half the calories are from fat in the separable lean portion. The separable lean of fresh ham contains no more fat than the separable lean of several cuts of beef. The percentage of calories from fat in the separable lean portion of a good-grade chuck rib is the same as in the separable lean of a medium-fat-class fresh ham (44 per cent in both instances).To keep the fat problem in perspective, half the calories in whole milk (3.7 per cent fat) are from fat and over half the fat is the saturated type.

The best choices of cuts for lean fresh pork are the ham and the picnic. Pork tenderloin is barely acceptable in limited amounts for a low-fat diet. Of the commercial light-cured hams, the picnic ham is a good choice as long as only the separable lean portion is used.

Public preference for vegetable shortening has greatly reduced the demand for lard in recent years. Even so, since lard is cheap, it is used in such commercial products as baked items and peanut butter. Lard is a classic example of an "empty-calorie" food which is all calories and contains no important amounts of any other nutrients. A 3½-ounce portion contains 900 calories (an exercise equivalent of walking 15 miles). Unlike beef or veal about 10 per cent of pork fat or lard is polyunsaturated fat.

Bacon should be used only in limited quantities if fats are restricted. Canadian bacon is the best kind because it contains less than a third as many calories as standard cured bacon and less than one fourth as much as fat. Nevertheless, a little more than half its calories are from fat.

The composition of various cuts of pork and pork products is listed in Table XXII, page 331.

In preparing pork the same principles apply as in cooking beef. Lean cuts may be pan-broiled or broiled over open coals, or under an electric or gas burner. Pork goes well with fruit, as in the following recipe.

#239 Pork Steaks with Grape Apples

1. Dredge

   2 pounds pork shoulder steaks (separable lean)

   in

   2 tablespoons flour.

2. Brown in hot prepared skillet.
3. Season with

   salt and pepper.

4. Add

   ¾ cup water.

5. Cover tightly and cook over low heat until tender, usually 45 minutes.
6. Remove meat and transfer fluid to refrigerator to cool.
7. Remove fat from chilled fluid.
8. Heat fluid to boiling in skillet and add

   ½ cup grape jelly.

9. Pare, core, and section

   3 large apples.

10. Add apples to fluid and cook until apples are tender. Serve with pork steaks.

TC	P	C	F	S	M	PU	CHOL
1893	756	520	616(32.5%)	218(11.5%)	254(13.4%)	55(2.9%)	636

Roasting lean pork is as simple as roasting beef. For best results use a meat thermometer and a low oven.

#240 Roast Pork

1. Place on rack in open roaster

   fresh pork (ham or picnic), separable lean.

2. Roast at oven temperature of 300° until meat temperature is 185° (usually about 50 minutes per pound).
3. Remove drippings (chill, remove fat, and return to roaster for gravy, or discard).

#241 Spicy Sauce for Roast Pork

1. Mix together

   2 small onions, minced
   2 tablespoons catchup
   1 tablespoon Worcestershire sauce
   1 tablespoon sugar
   ½ teaspoon paprika
   ½ cup vinegar
   ½ cup water.

2. Add to finished pork roast after drippings are removed (and fat separated or drippings discarded).
3. Cook together 5 minutes, or long enough to warm the roast if it was cooked ahead of time.

TC	P	C	F	S	M	PU	CHOL
186	10	169	2(1.1%)	T	T	T	—

#242 Roast Pork and Sweet Potatoes

1. Slice

   2 pounds roasted pork, Recipe #240

   and place in bake dish.
2. Use

   fat-free drippings

   or

   pork stock

   to make a low-fat gravy.
3. Pour part of gravy over sliced pork.
4. Place on top pork

   3 medium sweet potatoes, sliced.
5. Pour remainder of gravy over sweet potatoes.
6. Bake at 350° 30 minutes, or until sweet potatoes are tender.

Variation: Place marshmallows and sweet potatoes together on top of pork and gravy, baking as above.

TC	P	C	F	S	M	PU	CHOL
1893	793	468	635(33.5%)	221(11.7%)	257(13.6%)	63(3.3%)	636

#243 Glazed Pork and Sweet Potatoes

1. Slice and place in baking dish

   2 pounds roasted or boiled pork, Recipe #240 or #244.
2. Cover with

   3 medium sweet potatoes, sliced.
3. Pour over sweet potatoes mixture of

   1 cup orange juice
   ⅓ cup honey.
4. Bake at 350° until brown, about 30 minutes.

TC	P	C	F	S	M	PU	CHOL
3029	798	1594	640(21.1%)	221(7.3%)	257(8.5%)	63(2.1%)	636

Boiling pork is an excellent way to remove excess fat. If the water used in boiling is saved and the fat removed, it can be used for stock, white sauce, pork gravy, or for cooking vegetables to be served with pork.

The boiled pork meat is delicious served with applesauce, cooked apples, spiced apples, various jellies, and sweet relish. It may also be used in other recipes calling for cooked pork.

#244 Boiled Pork

1. Put in a kettle
   fresh pork (ham or picnic), separable lean
   and cover with
   water.
2. Cover kettle and simmer until meat is tender.
3. Remove meat and serve—save liquid, and chill for stock.

Smoked or cured hams with all the visible fat removed are acceptable in limited quantities for a low-fat diet. The smoked ham may be panbroiled in a prepared skillet or broiled in the oven or over coals. It can also be cooked with a variety of vegetables.

#245 Ham with Green Beans

1. Cover
   3 pounds smoked ham (separable lean)
   with
   water.
2. Simmer 2 hours.
3. Add
   1 quart green beans, cut
   6 medium potatoes, pared.
4. Cook until vegetables are tender.
5. Season to taste with
   salt and pepper
   and serve.

TC	P	C	F	S	M	PU	CHOL
3100	1345	724	1069(34.5%)	381(12.3%)	436(14.1%)	99(3.2%)	953

Of course for a low-fat diet you can bake smoked ham—preferably after the fat has been removed. The baked ham can be prepared with a variety of glazes (see Recipes #73 and #75), covered with pineapple slices, or served plain.

#246 Baked Smoked Ham

1. Remove rind and all visible fat from
   1 smoked picnic ham.
2. Place on rack in open roaster.
3. Bake at 300° until meat temperature is 150°.

#247 Basic Ham Loaf

1. Mix together
   ½ cup nonfat milk powder
   1 cup cold water.
2. Add to
   2 cups ground cooked ham (separable lean)
   1 cup bread crumbs
   2 egg whites
   1 cup carrots, ground
   2 tablespoons chili sauce (or 1 tablespoon mustard).
3. Shape into loaf and bake in prepared loaf pan at 350° for 45 minutes.

Lamb

In much of the world lamb or mutton is the principal meat. A major exception is the United States, where beef occupies the place of honor and the annual consumption of lamb is as low as four pounds a person. The amount of fat in the meat is determined by whether the animals are penned and fattened or allowed to graze on the hillside. Like beef, the carcass is graded as prime (40 per cent fat), choice (33 per cent fat), or good (30 per cent fat). The retail cuts listed in Table XXIII, page 332, are all choice grade.

There are no special advantages from a health point of view in eating lamb as opposed to beef. Actually, there is a higher percentage of saturated fat (50 per cent of the fat) in lamb than in any other commonly used meat. The separable lean meat of lamb, cut for cut, tends to have a little more fat than the separable lean of beef.

The basic principles of low-fat food preparation used for cooking beef apply to lamb and mutton as well. The two most satisfactory cuts for low-fat diets are the leg and the loin with all visible fat removed. Even the separable lean of other cuts tends to have lots of fat and if used in low-fat diets, it should be boiled to remove as much fat as possible.

#248 Barbecued Lamb

1. Remove all visible fat from leg of lamb.
2. Dredge in
   flour
   and place on rack over coals or in roasting pan in 350° oven.
3. Mix barbecue sauce or
   1 cup water
   ½ cup catchup
   2 tablespoons Worcestershire sauce
   ¼ teaspoon cayenne
   1 onion, sliced
   2 tablespoons A-1 sauce
   2 teaspoons salt.
4. About every 15 minutes turn lamb over and brush the top side with barbecue sauce. Cook until internal temperature is 175° (about 30 minutes for every pound) for medium-well-done lamb.

#249 Lamb Stew

1. Remove all visible fat from amount of meat sufficient to make
   2 pounds lamb cubes.
2. Boil cubes in enough water to cover until tender.
3. Remove meat and cool fluid in refrigerator; then remove all fat.
4. Place cooked cubes and fat-free fluid in pot and add
   6 potatoes, cubed
   6 carrots, sliced
   3 onions, sliced
   4 turnips, sliced
   1 cup peas
   and simmer for 30 minutes.
5. Add
   3 tomatoes, sliced
   and simmer 10 minutes longer.

6. Season to taste with
   salt and pepper
   and serve.

#250 Roast Leg of Lamb

1. Remove all visible fat and shank bone from
   leg of lamb.
2. Place lamb on rack in uncovered roasting pan and place in oven at 300°. Roast until internal temperature is 175°.
3. Season to taste with
   salt and pepper.
4. The drippings may be saved and cooled and the fat removed, then used for gravy or sauce.

You may choose to baste the leg of lamb with a variety of substances, including grape jelly, red wine, apricot juice, and Worcestershire sauce.

Cold Cuts, Sausage, and Luncheon Meats

If you wish to restrict calories or fat you should avoid these foods or use them in limited amounts. All of them are high in fat content. About 80 per cent of the calories in bologna is from fat; over 75 per cent of the calories in so-called all-meat frankfurters is from fat. If you really want to upset the fat ratio in your diet, however, eat a little pork sausage. Over 90 per cent of its calories is from fat, and 3½ ounces have an exercise equivalent of over eight miles. The cook who feeds the family these fat little morsels is either ignorant or lazy, or both. They are not rich in any essential nutrient except fat calories, and what nutrients they do contain are more abundant in other, less fatty foods. The composition of these foods is listed in Table XXIV, page 333. Those who care about the purity of their food should note that these foods are often loaded with additives.

Organ Meats

It is possible to eat some organ meats and restrict your fat intake. The real problem is their cholesterol content (see Tables V and XXV, pages 288 and 334). You can forget about eating brains if you need to limit your cholesterol at all. A 3½-ounce serving has 2000 milligrams, nearly seven times the daily limit recommended by the Inter-Society Commission on Heart Disease. In addition to this problem over 60 per cent of the calories in raw brains is from fat (before you conclude that most of the brain is fat, by weight only 8.6 per cent is fat and most of its weight is from its water content). Whether or not it suits your palate, brains and eggs scrambled in fat are hardly compatible with a low-fat, low-cholesterol diet.

Heart can be used on a low-fat, low-cholesterol diet, since only 30 per cent of its calories is from fat. Calf heart and pig heart with all the fat removed are also low-fat foods. A standard 3½-ounce serving of heart contains 150 milligrams of cholesterol, about half of the strict daily limitation of 300 milligrams.

#251 Baked Heart

1. Remove all fat and any arteries, veins, and hard parts from
   1 calf heart.
2. Partially fill cavities with stuffing of
   ½ pound bread pieces
   1 teaspoon salt
   ¼ teaspoon pepper
   2 teaspoons sage
   2 tablespoons onions, chopped
   1 egg white
   mixed with
   ½ cup nonfat milk powder
   dissolved in
   1 cup cold water.
3. Sew heart closed, place on rack in covered roasting pan, and bake at 325° about 3 hours or until tender.

TC	P	C	F	S	M	PU	CHOL
1315	438	561	309(23.5%)	125(9.5%)	154(11.7%)	14(1.1%)	699

#252 Sautéed Heart

1. Clean and remove all visible fat and cut into slices
   1 calf heart.
2. Roll it in
   flour
   and let dry on sheet of aluminum foil.

3. Sauté in prepared skillet until tender.
4. Season to taste with
   salt

   and serve.

Liver is a low-fat food. If all you wish to do is limit calories or limit fat intake, it is an excellent food. Liver is moderately high in cholesterol; a 3½-ounce serving contains 300 milligrams. It is wise to try to include a small serving of liver once a week. Fortunately, women in the childbearing years usually have low blood-cholesterol levels and can eat more liver than men or older women without any real problem. Liver is an excellent source of iron and necessary blood-forming elements. It can also be useful in reducing diets because of its low fat (24 per cent of its calories) and because of its low caloric value.

#253 Sautéed Liver

1. Cut into strips less than ½ inch thick
   1 pound liver.
2. Roll strips in
   flour

   seasoned with
   salt and pepper.
3. Dry on sheet of foil about 10 minutes.
4. Sauté in prepared skillet until brown on each side.

#254 Liver and Onions

1. Sauté as in Recipe #253
   1 pound liver.
2. After liver is browned on both sides remove it and add to skillet a small amount of
   water

   and additional
   flour

   to thicken; then add
   1 onion, thinly sliced.
3. Cover and simmer until onions are tender, about 10 minutes.
4. Pour onions over liver and serve.

The tongue is a muscle with special organs attached for taste. It is usually fairly fat. The tip of the tongue in front of its attachment to the floor of the mouth is mostly muscle, and the fat content increases behind this point. If you like tongue, choose calf's tongue rather than beef, hog, or lamb, which are heavier in fat (see Table XXV, page 334).

#255 Boiled Tongue

1. Cover

   calf or veal tongue

   with

   water.

2. Add

   1 teaspoon salt

   for each quart.

3. Simmer until tongue is tender when fork is inserted. For small tongues, about 1½ hours.
4. Allow to cool, peel, and slice to serve.

Sweetbreads are not forbidden; in fact, if all fat is removed they are very lean. The best choice for a low-fat diet is the calf thymus (the thymus gland is in the chest adjacent to the heart) since less than 20 per cent of the calories in a lean calf thymus is from fat, with only 250 milligrams of cholesterol in 3½ ounces (100 grams).

Sweetbreads should be partially or completely cooked by boiling before being used in most basic recipes.

#256 Parboiled Sweetbreads

1. Wash and remove extraneous material from

   fresh sweetbreads.

2. For each

   1 quart water

   add

   1 tablespoon vinegar
   1 teaspoon salt

   and simmer sweetbreads in the water for 20 minutes.

3. Drain and plunge sweetbreads in cold water.
4. Remove membranes or other remaining extraneous material.

#257 Broiled Sweetbreads

1. Parboil
   1 pound sweetbreads.
2. Slice and soak in
   sherry
   for 5 minutes (optional).
3. Sprinkle slices with
   salt and pepper.
4. Place on rack over drip pan and broil under moderate heat 5 minutes for each side.
5. Add a little sherry and mushrooms, if you like, to drippings and pour over sweetbreads.

#258 Sautéed Sweetbreads

1. Parboil and slice
   1 pound sweetbreads.
2. Sprinkle with
   salt and pepper.
3. Dip sweetbreads in
   egg white
   and roll them in
   flour.
4. Let stand 10 minutes on sheet of aluminum foil.
5. Sauté in prepared skillet over low heat until cooked.

#259 Creamed Sweetbreads

1. Precook and dice
   1 pound sweetbreads.
2. Combine with
   white sauce, Recipe #58, doubled, or curry sauce, Recipe #69, doubled.
3. Heat and serve.

TC	P	C	F	S	M	PU	CHOL
1118	339	114	657(58.8%)	291(26.0%)	318(28.4%)	15(1.3%)	1146

Variations of white sauce may be substituted.

Kidney is a relatively low-fat food containing a little more fat and a little more cholesterol than sweetbreads. It can be eaten occasionally if other foods are sufficiently low in cholesterol (see Table XXV, page 334).

The spleen is not often eaten in the United States, except in some rural areas where home butchering is common. It is a low-fat meat, with only about a fourth of its calories from fat. Commonly it is pan-broiled or dredged in flour and sautéed, and it can be very tasty.

CHAPTER 16

Desserts

The dessert has a purpose at the end of the meal. Most desserts are sweet, and the sudden intake of sugar raises the blood sugar abruptly. This in turn decreases the sensation of hunger, turning off the appetite. Every mother knows that if her children eat candy or desserts before a meal, they will not have any appetite. The blood sugar will rise after a meal even without sugar in any of the foods if you wait long enough. If you still feel hungry at the end of a meal, and you wait a while without eating dessert, the sensation of hunger often goes away as the blood sugar gradually rises.

Desserts are a frequent cause of gain in body fat, and the individual wishing to control his fat deposits should limit desserts to unsweetened fresh fruit, which, incidentally, is a healthy dessert for anyone.

It is possible to have desserts that are low in fat and desserts that contain more polyunsaturated fat than saturated fat. The principle is really very simple. Instead of using the shortening specified in most standard recipes, use one of the cooking oils; for example, corn oil or safflower oil. You will need a little less cooking oil than the amounts of solid shortening given in most recipes, which is fine, since it tends to decrease the fat content of the dessert. All of the dessert recipes in this book are standard recipes modified by the substitution of cooking oil for shortening and by the use of nonfat milk for ordinary milk. Of course, there are also a number of desserts that do not require any fat, such as fresh fruits and berries.

An excellent topping for desserts is the nonfat cream substitute, Recipe #2, or the nonfat whipped-cream substitute, Recipe #3. Flavor them with cinnamon or nutmeg if you wish. Low-fat puddings and ice creams which can be used with cakes are even lower in calories than most cake icings.

Unfortunately for the chocolate-lover, chocolate contains saturated fat. The person wishing to limit his saturated-fat intake will have to limit the amount of chocolate desserts he eats, or chocolate candy, chocolate malt shakes, and chocolate sauces (see Table IX, page 293). Some investigators have reported that the saturated fat in chocolate (steric acid) has no effect on the blood-cholesterol level, as do animal saturated fats or coconut oil. The fatty acid, steric acid, nevertheless contributes to the total fat intake.

Artificial sweetener can be used in some desserts. It is quite suitable for fresh berries and for such juicy desserts as cooked fruit, or even for puddings. When used in such bakery products as cakes and cookies it can cause difficulty, because the dry form of artificial sweetener causes the cake and cookie mixes to be far more dry and affects their texture. You can help matters by using only half artificial sweetener and half sugar, but you will still need to add water to obtain a batter of the consistency you are accustomed to achieving. Use the recipes offered by companies manufacturing artificial sweeteners, substitute nonfat milk for whole milk, and use about two thirds as much cooking oil as shortening. You will usually obtain good results.

A common problem in commercially prepared desserts and baked items is the use of saturated fats, egg yolks, and, in some instances, coconut. The egg yolks increase the cholesterol intake in the diet. In most instances a person will be better off reserving his limited cholesterol allowance for liver or shellfish. In doing your own baking you should avoid the use of shredded coconut or other forms of coconut (except artificial coconut extract) if you are trying to limit saturated-fat intake. Also avoid artificial milk and artificial whipped cream, usually made of coconut oil.

Puddings

There are a number of commercial puddings that can be used for diets limiting fat content. Others have more fat than is necessary. Some puddings use egg yolks, and if you follow the American Heart Association recommendation of only three egg yolks a week, you won't be able to eat many of these. If a recipe you like calls for egg yolks, you can often substitute egg whites, two egg whites for each whole egg. The composition of commercial puddings is given in Table XXVI, page 336.

Don't forget Jello, which is excellent combined with fruit. Gelatin is a source of protein and has no fat.

Blancmange can be served as a plain vanilla cornstarch pudding or used as a vehicle for other puddings with the addition of various flavors. Banana pudding, lemon pudding, and coconut pudding can be made from the basic cornstarch pudding, Recipe #266.

#260 Maple Pudding

1. Heat to boiling

   1 cup maple sirup

   and pour into prepared baking dish.
2. Mix thoroughly together

   1 tablespoon cooking oil
   3 tablespoons sugar
   ¼ cup nonfat milk powder.
3. Add gradually

   ½ cup cold water

   and stir until smooth.
4. Add and stir in thoroughly

   1 cup sifted cake flour
   2 teaspoons baking powder
   ¼ teaspoon salt.
5. After the above ingredients are thoroughly mixed, fold them into

   2 egg whites, beaten stiff.
6. Pour mixture over the hot sirup and bake at 400° approximately 25 minutes.

TC	P	C	F	S	M	PU	CHOL
1586	86	1352	130(8.2%)	13(0.8%)	36(2.3%)	68(4.3%)	6

#261 Maple-Walnut Pudding

1. Mix together

   ¼ cup cold water
   ⅓ cup cornstarch.

2. To mixture add

   2 cups water
   1½ cups brown sugar

   and heat over boiling water in double boiler until thickened. Continue cooking 20 minutes longer.
3. Remove from heat and fold into mixture

   3 egg whites, beaten stiff
   ½ cup English walnuts, chopped.
4. Chill.

TC	P	C	F	S	M	PU	CHOL
1844	80	1422	337(18.3%)	22(1.2%)	53(2.9%)	211(11.4%)	—

#262 Rice Pudding

1. Mix together

   4 cups cold water
   2 cups nonfat milk powder.
2. Add

   ½ cup washed raw rice
   ½ teaspoon cinnamon
   ½ cup sugar
   ½ teaspoon salt.
3. Bake in prepared bake dish at 275° for 2½ hours. Stir often during the first hour.
4. Stir into pudding

   ½ cup raisins

   and bake 30 minutes longer.

TC	P	C	F	S	M	PU	CHOL
1454	238	1200	13(0.9%)	T	T	T	44

Variation: Use ½ cup brown sugar instead of white.

TC	P	C	F	S	M	PU	CHOL
1480	238	1226	13(0.9%)	T	T	T	44

#263 Steamed Apple Pudding

1. Mix together
   1 cup sifted flour
   ½ cup cooking oil
   1 teaspoon baking powder
   ⅛ teaspoon salt.
2. Add
   cold water
   to make soft dough.
3. Separate dough and roll out into 2 separate rounds (about ¼ inch thick).
4. Line bottom of prepared pan with one round.
5. Fill with
   2 medium apples, sliced.
6. Sprinkle apples with
   ¼ cup sugar.
7. Cover with other round of dough.
8. Steam for 2 hours.

TC	P	C	F	S	M	PU	CHOL
1889	54	813	1006(53.2%)	100(5.3%)	276(14.6%)	521(27.6%)	—

Variations: Use
¼ cup brown sugar
in place of cane or beet sugar. Or use
¼ cup maple sugar.
Use various seasonings to taste—
cinnamon, nutmeg.

#264 English Pudding

1. Sift together
   3 cups sifted flour
   1 teaspoon baking soda
   1 teaspoon salt.
2. Stir together thoroughly with
   1 teaspoon cinnamon
   1 teaspoon cloves
   ½ cup cooking oil.

3. Add slowly, one at a time, while stirring
   1 cup buttermilk
   1 cup molasses.
4. Stir into mixture
   1 cup raisins.
5. Fill prepared molds or baking-powder cans ⅔ full and cover.
6. Steam for 3 hours.

TC	P	C	F	S	M	PU	CHOL
3648	194	2391	1007(27.6%)	104(2.8%)	282(7.7%)	531(14.6%)	7

#265 Molasses-Fruit Pudding

1. Mix together
   1 cup cake flour
   ½ cup bran
   ½ teaspoon baking soda
   1 teaspoon salt
   ¼ cup nonfat milk powder.
2. Stir into dry mixture
   3 tablespoons cooking oil
   ½ cup cold water.
3. Mix into above ingredients
   2 egg whites, slightly beaten.
4. Mix in
   ½ cup molasses
   ½ cup raisins.
5. Pour mixture into prepared mold ⅔ full, cover, and steam for 1½ hours.

TC	P	C	F	S	M	PU	CHOL
1516	96	1013	377(24.9%)	38(2.5%)	104(6.9%)	198(13.1%)	6

Variation: Substitute other fruit, such as dates, for raisins. Add chopped English walnuts.

#266 Blancmange

1. Mix together in top of double boiler
    ½ cup sugar
    5 tablespoons cornstarch
    ¼ teaspoon salt
    2 cups nonfat dry milk powder.
2. Gradually stir in
    3½ cups cold water.
   It may be necessary to use rotary beater to make smooth.
3. Heat over boiling water, stirring constantly until mixture thickens.
4. Cover and heat over water 20 minutes longer.
5. Remove from heat and stir in
    1½ teaspoons vanilla.
6. Set aside to cool. Makes about 4 cups.

TC	P	C	F	S	M	PU	CHOL
1021	208	799	8(0.8%)	T	T	T	44

Variation: Add
    3 tablespoons cocoa.

TC	P	C	F	S	M	PU	CHOL
1077	214	811	45(4.2%)	20(1.8%)	14(1.3%)	—	44

Add ½ brown sugar instead of white.

TC	P	C	F	S	M	PU	CHOL
1047	208	825	8(0.8%)	T	T	T	44

Pies

A wide variety of pies can be made with no more fat than it takes to make the crust. You can make the crust with polyunsaturated cooking oil and have a dessert low in saturated fats.

Pie crusts can be filled with pudding mixtures, which act as vehicles for flavoring. These can be made using either flour or cornstarch as a thickener and mixed with cooked or raw fruit. Fruit may also be held together with gelatin and topped with nonfat whipped-cream substitute. The pie shell can be filled with many kinds of fruit, such as apples, cherries, blueberries, or peaches. Just fill the pie shell with fresh fruit, sweeten to taste, and top with your favorite topping. If you keep some prepared pie shells on hand this can provide a tasty, easy dessert which is sure to please.

#267 Pie Crust

1. Sift together
   2 cups sifted flour
   ¾ teaspoon salt.
2. Cut in with knives or pastry blender
   ½ cup oil.
3. Add gradually a little at a time
   4 to 6 tablespoons cold water
   until mixture holds together.
4. Divide the dough in half and roll out each piece separately, on a floured board.
5. Use one piece of dough for bottom crust and the other for the top, or use for the bottoms of two open-faced pies.

If a prebaked shell is desired bake at 450° 10–15 minutes or until golden brown.

When rolled to proper thickness, dough should make a top and bottom shell for a 9-inch pie or the bottom shell for two 9-inch open-faced pies.

TC	P	C	F	S	M	PU	CHOL
1846	96	722	992(53.7%)	102(5.5%)	279(15.1%)	526(28.5%)	—

#268 Apple Pie

1. Prepare
   pie crust, Recipe #267.
2. Line pie pan with one shell of crust.
3. Pare and slice
   7 apples.
4. Mix together and add to apples
   1 cup sugar
   ½ teaspoon cinnamon
   ¼ teaspoon nutmeg.

5. Place fruit mixture in pie shell.
6. Cover mixture with remaining half of pie crust.
7. Make several holes or slices in top crust and bake at 450° for 15 minutes. Reduce temperature to 350° and bake for 45 minutes or until crust is golden brown. Makes 1 9-inch pie.

TC	P	C	F	S	M	PU	CHOL
3274	110	2087	1048(32.0%)	102(3.1%)	279(8.5%)	526(16.0%)	—

#269 Fresh Peach Pie

1. Prepare
   pie crust, Recipe #267.
2. Line pie pan with crust.
3. Sift together
   1 cup sugar
   1 tablespoon flour
   ¼ teaspoon salt.
4. Add dry mixture to
   4 cups fresh peaches, sliced.
5. Place fruit mixture in pie shell and cover with top crust.
6. Make holes or slices in top crust and bake at 450° for 15 minutes, then at 350° for 35 minutes, or until crust is golden brown. Makes 1 9-inch pie.

TC	P	C	F	S	M	PU	CHOL
2899	111	1750	1001(34.5%)	102(3.5%)	279(9.6%)	526(18.1%)	—

#270 Peach Pie

1. Prepare
   pie crust, Recipe #267.
2. Line pie pan with crust.
3. Drain and reserve liquid from
   3 cups sliced peaches, canned in heavy sirup.
4. Mix sirup with
   2 tablespoons cornstarch
   ½ teaspoon cinnamon
   and cook over low heat until thickened.

5. Add sliced peaches to sauce and place mixture in pie crust.
6. Cover with top pie crust, make holes or slices, and bake at 450° for 15 minutes, then at 350° for 35 minutes or until crust is golden brown. Makes 1 9-inch pie.

TC	P	C	F	S	M	PU	CHOL
2437	105	1298	1001(41.1%)	102(4.2%)	279(11.4%)	526(21.6%)	—

#271 Fresh Cherry Pie

1. Prepare

    pie crust, Recipe #267.
2. Line pie pan with crust.
3. Prepare fruit mixture of

    1 quart tart red cherries, washed and pitted
    1¼ cups sugar
    2½ tablespoons flour
    ¼ teaspoon salt.
4. Put fruit mixture in pie shell and cover with other pie crust. Make holes or slices in the top crust.
5. Bake at 450° for 10 mintues, then at 350° for 25 minutes or until crust is golden brown. Makes 1 9-inch pie.

TC	P	C	F	S	M	PU	CHOL
3248	144	2072	1006(31.0%)	102(3.1%)	279(8.6%)	526(16.2%)	—

#272 Cherry Pie

1. Prepare

    pie crust, Recipe #267.
2. Line pie pan with crust.
3. Drain and reserve juice from

    3 cups canned sweetened red cherries.
4. Mix together

    2 tablespoons cornstarch
    3 tablespoons sugar
    ⅛ teaspoon salt.
5. Add juice gradually to dry mixture; then cook slowly over low heat until thickened.
6. Add cherries to mixture and cool.

7. Pour fruit mixture into pie crust.
8. Place other pie crust on top of fruit mixture and make holes or slices.
9. Bake at 450° for 15 minutes, then at 350° for 25 minutes or until crust is golden brown. Makes 1 9-inch pie.

TC	P	C	F	S	M	PU	CHOL
2332	114	1175	1001(42.9%)	102(4.4%)	279(12.0%)	526(22.6%)	—

#273 Blackberry Pie

1. Prepare
   pie crust, Recipe #267.
2. Line pie pan with one crust.
3. Prepare fruit mixture of
   4 cups fresh blackberries
   1 cup sugar
   2 tablespoons flour
   2 tablespoons lemon juice
   ⅛ teaspoon salt.
4. Pour fruit mixture into pie crust.
5. Place other pie crust on top of fruit mixture and puncture with small holes or slices.
6. Bake at 450° for 10 minutes, then at 350° for approximately 30 minutes more, or until crust is golden brown. Makes 1 9-inch pie.

TC	P	C	F	S	M	PU	CHOL
3014	126	1809	1033(33.3%)	102(3.4%)	279(9.2%)	527(17.5%)	—

#274 Blueberry Pie

1. Prepare
   pie crust, Recipe #267.
2. Line pie pan with crust.
3. Prepare fruit mixture of
   4 cups blueberries
   1 cup sugar
   4 tablespoons flour
   ⅛ teaspoon salt
   1½ tablespoons lemon juice.
4. Pour fruit mixture into pie crust and cover with other crust.

5. Make holes or slices in top crust and bake at 450° for 10 minutes, then at 350° for an additional 30 minutes or until crust is golden brown. Makes 1 9-inch pie.

TC	P	C	F	S	M	PU	CHOL
3086	120	1904	1018(33.0%)	102(3.3%)	279(9.0%)	528(17.1%)	—

#275 Uncooked Blackberry Pie

1. Use

    ½ pie crust, Recipe #267.
2. Line pie pan with pie crust.
3. Bake at 450° 10–15 minutes or until golden brown.
4. To

    5 cups fresh blackberries

    add

    1 cup sugar

    and let stand until sugar is dissolved.
5. Just before serving add fruit to pie crust and top with

    whipped-cream substitute, Recipe #3.

TC	P	C	F	S	M	PU	CHOL
2113	78	1461	546(25.8%)	51(2.4%)	140(6.6%)	263(12.4%)	—

Variations:

With blueberries:

TC	P	C	F	S	M	PU	CHOL
2138	63	1526	526(24.6%)	51(2.4%)	140(6.5%)	263(12.3%)	—

With peaches:

TC	P	C	F	S	M	PU	CHOL
2013	63	1426	506(25.1%)	51(2.5%)	140(7.0%)	263(13.1%)	—

With strawberries:

TC	P	C	F	S	M	PU	CHOL
1978	63	1366	526(26.6%)	51(2.6%)	140(7.1%)	263(13.3%)	—

#276 Uncooked Banana Pie

1. Use

    ½ pie crust, Recipe #267.
2. Line pie pan with pie crust.
3. Bake at 450° 10–15 minutes or until golden brown.
4. To

    4 bananas, sliced

    add

    1 cup sugar.
5. Just before serving fill pie crust with bananas and top with

    whipped-cream substitute, Recipe #3.

NOTE: Do not prepare bananas until time to serve to avoid darkening.

TC	P	C	F	S	M	PU	CHOL
2205	72	1611	508(23.0%)	51(2.3%)	140(6.3%)	263(11.9%)	—

#277 Pumpkin Pie

1. Use

    ½ pie crust, Recipe #267.
2. Line pie pan with pie crust.
3. Sift together

    1 teaspoon cinnamon
    ¼ teaspoon nutmeg
    ½ teaspoon ginger
    ⅔ cup sugar
    ⅛ teaspoon salt
    ¾ cup nonfat milk powder.
4. Stir in

    4 egg whites, lightly beaten.
5. Add gradually

    1½ cups cold water.
6. Stir in

    2 cups cooked pumpkin, mashed.
7. Pour filling into pie crust.

8. Bake at 450° for 10 minutes, then at 350° for 35 minutes or until an inserted knife comes out clean.

TC	P	C	F	S	M	PU	CHOL
1844	204	1110	508(27.5%)	51(2.8%)	140(7.6%)	263(14.3%)	16

Variations: Substitute cooked squash or sweet potato for pumpkin.

#278 Cream Flour Filling for Pies

1. Mix together in top of double boiler
   ½ cup sugar
   6 tablespoons flour
   ½ teaspoon salt
   ¾ cup nonfat dry milk powder.
2. Gradually stir in
   1½ cups cold water
   2 egg whites
   and beat mixture with rotary beater.
3. Heat over boiling water until mixture thickens, stirring constantly.
4. Cover and heat 15–20 minutes longer. Makes about 1½ cups.
   Caution: If not cooked sufficiently a flour taste will be noticeable.

TC	P	C	F	S	M	PU	CHOL
768	128	627	7(0.9%)	T	2(0.3%)	2(0.3%)	16

Cakes

Don't forget that baking cakes at high altitudes may pose some problems with standard recipes (see Chapter 4). Most cakes have lots of calories, particularly if coated with a sweet icing. There are some cakes you simply cannot make and hope to have a low-fat, low-cholesterol product. All those cakes which require large numbers of egg yolks for their success are simply not suited for such diets. Many of your favorites, though, can be made by substituting one egg white for every egg yolk in the recipe.

Many commercial cake mixes contain egg yolks, and even more contain large amounts of saturated fat. Be careful about mixes with labels that simply state "vegetable oil"—the vegetable oil may well be coconut oil, which is 97 per cent saturated fat. You can avoid all these problems by baking your own cakes. There are some low-fat cake mixes available, but unless you are sure from reading the label, don't assume they are low-fat products. A good mix and an excellent choice for diets restricting calories, fat, and cholesterol is angel-food cake mix, which is free of fat and egg yolks. The angel-food cake is sometimes difficult to make from the basic ingredients but you can rely on the commercial mixes. The chocolate angel-food cake mix, however, contains fat from the chocolate. (See page 63 for information about baking powder.)

#279 Chocolate Devil's-Food Cake

1. Sift into a bowl
   2¼ cups sifted cake flour
   1¾ cups sugar
   ½ teaspoon baking powder
   1¾ teaspoon soda
   1 teaspoon salt
   ⅔ cup cocoa.
2. Add and stir vigorously for two minutes
   ½ cup cooking oil
   ½ cup cold water.
3. Add and stir 2 minutes more
   1 teaspoon vanilla
   4 egg whites
   ½ cup cold water.
4. Pour into prepared pans and bake at 350° for 45 minutes or until done. Makes 2 9-inch layers.

Note: This is not an exceptionally sweet cake—you may wish to use a sweet icing.

TC	P	C	F	S	M	PU	CHOL
3409	148	2104	1120(32.8%)	173(5.1%)	327(9.6%)	525(15.4%)	—

#280 Silver Cake

1. Sift together into bowl
   ½ cup nonfat milk powder
   ¾ teaspoon salt
   3 teaspoons baking powder
   1⅓ cups sugar
   2 cups sifted cake flour.

2. Add

   ⅓ cup cooking oil
   ½ cup cold water

   and stir well.
3. Add

   4 egg whites
   2 teaspoons flavoring

   and stir until smooth.
4. Pour batter into prepared pans.
5. Bake in a 350° oven for 45 minutes or until done. Makes 1 9-inch layer.

TC	P	C	F	S	M	PU	CHOL
2612	172	1743	664(25.4%)	67(2.6%)	186(7.1%)	352(13.5%)	11

#281 Angel Ginger Cake

1. Sift together into mixing bowl

   ½ cup sugar
   2 cups cake flour
   1 teaspoon baking soda
   ¼ teaspoon salt
   1 teaspoon ginger.
2. Add

   ¼ cup cooking oil
   ½ cup buttermilk

   and stir well.
3. Add

   ¼ cup molasses
   4 egg whites

   and stir until smooth—don't overstir.
4. Pour into prepared pans and bake at 350° for 40 minutes or until done. Makes 1 9-inch layer.

TC	P	C	F	S	M	PU	CHOL
1911	139	1242	501(26.2%)	51(2.7%)	140(7.3%)	266(13.9%)	4

#282 Orange Cake

1. Sift together into mixing bowl
   1 cup sugar
   1½ cups cake flour
   1½ teaspoons baking powder
   ¼ teaspoon salt.
2. Add
   ⅓ cup cooking oil
   4 egg whites, unbeaten
   1 teaspoon grated orange rind
   and stir well.
3. Add a little at a time
   ½ cup orange juice
   and stir until smooth.
4. Pour into prepared pans and bake at 350° for 30 minutes or until done. Makes 1 9-inch layer.

NOTE: Cake will not be brown.

TC	P	C	F	S	M	PU	CHOL
2097	109	1299	662(31.6%)	66(3.1%)	185(8.8%)	350(16.7%)	—

#283 Orange Tea Cake

1. Sift together into mixing bowl
   1 cup sugar
   2 cups cake flour
   ¼ teaspoon nutmeg
   ¼ teaspoon salt
   3 teaspoons baking powder.
2. Add
   6 tablespoons cooking oil
   4 egg whites, lightly beaten
   grated rind of 1 orange
   and stir well.
3. Stir in gradually
   ¾ cup orange juice
   and mix well.

4. Pour into prepared pans and bake at 350° for 50 minutes. Makes 1 9-inch layer.

TC	P	C	F	S	M	PU	CHOL
2432	124	1527	746(30.7%)	76(3.1%)	208(8.6%)	396(16.3%)	—

#284 Corn-Sirup Spicecake

1. Sift together into mixing bowl
   2 cups cake flour
   ½ teaspoon salt
   ½ teaspoon mace
   ½ teaspoon cinnamon
   2 teaspoons baking powder
   ¼ teaspoon cloves
   ¼ teaspoon allspice
   ¼ cup nonfat milk powder.
2. Add and stir well
   6 tablespoons cooking oil
   ½ cup cold water.
3. Add and stir well
   4 egg whites
   1 cup dark corn sirup.
4. Pour mixture into prepared pans and bake at 350° for 45 minutes or until done. Makes 1 8- or 9-inch layer.

TC	P	C	F	S	M	PU	CHOL
2478	146	1556	743(30.0%)	76(3.1%)	208(8.4%)	396(16.0%)	6

#285 Honey Cake

1. Sift together into mixing bowl
   2 cups cake flour
   1 teaspoon baking soda
   ½ teaspoon ginger
   ½ teaspoon cinnamon
   ¼ teaspoon salt.
2. Add and stir well
   6 tablespoons cooking oil
   ½ cup buttermilk.

3. Add

2 egg whites
1 cup honey

and mix well.

4. Pour into prepared pan and bake at 350° for 40 minutes or until done. Makes 1 9-inch layer.

TC	P	C	F	S	M	PU	CHOL
2558	107	1679	743(29.0%)	76(3.0%)	208(8.1%)	396(15.4%)	4

#286 White Cake

1. Sift together into mixing bowl

3 cups cake flour
1½ cups sugar
½ cup nonfat milk powder
3 teaspoons baking powder
½ teaspoon salt.

2. Add

6 tablespoons cooking oil
5 egg whites
¾ teaspoon vanilla
¼ teaspoon almond extract

and stir well.

3. Add gradually while stirring

1 cup cold water

and mix well.

4. Pour into prepared pans and bake at 350° for 50 minutes or until done. Makes 2 8-inch layers.

TC	P	C	F	S	M	PU	CHOL
3202	196	2186	751(23.4%)	77(2.4%)	210(6.6%)	400(12.5%)	11

#287 Gingerbread Cake

1. Sift together into mixing bowl

2½ cups cake flour
2 teaspoons ginger
1¾ teaspoons baking soda
½ teaspoon salt.

2. Add

6 tablespoons cooking oil
½ cup buttermilk

and stir well.

3. Add

2 egg whites, well beaten
1 cup molasses
½ cup buttermilk

and mix well.

4. Pour into prepared pans and bake at 350° for 30 minutes or until done. Makes one 8-by-10-inch cake.

TC	P	C	F	S	M	PU	CHOL
2469	133	1558	746(30.2%)	76(3.1%)	206(8.3%)	393(15.9%)	8

#288 Marble Cake

1. Sift together into mixing bowl

2 cups cake flour
2½ teaspoons baking powder.
¼ teaspoon salt
1 cup sugar
⅓ cup nonfat milk powder.

2. Add

3 tablespoons cooking oil
2 egg whites
¾ cup cold water
1 teaspoon vanilla.

3. Beat mixture until smooth.
4. Divide the batter into 2 equal parts.
5. To one half of batter add 1 ounce unsweetened chocolate, melted, and blend thoroughly.
6. Place batter in prepared baking pan, alternating spoonfuls of chocolate and plain batter.
7. Bake in preheated oven at 350° 30–40 minutes or until done.

TC	P	C	F	S	M	PU	CHOL
2027	155	1461	379(18.7%)	39(1.9%)	106(5.2%)	202(10.0%)	7

#289 Angel-Food Cake

1. Sift together six times

   1 cup sifted cake flour

   ¼ cup sugar.

2. Beat until foamy

   10 egg whites

   ½ teaspoon salt.

3. Add

   1 teaspoon cream of tartar

   and beat until egg white will stand in peaks.

4. Fold in 2 tablespoons at a time

   1 cup sugar

   and beat each time after adding sugar.

5. Fold in

   ¾ teaspoon vanilla

   ¼ teaspoon almond extract.

6. Sift ¼ cup of dry ingredients at a time into egg-white mixture and fold in until all is used.
7. Pour batter into large ungreased tube pan. Bake at 350° 45–60 minutes or until done.
8. Cool with cake hanging upside down. Makes 1 9-inch cake.

TC	P	C	F	S	M	PU	CHOL
729	188	519	7(1.0%)	1(0.1%)	2(0.3%)	4(0.5%)	—

#290 Chocolate Angel-Food Cake

1. Sift together six times

   ¾ cup sifted cake flour

   1¼ cups sugar

   ¼ cup cocoa

   ¼ teaspoon salt.

2. Beat until foamy

   12 egg whites.

3. Add

   1 teaspoon cream of tartar

   and continue beating until egg whites will stand in peaks.

4. Fold into whites

1 teaspoon vanilla.

5. Sift over egg whites ¼ cup of dry ingredients at a time and fold into egg-white mixture until all is used.
6. Pour into ungreased tube pan and bake at 350° for 60 minutes or until done.
7. Hang upside down to cool. Makes 1 10-inch layer.

TC	P	C	F	S	M	PU	CHOL
1517	221	1229	55(3.6%)	28(1.8%)	21(1.4%)	3(0.2%)	—

#291 Baked Meringue Frosting

1. Beat until very stiff

2 egg whites.

2. Mix together and fold into whites

1 cup brown sugar
⅛ teaspoon salt.

3. Spread mixture over cake batter and bake with the cake.

TC	P	C	F	S	M	PU	CHOL
855	32	823	—	—	—	—	—

#292 Peppermint Icing

1. Mix together

¼ cup nonfat milk powder
½ cup cold water.

2. Melt in milk over hot water

¼ cup crushed peppermint-stick candy.

3. Add and stir in

1 pound confectioner's sugar.

TC	P	C	F	S	M	PU	CHOL
2002	26	1974	1	—	—	—	6

#293 White Icing

1. Heat to 240° and cook to threading stage
   1 cup sugar
   1 teaspoon corn sirup
   ⅓ cup water.
2. Pour resulting sirup gradually into
   3 egg whites, stiffly beaten
   stirring constantly.
3. Continue stirring until cool; then add
   1 teaspoon vanilla.

TC	P	C	F	S	M	PU	CHOL
841	48	793	—	—	—	—	—

Variation: Add ½ teaspoon instant coffee for coffee icing or substitute strong coffee for water.

#294 Chocolate Frosting

1. Melt over boiling water
   2 squares chocolate.
2. Mix together until smooth
   1 cup nonfat milk powder
   1⅓ cups cold water
   and add to melted chocolate.
3. Add
   6 tablespoons sugar.
4. Heat over boiling water to desired thickness.
5. Stir in
   1 teaspoon vanilla.
   Will frost 1 9-inch layer.

TC	P	C	F	S	M	PU	CHOL
817	116	448	252(30.8%)	140(17.1%)	92(11.3%)	4(0.5%)	22

Cookies

You can make delicious cookies by using cooking oils high in polyunsaturated fat for shortening. Most of the principles discussed in baking cakes apply equally well to baking cookies. The recipes in this section should serve as an example of how you can modify other standard favorites and still limit the saturated-fat intake. There are even such things as nonfat cookies. Try the simple meringue cookies, Recipe #305. If you want a variety of flavors, add chopped dried fruits (dates, figs, raisins, peaches) or candied fruits to them.

#295 Applesauce-spice Cookies

1. Sift together into mixing bowl

    2 cups cake flour
    1 cup sugar
    1 teaspoon baking powder
    ½ teaspoon soda
    ½ teaspoon salt
    ½ teaspoon cinnamon
    ¼ teaspoon cloves.

2. Mix dry ingredients with

    ⅓ cup cooking oil
    2 egg whites, lightly beaten.

3. Mix with dough

    1 cup thick applesauce, unsweetened.

4. Drop dough onto prepared cookie sheet and bake at 375° for 15 minutes.

NOTE: If dough is thinner than you wish, you can add extra flour. The flavor will be better if you can avoid this.

TC	P	C	F	S	M	PU	CHOL
2418	88	1635	664(27.5%)	67(2.8%)	186(7.7%)	352(14.6%)	—

#296 Basic Drop Cookies

1. Sift together into mixing bowl

    2 cups cake flour

¾ cup brown or white sugar
2 tablespoons nonfat milk powder
1 teaspoon baking powder
¼ teaspoon salt.

2. Stir in and mix thoroughly
¼ cup cooking oil
1 teaspoon vanilla
2 egg whites, lightly beaten.

3. Stir in gradually
⅓ cup cold water.

4. Drop dough onto prepared cookie sheet and bake at 375° for 15 minutes.

TC	P	C	F	S	M	PU	CHOL
1901	101	1268	500(26.3%)	51(2.7%)	140(5.3%)	266(14.0%)	3

Variations: May be used with fruits, such as raisins or dates, or nuts, or spices may be added for spice cookies.

#297 Cocoa Drops

1. Sift together into mixing bowl
4 cups cake flour
1⅓ cups brown sugar
½ cup nonfat milk powder
¾ cup cocoa
3 teaspoons baking powder
1 teaspoon salt.

2. Mix in thoroughly
½ cup cooking oil
3 egg whites.

3. Slowly mix in
1 cup cold water
2½ teaspoons vanilla.

4. Stir into mixture
1 cup chopped English walnuts.

5. Drop dough from teaspoon onto prepared cookie sheet and bake at 350° for 15 minutes.

TC	P	C	F	S	M	PU	CHOL
4760	299	2568	1825(38.3%)	227(4.8%)	443(9.3%)	954(20.0%)	11

#298 Chocolate-Chip Cookies

1. Sift together into a mixing bowl
   1 1/8 cups flour
   1/4 cup brown sugar
   1/2 cup white sugar
   1/2 teaspoon salt
   1/4 teaspoon soda.
2. Cream dry ingredients with
   1/3 cup cooking oil
   2 egg whites, lightly beaten.
3. Add
   1 teaspoon vanilla
   1/2 cup chopped English walnuts
   1/2 pound semisweet chocolate chips.
4. Drop dough from teaspoon onto prepared cookie sheet and bake at 350° about 10 minutes.

TC	P	C	F	S	M	PU	CHOL
3241	114	1080	1372(42.3%)	297(9.2%)	389(12.0%)	560(17.3%)	—

#299 Banana-Nut Cookies

1. Sift together into mixing bowl
   2 1/4 cups flour
   1 cup sugar
   2 teaspoons baking powder
   1/2 teaspoon salt
   1/4 teaspoon soda.
2. Cream dry ingredients with
   1/3 cup cooking oil
   3 egg whites, lightly beaten.
3. Stir into mixture
   1/2 teaspoon vanilla
   1/4 teaspoon lemon extract
   1/2 cup chopped English walnuts.
4. Gradually add to dough, stirring all the while
   1 cup mashed bananas.

5. Drop dough from teaspoon onto prepared cookie sheet and bake at 350° for about 15 minutes.

TC	P	C	F	S	M	PU	CHOL
2938	154	1746	1006(34.2%)	89(3.0%)	240(8.2%)	564(19.2%)	—

#300 Vanilla Wafers

1. Sift together into mixing bowl
   2 cups flour
   1 cup sugar
   2 tablespoons nonfat milk powder
   2 teaspoons baking powder
   ½ teaspoon salt.
2. Cream dry ingredients with
   ¼ cup cooking oil
   2 egg whites, lightly beaten.
3. Stir into dough
   ¼ cup cold water
   3 teaspoons vanilla.
4. Drop dough from teaspoon onto prepared cookie sheet and bake at 300° for 20 minutes.

Note: May not be brown, will be soft.

TC	P	C	F	S	M	PU	CHOL
2061	101	1427	500(24.3%)	51(2.5%)	140(6.8%)	266(12.9%)	3

#301 Molasses Cookies

1. Sift together into mixing bowl
   2½ cups flour
   ½ cup brown sugar
   1 teaspoon baking powder
   1 teaspoon cinnamon
   ½ teaspoon ginger
   ½ teaspoon cloves
   ½ teaspoon salt
   ¼ teaspoon soda.

2. Cream dry ingredients with

   ⅓ cup cooking oil
   2 egg whites, lightly beaten.

3. Stir into dough

   1 tablespoon vinegar
   ½ cup molasses
   ½ cup buttermilk
   ½ cup raisins.

4. Drop dough from teaspoon onto prepared cookie sheet and bake at 350° for 15 minutes.

TC	P	C	F	S	M	PU	CHOL
2694	128	1860	669(24.8%)	68(2.5%)	187(6.9%)	354(13.1%)	4

#302 Brownies

1. Sift together into mixing bowl

   1 cup cake flour
   1 cup sugar
   ½ teaspoon baking powder
   ¼ teaspoon salt.

2. Cream dry ingredients with

   ¼ cup cooking oil
   3 egg whites, lightly beaten.

3. Stir into dough

   2 ounces chocolate, melted.

4. Mix into dough

   ½ teaspoon vanilla
   1 cup English walnuts, chopped.

5. Spread about ½ inch deep in prepared 8-inch bake dish and bake at 350° for 30 minutes or until done.

TC	P	C	F	S	M	PU	CHOL
2776	152	1193	1415(51.0%)	233(8.4%)	366(12.1%)	688(24.8%)	—

#303 Gingersnaps

1. Sift together into mixing bowl

   2½ cups cake flour
   ½ cup sugar

1 teaspoon ginger
½ teaspoon cloves
½ teaspoon cinnamon
½ teaspoon soda
½ teaspoon salt.

2. Cream dry ingredients with
   ⅓ cup cooking oil.
3. Stir into mixture
   ⅓ cup molasses
   ⅓ cup hot coffee.
4. Chill dough thoroughly.
5. Roll dough to ⅛ inch thick on a pastry cloth.
6. Cut dough to desired size and shape.
7. Place on prepared cookie sheet.
8. Bake at 350° for 17 minutes.

TC	P	C	F	S	M	PU	CHOL
2210	70	1437	666(30.1%)	68(3.1%)	187(8.5%)	354(16.0%)	—

#304 Chocolate Nut Kisses

1. Beat until foamy
   5 egg whites.
2. Add
   ¼ teaspoon cream of tartar
   ¼ teaspoon salt
   and beat until stiff.
3. Add a little at a time
   1½ cups sugar
   and beat mixture after each addition.
4. Fold into beaten mixture
   1 teaspoon vanilla
   ½ pound semisweet chocolate chips or nuggets
   1 cup English walnuts, chopped.
5. Drop from spoon onto prepared cookie sheet and bake at 300° for 25 minutes.

TC	P	C	F	S	M	PU	CHOL
3212	162	1337	1053(32.8%)	252(7.8%)	258(8.0%)	422(13.1%)	—

#305 Simple Meringue Cookies

1. Boil together until they reach the thread stage or 238° registers on candy thermometer

3 cups sugar
1½ cups water.

2. To

8 egg whites, beaten stiff

add

¼ teaspoon salt
½ teaspoon cream of tartar.

3. While beating the egg whites (a mixer is best for this step) gradually pour in the hot sirup.
4. Add

1½ teaspoon vanilla

and continue beating until mixture is cold.

5. Drop mixture from a teaspoon onto prepared bake sheet that has been lightly covered with cornstarch.
6. Bake at 250° about 45 minutes.

TC	P	C	F	S	M	PU	CHOL
2447	128	2319	—	—	—	—	—

Variations: Add chopped dried fruit to final mixing (dates, raisins, figs, peaches) or chopped candied fruit, or finely broken sugar candy, such as peppermint sticks.

Ice Cream and Frozen Custard

The consumption of ice cream has risen steadily in the industrialized nations, probably because of refrigeration and modern marketing methods. Whereas ice cream was once a special treat reserved for holidays and special occasions it is now a daily household item in the United States. It is also a source of many calories and lots of saturated fat. Commercial frozen pudding must contain egg yolks to meet marketing standards in the United States, which increases the cholesterol of such products. The end result is a high-calorie, high-saturated-fat, high-cholesterol food, and it is delicious. Over 50 per cent of the calories in commercial ice cream are usually from fat, and a 3½-ounce (100 grams) portion contains over 200 calories.

There are ice-cream substitutes on the market. These are often called ice milk and some may contain as little as 4 per cent fat (by volume, not by calorie count). They are still high-fat foods, but in limited amounts they are tolerable for a low-fat diet. The sherbets made without milk or cream pose no problem as to fat or cholesterol restriction, but they too contain a lot of calories. The diet ice-cream substitutes contain artificial sweeteners to decrease the calorie content and may be acceptable to a point, but with the rapidly changing views on these products it is best to check with your doctor before using them in any quantity.

You can still enjoy ice-cream-like desserts and be on a fat-restricted, low-cholesterol diet. You can even make your own ice cream in such a way that it becomes a source for polyunsaturated fat and is low enough in fat to help balance the high fat content in other foods.

There are many ways of making ice cream; some people prefer to use a cooked mixture or at least some scalded milk, while others prefer a completely raw product. The flavor is affected by cooking before freezing. If the recipe for vanilla ice cream suits your taste, then you can use it as a base for chocolate ice cream, any fruit-flavored ice cream, or nut ice cream. Most ice-cream recipes use whole eggs or egg yolks, milk, cream, and a thickening agent such as flour, cornstarch, or gelatin. The old-fashioned ice cream of yesteryear on the farm often contained no thickener because it was so thick with cream and eggs that it didn't require it. You will not find commercial ice cream with these characteristics, though, because the cost would not be competitive.

Four basic vanilla ice-cream substitutes are described in this book to suit varied conditions and tastes. You will probably find one of the four to your liking. None is high in fat content. All are low in cholesterol, and one is a satisfactory source for polyunsaturated fat. If you cannot obtain fortified skim milk for this recipe, you can use 1 per cent or 2 per cent low-fat milk, although this will increase the saturated-fat content somewhat. The flavor of dry milk powder is sometimes difficult to mask and may be noticeable in vanilla ice-cream substitute, but it is less apparent when stronger flavors such as chocolate or strawberry are added. Remember that more flavoring is necessary in frozen foods since the cold decreases the effect of flavoring agents, including sugar.

The ice-cream substitutes described in this book are all for use in a home freezer. Freshly made, they can be delicious or even superior in taste to many commercial products as well as a plus factor for a low-fat diet.

#306 Polyunsaturated Vanilla Ice Cream

1. In top of double boiler, soak until softened

   2 tablespoons (envelopes) Knox gelatine

   in

   ½ cup fortified skim milk.

2. Beat together

   3½ cups fortified skim milk
   12 tablespoons sugar
   4 egg whites
   3 teaspoons vanilla
   4 tablespoons safflower oil.

3. Heat gelatine over boiling water until dissolved; then add to above mixture while stirring.
4. Freeze.

TC	P	C	F	S	M	PU	CHOL
1234	128	608	497(40.3%)	40(3.2%)	76(6.2%)	356(28.8%)	4

Note: The fat contributes to the creamy texture. If you want a more creamy texture you can increase the amount of safflower oil, but you will need to recalculate the food value by adding the values for the additional oil. If safflower oil is not available, then corn oil may be used, although the ice cream will have slightly more saturated fat and less polyunsaturated fat.
Variation: Without oil:

TC	P	C	F	S	M	PU	CHOL
738	128	608	1(0.1%)	—	—	—	4

#307 Nonfat Vanilla Ice Cream I

1. In top of double boiler, soak until softened

   2 tablespoons (envelopes) Knox gelatine

   in

   ½ cup fortified skim milk.

2. Beat together

   3½ cups fortified skim milk

12 tablespoons sugar
4 egg whites

and add to softened gelatine.

3. Heat over boiling water for 15 minutes, remove from heat, and add
   3 teaspoons vanilla.
4. Freeze.

TC	P	C	F	S	M	PU	CHOL
1099	283	806	10(0.9%)	T	T	T	30

#308 Nonfat Vanilla Ice Cream II

1. In top of double boiler soak until softened
   2 tablespoons (envelopes) Knox gelatine
   in
   ½ cup cold water.
2. Beat together
   4 cups nonfat milk powder
   3½ cups cold water
   2 teaspoons lemon juice
   2 tablespoons honey
   10 tablespoons sugar
   4 egg whites
   dash salt.
3. Add mixture to softened gelatine and heat over boiling water for 15 minutes, while stirring.
4. Remove and add
   3 teaspoons vanilla.
5. Freeze.

TC	P	C	F	S	M	PU	CHOL
1708	522	1166	16(0.9%)	T	T	T	88

#309 Chocolate Ice Cream

1. Make your favorite
   nonfat vanilla ice cream.
2. To it add
   3 ounces (squares) chocolate, melted.

3. Beat with rotary beater until smooth.
4. Freeze.

Calculation based on Recipe #306:

TC	P	C	F	S	M	PU	CHOL
1657	146	641	869(52.4%)	250(15.1%)	214(12.9%)	362(21.8%)	4

#310 Caramel Ice Cream

1. Caramelize half the sugar for your favorite
   nonfat vanilla ice cream
   and proceed with recipe.
2. Freeze.

#311 Peach Ice Cream

1. Make your favorite
   nonfat vanilla ice cream
   but omit the vanilla.
2. To the mixture add
   2 cups peach pulp, mashed.
3. Freeze.

Calculation based on Recipe #306:

TC	P	C	F	S	M	PU	CHOL
1407	219	767	502(35.7%)	40(2.8%)	76(5.4%)	356(25.3%)	4

#312 Black-Walnut Ice Cream

1. Make your favorite
   nonfat vanilla ice cream.
2. To the mixture add
   1 cup black walnuts, finely chopped.
3. Freeze.

NOTE: You may wish to add black-walnut flavoring to the mixture or to caramelize half the sugar.

Calculation based on Recipe #306:

TC	P	C	F	S	M	PU	CHOL
2025	217	684	1122(55.4%)	83(4.1%)	298(14.7%)	653(32.2%)	4

CHAPTER 17

Appetizers and Hors d'Oeuvres

Often these little tidbits contain enough calories for a whole meal. In fact, a whole succulent *smörgåsbord* can be made up of them. If you are interested in restricting your calories and your intake of saturated fat and cholesterol, don't neglect to count the values in appetizers and hors d'oeuvres. Through a little planning you can serve excellent appetizers and stay well within the bounds of most dietary requirements. Many different kinds of hors d'oeuvres can be made by following a few simple principles. They can run the gamut of food items, from vegetables, meats, and seafood to relishes, nuts, and breads.

Breads, Chips, and Sticks

Many appetizers require a small piece of bread or a potato chip for a base. For fat-restricted diets the best choices are small pieces of toasted bread, toasted bread sticks, melba toast of all varieties, and bread rounds, as long as they are not flavored with cheese or fats. Don't forget wheat cereal biscuits or wheat wafers, which are an excellent base for appetizers.

For fat-restricted diets you can use limited amounts of soda crackers, but you should avoid all crackers rich in cheese or butter (see Chapter 7 on breads).

Potato chips and similar snack items are not acceptable if you are trying to restrict your fat intake. You can use foods made with oils containing mostly polyunsaturated fat, but they are still very high in fat content.

Do's and Don'ts of Dips

The presence of processed and cured cheese in dips and cheese spreads makes them a common source of many saturated-fat calories. You can still have dips and remain on a low-fat diet, but it is all a matter of how you make the dip—which means that you have to make your own. It is really very easy, however. The base for a variety of dips can be uncreamed cottage cheese, which is essentially fat-free yet filled with all the nutritional value of milk. Beat it until smooth in an electric mixer or a blender, and add onions, chives, tomatoes, pimientos, or whatever suits your palate.

#313 CHIVE CHEESE

1. Place in an electric mixing bowl

   12 ounces uncreamed cottage cheese

   and beat until smooth.
2. Add

   chopped chives
   salt and pepper

   to taste.

#314 PIMIENTO-CHEESE SPREAD

1. Place in electric mixing bowl or blender

   12 ounces uncreamed cottage cheese

   and beat until smooth.
2. Add

   1 4-ounce can pimientos
   salt and pepper to taste

   and mix thoroughly.

#315 Tomato-Cheese Spread

1. Place in electric mixing bowl or blender
   12 ounces uncreamed cottage cheese
   1 cup cooked tomatoes
   salt and pepper to taste
   and mix until smooth.

You needn't limit yourself to cheese spreads for dips or stuffings. Turn to the recipes for chicken or fish salad, which can be served on bread rounds or tiny sections of toast.

Nutty Things

The bowl of nuts is usually a must for the cocktail hour, and too often nuts are used for flavoring other foods. A few nuts go a long way: a 3½-ounce portion usually contains nearly 600 calories. The reason is simply that three fourths of their calories are from fat—saturated fat, monounsaturated fat, and polyunsaturated fat. There are only three common items in the nut group that are high in polyunsaturated fat: sunflower seeds, black walnuts, and English walnuts. Of these the English walnut tops the list (see Table XXVII, page 339). Coconut meat is almost all saturated fat, and the other common nuts contain a little bit of everything, but mostly monounsaturated fat. If you want to avoid calories, avoid all nuts. If you can stand the calories but not the saturated or monounsaturated fats, stick to English walnuts.

A good substitute for the nut bowl is popcorn. It takes a lot of popcorn to make many calories, and what natural fat it contains is mostly polyunsaturated. It is suitable for almost any diet—as long as you don't soak it in butter or pop it in large amounts of fat.

Fishy Bits

You can use seafood for hors d'oeuvres if you are selective. Boiled shrimp are fine if you don't have to limit the amount of cholesterol in your diet too severely. Even then 3½ ounces of shrimp contain only half as much cholesterol as one egg yolk, or a little more than a third of a daily allowance of 300 milligrams of cholesterol. Lobster has a little more cholesterol, but crab and scallops are low in both fat and cholesterol. A recent analysis of oysters indicates they are actually lower in cholesterol than was reported earlier. Shellfish are all low in fat content and high in protein, so if cholesterol is not a consideration, there is no need to limit them. Since weight loss or removal of fat is sometimes more important than a severe restriction of cholesterol, weight-reducing diets often include shellfish.

Shellfish can be boiled or broiled and served alone on toothpicks or with any variety of sauces, from tartare sauce to shrimp sauce (see Chapter 13).

Not all fish are satisfactory for low-fat diets. Sardines are a classic example. Over half the calories in sardines packed in mustard or tomato sauce are from fat, and the ones packed in any form of oil contain even more fat. The same is true of pickled herring. Don't assume that just because it is fish it is all right to include in the diet. Half the calories in salmon are fat calories; smoked salmon is a little better but it is far from being a low-fat item. Broiled fish bits are a good choice for appetizers if you use the right fish. (See Table XVIII, page 319, for food composition of fish.) Fish low in fat content can be used to make salads that are satisfactory for spreads and dips. Tuna fish packed in water is an excellent low-fat ingredient for such a salad.

The "Devil's Eggs"

If you must restrict your intake of cholesterol you must limit the number of egg yolks. This means all egg yolks, including those slipped into sauces or baked items or appetizers. Deviled eggs are a common appetizer. One egg yolk contains about as much cholesterol as 7 ounces of shrimp or three-fourths of a pound of beef. Egg yolks also add significantly to the fat intake since over three fourths of the calories come from fat and over a third of that is saturated fat.

The egg white, as has been stressed, is suitable in all diets unless a person needs to restrict protein (which happens only in certain rare diseases). An attractive replacement for the deviled egg is a boiled egg white with a stuffing of chicken salad, tuna salad, or similar salad. A tray of these will make everyone forget deviled eggs and will not tax the fat or cholesterol budget.

The Garden Path

Help yourself to vegetables. Since they do not contain either significant amounts of fat or cholesterol and are low in calories, they are ideal for appetizers. Raw vegetables are the best. Just don't serve them with rich sauces containing lots of fat or egg yolks or butter, if you need to restrict fat or cholesterol. The low-fat cheese dips described above in this section make excellent stuffings. Hollowed-out cocktail tomatoes or tomato wedges stuffed with chicken salad or tuna salad are excellent appetizers which leave plently of room for the main course, even on a calorie-restricted low-fat diet.

Pickles and relishes are fine, but both olives and avocados must be used sparingly since they contain lots of fat. Most of it is monounsaturated fat with very little polyunsaturated fat. Over 80 per cent of the calories in avocados is from fat and over 90 per cent of the calories in green or ripe olives is from fat. See Tables XVI and XVII, pages 304 and 312, for food values of pickles, relishes, and avocados.

The Meat of the Situation

The same principles used in preparing meat dishes apply to their use in making appetizers. Low-fat diets simply cannot include any significant quantity of bacon, sausages, cold cuts (especially those including processed and cured cheeses); even those delightful little meatballs made of hamburger must be replaced with something else. Make your own little meatballs from lean ground round steak (with all visible fat removed before grinding) mixed with Worcestershire sauce or any seasoning recommended in the meat chapter.

Small steak bits make excellent appetizers. When properly prepared only about one third of their calories is from fat and only half of these from saturated fat.

#316 Steak Tidbits

1. Prepare by removing all visible fat a quantity sufficient to make
   1 pound lean round steak.
2. Pound steak until tender and cut into desired sizes.
3. Place steak bits on cookie sheet or foil.

4. Dab each steak bit with
   Worcestershire sauce
   seasoning to taste.
5. Place under broiler grill and cook desired amount. Turn each steak bit once.

#317 Miniature Shish Kebab

1. Prepare by removing all visible fat from quantity sufficient to make
   1 pound lean round steak.
2. Pound steak until tender.
3. Cut into small squares to desired size for miniature shish kebab.
4. Marinate meat in bowl of
   Worcestershire sauce
   or
   dry red wine
   or
   meat sauce of your choice
   for about one hour.
5. Place meat pieces on skewer, alternating pieces with small pieces of
   onions
   green peppers
   tomatoes (shell of larger ones or slices of cocktail tomatoes).
6. Broil and season to taste.

Ham, if lean enough and sliced thin enough, is acceptable for use in preparing appetizers. This is the best answer to the cold-cut question. Even so, ham must be used sparingly by the person severely restricted to a low-fat diet.

#318 Ham-and-Cheese Roll

1. Spread on top of thin slice of
   cooked ham
   about
   ¼-inch thickness of cheese spread, Recipes #313, #314, or #316.
2. Roll slice of ham into oblong the shape of a hot dog. Hold in place with toothpicks and place in refrigerator to cool.

3. Slice cooled ham roll as if you were slicing a bologna and serve individually or place on a suitable bread round.

#319 Chicken-Salad Ham Roll

1. Spread over thin slice of
   cooked ham
   a layer about ¼ inch thick of
   chicken salad, Recipe #164.
2. Roll ham into oblong with salad inside. Then place in the refrigerator to cool.
3. Slice cooled ham roll as you would slice a loaf of bread and serve the individual slices alone or place on suitable bread rounds or other base for appetizers.

Chickening Out

The principles that apply to cooking chicken for the main course apply as well to chicken appetizers. It all depends upon how much you want to include in appetizers. Broiled chicken legs are easily served and you can remove the skin first to limit the fat. Remember to use fryers since they have less fat than older birds. Fryer breast may be broiled or roasted and then, if you wish, stripped from the bone, seasoned, and served as chicken tidbits. Chicken livers are low in total fat and saturated fat but moderately high in cholesterol content. There are many uses of chicken salad for small open-faced sandwiches, stuffings, or dips. Or you can take small pieces of cooked chicken, bind them with a thick white sauce, mold them into small croquettes, and pan-broil or grill before serving. The imaginative chef will have no difficulty devising ways of using chicken for appetizers, hors d'oeuvres, or the *smörgåsbord.*

CHAPTER 18

Sandwiches

It is quite possible to eat sandwiches on a low-fat, low-cholesterol diet. The kind of sandwiches you eat depends entirely on the diet you wish to follow. The only requirement is that the principles discussed earlier concerning the basic food elements be applied to the ingredients used for sandwiches. Bread itself is not forbidden. You can use thin slices to reduce the calorie content, and you can make your own bread to limit the fat content. There are a sufficient number of breads on the market today that are low enough in fat to satisfy most dietary requirements. The important consideration is the filling.

There is usually no reason to limit the amount of most vegetables in sandwiches. Fresh sliced tomatoes, slices of pickles, a leaf of lettuce all help to dress up a sandwich and give it character without affecting the most severely restricted-fat-or-cholesterol diet.

Many spreads can be used, and mustard is no problem. Use our non-fat and eggless mayonnaise or, for a more tangy sandwich, the special tartare sauces described in Chapter 8. Of course if fat and calories are restricted, you cannot use much margarine or any butter. If fat is not restricted except to limit the saturated fats, and if calories are not a problem, then you can use margarine containing large amounts of poly-unsaturated fat.

Salad Fillings

There are a host of salad fillings that can be used for sandwiches. Consult the recipes for chicken salad, turkey salad, ham and chicken salad, tuna salad, fish salad, or shrimp salad (see Chapter 12).

Chicken Sandwiches

Follow the principles already outlined for selecting chicken. Use fryer chicken without the skin for the lowest fat portions. Slices of breast of chicken or young turkey with nonfat mayonnaise make an excellent low-fat sandwich.

Beef Sandwiches

Lean beef roasted in such a way as to minimize the fat content should be the source for all roast-beef sandwiches. Garnish the beef with a leaf of lettuce between thin slices of bread, spread with nonfat mayonnaise, and no one will know he is on a low-fat diet.

If a steak sandwich is desired, use lean round steak with all the visible fat removed, tenderize it, and grill it. You can use one of the meat sauces during the broiling if you wish. Since only 31 per cent of the calories in the raw lean round steak is from fat and only half of these is saturated fat, the addition of bread and perhaps sliced tomatoes produces a sandwich with an acceptably low percentage of the total calories as fat. Of course you won't get any polyunsaturated fat in such a sandwich.

The all-American favorite, the hamburger, can fit in almost any diet. Make the low-fat beef burger, Recipe #224, and serve it on a bun with your favorite condiments—nonfat mayonnaise, mustard, pickle, onion, or sliced tomato.

Fish Sandwiches

Pan-broiled fish are fine for sandwiches, served with or without tartare sauce. Select a fish that is low in fat if you want to limit the calories and the fat in the diet. Codfish and flounder are good choices.

Ham Sandwiches

Very lean slices of cooked ham can be used occasionally, since ham does not contain prohibitive amounts of fat. Garnish with lettuce and nonfat mayonnaise. If the rest of the meal has enough nonfat or sufficiently low-fat calories, the ham is quite acceptable. For the person who can stand the calories, a low-fat potato salad, Recipe #161, or a salad served without a dressing or with a nonfat dressing with the ham sandwich balances out to an acceptably low percentage of the total calories in the form of fat.

Egg Sandwiches

Forget these unless you can make an omelette sandwich from one of the low-fat, low-cholesterol egg products now available on the market.

Cold Cuts

These must be severely limited for low-fat diets. Most available cold cuts contain so much fat, which is usually saturated fat, that they cannot be included in low-fat diets or diets restricting saturated fat. Processed creamed cheese products are equally troublesome.

Cottage-Cheese Sandwiches

The cheese-lover can use uncreamed cottage cheese prepared as a spread with jelly or jam and spread on thin slices of Boston brown bread or similar breads.

Peanut Butter and Jelly

Peanut butter isn't absolutely forbidden, but any dieter restricting fat will need to use this item sparingly and compensate for its high fat content by eating a lot of other foods that have little or no fat. You may be able to tolerate peanut-butter sandwiches if you stick to baked lean fish and serve nonfat mayonnaise and salads without fat for other meals.

The jellies and jams, like applesauce and apple butter, are low in fat and free of cholesterol. The only problem is the calories, but there are some low-calorie preparations available on the diet shelf in supermarkets. (The composition of jellies and jams is listed in Table III, page 286.)

CHAPTER

19

Beverages

Primitive man soon learned there was more to drink than just water. Undoubtedly his first beverage after maternal milk and water was fruit or berry juice. It was a short step from there to learning about fermentation. The art of wine-making and brewing beer was already far advanced in the time of the ancient Egyptian civilization. The Egyptian feasts, which were something to behold, included a wide variety of breads, meats, poultry, and vegetables, commonly washed down with wine or beer. The ancient Greeks and then the Romans knew the pleasures of wine. After alcohol came the adult use of milk, tea, coffee, soda-water drinks of all descriptions, and, in recent years, diet drinks for fat-watchers. The variety of fruit drinks, such as lemonade, and of frozen milk drinks, including the malts and ice-cream floats, is sufficient to stagger the imagination.

Alcoholic Beverages

Alcohol does not contain cholesterol or fat of any type. From this point of view it is no problem in restricted diets, but it does contain calories—and a lot of them. Some affluent individuals who lead apparently normal lives, pursuing important occupations, obtain over 20 per cent of their calories from alcohol. Each gram of alcohol contains about 7 calories, and 3½ ounces (100 grams) of pure alcohol contain 700 calories, a great deal more than a similar amount of pure sugar, nearly as many calories as a similar weight of butter. (For details of the composition of alcoholic beverages consult Table XXVIII, page 341.)

Alcohol does not prevent fat deposits in the arteries, although some alcoholics do not eat enough other food and have limited amounts of fatty changes in their arteries because of malnutrition. Some individuals because of liver disease related to excess alcoholic consumption are nearly free of atherosclerosis, but severe liver disease can be as serious a medical problem as heart disease. So drinking is not a very satisfactory way to prevent atherosclerosis or heart and vascular disease. Because will power usually vanishes after a drink or two, the moderate drinker often indulges in too many calories and eats foods rich in saturated fat and cholesterol. For the person who drinks, it is wise to plan the meal to limit the need for will power. A table of suitably low-fat dishes will prevent the disaster. And snacks at a cocktail party can be prepared to provide a wide variety of low-fat appetizers (see Chapter 18).

Wines and brandies do provide good seasoning for a variety of dishes. In the cooking process the alcohol evaporates, leaving the flavorful elements.

Alcohol is one of the few substances that can qualify as both a food and a toxic drug. Other foods contain drugs or poisons but the drug or poison itself, like caffein in coffee, has no calories. Alcohol can and does cause cell damage. It can cause liver damage, either directly or because of associated malnutrition. It can damage the pancreas and the brain. Chronic use of large amounts of alcohol can lead to early sexual inadequacy in the male, and is a frequent factor in the high incidence of impotence in modern society (sometimes before the age of forty). While alcohol may release inhibitions by its anesthetic effect on the brain, larger amounts cause incapacitation. Alcohol has been demonstrated to be toxic to the heart-muscle cells. With sufficient damage to the heart muscle, actual heart failure may occur, with accumulation of fluid in the lungs, abdomen, and legs. When the alcohol is stopped, the heart recovers and health is restored, if matters have not progressed too far. The problem recurs again as soon as drinking is resumed. Alcohol is included in this book because it is a food with caloric content. When used with restraint it can be an adjunct to eating, but with loss of discretion goes loss of health.

Since alcoholic beverages contain no significant amounts of fat or cholesterol you can follow standard recipes. The exceptions are those few drinks, such as eggnog, that use cream or egg yolks. These should be avoided or limited in a diet restricting saturated fat or cholesterol.

Coffee

There is a relationship between coffee-drinking and health. Coffee is another example of a cultural habit that man has acquired to the detriment of his health. There is some evidence that drinking five or six cups of coffee a day is associated with an increase in heart attacks. The principal reason that coffee has an adverse effect on the body is its caffein content. A single 6-ounce cup of coffee contains from 70 to 150 milligrams of caffein, a potent drug that stimulates the central nervous system. One gram of caffein, which is equivalent to about ten cups of coffee, can cause a severe drug reaction including delirium, ear ringing, flashing of light, and tremulousness. Caffein also stimulates the stomach to pour out large amounts of acid, sometimes four times as much as it does without the coffee. This in turn leads to burning in the pit of the stomach and aggravates peptic ulcers of the stomach and duodenum. Often the cause of indigestion is too much coffee, but this is not revealed by X-ray studies or other diagnostic methods, so that, too often a patient is put on tranquilizers and goes home to wash them down with a stimulating cup of coffee.

Anyone with digestive disturbances should stop drinking coffee. The heavy coffee-drinker may experience withdrawal symptoms—including a severe headache and drowsiness. The headache can be quickly relieved by one cup of coffee. A sensible way to stop the coffee habit is to cut down to one or two cups a day for a week, then eliminate it altogether. If you like the taste, you can use a decaffeinated brand which will protect you from the adverse effects of caffein.

Coffee also will cause the heart to beat too fast. Even a healthy person may have a resting heart rate of fifteen to twenty beats a minute more than if he didn't drink coffee. This in turn leads to a decreased functional capacity of the heart and increases the likelihood of heart irregularities. Anyone having recurrent attacks of palpitation of the heart or attacks of rapid heart rates should stop coffee at once.

The use of sugar and cream in coffee increases its caloric content from zero to about 70 calories, more energy than it takes to walk a mile. The coffee alone contains very few calories, about 2 calories a cup. If you use cream, remember that *commercial artificial cream or coffee-whitener is made from coconut oil. Over 90 per cent of the fat is saturated fat.* You will be better off using real cream and much better off using nonfat cream substitute, Recipe #2, if you want to limit your saturated-fat intake.

Coffee was not a common beverage in the Western world until the seventeenth century. Originally a drink of the Arabic world, it was first discovered in Ethiopia in the ninth century. With its spread to Europe it was also transported to tropical areas and particularly to Latin America, where today most of the world's coffee is raised. Coffee consumption in the United States has grown tremendously since the beginning of the twentieth century, paralleling the increase in heart disease and peptic ulcers. Before World War I the average person used only 9 pounds of coffee a year and by the time of World War II, the consumption had risen to nearly 16 pounds per person, which is about its present level. Over 70 per cent of the world's coffee supply is consumed by the United States. The Scandanavian countries are the only other group to outdo the United States on a per capita basis; the Swedes use 30 pounds per person each year.

Tea

The habit of tea-drinking is much older than coffee-drinking, and it was known to be popular in China as early as the eighth century. Tea was brought to Europe with the spice trade but did not become an important drink until the eighteenth century. It was introduced in the American colonies in Boston in 1690 and may well have changed the course of history, since British taxation of tea led to the famous Boston Tea Party of 1773 and ignited the American Revolution.

Tea leaves actually contain more caffein than the coffee bean. The brewing makes the difference, and the usual cup of tea contains far less caffein than coffee. Figures vary from 36 to 48 milligrams of caffein to as much as is in coffee. Tea also contains theophylline, a related drug. This drug is a more powerful stimulant to the heart than caffein. It is doubtful that there is any advantage to drinking tea in place of coffee other than the possible lesser amounts of caffein ingested. In the United States tea-drinkers seldom drink anywhere near as much tea as the quantity of coffee drunk by dedicated coffee-drinkers.

Cocoa and Chocolate

Drinks prepared from the cacao beans came from the Aztecs of Mexico. When the Spaniards arrived in what is now Mexico City they found the

Aztecs drinking a brew made from cacao beans and flavored with vanilla, also originally from Mexico. The Spaniards added sugar, and around 1700 the English added milk.

Cocoa, like coffee and tea, contains caffein, about 50 milligrams a cup. It is about comparable to tea in its drug effect. Cocoa also contains theobromine, a less potent stimulant of the nervous system.

The percentage of calories from fat in a cup of cocoa can be rather high. Over two thirds of its calories in the powder are from fat and over half the fat is saturated. Baking chocolate likewise is high in fat content. You can still prepare a low-fat drink of cocoa or hot chocolate by following a few basic principles. Expand the calories in the drink by using plenty of nonfat milk and sugar. Limit the amount of chocolate or cocoa to the minimum required to impart a suitable flavor. Using the recipe below, you can make cocoa with less than 15 per cent of its calories from fat and less than 10 per cent of its calories of the saturated-fat type. Note that you cannot achieve this same effect by using water in place of nonfat milk. The diluted chocolate will have a higher percentage of its calories from saturated fat.

#320 Hot Cocoa

1. Mix thoroughly
   5 level tablespoons cocoa powder
   ½ cup sugar
   2 cups nonfat milk powder
   dash salt.
2. Stir in a small amount from
   4 cups cold water
   to make a paste; then gradually stir in remainder.
3. Heat thoroughly to desired temperature but *do not boil.*
4. Remove from heat and add
   ¼ teaspoon vanilla
   and serve.

TC	P	C	F	S	M	PU	CHOL
972	218	681	70(7.2%)	34(3.5%)	23(2.4%)	T	44

Bouillon and Gelatin

A happy choice for a warm drink without the caffein of coffee, tea, or cocoa is a cup of bouillon. You can make your own and skim off the fat, providing a fat-free beverage, or you can use commerical bouillon cubes. These contain very little fat, and a cup of bouillon has about 7 calories.

Gelatin, which is all protein and no fat, can be used for cold drinks, and it is often flavored with fruit extracts. Fruit and vegetable juices are also excellent. They may contain more calories but they are rich in vitamin C and essential vitamins and minerals, a decided improvement over the ills induced by coffee and tea when drunk to excess. There are no drugs in fruit and vegetable juices!

Carbonated Beverages

The numerous soda-pop and nonalcoholic cola drinks are a fairly recent addition to man's drinking habits. Soda water was first introduced in 1833 and the French added sirups, giving birth to soft drinks flavored with grape, orange, cherry, lemon, strawberry, and root beer, to mention a few. These became popular throughout the world and particularly in the United States. These fairly harmless beverages have no fats or cholesterol. Their only drawback is in contributing calories without other important nutrients to the diet. Most of their energy comes from sugar; a 6½-ounce bottle will contain about 85 calories.

It is true that a soda-pop beverage can digest an egg through the action of its carbonic acid, but it does not do so nearly as fast as the much stronger acid hydrochloric acid, which is naturally formed in much larger quantities by the stomach. Unless you need to watch your calorie intake or are trying to control acidity there is no harm in drinking copious amounts of soda pop, if you still eat a balanced diet.

A sirup was developed which originally contained traces of the cola nut and extract of coca leaves. This sirup was added to soda water and eventually became the world-famous Coca-Cola, which has spawned a host of other cola beverages now commonplace. Today's Coca-Cola contains only trace amounts of either cocaine (the company claims the beverage contains a nonnarcotic extract of coca leaves) and even less cola. Aside from the sugar content that causes each 6-ounce bottle to contain over 80 calories, the most important ingredient is caffein. A 6½-

ounce bottle contains about 26 milligrams of caffein, or about a fourth as much as an equal amount of most coffee. Drinking large amounts of cola beverages containing this amount of caffein can have an effect similar to coffee, but obviously one needs to drink about four times as much.

In more recent times dietetic drinks have been developed. They differ only in using a sugar substitute—which from time to time generates heated controversies. These drinks are just as safe as the artificial sweetener used, no more and no less.

CHAPTER

20

Planning Your Diet

The key to success in any diet plan is *variety*. Some people are able to follow a diet fad that helps them for a little while, but most soon tire of the limited foods available and return to the same eating habits that caused their original problem.

Variety is also the key to a well-balanced diet. The reason so many people eat excess amounts of fat, particularly saturated fat, and too much cholesterol is simply that they are not eating a well-balanced diet. Their foods are too limited to those high in fat, with inadequate amounts of vegetables, fruits, and cereals.

To help you plan a well-balanced diet, a master food-exchange list has been developed for this book. By using it wisely you can enjoy eating a variety of foods. It is not necessary to eliminate any particular food entirely from your diet. The list provides a means of eating the foods you like rather than taking the usual approach of forbidding foods.

Of course, you may need to limit the amounts and frequency of some foods. But you can lessen even this drawback by choosing the right *kinds* of meat, if that is your main gastronomic delight, and by being careful how they are prepared.

Like most aspects of life, a balanced diet sometimes requires compromises and choices. If you eat a meal with a main course that contains lots of fat, then the dessert you choose should not be a chocolate devil's-food cake but rather an angel-food cake, which is essentially fat-free.

The Food-Exchange Table

Table XXIX, the Master Food-Exchange List (pp. 342–393), will help you follow any reasonable diet plan without resorting to higher mathematics. You can follow a low-calorie diet, a low-fat diet, a low-saturated-fat diet, a balanced ratio of polyunsaturated fat to saturated fat, a low-cholesterol diet, or any combination of these. All the values are given for household measurements. If you don't have any simple kitchen scales, get a set that measures food in either ounces or grams. Use standard measuring cups, not the smaller coffee cups in common use. The 3½-ounce (100 grams) quantity is the most common measurement given in the table because it is considered an average serving of meat, fish, and similar foods.

The caloric value of all food items will tell you if a food is rich or poor in calories for a given weight. A serving of bacon contains lots of calories while a serving of uncreamed cottage cheese is low in calories.

The food items are all evaluated for their total fat content in terms of *white points* or *black points.* All foods with 35 per cent or less of their calories from any kind of fat are white-point foods. Foods with more than 35 per cent of their calories from any kind of fat are black-point foods. The whole purpose is to make it simple for you to plan meals that provide a diet with 35 per cent or less of the calories from fat. By balancing foods that contain lots of fat with sufficient amounts of foods that contain little or no fat you can plan a diet that provides an average of 35 per cent or less of its calories from fat. All you need to do is choose enough food items with white points to be sure the diet contains as many or more white points as black points.

The exchange list also includes a rating of all food items in terms of their saturated-fat content. All foods with 10 per cent or less of their calories from saturated fat are rated in *green-point* values. A food with more than 10 per cent of its calories from saturated fat is rated in terms of *red points.* All you need to do to limit your saturated-fat intake to less than 10 per cent of your calories is simply to choose enough food items to provide as many or more green points as red points in your diet.

Some diets are planned to provide as much polyunsaturated fat as saturated fat. To help you do this the food items are rated in terms of calories of saturated fat, *blue points,* and calories of polyunsaturated fat, *gold points.* To ensure that your diet contains as much or more polyunsaturated fat as saturated fat, just choose enough foods with sufficient gold points to equal or exceed the blue points.

Opinions vary on how severely cholesterol should be restricted in the diet. To satisfy any goal the cholesterol content of each food item is also listed.

The food-exchange list is organized into four major lists which separate the different classes of food. One list contains all the foods with *white- and green-point* ratings. These are foods that are low in fat and low in saturated fat. A second list includes only those foods that have *white- and red-point* ratings, or those foods low in total fat but with more than 10 per cent of their calories from saturated fat, the white and red list. A third list includes only those food items with *black- and green-point* ratings, or those foods with over 35 per cent of their calories as fat but less than 10 per cent of their calories from saturated fat. The fourth list contains only those foods that have *black- and red-point* ratings, or foods with more than 35 per cent of their calories from fat and over 10 per cent of their calories from saturated fat.

Within each of the four main food groups the items have been separated into foods that contain no cholesterol, such as fruits and vegetables; foods that are low in cholesterol, containing 100 milligrams of cholesterol or less; foods containing moderate amounts of cholesterol, from 100 milligrams to 300 milligrams; and foods containing large amounts of cholesterol, over 300 milligrams. In each case the cholesterol rating is based on the amount of cholesterol in 3½ ounces (100 grams) of the food item, although the amount of cholesterol shown on the table will refer to the amount in the household measure given in the table. Thus the amount of cholesterol listed for whole milk will be for a cupful, not for 3½ ounces (100 grams). If you need to know the amount of cholesterol in a standard 3½-ounce portion you can find it in the individual tables for different food categories, in this instance, for milk, in Table XII for dairy products.

The last division of each listing includes the recipes from this book that have been completely analyzed.

With food items listed in this manner you can easily choose items from the white and green list to balance items from the black and red list. You will also observe that to balance a diet in terms of fat content you will really need to use a variety of foods, which will include vegetables, fruits, and cereals on one hand and meats or some dairy products on the other. This also helps to ensure a balanced diet.

Foods for a Balanced Diet

To ensure that your diet is a healthy one you need to follow only a few basic principles. The diet should contain enough calories to meet your daily energy expenditures, unless you want to lose undesirable body fat, in which case you can decrease the number of calories. The number of calories needed will depend on your body size and the amount of daily activity.

You will want to be sure you get enough protein. This isn't hard to do since so many foods contain protein, but you should try to use several different sources of protein to make sure that you are getting all the necessary types of amino acids in proteins to maintain such body tissue as muscle. All the essential amino acids can be obtained by eating just whole wheat and gelatin, though neither of these alone is adequate. Even a diet that severely restricts fat and cholesterol can still provide enough protein. You could use only items from the white and green list in the no-cholesterol group, plus uncreamed cottage cheese and fortified skim milk or the fish from the white and green list and have all the essential proteins you need, even for growth.

Your diet should include enough food elements to provide all the essential vitamins and minerals. This will be no problem if you can eat an adequate amount of vegetables and fruit as part of your diet. Try to include vegetables with color, such as lettuce, carrots, and fresh ripe tomatoes. Tomatoes are a good source of both vitamins A and C. The B-complex vitamins are plentiful in cereal that hasn't been over-refined or in enriched cereal products. Vitamin E is found in a wide variety of vegetables and cereals. Mature beans are a good source of iron, as well as protein.

You need calcium, and even a very restricted diet will tolerate nonfat milk powder and fortified skim milk, which is fine for drinking. Milk is often enriched with additional vitamins. If you can't tolerate milk because of lactose intolerance, use uncreamed cottage cheese for calcium.

You will need some fat in your diet and you can hardly escape it. Even vegetables, fruit, and cereal have varying amounts of fat. Corn, for example, will yield a reasonable amount of fat and a good portion of it is polyunsaturated fat. Some authorities believe that man needs certain polyunsaturated fats in the diet which the body cannot manfacture in sufficient quantity. There are studies that show that fish oil, which contains some of these polyunsaturated fats, markedly lowers blood-cholesterol levels in some people.

Very few people need encouragement to eat meat. You can live without it, even as a complete vegetarian, and remain in good health. But you don't need to live without it for your health. Meat, chicken, and fish are all good sources of protein and a number of vitamins. It is a good practice to rotate your main dish for meals between meat, fish, and poultry.

Calorie-Counting

In the final analysis, if you want to prevent accumulation of body fat you should limit the calories you eat. The amount of fat on the body will indicate whether you are limiting them sufficiently. Many people are able to improve their health significantly by simply correcting their obesity. You can also lower your blood-cholesterol level significantly and eat high-cholesterol foods, but to achieve this result you must become really lean.

In general, foods that are high in fat content or contain little water or roughage are the ones that add the calories. They include sugars, sirups, and similar carbohydrates that are found in the white and green listing. They also include the fat meats, some dairy products, and other fatty foods, such as nuts. Flour and hard-grain products also contain lots of calories.

To have a satisfactory diet that is limited in calories choose foods that contain lots of water and not too much fat. This includes the lean fish from the white and green listing, the vegetables and fruits from the white and green listing, certain soups, low-fat and nonfat dairy products, egg whites, poultry from the white and green listing and certain food items from the white and red listing. Look at Figure 1 again to see how water content influences the number of calories in food.

Lean round steak is a good example of a food that can be used in large amounts and still not add too many calories to the diet if it is prepared properly. Three servings (10½ ounces, or 300 grams) contain about as much protein as you need for the day and only 405 calories. You could eat three times this much lean round steak every day and still consume only about 1200 calories. Most adults would lose weight on such a diet, not only because it has only a few calories, but also because without carbohydrates in the diet the body loses a lot of water. The water comes back, however, after you go back to a regular diet.

A diet of lean round steak alone is not a balanced diet and cannot be healthy. You could tolerate it for a few days but soon you would feel weak, and you would have vitamin and mineral deficiencies. The same principle applies naturally to fish, which also contains a lot of water, and to chicken. As long as you choose lean fish or lean pieces of chicken you can significantly lower your calorie intake.

The most satisfactory way of limiting your caloric intake and still having a balanced diet you can enjoy without monotony is to choose a limited amount of vegetables, fruit, cereals, lean meats, fish, and poultry. By eliminating excessive amounts of fats and limiting such high-calorie items as the sugars, sirups, and flour, or products made from them, you can achieve such an objective. Remember, hunger is satisfied by bulk. Eat the foods that are bulky from water or cellulose, and you will feel just fine. This is basically the principle used in some of the more successful and popular diet programs, which are sometimes coupled with psychological gimmicks.

It is doubtful that any diet will be successful in preventing fatty deposits in the arteries to the heart, brain, kidney, and elsewhere unless body fat is eliminated. There are a few people who can tolerate large amounts of body fat and remain in good health, but they are a distinct minority.

Limiting Total Fat Intake

The most universal opinion at present among medical scientists concerned with heart, brain, and other diseases caused by fatty deposits in the arteries is that the fat intake should be limited to 35 per cent of your calories. That includes all types of fat (animal, vegetable, saturated, or unsaturated). You can do this very easily with the help of your food-exchange chart. You can use the uncured separable lean of ham with half as much (by weight) canned sweetened applesauce and presto, the combination yields an equal number of white and black points, so that only 35 per cent of the calories from the combination is from fat. You can also use one half as much sweet potatoes as ham with the same results. If you eat a beef steak, remove all the fat and balance it with baked potatoes garnished with sour-cream substitute, Recipe #4. You can balance fat fish with potatoes or other vegetables. Salads can also balance items with more fat. Then you can eat a nonfat dessert if you wish.

Don't overlook the value of using nonfat milk in preparing side dishes such as gravy for meat. A cup of fortified skim milk contains 34 white points, so if you drink two cups of it you can eat 14 ounces (400 grams) of separable lean of choice porterhouse steak or 28 ounces (800 grams) of the separable lean of grade good T-bone steak and still obtain only 35 per cent of your calories from fat.

The secret is not to overload the side dishes with additional fat when you eat a meat, fish, or poultry from the black and red list. If you must add butter or lard to vegetables or use processed cheese with macaroni, these natural foods will no longer be able to balance out the high fat content of the main dish. If you must add fat to natural vegetables then you will need to restrict the other food items in the meal to those items from the white and green list.

To restrict your calories and also limit the number of calories from fat you will naturally need to decrease the amount of each. Don't eat just foods from the black and red list or just foods from the white and green list.

If your doctor wants you to keep your fat intake well below 35 per cent, an easy way to do it is to limit yourself to foods listed on the white and green list or the white and red list. None of these foods exceeds the 35 per cent limit of calories for fat, and when you plan a balanced diet using vegetables, fruits, cereals, breads, pastas, low-fat dairy products, and low-fat desserts, you will have a diet considerably lower in fat than the 35 per cent limit.

Another approach would be to sit down and patiently develop a diet from the basic tables for each food category which precedes the master exchange list. You can do it because all the foods are listed in terms of their calorie content for total fat.

Limiting Saturated-Fat Intake

In addition to limiting calories sufficiently to prevent obesity and limiting total fat intake to less than 35 per cent of all calories, the Inter-Society Commission on Heart Disease also recommends that the saturated-fat intake should be limited to 10 per cent of the total calories. Your food-exchange list will make this possible. Of course you can meet all these requirements by simply limiting your diet to those items listed on the white and green list, since all those foods meet the requirements.

Unless you need to restrict the total fat in your diet you can also use those items listed on the black and green list. If you need to limit total fats the black points will need to be balanced by foods with white points.

If you use foods from the white and red list or from the black and red list you should balance them with items from the white and green or black and green list. The principle is to select enough foods with green points so that the total green points equal or exceed the total red points.

Just as you balance black points with white points in achieving a balanced diet, you can do the same for saturated fat. If you choose the separable lean of uncured ham you can elect to use an equal amount of applesauce, or an equal amount of sweet potatoes. Or just use half as much sweetened applesauce and half as much sweet potatoes as you use ham. In both instances less than 10 per cent of the total calories will be from saturated fat.

You will find that adding the restriction of limiting saturated fat will force you to select fewer items from the black and red list, or to use smaller quantities of these foods. If you want to eat the separable lean of a good-grade T-bone steak, you can only eat two servings (7 ounces, or 200 grams) if you plan to balance it with two cups of fortified skim milk. Of course, you don't need to balance your meat item with just milk or even just potatoes. You can use bread, biscuits, fresh fruit, and desserts that are low in fat or made with polyunsaturated fat to balance saturated fat.

You will find that some foods on the black and red list are so high in both black and red points that you will have to use them in very small quantities. This isn't a very big handicap or even a significant dietary sacrifice, since there is usually a similar item that works better. It is no great sacrifice to forgo eating the fat around a T-bone steak if you still have the opportunity to eat the steak.

Improving Your Polyunsaturated- to Saturated-Fat Ratio

This is a little more difficult. You must select foods with sufficient gold points to equal or exceed the blue points. Many types of fish will have about the same amount of both fats and are satisfactory as a main course. The same is true for fryer chicken and young turkey. Such meats as beef, pork, and lamb, however, have limited amounts of polyunsaturated fat. You will need to use fruits, vegetables, cereals, and cereal products to help with this problem. You can add a little extra polyunsaturated fat to your diet if you wish by being certain to use safflower oil or corn oil, for example in salads or in making desserts or baked products.

Planning the Day's Menu

Menu-planning is simple using the Master Food-Exchange List (Table XXIX, page 342). After you have planned menus for a few weeks you will become an expert in knowing what combinations you should use. It will help to make a simple table to list all the items you include in the menu so you can fill in the amounts and add the values. An example of one day's menu for one person is as follows:

	TC	W	B	G	R	Bl	Gld	Chol*
BREAKFAST								
Grapefruit, 1 cup	82	28	0	8	0	0	0	0
Oatmeal, ⅓ cup (1 cup cooked)	107	20	0	8	0	2	5	0
Sugar, 2 tsp.	32	12	0	4	0	0	0	0
Milk, skimmed, fortified with 2% nonfat solids, ½ cup	52	17	0	5	0	0	0	4
Coffee, 1 cup	2	0	0	0	0	0	0	0
Sugar, 2 tsp.	32	12	0	4	0	0	0	0
Sweet-cream substitute (about 1/12 recipe), 1 tbsp.	22	7	0	2	0	0	0	1
TOTAL for Breakfast	329	96	0	31	0	2	5	5
LUNCH								
Chicken-noodle soup, Campbell's, 100 gms. (3½ oz.)	55	5	0	2	0	3	3	5
Salad								
Tomato, 1,200 gms. (7 oz.)	44	12	0	4	0	0	2	0
Nonfat mayonnaise, Recipe #83, 1 tbsp.	12	4	0	1	0	0	0	1
Flounder (broiled, pan-broiled, or baked), 200 gms. (7 oz.)	158	40	0	12	0	4	4	82

* TC, total calories; W, white points; B, black points; G, green points; R, red points; Bl, blue points; Gld, gold points; Chol, cholesterol in milligrams.

	TC	W	B	G	R	Bl	Gld	Chol
Tartare sauce, Recipe #89, 1 tbsp.	13	4	0	1	0	0	0	0
Beans, snap, 1 cup, 100 gms. (3½ oz.)	27	8	0	3	0	0	1	0
Cole slaw, ¼ Recipe #163	78	27	0	8	0	0	0	2
Bread, whole-wheat, 2 slices	134	34	0	12	0	2	2	2
Margarine, Fleischmann's, ½ tbsp.	50	0	32	0	3	8	13	0
Milk, skimmed, fortified with 2% nonfat solids, 1 cup	125	20	0	0	0	12	0	12
Banana-nut cookies, 1/15 Recipe #299	196	2	0	14	0	6	38	0
TOTAL for Lunch	892	156	32	57	3	35	63	104

DINNER

	TC	W	B	G	R	Bl	Gld	Chol
Salad								
Lettuce, romaine, 1 cup broken pieces	8	2	0	1	0	0	0	0
Pepper, sweet green, ½ pod	8	2	0	0	0	0	0	0
Radishes, 2 small	4	1	0	0	0	0	0	0
Tomato, ½ chopped	22	6	0	2	0	0	1	0
Thousand Island dressing, Recipe #88, 2 tbsp. (about 1/20 of recipe)	28	10	0	3	0	0	0	1
Sirloin steak, double bone, good grade lean only, 200 gms. (7 oz.)	270	10	0	0	12	40	16	140
Broccoli, boiled and drained, 1 cup, 155 gms. (5⅖ oz.)	40	11	0	5	0	0	2	0
Corn, sweet, 1 cup, 168 gms. (5 9/10 oz.)	139	25	0	13	0	2	7	0
Margarine, Fleischmann's, ½ tbsp.	50	0	32	0	3	8	13	0

	TC	W	B	G	R	Bl	Gld	Chol
Bread, whole-wheat, 2 slices	134	34	0	12	0	2	2	2
Margarine, Fleischmann's, ½ tbsp.	50	0	32	0	3	8	13	0
Fresh cherry pie, 1/6 Recipe #271	541	22	0	37	0	17	88	0
Milk, skimmed, fortified with 2% nonfat milk solids, 2 cups, 492 gms. (17 oz.)	250	40	0	0	0	24	0	24
TOTAL for Dinner	1544	163	74	73	18	101	142	167
TOTAL for the Day	2765	415	106	161	21	138	210	276

The example used provides sufficient calories, unless the individual is very active, in which case additional food items that contain little or no cholesterol (to stay under 300 milligrams) may be added, including more vegetables, fruit, even margarine, nuts, or more dessert.

Look at the sample menu carefully. It meets all the criteria recommended by the Inter-Society Commission for Heart Disease. The calories from all fat are far less than the 35 per cent limit, since there are more white points than black points. Less than 10 per cent of the calories are from saturated fat since there are far more green points than red points. The total cholesterol intake is less than 300 milligrams. In addition, a generous portion of the fat is polyunsaturated fat since there are more gold points than blue points. All of this is easily accomplished and still the menu includes a variety of healthful nutritious food, packed with vitamins, calcium, and other minerals with abundant proteins.

Note that the main restriction on the nature of the diet really is the cholesterol content of the food. Clearly, adding egg yolks to the diet would make it impossible to enjoy the generous serving of meat and fish and still stay within the recommended cholesterol limitation.

The menu could easily include hot cakes with margarine and sirup rather than oatmeal, since there is ample room for increasing the fat intake without exceeding the limits.

If you plan a menu that does not concern itself with cholesterol intake you can be more generous with animal products. The fewer the restrictions, the easier it is to tabulate a menu and stay within the restrictions.

Limiting Cholesterol

Most authorities studying the problems of fatty deposits in the arteries agree that the cholesterol in the diet should be limited. How severely it should be limited depends upon the individual. The Inter-Society Commission recommends that cholesterol be limited to 300 milligrams a day. You can meet this limitation by eating only those foods in the four main food charts that are listed as having no cholesterol. You would still be able to eat vegetables, fruit, cereals, candy, breads, many desserts, and in general all nonanimal food products, plus egg white.

You can add to the list the products very low in cholesterol, such as uncreamed cottage cheese, fortified skim milk, and nonfat milk powder. This combination is sufficiently varied to provide a balanced diet. You might wish to eat more mature beans than you have been used to eating and identify vegetable-protein sources. If a person avoids other sources of cholesterol this limitation still allows him a sufficient varied protein intake. It takes approximately a pound (454 grams) of meat to provide 300 milligrams of cholesterol, and slightly more of chicken or turkey (weighed after the bone and skin are removed). The cholesterol analysis of all different kinds of fish is not available, but some are very low in cholesterol content. Red or gray snapper (flesh only) contains only 33 milligrams a serving, and it would be possible to eat nearly two pounds (908 grams) a day within the 300-milligram limit. Flounder, sole, and haddock have similar counts. A varied diet including meat, fish, and poultry is therefore entirely possible even when cholesterol intake is limited to 300 milligrams a day.

You can even eat whole eggs, but remember that one yolk wipes out nearly the rest of the day's allowance for cholesterol. Other animal products contain cholesterol but usually not in such large quantities. Don't forget Eggstra, the low-fat, low-cholesterol egg product now available. Brains are a rich source of cholesterol but they are not so commonly eaten. Liver is moderately high in cholesterol, but on the days you choose liver you can avoid all other food products that contain cholesterol in any sizable amount.

If your doctor agrees that you can use more cholesterol in your diet, you can be a little more liberal in the quantities of foods containing cholesterol. Note that the margarines made from vegetable products contain no cholesterol, whether or not they have been hydrogenated.

How Good Is Your Present Diet?

Now you can look at the distribution of foods on the food-exchange list and get a pretty good idea about how good or bad your diet really is in terms of fat and cholesterol intake. If most of your diet comes from the black and red list you are in trouble. You can eat almost any item on this list some of the time if you are reasonably healthy, *but* you can't eat all your food from such a list. This is analogous to eating a diet of ice cream and cake exclusively. If you have a lot of items from the white and green list as well as items from the other lists the chances are that you are doing all right. By using the point system, though, you can see readily what the facts are. You can also see how you are doing on your choice of individual items; for instance, do you always eat the dark meat of chicken instead of the breast, and do you eat the skin? Do you add butter or margarine to your normally low-fat vegetables? What are you using for fat in preparation of desserts? If you don't like how your points balance after reviewing your diet, perhaps you should make some changes.

What About Breakfast?

Breakfast is not necessary for health. That statement will be shocking to many people. For years in the United States well-meaning school teachers and a number of uninformed members of the medical and health profession have preached the virtues of a healthy breakfast. No single other development has contributed so much to the high incidence of fatty deposits in the arteries of Americans and Englishmen. The body adjusts to almost anything and if you are accustomed to eating a large breakfast, you will miss it—with a midmorning feeling of "faintness" which will last a few days until your body readjusts to the realities of little or no breakfast.

Most of the world's people *do not* eat a big breakfast, if any at all, and they are usually less fat and have fewer problems with heart and circulatory diseases caused by fatty deposits in the arteries.

For centuries men were content with a piece of bread and sometimes a beverage such as ale for their first snack of the day. It was the English who started the tradition of beginning the day with a full meal. France and the Mediterranean parts of the world never developed the habit.

In countries where breakfast is not a tradition, a midmorning snack of coffee, tea, or other beverage with bread or cake is common. In defense of the English habit, it must be said that breakfast began when lunch was often not available or not eaten. Today, with lunch once more established, English breakfast feasts should be a thing of the past. The British did have the good sense to rely heavily on fish for breakfast, which, in terms of health, is much better than the American habit that persists in many families today.

In the United States, breakfast became a tradition, and not because lunch wasn't available. For the farmer breakfast usually followed a good deal of work—tending the cattle and other livestock, doing the milking by hand and strong-arming a mechanical cream-separator. After all that work, a man was ready for breakfast before going on to the rest of the day's work.

If you need the calories, eating breakfast is not a bad idea. The only problem is that far too many people don't need the calories and eat the wrong thing. If you take away their eggs, bacon, and toast with butter they don't know what to eat. Add to the cholesterol in two eggs the fat in bacon and the butter on the toast, and you will find you are starting the day with far too much fat of any kind, saturated fat in particular, and insulting the principle of health by exceeding the entire daily allowance for cholesterol. No wonder Americans have one of the highest incidences of fatty deposits in their arteries of any people on the earth.

Breakfast can be a plus factor in your diet program. You can start the day with an excess balance of white and green points that will permit you to eat more items from the black and red list that you may enjoy. All of the cereals are good sources for polyunsaturated fat, and their total fat content is low. Don't turn up your nose at breakfast food, prepared or homemade. You can use fortified skim milk with it or make a richer mix using nonfat milk powder, which contains very little saturated fat. You can add fruit to the cereal or eat it separately. Fruit or tomato juice is a good starter. You can eat melon or berries. If you like toast, why not try it spread with cinnamon and the nonfat cream substitute? Or do the same with low-fat pancakes spread with jelly, jam, or nonfat cream substitute. All these items are from the green and white list. The fortified skim milk will add to your protein intake, and you will get more gold points than blue ones from these foods. Except for the small amount of cholesterol in the nonfat or low-fat milk products, there is no cholesterol in any of these foods. What an improvement over eggs with bacon or sausage!

If you feel you should get more protein for your breakfast, don't get it by ruining your diet plan. How about using dried beef creamed in nonfat white sauce and served on toast? If you have an aversion to that, try one of the low-fat chicken à la king recipes for breakfast. There is nothing wrong with fish for breakfast, either.

If you must have an egg for breakfast you would be wise to use the low-fat, low-cholesterol egg products now available. And of course you can use all the egg white you wish. If you want to indulge in bacon, try Canadian bacon, which will introduce less fat than regular bacon into your morning meal; try using lean ham instead of bacon.

Special Medical Considerations

The diet plan recommended in this book is for a general diet for people who enjoy normal health. Like any daily fare it may have to be modified for special medical considerations. Since all the foods are listed in terms of their calorie content for carbohydrate, protein, fat, saturated fat, monounsaturated fat, polyunsaturated fat, total calories, and cholesterol content, this information can be used for nearly any diet plan.

A diabetic can plan his meals using the information included in this book. Since diabetic individuals are more prone to develop fatty deposits in the arteries, it is particularly important that they should plan a healthy diet in terms of caloric restriction and the recommendations relative to fat and cholesterol intake. By using the charts listing the calorie values for all the different food items, and the recipes that are analyzed, the diabetic can follow any plan his doctor recommends.

For the diabetic who wishes to enjoy desserts and prepared food items that normally contain sugar, artificial sweetener can be substituted in most recipes. The major exception is dry baked products, specifically cakes and cookies. To use these recipes with artificial sweetener it will be necessary to add water to the ingredients.

The calories of carbohydrate given for the recipes can be reduced by the amount of calories in the sugar that is replaced with artificial sweetener. Since this will reduce the total number of calories in the recipe it will increase the percentage of the remaining calories that are provided by fat and saturated fat. This won't be important in such items as fresh fruit pies but may be of some importance in foods that contain considerable fat, such as cakes. Puddings and cream pies will not require additional water when artificial sweetener is used.

Neither insulin nor pills will take the place of a good basic diet for a diabetic. Many mild diabetics can control their diabetes by dietary measures directed toward elimination and prevention of body-fat deposits.

In some medical cases, it is necessary to limit the amount of salt in the diet. Within reasonable limits there is no evidence that normal salt consumption is in any way damaging to the health. In fact, laborers in hot weather who sweat a lot may lose excess amounts of salt from the body and must take salt pills to replace the body's needs. In many parts of the world, foods that contain sufficient iodine are in short supply and the chief source of iodine is iodized salt. It is important to realize that the body normally contains and must have salt. The blood and body fluids contain about the same amount of salt as sea water. Salt is composed of two chemicals, sodium and chlorine, united to form sodium chloride, or ordinary table salt. Sodium occurs naturally in a host of foods, including vegetables, meat, fish, and dairy products. Even the water supply of some cities contains significant amounts of sodium. It is the sodium that is of particular importance in the consideration of salt in the diet.

At the opposite end of the spectrum from diabetes is low blood sugar (hypoglycemia), which is surprisingly common. In rare instances attacks of low blood sugar are caused by tumors of the pancreas that cause the overproduction of insulin or disorders of the liver and endocrine system, but in the majority of cases, attacks of low blood sugar result from the imperfect functioning of normal digestive mechanisms, and are frequently related to the diet.

Even in normal people there is a chain of events that can be called a "rebound" reaction. If the level of blood sugar is sharply elevated, more insulin will be produced to enable the body to use the sugar. When the body overdoes it, too much insulin may be produced for too long a period of time and the blood sugar will drop to low levels. This alone will cause some weakness, since the sugar is necessary for energy. The body has another defense mechanism it can use to help restore the blood sugar to normal levels, the pouring out of adrenalin, the substance that mobilizes the body for "fight or flight." One action of adrenalin is to free stores of sugar in the body and again elevate the blood sugar. In a sense adrenalin is an antidote to insulin.

Adrenalin has other actions, though, and it induces nervousness, rapid heart beat with a strong pounding pulse, sweating, and sometimes a pale skin. Faintness is not unusual. These are the symptoms most people complain about that are associated with "rebound low blood sugar."

Most people with this problem soon learn that they can relieve their symptoms by taking something sweet, just as the diabetic may take sugar on a slice of orange to relieve hypoglycemia from taking too much insulin. The attack of low blood sugar also makes the person hungry. Thus the individual eats, usually something sweet. This provides temporary relief but actually makes matters worse since it sets the stage for still another episode of low blood sugar.

There are two principal factors that lead to an excessive elevation of blood sugar which can induce rebound low blood sugar. One is the amount of sugar in the food that is available to be readily absorbed into the blood stream. If you eat a lot of candy, the sugar will be absorbed rapidly and there will be a sharp rise in the blood sugar. The second factor is the rate of emptying of the stomach. If the food in the stomach is emptied slowly into the intestine, there will be a delay in absorption of sugar from the intestine into the blood stream.

The time required for stomach-emptying is a very important factor. Sugars and refined carbohydrates alone are retained in the stomach only a very short time before they are emptied directly into the intestine. Liquids pass almost immediately through the stomach into the intestine. Hence a very sweet liquid enters the intestine immediately and causes an abrupt rise in the blood sugar. The sugar-tolerance test used in studying patients for diabetes is based on this principle. The patient drinks a concentrated solution of sugar water, and within thirty minutes the blood sugar is normally elevated sharply above its previous level. By an hour it usually reaches its highest level.

By contrast roughage must be churned and digested before it can be emptied directly into the small intestine for absorption. Proteins require a longer time for digestive action within the stomach and fats require several hours.

Clearly, to avoid the problem of rapid emptying of the stomach it is best to concentrate on food that contains solid roughage, proteins, and fat. This means avoiding concentrated sweets and particularly sweet liquids. Such a diet also decreases the available sugar that would be absorbed to cause a peak rise in blood sugar. This is the basis for a proper diet to avoid attacks of low blood sugar.

The diet in the management of low blood sugar should contain carbohydrates from raw vegetables, lettuce, cabbage, corn, beans, peas and similar items. It should be reasonably high in protein, which can be obtained from items relatively low in fat content, such as lean meats, lean fish, and lean poultry. Within the limits of 35 per cent of the calories as fat, one can eat enough fat with each meal to help slow down the emptying of the stomach. The fat, whether saturated, monounsaturated, or polyunsaturated, will induce the same effect.

The items to avoid are sweets, sugars, sirups, jams, jellies, flour, and products made from these items. Liquid sweets, such as soft drinks and sweetened beverages, should be avoided.

Because many people eat a breakfast that is principally of carbohydrates and often contains lots of sweets and sweet liquids, this is the meal that usually starts the day's problems. Individuals with this difficulty should make a point of eating a breakfast that contains some protein, preferably in solid form. Lean fish is a good choice; salmon patties or fish cakes are excellent. If it contains enough meat, creamed beef or chicken à la king is fine. Even a lean breakfast steak is preferable to a sweet starch breakfast for people with low-blood-sugar problems. Breads, rolls, pancakes, sweetened refined breakfast foods, sweetened beverages (including fruit juice) can be a problem. It is better for these individuals to eat their fruit or drink fruit beverages after a solid meal. Fruit can be used as a replacement for dessert.

If necessary, in-between-meal snacks of allowable items can be used to smooth out the level of blood sugar. By following such a regime a person can avoid attacks of low blood sugar and uncontrollable desires to eat that lead to obesity.

Individuals with high blood pressure, heart failure, certain kidney diseases, liver disease, and a few other medical problems may be required to limit their sodium intake significantly. Diets for these individuals can still use the same principles advocated for a low-fat, low-cholesterol diet. It will be necessary to eliminate certain food items as well as the use of salt in cooking. How severe the limitation must be will depend upon the individual patient's problem. To illustrate the degree of restriction that is sometimes used, one diet that has been used by a number of doctors allows only rice and fruit. Fruit contains more potassium than sodium (a similar chemical element) and the combination provides a very low salt diet. Most doctors feel that it is not necessary to use this severe a limitation for most patients, but in some instances it is justified. Such a diet is obviously cholesterol-free and nearly fat-free.

In the United States, the average diet contains ten grams (⅓ ounce) of sodium chloride. By eliminating any added salt in cooking or eating, the amount can easily be decreased to two to four grams a day. Salt substitutes can be used if desired. If it is necessary to restrict the salt intake still further, then foods that contain appreciable amounts of salt must be eliminated from the diet. The master food-exchange list in this book can still be used, but only for those foods allowed, to meet the objectives of salt restriction. In this way, it is possible to combine a fat-restricted, low-cholesterol diet with a low salt requirement. Many of the foods eliminated because of high salt content are also foods that contain lots of fat. In general, the salt restriction will require a diet that is a low-fat, low-cholesterol diet.

Even on a diet severely restricted in salt intake, the following foods can be used: fruit (raw or cooked), fresh or frozen vegetables (except beets, celery, kale, lima beans, sauerkraut, spinach, swiss chard, mustard greens, and frozen green peas if salt has been added), rice, puffed rice, puffed wheat, shredded wheat, barley, farina, hominy, macaroni, oatmeal, cooked cereals prepared without salt, special breads made without salt or ordinary milk (yeast breads), unsalted butter or margarine, shortenings or oils, limited amounts of special desalted milk, one serving of 3½ ounces (100 grams) of fish, meat, or poultry a day, puddings and desserts made without salt or ordinary milk or baking powder, unsalted soups, and most beverages.

To use a low-salt diet successfully food must be prepared with a variety of spices. Some commercially prepared spices contain salt and this must be avoided. The same is true of many commercially prepared sauces, such as those used for meats, or catchup. Such spices as nutmeg, cinnamon, pepper, curry powder, and many other natural varieties are quite satisfactory.

There are individuals who have special problems related to fat metabolism which causes elevation in cholesterol and in certain fat particles in the blood. In many ways, these individuals may be regarded as the extremes of the broader problem that affects the general population in modern society, causing the almost universal problem of fatty deposits in the arteries. Some of these individuals appear to have rare inherited disorders. These observations have led to an effort to classify people with abnormally high cholesterol levels into types I, II, III, IV, and V. Most practicing heart specialists agree that all these individuals regardless of type benefit markedly from elimination of excess body fat by restricting the number of calories ingested. In line with the recommendations of the Inter-Society Commission on Heart Disease, all individuals with these kinds of abnormalities should limit their total fat intake to 35 per cent of the total calories and should limit their saturated fat while making certain that about one third of the fat used is polyunsaturated fat. Limitation of cholesterol intake also is important, particularly if the amount in the blood is markedly elevated.

Although much has been said about the beneficial effects of limiting carbohydrates, particularly sweets such as sugar, sirups, and candy, in certain types of these disorders it appears likely that the beneficial effects of limiting carbohydrates come from the loss of excess body fat resulting from a significant decrease in the number of calories consumed. If you should be classified as having a fat-metabolism problem, technically called "hyperlipidemia," regardless of whether you are type I, II, III, IV, or V the principles of diet outlined in this book do apply. Number one on the list of these principles is elimination or prevention of excess body-fat stores. It will be necessary for most people to limit their carbohydrate intake to lose body fat, especially such calorie-rich carbohydrate foods as sugar, sirups, jelly, jams, flour, and products made from these food items.

Failures in successful treatment of individuals with these problems are often the result of inadequate weight reduction. A man who has an excess of fifty pounds of fat will not reach an optimal level of blood fats by losing only twenty pounds.

When to Begin the Balanced-Diet Plan

Too often people think that a special diet should be started when trouble makes itself evident or in later years. Nothing could be further from the truth. The right time to begin good eating habits that provide for a balanced diet is with a baby's first mouthful of food. Infants do get some protection against excess intake of cholesterol but this soon disappears, and very young people can be and sometimes are adversely affected by a diet overbalanced with saturated fat. The child should learn to enjoy a diet balanced between vegetables, fruit, cereals, low-fat dairy products, lean meats, fish, and poultry. Such a diet can be planned to include sufficient amounts of protein. Although many baked desserts are far less helpful in providing necessary food elements, even these items that children like so much can be prepared with limited amounts of fat, and by using polyunsaturated fat in their preparation they can be a plus factor in the diet.

The simple plan of a balanced diet is, really, a more natural diet, a diet more in keeping with man's natural origins. The greater emphasis on vegetables, fruits, cereals, lean meats, and lean poultry as well as fish is really the natural way. It is not surprising that the natural way is the right way from birth on. It is never too late to change back to a more natural way. The benefits include not only the likelihood of a longer life, but most important, the good health to enjoy it.

Tables

Using the Food-Value Tables

The food-value tables in this book are of particular importance to any diet pattern you wish to use. No diet can be constructed properly without applying the actual food values for the items eaten. Such data are not readily available, hence most people have a problem in constructing any successful diet.

Household Measurements

There are three common ways foods can be measured, by weight (grams or ounces), by volume (teaspoons or cups), and by energy content (calories). All three measurements of many food items are presented in the tables to make it easy for the cook to use the information in any recipe or diet plan.

Because recipes and servings are usually expressed in such household measurements as teaspoons, cups, one carrot, two peppers, or one head of lettuce, the cook needs to know the food values in these terms. In many instances a serving is a 3½-ounce (100-gram) portion. All food values are given for a 3½-ounce portion of raw, unless otherwise specified, of only the edible portion of the item in Tables III through XXVIII. Bones, seeds, pits, feathers, or other inedible parts of the food are not included in the weight measurement of the food item. The weight refers only to what is left that is edible. Expressing food values in this way will enable you to compare the nutritive value of all foods with one another in terms of the actual weight of the item.

Household measurements are listed in the left-hand margin for each food item. If a cup of an item weighs 250 grams (8¾ ounces), you can tell this by looking in the left-hand column, *but* the value of the food item in the table will be given for a 100-gram (3½-ounce) portion, except for Table XXIX. To find the value for a cupful you would need to multiply the values listed in the table by two and a half (100 grams times 2.5 = 250 grams). In a similar fashion all of the food values can be converted to household measurements other than weight.

The values of items for household measurements are given directly in Table XXIX, the Master Food-Exchange List. For simple food exchange for calories, fat composition, or cholesterol you can often use the values from this table directly without additional computation.

To help you avoid the confusion between ounces and grams, either of which are commonly used on packaged food items, the weight is given in both ounces and grams. Not only is the 3½-ounce (100-gram) portion a common one-serving size, but it is also the amount used for most food-analysis measurements throughout the world.

Calories

There is an important difference in whether the composition of foods is expressed in calories (the actual energy available) or in weight (grams or ounces). Because of the common practice of expressing composition of food in grams or percentage of something (usually not specified) it is almost impossible for a person to know how many calories, and of what, he is actually eating. Any diet for any purpose must include the consideration of how many calories of what a person eats. The secret of many fad diets is foods containing lots of bulk but a limited number of calories.

The tables in this book express the value of the components of food items in actual calories. You can read directly the caloric value for the entire item, the caloric value for the carbohydrates, proteins, and fats it contains, and even the caloric values for the saturated, monounsaturated, and polyunsaturated fat elements. This is very important since special diets like those for diabetics usually require a person to eat a diet with a specified number of calories from each food element. Weight-reducing diets or weight-gaining diets also must rely on actual caloric content. In this sense you can use the tables in this book for most diet requirements as a handy source for the actual caloric composition of foods.

You will note that the sum of the calories for carbohydrates, protein, and fat usually does not equal the total caloric value listed. This is because not all of the food elements have been measured. Some types of fat may not be accounted for by some methods of analysis. The usual practice is to ignore this and use an elementary way of accounting for the calories. This is not the case here, and the actual available measurements are listed.

The calculations of the caloric values are done in the manner used in the *United States Department of Agriculture Handbook No. 8.* The usual practice of assuming that carbohydrates and proteins yield 4 calories per gram and that fat yields 9 calories is *not correct.* The calories the body uses from any food depend upon its digestibility. A food does not provide any calories unless it is absorbed and used. For this reason the caloric value of different types of fat may vary from over 9 calories for each gram to little more than 8. Similarly, the amount of calories from different food items available to the body varies greatly. Using the information available in the *United States Department of Agriculture Handbook,* we have converted all of the food items to the actual values for calories the body obtains for each different food item. You needn't worry about these technicalities since the calculations to provide the actual caloric values have solved this problem for you and provided the real values, not some oversimplification.

Abbreviations and Symbols

Abbreviations and symbols are used in the tables and in the tabulations of values at the bottom of many recipes. They are as follows:

TC	Total calories for item or recipe
EE	Food energy equivalent to miles of walking
P	Protein
C	Carbohydrate
F	Fat
S	Saturated fat
M	Monounsaturated fat
PU	Polyunsaturated fat
Chol	Cholesterol
( )	Imputed or derived value

Approximations

Values are rounded to the nearest calorie or nearest one tenth. Because unrounded values are used in the calculation of percentages, the same caloric values for fractions of fat show minor variations in the percentage of calories for the same item.

In all instances the values have to be approximations. The amount of any substance varies from one measurement to the next, even in a tablespoon. The size, weight, and caloric value of an apple, an orange, a banana, or a potato obviously must vary. These variations inherent in foods and cooking will not, however, significantly detract from the practical application of the data to any diet plan.

TABLE I: WATER CONTENT AND CALORIC VALUE OF DIFFERENT TYPES OF FOODS 3 1/2 Ounces (100 Grams) Edible Portion

	Water Percentage	*Total Calories*	*Carbohydrate Calories*	*Protein Calories*	*Fat Calories*
Egg white	87.6	51	3	48	0
Drum (red) redfish	80.2	80	0	77	4
Potatoes	79.8	76	69	8	1
Shrimp	78.2	91	6	77	7
Fryer chicken, light meat without skin	77.2	101	0	88	14
Bananas	75.7	85	80	4	2
Round steak, separable lean	72.7	135	0	92	42
Butter	15.5	716	2	3	712
Wheat flour, all-purpose, enriched	12.0	364	301	40	8
Sugar	0.5	385	385	0	0
Lard	0.0	902	0	0	902

TABLE II: CALORIES USED IN WALKING AT THREE MILES PER HOUR

Body Weight	*Total Calories Used in Walking One Mile*	*Calories Used for Basal Metabolism While Walking One Mile*	*Net Calories Used for Walking One Mile*	*Mile-Equivalent Factor*
100 pounds (45.4 kilos)	63.0	18.3	44.7	1.38
110 pounds (50.0 kilos)	67.4	19	48.4	1.27
120 pounds (54.5 kilos)	71.6	20	51.6	1.19
130 pounds (59.1 kilos)	75.8	21	54.8	1.12
140 pounds (63.6 kilos)	80.0	21.7	58.3	1.05
150 pounds (68.2 kilos)	84.2	22.7	61.5	1.00
160 pounds (72.7 kilos)	88.4	23.3	65.1	.94
170 pounds (77.3 kilos)	92.6	24	68.6	.90
180 pounds (81.8 kilos)	96.8	25	71.8	.86
190 pounds (86.4 kilos)	101.0	26	75.0	.82
200 pounds (90.9 kilos)	105.2	27	78.2	.79
210 pounds (95.4 kilos)	109.4	28	81.4	.76
220 pounds (100.0 kilos)	113.6	28.7	84.9	.72
230 pounds (104.5 kilos)	117.8	30	87.8	.70

TABLE III: **COMPOSITION OF SUGARS, SIRUPS, JELLIES, AND JAMS 3 1/2 Ounces (100 Grams)***

		Water Percentage	*TC*	*EE*	*Calcium MG.*	*Iron MG.*
Honey	1 tbsp = 21 gms. (3/4 oz.)	17.2	304	5.0	0	0
Jams and Preserves	1 tbsp = 20 gms. (3/4 oz.)	29.0	272	4.5	20	1.0
Jellies	1 tbsp = 20 gms. (3/4 oz.)	29.0	273	4.5	21	1.5
Molasses, Cane	1 tbsp = 20 gms. (3/4 oz.)					
Light		24.0	252	4.2	165	4.3
Medium		24.0	232	3.9	290	6.0
Blackstrap		24.0	213	3.6	684	16.1
Sirups	1 tbsp = 21 gms. (3/4 oz.)					
Cane		26.0	263	4.4	60	3.6
Corn		24.0	290	4.8	46	4.1
Maple		33.0	252	4.3	104	1.2
Sorgum		23.0	257	4.3	172	12.5
Table (cane and maple)		33.0	252	4.2	16	T
Sugar						
Brown	1 cup = 220 gms. (7 3/4 oz.)	2.1	373	6.2	85	3.4
Maple	1 cup = 220 gms. (7 3/4 oz.)	8.0	348	5.8	143	1.4
White granulated	1 cup = 200 gms. (7 oz.)	0.5	385	6.4	0	0
White powdered	1 cup = 120 gms. (4 1/4 oz.)	0.5	385	6.4	0	0

*See page 283 for abbreviations and symbols.

TABLE IV: COMPOSITION OF FATS AND OILS
3 1/2 Ounces (100 Grams)*

	TC	*EE miles*	*S cal*	*M cal*	*PU cal*
Butter					
Stick = 1/2 cup = 113 gms. (4 oz.) 1 tbsp = 14 gms. (1/2 oz.)	716	11.9	404 56.4%	237 33.1%	18 2.5%
Lard					
1 cup = 205 gms. (7 oz.) 1 tbsp = 13 gms. (1/2 oz.)	902	15.0	342 37.9%	414 45.9%	90 10.0%
Margarine					
Stick = 1/2 cup = 113 gms. (4 oz.) 1 tbsp = 14 gms. (1/2 oz.)					
Bluebonnet, regular	720	12.0	152 21.1%	430 59.7%	125 17.4%
Bluebonnet, soft	720	12.0	114 15.8%	405 56.3%	189 26.3%
Fleischmann's, diet	357	6.0	63 17.6%	151 42.2%	139 38.9%
Fleischmann's, salted	720	12.0	114 15.8%	405 56.3%	189 26.3%
Fleischmann's, unsalted	720	12.0	114 15.8%	405 56.3%	189 26.3%
Fleischmann's, soft	720	12.0	125 17.4%	304 42.2%	278 38.6%
Mazola, diet	350	5.8	53 15.1%	144 41.1%	148 42.3%
Mazola, salted or unsalted	720	12.0	118 16.4%	375 52.0%	206 28.6%
Nucoa, regular	720	12.0	126 17.5%	382 53.0%	192 26.7%
Nucoa, soft	720	12.0	134 18.6%	262 36.4%	305 42.4%
Oils					
1 cup = 220 gms. (7 3/4 oz.) 1 tbsp = 14 gms. (1/2 oz.)					
Coconut oil	884	17.1	760 86.0%	51 5.8%	2 0.2%
Corn oil	884	17.1	88 10.0%	248 28.0%	469 53.0%
Cottonseed oil	884	17.1	221 25.0%	186 22.0%	442 50.0%
Olive oil	884	17.1	97 11.0%	672 76.0%	62 7.0%
Peanut oil	884	17.1	159 18.0%	415 47.0%	256 29.0%
Safflower oil	884	17.1	71 8.0%	133 15.0%	637 72.0%
Sesame oil	884	17.1	124 14.0%	336 38.0%	371 42.0%
Soy oil	884	17.1	133 15.0%	177 20.0%	460 52.0%

*See page 283 for abbreviations and symbols.

TABLE V: **CHOLESTEROL CONTENT OF 3 1/2 OUNCES (100 GRAMS) OF EDIBLE FOOD (RAW)***

Beef	70** Milligrams
Brains	> 2,000
Butter (8 tablespoons)	250
Caviar or fish roe	300
Cheese	
Cheddar	100
Cottage, creamed	15
Cream	120
Cheese spread	65
Chicken	60
Crab meat	125*
Egg	
(2 whole)	550
(3 whites)	0
(6 yolks)	1,500
Fish	70*
Heart	150
Ice Cream	45
Kidney	375
Lamb	70
Lard (8 tablespoons)	95
Liver	300
Lobster	200
Margarine	
All-vegetable fat	0
Two-thirds animal fat	65
Milk	
Whole (2/5 cup)	11
Skim (2/5 cup)	3
Mutton	65
Oysters	> 200*
Pork	70***
Shrimp	125
Sweetbreads (thymus)	250
Veal	90

*These values are from *U.S.D.A. Handbook No. 8.* Items marked * are said to have lower values by more recent analysis (see table for fish and shellfish).

**Beef muscle is reported to have values from 54.8 to 62.5 milligrams and beef fat 56.2 milligrams, as reported by the *Journal of Food Science*, 1967.

***Pork muscle is reported to have values from 61.6 to 69.5 milligrams and pork fat 42.7 milligrams as reported by the *Journal of Food Science*, 1967.

TABLE VI: **VITAMIN A CONTENT (UNITS) OF COMMON FOODS 3 1/2 OUNCES (100 GRAMS) EDIBLE PORTION**

Apricots	
Raw	2,700
Dried	10,900
Asparagus (not white)	900
Bacon	0
Bananas	190
Beans, frozen, cooked	600
Beef	50
Beets, red, cooked	20
Broccoli	2,500
Brussel sprouts, cooked	520
Butter	3,300
Carrots, cooked	10,500
Chard, Swiss, cooked	5,400
Cheese	
Cheddar	1,310
Uncreamed cottage	10
Cherries, sour red	
Canned	680
Frozen unsweetened	1,000
Chicken	
Skin	550
Light meat without skin	60
Dark meat without skin	150
Giblets	4,290
Chives, raw	5,800
Collards, frozen, cooked	6,800
Crab, cooked, steamed blue Dungeness, rock, king	2,170
Cream, light whipping	1,280
Cress, raw	9,300
Dandelion greens	11,700
Egg yolk	3,400
Egg white	0
Endive	3,300
Lettuce	
Leaf	1,900
Crisp head	330
Liver, beef, fried	53,400
Mangos, raw	4,800
Margarine	3,300
*Milk (3.7% fat)	150
Muskmelon cantaloupe and netted	3,400
Mustard greens, cooked	5,800
Nectarine, raw	1,650
Onion tops	4,000
Orange, raw	200
Papayas, raw	1,750
Parsley, raw	8,500
Peaches	
Raw	1,330
Dried	3,390
Pepper, mature	
Red sweet	4,450
Green sweet	420
Prunes, dried	1,600
Pumpkin, canned	6,400
Spinach, frozen cooked	7,900
Squash, cooked	
Summer	390
Winter	3,500
Acorn	1,400
Butternut	6,400
Hubbard	4,800
Sweet potato, raw	8,800
Swordfish, raw	1,580
Tangerine, raw	420
Tomatoes, raw	900
Turnip greens	6,900
Whitefish, raw	2,260

*May contain much more if "fortified" with additional Vitamin A. This also applies to low-fat products. Consult the container label.

TABLE VII: **CALCIUM CONTENT OF COMMON FOODS (MILLIGRAMS) IN 3 1/2 OUNCES (100 GRAMS) EDIBLE PORTION**

	Milligrams
Baking powder (7 tablespoons or 22 teaspoons)	
Sodium aluminum sulfate	
With monocalcium phosphate monohydrate	1,932
With monocalcium phosphate monohydrate and calcium carbonate	5,778
With monocalcium phosphate monohydrate and calcium sulfate	6,320
Straight phosphate	6,279
Cheddar cheese	750
Uncreamed cottage cheese	90
Beef	10
Bread, enriched white	84
Collards	250
Fish flour	
From whole fish	4,610
From filets	920
Mackerel, canned	260
Milk, nonfat powder (Scant 1 1/2 cups)	1,292
Milk, skimmed (2/5 cup)	120
Milk, partially skimmed with 2% non-fat solids added (2/5 cup)	143
Sardines	
Atlantic	
Solids and liquid	354
Drained solids	437
Pacific in tomato sauce, solids and liquid	449
Salmon, canned (solids and liquid)	
Chum	249
Coho (silver)	244
Pink	196
Red (sockeye)	259

TABLE VIII: SPICES FOR ALL OCCASIONS

Allspice	Desserts, fruit dishes, pickles, relishes
Anise	Breads, cakes, cookies
Balm	Soups, salads
Basil	Soups, sauces, fish, vegetables (eggplant, squash, tomatoes, onions, green salads) fruit compote
Bay leaves	Soups, meat stews and roasts, poultry fricassee, vegetables (potatoes, carrots, tomatoes)
Borage	Vegetable salads
Capers	As a condiment
Caraway seed	Breads, cakes, baked fruit, soups
Cardamom	A condiment, especially good with honey
Cayenne pepper	Meat dishes, gravies, vegetables, salad dressings
Celery seed	Soups, stews, pickles, salads
Chervil	Soups, salads
Chili	Chili sauce, spicy dishes
Chili powder	Sauces, seafood cocktails, chili, meats, beans, vegetables
Cinnamon	Desserts, rolls, fruit compote
Cloves	Pickles, relishes, other spice combinations
Coriander	Desserts, confections, pickles, relishes
Cumin	Pickles, relishes, meats, curry powder
Curry powder	Sauces (curry sauce), vegetables, meat, poultry, fish
Dill	Pickles, fish
Fennel seed	Pies, baked fruit
Fennel leaves	Steamed or baked fish
Garlic	Meats, salads
Ginger	A condiment, other spice combinations (pumpkin-pie spice)
Mace	Soups, sauces, pies, cakes, pickles, relishes
Marjoram	Soups, stuffings, meat, fowl, fish, salads, vegetables (carrots, peas, squash), white sauce and its variations
Mincemeat spice	Mincemeat, cakes, cookies and sauces
Mint	Jellies, preserves, ices, sauces (especially for meat) beverages, salads, fruit beverages, carrots, peas, apple dishes
Mustard	Paste for meats, sauces, pickles, salad dressings
Nutmeg	Soups, meat dishes, desserts, breads, with other spices for pickles and relishes
Paprika	For imparting browning color for broiling or baking. Meats, soups, vegetable salads, vegetable garnish
Pepper	Meats, vegetable dishes, soups, salads, uncreamed cottage cheese, stuffings, fish, poultry
Poppy seed	Breads, cakes, cookies, rolls
Pumpkin-pie spice	Pumpkin, squash, sweet-potato pie

TABLE VIII (continued)

Rosemary	Flavor stews, sauces, fish, fruit cup, soups, (chicken, pea, spinach) meats, poultry, vegetables, fruit salads, white sauce
Saffron	Breads, meats, fish, veal, beef, chicken, vegetables, fish sauces, curry powder, yellow coloring for any purpose
Sage	Soups, stuffings, stews, tomatoes
Salt	Universal application
Savory	Vegetable juices, soups, broiled fish, stuffings, beans, rice, mixed greens, salad dressings, poultry seasoning
Sesame	Rolls and cookies
Soy sauce	Chinese cooking, rice, vegetables, stews
Tabasco sauce	Seafood sauce, spicy sauces, soups, vegetables, meats
Tarragon	Seafood sauce, chicken or tomato soup, salads, broiled or baked fish, chicken, mushrooms, potatoes, pickles, relishes
Thyme	Vegetable juice, meat, poultry, clams, baked fish, broiled fish, meat loaf, stuffings, carrots, beets, salads

TABLE IX: COMPOSITION OF MISCELLANEOUS COMMON INGREDIENTS 3 1/2 Ounces (100 Grams)*

	TC	*EE miles*	*C cal*	*P cal*	*F cal*	*S cal*	*M cal*	*PU cal*	*Chol. mg.*
Baking Powder									
Sodium aluminum sulfate									
With monocalcium phosphate monohydrate									
1 tbsp = 14 gms. (1/2 oz.)									
1 tsp = 4.5 gms. (1/6 oz.)	129	2.2	115	0	0	0	0	0	0
With monocalcium phosphate monohydrate and calcium carbonate									
1 tbsp = 14 gms. (1/2 oz.)									
1 tsp = 4.5 gms. (1/6 oz.)	78	1.3	70	0	0	0	0	0	0
With monocalcium phosphate monohydrate and calcium sulfate									
1 tbsp = 14 gms. (1/2 oz.)									
1 tsp = 4.5 gms. (1/6 oz.)	104	1.7	93	0	T	0	0	0	0
Straight phosphate									
1 tbsp = 14 gms. (1/2 oz.)									
1 tsp = 4.5 gms. (1/6 oz.)	121	2	109	0	T	0	0	0	0
Cream of tartar	78	1.3	70	0	T	0	0	0	0
Bouillon Cubes, Wyliess									
16 cubes = 100 gms. (3 1/2 oz.)									
1 cube = 7 calories	(182)	3.0	(30)	(86)	(2.5%)	(T)	(T)	(T)	(2)
Chocolate									
Bitter or baking	505	8.4	38	20	444	251	165	8	0
1 sq. = 28 gms. (1 oz.)					87.9%	49.7%	32.7%	1.6%	
Semi-sweet, small pieces	506	8.4	41	8	167	92	67	T	0
1 cup = 170 gms. (6 oz.)					33.0%	18.1%	13.2%		
Chocolate Sirup									
Thin	245	4.0	83	4	17	8	8	T	0
1 cup = 300 gms. (10 1/2 oz.)					6.9%	3.3%	3.3%		
Fudge type	330	5.5	72	9	115	58	42	T	0
1 cup = 285 gms. (10 oz.)					34.8%	17.6%	12.7%		
Cocoa, dry powder									
Plain, high fat	299	5.0	64	31	198	109	75	T	0
1 cup = 100 gms. (3 1/2 oz.)					66.2%	36.5%	25.2%		
Medium-low fat	265	4.4	68	32	159	92	58	T	0
					60.0%	34.7%	21.9%		
Low fat	187	3.1	27	37	66	34	25	T	0
					35.3%	18.1%	13.4%		
Gelatine									
1 envelope Knox = 28 cal.	335	5.6	0	334	1	0	0	0	0
					0.3%				

*See page 283 for abbreviations and symbols.

TABLE X: COMPOSITION OF CEREAL PRODUCTS
3 1/2 Ounces (100 Grams)*

	TC	*EE miles*	*C cal*	*P cal*	*F cal*	*S cal*	*M cal*	*PU cal*	*Chol. mg.*
Barley									
Pearled	349	5.8	311	29	8	0	4	4	0
1 cup = 200 gms. (7 oz.)					24%		1.2%	1.2%	
Pat or Scotch	348	5.8	305	34	9	0	4	4	0
1 cup = 200 gms. (7 oz.)					2.7%		1.2%	1.2%	
Buckwheat Flour									
Dark	333	5.6	272	39	21	0	0	0	0
1 cup = 100 gms. (3 1/2 oz.)					6.3%				
Light	347	5.8	314	23	10	0	0	0	0
1 cup = 100 gms. (3 1/2 oz.)					2.9%				
Corn Grits (also Hominy Grits)									
Enriched	362	6.0	315	24	7	1	2	2	0
1 cup = 245 gms. (8 1/2 oz.)					1.9%	0.3%	0.6%	0.6%	
Cornmeal									
Whole ground, unbolted, dry	355	5.9	298	25	33	T	8	17	0
1 cup = 122 gms. (4 1/2 oz.)					9.2%		2.4%	4.7%	
Bolted, nearly dry	362	6.0	300	25	28	T	8	17	0
1 cup = 122 gms. (4 1/2 oz.)					7.9%		2.3%	4.6%	
Degermed, enriched	364	6.0	326	27	10	T	8	17	0
1 cup = 138 gms. (4 3/4 oz.)					2.8%		2.3%	4.6%	
Cornstarch									
1 cup = 125 gms. (4 1/2 oz.)	362	6.0	352	1	0	0	0	0	0
Farina									
Enriched, regular	371	6.2	304	43	8	2	2	4	0
1 cup = 245 gms. (8 1/2 oz.)					2.0%	0.4%	0.6%	1.0%	
Hominy Grits (see Corn Grits)									
Oatmeal									
Rolled oats	390	6.5	282	49	62	8	17	17	0
1 cup = 82 gms. (2 3/4 oz.)					15.9%	2.0%	4.4%	4.4%	
Popcorn									
Unpopped	362	6.0	291	32	39	8	8	25	0
					10.9%	2.3%	2.3%	6.9%	
Popped, plain	386	6.4	310	35	42	8	8	25	0
1 quart = 24 gms. (5/6 oz.)					10.8%	2.3%	2.3%	6.5%	
Rice, uncooked									
Brown	360	6.0	318	26	16	3	3	9	0
1 cup = 185 gms. (6 1/2 oz.)					4.4%	0.9%	0.9%	2.7%	
Instant dry	374	6.2	344	29	2	0	0	0	0
1 cup = 86 gms. (3 oz.)					0.4%				
White enriched	363	6.0	334	25	3	0	0	0	0
1 cup = 185 gms. (6 1/2 oz.)					0.8%				
Rye Flour									
Light	357	6.0	336	26	2	0	0	0	0
1 cup = 100 gms. (3 1/2 oz.)					0.5%				
Medium	350	5.8	299	37	14	3	3	9	0
1 cup = 100 gms. (3 1/2 oz.)					4.0%	0.8%	0.8%	2.6%	
Dark	327	5.4	258	48	22	4	4	12	0
1 cup = 128 gms. (4 1/2 oz.)					6.7%	1.2%	1.2%	3.7%	

TABLE X (continued)

	TC	EE miles	C cal	P cal	F cal	S cal	M cal	PU cal	Chol. mg.
Wheat Flour									
All-purpose	364	6.1	301	40	8	2	3	4	0
1 cup = 120 gms. (4 1/4 oz.)					2.3%	0.5%	0.7%	1.2%	
Cake or bakery	364	6.1	314	28	7	1	2	4	0
1 cup = 100 gm.s (3 1/2 oz.)					1.8%	0.4%	0.5%	0.9%	
Gluten	378	6.3	186	157	16	3	4	8	0
1 cup = 125 gms. (4 1/4 oz.)					4.2%	0.9%	1.1%	2.2%	
Self-rising, enriched	352	5.9	293	35	8	2	3	4	0
1 cup = 125 gms. (4 1/4 oz.)					2.4%	0.5%	0.7%	1.2%	
Whole-wheat	333	5.6	268	48	17	3	5	8	0
1 cup = 120 gms. (4 1/4 oz.)					5.0%	1.0%	1.5%	2.4%	
Wheat Germ									
1 cup = 114 gms. (4 oz.)	363	6.0	176	95	91	17	25	42	0
					25.1%	4.8%	6.9%	11.5%	
Wheat, whole-meal	338	5.6	273	48	17	3	3	8	0
						1.0%	0.7%	2.5%	
Wild Rice									
1 cup = 160 gms. (5 1/2 oz.)	353	5.9	298	50	6	0	0	0	0
					1.7%				

*See page 283 for abbreviations and symbols.

TABLE XI: **COMPOSITION OF PREPARED BREAKFAST CEREALS**
3 1/2 Ounces (100 grams)*

	TC	*EE miles*	*C cal*	*P cal*	*F cal*	*S cal*	*M cal*	*PU cal*	*Chol. mg.*
Bran Flakes									
40% brand	303	5.0	189	18	15	0	0	0	0
1 cup = 35 gms. (1 1/4 oz.)					5.0%				
With raisins	287	4.8	186	15	3	0	0	0	0
1 cup = 50 gms. (1 3/4 oz.)					0.9%				
Corn Flakes									
Added nutrients	386	6.4	344	22	3	0	0	0	0
1 cup = 24 gms. (7/8 oz.)					0.9%				
Corn, puffed									
Added nutrients	399	6.4	81	22	35	(3)	(10)	(18)	0
					8.8%	(0.9%)	(2.5%)	(4.6%)	0
Oats, puffed									
Added nutrients	397	6.2	310	41	46	(5)	(9)	(9)	0
1 cup = 25 gms. (7/8 oz.)					11.6%	(1.3%)	(2.3%)	(2.3%)	
Rice Flakes									
Added nutrients	390	6.5	361	20	2	(T)	(T)	(T)	0
					0.6%				
Rice, puffed									
Added nutrients	399	6.6	368	19	3	(1)	(1)	(1)	0
1 cup = 15 gms. (1/2 oz.)					0.8%	(0.2%)	(0.2%)	(0.4%)	
Wheat Flakes									
Added nutrients	354	5.9	304	37	13	(2)	(3)	(7)	0
1 cup = 30 gms. (1 oz.)					3.8%	(0.7%)	(0.9%)	(1.8%)	
Wheat, puffed									
Added nutrients	363	6.0	297	54	13	(2)	(3)	(7)	0
1 cup = 15 gms. (1/2 oz.)					3.5%	(0.7%)	(0.9%)	(1.8%)	
Wheat, shredded									
1 biscuit = 25 gms. (5/6 oz.)	354	5.9	302	36	17	(3)	(5)	(8)	0
1 cup = 30 gms. (1 oz.)						(0.9%)	(1.4%)	(2.4%)	

*See page 283 for abbreviations and symbols.

TABLE XII: COMPOSITION OF DAIRY PRODUCTS
3 1/2 Ounces (100 grams)*

	TC	*EE miles*	*C cal*	*P cal*	*F cal*	*S cal*	*M cal*	*PU cal*	*Chol. mg.*
Butter									
Stick = 1/2 cup = 113 gms. (4 oz.)	716	11.9	2	3	712	404	237	18	250
1 tbsp = 14 gms. (1/2 oz.)					99.4%	56.4%	33.1%	2.5%	
Cheese									
Natural									
Blue or Roquefort	368	6.1	8	92	268	158	96	9	100
					72.8%	42.7%	26.3%	2.4%	
Brick	370	6.1	7	95	268	158	97	9	100
					72.5%	42.7%	26.3%	2.4%	
Camembert	299	5.0	7	75	217	132	79	9	100
					72.5%	44.1%	26.4%	2.9%	
Cheddar (American domestic)	398	6.6	8	107	283	158	97	9	100
					71.0%	39.7%	24.3%	2.2%	
Cottage, creamed	106	1.8	11	58	37	18	9	T	15
					34.8%	16.6%	8.3%		
Cottage, uncreamed	86	1.4	10	72	3	T	T	T	15
1/2 cup = 100 gms. (3 1/2 oz.)					3.1%				
Cream	374	6.2	8	34	331	185	105	9	120
					88.5%	49.4%	28.1%	2.4%	
Limburger	345	5.8	8	90	246	132	79	9	100
					71.4%	38.3%	22.9%	2.6%	
Parmesan	393	6.6	11	154	229	132	79	9	100
					58.3%	33.6%	20.1%	2.2%	
Swiss	370	6.2	7	117	246	132	79	9	100
					66.5%	35.6%	21.4%	2.4%	
Pasteurized									
American	370	6.2	7	99	264	132	79	9	100
					71.3%	35.6%	21.4%	2.4%	
Swiss	355	5.9	6	113	236	132	79	9	100
					66.5%	37.2%	22.2%	2.5%	
Spread									
American	288	4.8	32	68	188	132	79	9	100
					65.3%	45.8%	27.5%	3.0%	
Cream									
Half cream and half milk	150	2.5	17	14	98	53	32	4	406
1 cup = 242 gms. (8 1/2 oz.)					65.6%	35.2%	21.1%	2.3%	
Light (coffee or table)	211	3.5	17	13	180	99	59	4	706
1 cup = 240 gms. (8 1/2 oz.)					85.3%	46.9%	28.0%	1.7%	
Sour	211	3.5	17	13	180	99	59	4	(95)[b,c]
1 cup = 230 gms. (8 oz.)					85.3%	46.9%	28.0%	1.7%	
Whipped (in pressurized container)	225	3.7	16	6	82	46	29	T	(42)[b,d]
1 cup = 60 gms. (2 oz.)					36.3%	20.7%	12.9%		
Whipping, light	300	5.0	14	11	275	151	92	7	(70)[b,d]
1 cup = 239 gms. (8 1/2 oz.)					91.8%	50.3%	30.8%	2.4%	
Whipping, heavy	352	5.9	12	9	330	185	111	11	1206
1 cup = 238 gms. (8 1/2 oz.)					93.8%	52.5%	31.6%	3.2%	
Cream, imitation									
Powdered (from vegetable fat)	508	8.5	213	18	308	290	9	T	0
1 cup = 94 gms. (3 1/3 oz.)					60.7%	57.0%	1.7%		
Sour (from nonfat dry milk and vegetable oil)	187	3.2	28	16	141	131	4	T	(6)[e]
1 cup = 235 gms. (8 1/4 oz.)					75.4%	70.0%	1.9%		
Whipped topping, pressurized	271	4.5	50	5	214	188	12	T	0
1 cup = 70 gms. (2 1/2 oz.)					78.9%	69.3%	4.5%		

TABLE XII (continued)

	TC	*EE miles*	*C cal*	*P cal*	*F cal*	*S cal*	*M cal*	*PU cal*	*Chol. mg.*
Eggs									
Whole	163	2.7	3	56	104	36	40	9	550
1 egg = 50 gms. (1 3/4 oz.)					63.9%	22.2%	24.6%	5.5%	
Whites	51	0.8	3	48	T	T	T	T	0
1 white = 33 gms. (1 1/6 oz.)									
Yolks	348	5.8	2	70	276	90	117	18	1500
1 yolk = 17 gms. (6/10 oz.)					79.4%	25.9%	33.6%	5.7%	
Eggstra (Tillie Lewis)									
Reconstituted 1 to 4, large eggs– 50 gms. (1 3/4 oz.)	86	1.4	16	48	22	(7)	(8)	(2)	114
					25.5%	(8.1%)	(9.0%)	(2.3%)	
Milk, cow's									
Whole	66	1.1	19	15	32	18	9	T	11
1 cup = 244 gms. (8 1/2 oz.)					49.2%	26.7%	13.3%		
Skimmed	36	0.6	20	15	1	T	T	T	3
1 cup = 245 gms. (8 1/2 oz.)					2.4%				
Skimmed (fortified with 2% nonfat milk solids added)	42	0.7	23	18	1	T	T	T	(3)[a]
1 cup = 246 gms. (8 1/2 oz.)					2.1%				
Skimmed, partially (1% fat) (with 2% nonfat milk solids added)	51	0.8	23	18	10	5	3	T	(5)[a]
1 cup = 246 gms. (8 1/2 oz.)					19.6%	9.8%	5.9%		
Skimmed, partially (2% fat) (with 2% nonfat milk solids added)	58	1.0	23	17	19	10	7	T	(7)[a]
1 cup = 246 gms. (8 1/2 oz.)					33.3%	18.1%	12.1%		
Canned									
Condensed, sweetened	321	5.4	210	35	76	40	29	T	(22)[a]
1 cup = 306 gms. (10 1/2 oz.)					23.8%	12.3%	9.0%		
Evaporated, unsweetened	137	2.3	38	30	69	35	26	T	(22)[a]
1 cup = 252 gms. (8 3/4 oz.)					50.6%	25.7%	19.3%		
Buttermilk (cultured from skim milk)	36	0.6	20	15	1	T	T	T	(3)[a]
1 cup = 245 gms. (8 1/2 oz.)					2.4%				
Dry, nonfat powdered									
Diluted (1 1/3 cup per quart)									
1 cup = 245 gms. (8 1/2 oz.)	33	0.6	18	14	T	T	T	T	(3)[a]
Undiluted									
1 cup = 68 gms. (2 1/3 oz.)	363	6.0	203	153	6	T	T	T	(33)[a]
Milk, goat's									
Whole	67	1.1	18	14	35	18	9	T	(11)[a]
1 cup = 244 gms. (8 1/2 oz.)					52.4%	26.3%	13.1%		

*See page 283 for abbreviations and symbols.

[a]Derived from *U.S.D.A. Handbook No. 8.*

[b]From Fetcher *et al.*

[c]Value for medium cream used.

[d]Derived from light cream.

[e]Double the value of skim milk.

TABLE XIII: COMPOSITION OF BREAD, ROLLS, AND PASTAS 3 1/2 Ounces (100 Grams)*

	TC	EE miles	C cal	P cal	F cal	S cal	M cal	PU cal	Chol. mg.
Bread									
French or Vienna, enriched	290	4.8	220	36	27	6	15	4	(3)
1 loaf = 454 gms. (16 oz.)					9.3%	2.0%	5.3%	1.3%	
Italian, enriched	276	4.6	226	36	7	T	2	4	(3)
1 loaf = 454 gms. (16 oz.)							0.6%	1.3%	
Raisin									
1 loaf = 454 gms. (16 oz.)	262	4.4	214	26	25	6	15	4	(3)
4 slices = 100 gms. (3 1/2 oz.)					9.5%	2.2%	5.8%	1.4%	
Rye									
American									
1 loaf = 454 gms. (16 oz.)	243	4.0	208	36	10	–	–	–	(3)
4 slices = 100 gms. (3 1/2 oz.)					4.1%				
Pumpernickel	246	4.1	212	36	11	–	–	–	(3)
1 loaf = 454 gms. (16 oz.)					4.5%				
White, enriched									
Firm-crumb type									
1 loaf (34 slices) =	275	4.6	200	34	31	7	18	4	(3)
907 gms. (32 oz.)					11.2%	2.6%	6.6%	1.3%	
Soft-crumb type									
1 loaf (24 slices) =	269	4.5	202	35	29	7	16	4	(3)
680 gms. (24 oz.)					10.8%	2.4%	5.9%	1.5%	
Whole wheat									
1 loaf (16 slices) =	241	4.0	197	36	23	4	12	4	(3)
454 gms. (16 oz.)					9.5%	1.5%	4.7%	1.5%	
Bread Crumbs, dry, grated									
1 cup = 100 gms. (3 1/2 oz.)	390	6.5	292	52	45	9	18	9	(3)
					11.5%	2.3%	4.6%	2.3%	
Biscuits									
Pillsbury fresh-dough products									
Buttermilk	254	4.2	182	26	38	11	22	4	3
10 biscuits = 229 gms. (8 oz.)					15.0%	4.3%	8.6%	1.6%	
Butter Tastin'	338	5.6	158	21	155	46	93	15	2
					45.8%	13.7%	27.5%	4.4%	
Country style	252	4.2	182	25	37	11	22	4	2
10 biscuits = 229 gms. (8 oz.)					14.7%	4.4%	8.7%	1.6%	
Extra-light buttermilk	253	4.2	170	29	50	14	30	5	4
10 biscuits = 229 gms. (8 oz.)					19.8%	5.5%	11.9%	2.0%	
Flaky baking powder	331	5.5	156	25	149	44	90	14	3
					45.0%	13.3%	27.2%	4.2%	
Flaky buttermilk	347	5.8	154	25	167	50	100	16	4
					48.1%	14.4%	28.8%	4.6%	
Hungry Jack buttermilk	266	4.3	170	28	60	18	36	6	4
10 biscuits = 271 gms. (1/2 oz.)					22.6%	6.8%	13.5%	2.3%	
Kentucky-style light buttermilk	337	5.6	156	26	149	45	90	14	4
					44.2%	13.4%	26.7%	4.2%	
Oven-ready	251	4.2	181	25	37	11	22	4	2
					14.7%	4.4%	8.8%	1.6%	
Crackers									
Graham									
4 crackers (2 1/2" square) =	384	6.4	293	32	85	(19)	(53)	(9)	(3)
28 gms. (1 oz.)					22.1%	(4.8%)	(13.8%)	(2.4%)	
Saltine	433	7.2	286	36	108	24	68	12	(3)
4 crackers = 11 gms. (1/3 oz.)					24.9%	5.5%	15.6%	2.7%	

TABLE XIII (continued)

	TC	EE miles	C cal	P cal	F cal	S cal	M cal	PU cal	Chol. mg.
Doughnuts, cake type									
1 doughnut = 32 gms. (1 1/6 oz.)	391	6.5	205	18	167 42.7%	38 9.8%	102 25.6%	12 3.1%	83a
Macaroni	369	6.2	30	50	11 2.9%	T	T	T	(T)
Pizza Dough with Sauce	173	2.9	125	24	23 13.3%	7 4.0%	14 8.1%	2 1.2%	1
Pretzels	390	6.5	304	39	40 10.2%	9 2.2%	25 6.4%	4 1.1%	(3)
Rolls and Buns									
Commercial									
Partially baked 1 roll = 28 gms. (1 oz.)	299	5.0	202	32	61 20.4%	14 4.8%	36 12.0%	7 2.4%	(3)
Ready-to-serve hard rolls 1 roll = 50 gms. (1 3/4 oz.)	312	5.2	238	39	29 9.3%	7 2.2%	17 5.4%	3 1.1%	(3)
Plain or cloverleaf (pan rolls) 1 roll = 28 gms. (1 oz.)	298	5.0	212	33	50 16.7%	12 3.9%	30 9.8%	6 2.0%	(1)
Dinner Rolls									
Pillsbury fresh-dough products									
Butterflake 12 rolls = 229 gms. (8 oz.)	283	4.7	168	27	82 29.0%	24 8.5%	50 17.7%	8 2.8%	31
Crescent 12 rolls = 229 gms. (8 oz.)	330	5.5	155	22	148 44.8%	44 13.3%	88 26.7%	14 4.2%	14
Hungry Jack, hot	296	4.9	167	27	95 32.1%	29 9.8%	57 19.3%	9 3.0%	16
Parkerhouse	265	4.4	178	26	54 20.3%	16 6.0%	32 12.1%	5 1.9%	22
Snowflake	296	4.9	19	27	95 32.1%	29 9.8%	57 19.3%	9 3.0%	2-8
Sweet Rolls									
Bakery	422	7.0	–	–	212 50.2%	63 14.9%	–	18 4.3%	70
Packaged	316	5.3	–	–	82 25.9%	18 5.7%	–	9 2.8%	70
Pillsbury soft-dough products									
Almond Danish	362	6.0	191	22	151 41.7%	45 12.4%	91 25.1%	15 4.1%	10
Caramel Danish 8 rolls = 343 gms. (12 oz.)	376	6.3	190	21	167 44.4%	39 10.4%	78 20.7%	16 4.3%	12
Cinnamon Danish	353	5.9	203	19	133 37.7%	40 11.3%	80 22.7%	14 4.0%	10
Cinnamon with icing 8 rolls = 271 gms. (9.5 oz.)	353	5.9	198	19	137 38.8%	41 11.6%	82 23.2%	14 4.0%	4
Orange Danish	354	5.9	196	18	140 39.5%	41 11.6%	84 23.7%	14 4.0%	10
Swirls									
Pillsbury fresh-dough products									
Caramel	364	6.1	236	18	111 30.5%	33 9.1%	67 18.4%	11 3.0%	4-7
Cinnamon	364	6.1	236	18	111 30.5%	33 9.1%	67 18.4%	11 3.0%	4-7
Orange	364	6.1	236	18	111 30.5%	33 9.1%	67 18.4%	11 3.0%	4-7
Spaghetti	369	6.2	301	50	11	T	T	T	(T)

*See page 283 for abbreviations and symbols.

TABLE XIV: **COMPOSITION OF COMMERCIAL SAUCES AND SALAD DRESSINGS 3 1/2 Ounces (100 Grams)***

	TC	*EE miles*	*C cal*	*P cal*	*F cal*	*S cal*	*M cal*	*PU cal*	*Chol. mg.*
Barbecue Sauce									
1 cup = 250 gms. (8 3/4 oz.)	91	1.5	30	5	61	6	18	33	0
1 tbsp = 15 gms. (1/2 oz.)					67.0%	6.4%	19.3%	36.4%	
Horseradish, prepared									
1 cup = 258 gms. (9 oz.)	38	0.6	37	4	2	T	T	T	0
					5.3%				
Mayonnaise, Hellmann's									
1 tbsp = 15 gms. (1/2 oz.)	720	12.0	6	4	698	110	261	320	50
					96.9%	15.3%	36.2%	44.4%	
Mustard									
1 tbsp = 15 gms. (1/2 oz.)	72	1.2	23	14	33	(5)	(12)	(15)	T
					45.8%	(7.2%)	(17.1%)	(21.0%)	
Salad Dressings, commercial									
Blue and Roquefort cheese									
Regular	504	8.4	27	16	462	97	97	221	27a
1 tbsp = 15 gms. (1/2 oz.)					91.6%	19.2%	19.2%	43.9%	
Low-fat (approximately 5 cal. per 1 tsp.)	76	1.3	15	10	52	26	18	T	(3)a
1 tbsp = 15 gms. (1/2 oz.)					68.4%	34.3%	23.6%		
Low-fat (approximately 1 cal. per 1 tsp.)	19	0.3	5	5	10	T	T	T	(T)
1 tbsp = 15 gms. (1/2 oz.)					51.0%				
French									
Regular	410	6.8	65	2	344	62	71	177	0
1 tbsp = 16 gms. (1/2 oz.)					83.9%	15.1%	17.3%	43.2%	
Low-fat (approximately 5 cal. per 1 tbsp)	96	1.6	58	1	38	9	9	18	0
1 tbsp = 15 gms. (1/2 oz.)					39.6%	9.4%	9.4%	19.8%	
Low-fat (approximately 1 cal. per 1 tsp)	10	0.2	7	1	2	T	T	T	0
1 tbsp = 15 gms. (1/2 oz.)					20.0%				
Italian									
Regular	552	9.2	26	7	530	88	115	279	0
1 tbsp = 15 gms. (1/2 oz.)					96.0%	16.0%	20.8%	49.6%	
Low-calorie (approximately 2 cal. per 1 tsp)	50	0.8	10	1	41	9	9	18	0
1 tbsp = 15 gms. (1/2 oz.)					82.0%	18.0%	18.0%	36.0%	
Russian	494	8.2	38	7	449	80	97	230	0
1 tbsp = 15 gms. (1/2 oz.)					90.8%	16.2%	19.6%	46.6%	
Thousand-island									
Regular	502	8.4	57	3	444	80	97	221	0
1 tbsp = 15 gms. (1/2 oz.)					69.6%	15.9%	19.3%	44.0%	
Low-calorie (approximately 10 cal. per 1 tsp)	180	3.0	58	3	121	18	26	62	0
1 tbsp = 16 gms. (1/2 oz.)					67.2%	10.0%	14.4%	34.4%	
Tartar Sauce, Hellmann's									
1 tbsp = 15 gm.s (1/2 oz.)	520	8.7	8	3	500	80	186	229	T
					96.2%	15.4%	35.8%	44.0%	
Vinegar, cider									
1 tbsp = 15 gms. (1/2 oz.)	14	0.2	14	T	0	0	0	0	0
Worcestershire Sauce, French's									
1 tbsp = 15 gms. (1/2 oz.)	40	0.7	32	2	2	T	T	T	0
					4.2%				

*See page 283 for abbreviations and symbols.

TABLE XV: **COMPOSITION OF SOUPS (CAMPBELL SOUP COMPANY PRODUCTS) 3 1/2 Ounces (100 Grams)***

	TC	*EE miles*	*C cal*	*P cal*	*F cal*	*S cal*	*M cal*	*PU cal*	*Chol. mg.*
Heat-Processed									
Asparagus, cream of	70	1.2	38	8	25	14	–	5	(1-6)
					35.7%	20.0%		7.1%	
Bean with bacon	133	2.2	68	27	38	10	–	10	(1-6)
					28.6%	7.5%		7.5%	
Beef	87	1.4	37	32	18	7	–	T	(1-6)
					20.7%	8.0%			
Beef broth	22	0.4	8	14	0	0	–	0	(1-6)
Beef noodle	58	1.0	29	13	17	6	–	2	6
					29.3%	10.3%		3.4%	
Black bean	80	1.3	49	19	13	1	–	6	(1-6)
					16.3%	1.3%		7.5%	
Celery, cream of	66	1.1	26	5	35	11	–	12	(1-6)
					53.0%	16.7%		18.2%	
Cheddar cheese	125	2.1	34	16	69	29	–	17	(1-6)
					55.2%	23.2%		13.6%	
Chicken broth	36	0.6	3	30	9	3	–	3	(1-6)
					25.0%	8.3%		8.3%	
Chicken, cream of	76	1.3	25	11	40	11	–	9	(1-6)
					52.6%	14.5%		11.8%	
Chicken gumbo	49	0.8	29	9	10	2	–	3	(1-6)
					20.4%	4.1%		6.1%	
Chicken 'n Dumplings	83	1.4	17	23	43	10	–	12	(1-6)
					51.8%	12.0%		14.5%	
Chicken noodle	55	0.9	29	12	14	3	–	3	5
					25.5%	5.5%		5.5%	
Chicken Noodle-O's	59	1.0	32	12	15	4	–	4	5
					25.4%	6.8%		6.8%	
Chicken with rice	43	0.7	20	11	12	3	–	3	(1-6)
					27.9%	7.0%		7.0%	
Chicken & Stars	50	0.8	24	14	12	3	–	3	(1-6)
					24.0%	6.0%		6.0%	
Chicken vegetable	60	1.0	30	14	16	3	–	4	(1-6)
					26.7%	5.0%		6.7%	
Chili beef	131	2.2	73	25	33	15	–	1	(1-6)
					25.2%	11.5%		0.8%	
Clam chowder	63	1.1	37	8	19	2	–	9	(1-6)
					30.2%	3.2%		14.3%	
Consommé	28	0.5	9	20	0	0	–	0	(1-6)
Golden mushroom	70	1.2	27	12	32	11	–	5	(1-6)
					45.7%	15.7%		7.1%	
Green pea	116	1.9	74	28	14	9	–	1	(1-6)
					12.1%	7.8%		0.9%	
Hot-dog bean	153	2.6	7.4	30	48	15	–	9	(1-6)
					31.4%	9.8%		5.9%	
Ministrone	72	1.2	37	13	22	4	–	10	(1-6)
					30.6%	5.6%		13.9%	
Mushroom, cream of	115	1.9	30	7	78	26	–	30	1
					67.8%	22.6%		26.1%	
Noodles and ground beef	80	1.3	32	14	33	14	–	1	(1-6)
					41.3%	17.5%		1.3%	
Onion	37	0.6	12	12	13	5	–	T	(1-6)
					35.1%	13.5%			
Oyster stew	57	0.9	21	7	29	17	–	1	(1-6)
					50.9%	29.8%		1.8%	

TABLE XV (continued)

	TC	*EE miles*	*C cal*	*P cal*	*F cal*	*S cal*	*M cal*	*PU cal*	*Chol. mg.*
Heat-Processed–continued									
Pepper pot	83	1.4	30	24	29	11	–	2	(1-6)
					34.9%	13.3%		2.4%	
Potato, cream of	59	1.0	36	4	17	7	–	4	(1-6)
					28.8%	11.9%		6.8%	
Scotch broth	74	1.2	34	18	22	11	–	3	(1-6)
					29.7%	14.9%		4.1%	
Split pea	141	2.3	76	41	23	10	–	2	(1-6)
					16.3%	7.1%		1.4%	
Tomato	69	1.2	49	6	14	2	–	6	3
					20.3%	2.9%		8.7%	
Tomato, bisque of	101	1.7	44	9	19	11	–	1	(1-6)
					18.8%	10.9%		1.0%	
Tomato rice, old-fashioned	87	1.5	59	6	23	5	–	10	(1-6)
					26.4%	5.7%		11.5%	
Turkey noodle	63	1.1	26	13	23	6	–	6	(1-6)
					36.5%	9.5%		9.5%	
Turkey vegetable	64	1.1	28	11	25	6	–	6	(1-6)
					39.1%	9.4%		9.4%	
Vegetable	68	1.1	44	11	13	3	–	5	3
					19.1%	4.4%		7.3%	
Vegetable beef	66	1.1	26	20	21	5	–	T	5
					31.8%	7.6%			
Vegetable beef stockpot	79	1.3	30	18	31	7	–	11	(1-6)
					39.2%	8.9%		13.9%	
Vegetable, old-fashioned	53	0.9	31	11	15	5	–	5	(1-6)
					28.3%	9.4%		9.4%	
Vegetarian vegetable	62	1.0	41	7	14	2	–	6	6
					22.6%	3.2%		9.7%	
Frozen									
Clam chowder	108	1.8	35	15	58	26	–	11	(1-6)
					53.7%	24.1%		10.2%	
Green pea with ham	109	1.8	59	30	21	7	–	2	(1-6)
					19.3%	6.4%		1.8%	
Oyster stew	102	1.7	28	18	57	32	–	3	(1-6)
					55.9%	31.4%		2.9%	
Potato, cream of	90	1.5	40	11	39	22	–	4	(1-6)
						24.4%		4.4%	
Shrimp, cream of	132	2.2	27	16	90	36	–	24	(1-6)
					8.2%	27.3%		18.2%	
Vegetable with beef, old-fashioned	68	1.1	26	22	21	9	–	3	(1-6)
					30.9%	13.2%		4.4%	

*See page 283 for abbreviations and symbols.

TABLE XVI: COMPOSITION OF VEGETABLES
3 1/2 Ounces (100 Grams) Edible Portion*#

	TC	EE miles	C cal	P cal	F cal	S cal	M cal	PU cal	Chol. mg.
Artichokes									
	28	0.5	22	6	2	(T)	(T)	(1)	0
					6.7%	(1.2%)	(1.2%)	(3.3%)	
Asparagus									
Raw	26	0.4	18	6	2	(T)	(T)	(1)	0
					6.3%	(1.2%)	(1.0%)	(3.2%)	
Canned	21	0.4	12	6	3	(1)	(1)	(2)	0
1 cup = 145 gms. (5 oz.)					15.9%	(3.5%)	(2.7%)	(8.3%)	
Frozen	24	0.4	14	8	2	(T)	(T)	(1)	0
					6.7%	(1.5%)	(1.1%)	(3.5%)	
Bamboo Shoots									
	27	0.4	19	6	2	(T)	(T)	(1)	0
					7.4%	(1.6%)	(1.3%)	(3.8%)	
Beans									
Lima									
Immature seeds	123	2.0	90	29	4	(1)	(1)	(2)	0
					3.3%	(0.7%)	(0.6%)	(1.6%)	
Immature seeds, canned, drained solids	96	1.5	74	19	2	(1)	(T)	(1)	0
1 cup = 170 gms. (6 oz.)					2.6%	(0.6%)		(1.3%)	
Immature seeds, baby limas,	122	2.0	94	26	2	(T)	(T)	(1)	0
frozen–Not Thawed					1.4%			(0.7%)	
Mature seeds	345	5.8	260	71	13	(2)	(3)	(7)	0
1/2 cup = 79 gms. (2 3/4 oz.)					3.8%	(0.6%)	(0.8%)	(2.0%)	
Mung	340	5.7	245	84	11	(2)	(2)	(6)	0
Mature seeds					3.2%	(0.7%)	(0.6%)	(1.7%)	
Pinto, calico or red Mexican									
Mature seeds	349	5.8	259	80	10	(2)	(2)	(5)	0
1 cup = 100 gms. (3 1/2 oz.)					2.9%	(0.4%)	(0.8%)	(1.5%)	
Red									
Mature seeds	343	5.7	252	78	13	(2)	(6)	(7)	0
1/2 cup = 100 gms. (3 1/2 oz.)					3.7%	(0.6%)	(0.8%)	(2.0%)	
Mature seeds, canned	90	1.5	67	20	3	T	(1)	(2)	0
1 cup = 255 gms. (9 oz.)					3.6%		(0.7%)	(1.7%)	
Snap, green									
Raw	32	0.5	25	5	2	T	T	(1)	0
1 cup = 100 gms. (3 1/2 oz.)					5.2%			(2.7%)	
Canned, drained solids	24	0.4	20	4	2	T	T	(1)	0
1 cup = 125 gms. (4 3/8 oz.)					6.6%			(3.6%)	
Frozen, not thawed	26	0.4	21	4	1	(T)	(T)	(T)	0
					3.2%				
Snap, yellow or wax									
Raw	27	0.4	21	4	2	(T)	(T)	(1)	0
1 cup = 100 gms. (3 1/2 oz.)					6.1%			(3.0%)	
Canned, drained solids	24	0.4	21	5	2	(T)	(T)	(1)	0
1 cup = 125 gms. (4 3/8 oz.)					10.4%			(5.0%)	
Frozen	28	0.5	23	4	1	(T)	(T)	(T)	0
					3.0%				
White									
Mature seeds	340	5.7	249	78	13	(2)	(6)	(7)	0
1/2 cup = 100 gms. (3 1/2 oz.)					3.9%	(0.6%)	(1.8%)	(2.0%)	
Mature seeds, canned with pork and tomato sauce	122	2.0	77	21	22	(8)	(8)	(T)	T
1 cup = 225 gms. (9 oz.)					18.0%	(6.6%)	(6.6%)		

TABLE XVI (continued)

	TC	*EE miles*	*C cal*	*P cal*	*F cal*	*S cal*	*M cal*	*PU cal*	*Chol. mg.*
Beans, White—continued									
Mature seeds, canned with pork									
and sweet sauce	150	2.5	77	21	39	(17)	(17)	(T)	0
1 cup = 255 gms. (9 oz.)					26.0%	(11.3%)	(11.3%)		
Mature seeds, canned without pork	120	2.0	94	22	4	(1)	(1)	(2)	0
1 cup = 190 gms. (6 2/3 oz.)					3.3%	(0.5%)	(0.7%)	(1.7%)	
Beets									
Common red									
Raw	43	0.7	38	4	1	(T)	(T)	(T)	0
1 2" beet = 50 gms. (1 3/4 oz.)					1.9%				
Cooked, drained									
1 cup sliced or diced =	37	0.6	34	3	1	(T)	(T)	(T)	0
170 gms. (6 oz.)					2.2%				
Canned	34	0.6	30	2	1	(T)	(T)	(T)	0
1 cup = 246 gms. (8 1/2 oz.)					2.5%				
Beet Greens	24	0.4	16	5	2	(T)	(T)	(1)	0
					10.5%			(5.2%)	
Black-Eyed Peas (See Cowpeas)									
Broad Beans									
Immature seeds	105	1.8	72	29	3	(T)	(T)	(2)	0
					3.1%			(1.5%)	
Mature seeds	338	5.6	208	61	14	(2)	(3)	(7)	0
					4.2%	(0.6%)	(0.8%)	(2.1%)	
Broccoli									
Raw	32	0.5	21	9	2	(1)	(T)	(1)	0
					7.8%	(1.7%)		(3.8%)	
Cooked spears, boiled, drained	26	0.4	16	8	2	T	T	(1)	0
1 cup = 155 gms.					9.6%			(3.2%)	
Spears, frozen, not thawed	28	0.5	18	8	2	(T)	(T)	(1)	0
					6.0%			(3.0%)	
Brussels Sprouts									
Raw	45	0.8	30	12	3	(1)	(1)	(2)	0
					7.4%	(1.3%)	(1.2%)	(3.8%)	
Frozen, not thawed	36	0.6	26	8	2	(T)	(T)	(1)	0
					4.8%			(2.3%)	
Cabbage									
Common									
1 average head = 1135 gms. (4 oz.)									
1 cup shredded = 80 gms.	24	0.4	19	3	2	(T)	(T)	(1)	0
(2 3/4 oz.)					6.7%			(3.4%)	
Cooked	20	0.3	15	3	2	(T)	(T)	(1)	0
1 cup = 145 gms. (5 oz.)					8.4%			(4.0%)	
Chinese	14	0.2	11	3	1	(T)	(T)	(T)	0
1 cup cut = 75 gms. (2 2/3 oz.)					5.8%				
Spoon	16	0.3	10	4	2	(T)	(T)	(1)	0
					10.4%			(5.2%)	
Carrots									
Raw									
2 carrots = 100 gms. (3 1/2 oz.)	42	0.7	37	3	2	(T)	(T)	(1)	0
1 cup diced = 143 gms. (5 oz.)					4.0%			(2.0%)	
Canned	28	0.5	25	2	2	(T)	(T)	(1)	0
1 cup diced = 145 gms. (5 oz.)					5.0%			(3.0%)	

TABLE XVI (continued)

	TC	EE miles	C cal	P cal	F cal	S cal	M cal	PU cal	Chol. mg.
Cauliflower									
Raw									
1 average head = 908 gms. (32 oz.)	27	0.4	19	7	2 6.2%	(T)	(T)	(1) (3.1%)	0
Cooked 1 cup = 120 gms. (4 1/4 oz.)	22	0.4	15	6	2 9.1%	(T)	(T)	(1) (4.5%)	0
Frozen	22	0.4	15	5	2 7.6%	(T)	(T)	(1) (3.3%)	0
Celeriac Root	40	0.7	30	4	3 6.3%	(T)	(T)	(1) (3.1%)	0
Celery 1 stalk = 40 gms. (1 1/2 oz.) 1 cup chopped = 100 gms. (3 1/2 oz.)	17	0.3	14	2	1 4.9%	(T)	(T)	(T)	0
Chard, Swiss	25	0.4	16	6	3 10.0%	(T)	(T)	(1) (5.0%)	0
Chickpeas, mature seeds	360	6.0	248	71	40 11.2%	(T)	(17) (4.6%)	(17) (4.6%)	0
Chicory									
Witloof	15	0.3	11	2	1 5.6%	(T)	(T)	(T)	0
Greens	20	0.3	14	4	3 12.6%	(T)	(T)	(1) (6.3%)	0
Chives	28	0.5	21	4	3 9.0%	(T)	(T)	(1) (4.5%)	0
Collards									
Leaves	45	0.8	27	12	7 14.9%	(2) (3.4%)	(1) (2.6%)	(4) (7.7%)	0
Frozen, not thawed	32	0.5	21	8	3 10.5%	(1) (2.3%)	(1) (1.8%)	(2) (5.4%)	0
Corn									
Field, whole-grain mature	348	5.8	258	22	33 9.4%	T	8 2.4%	17 4.8%	0
Sweet									
edible portion of corn on the cob (55%)	96	1.6	79	9	8 8.7%	1 0.9%	2 2.3%	4 4.4%	0
Cooked, drained 1 cup = 168 gms. (5 9/10 oz.)	83	1.4	76	9	8 10.1%	1 1.0%	2 2.4%	4 5.4%	0
Canned, cream-style	82	1.4	71	5	5 6.1%	T	1 1.7%	3 3.2%	0
Canned, whole kernel 1 cup = 170 gms. (6 oz.)	66	1.1	56	5	5 7.6%	T	1 1.7%	2 3.2%	0
Frozen, not thawed	82	1.4	70	8	4 5.1%	T	1 1.4%	2 2.7%	0
Cowpeas									
Mature seeds	343	5.7	251	79	12 3.6%	(2) (0.5%)	(2) (0.7%)	(6) (1.8%)	0
Canned	70	1.2	50	17	2 3.6%	(T)	(T)	(1) (1.9%)	0
Frozen, not thawed	131	2.2	96	31	3 2.6%	(1) (T)	(1) (0.5%)	(2) (1.3%)	0

TABLE XVI (continued)

	TC	*EE miles*	*C cal*	*P cal*	*F cal*	*S cal*	*M cal*	*PU cal*	*Chol. mg.*
Cress, Garden	32	0.5	20	6	6 18.3%	(1) (4.1%)	(1) (3.1%)	(3) (9.4%)	0
Cucumbers 1 7 1/2″ by 2″ cuc. pared = 207 gms. (8 oz.)	15	0.3	12	2	1 5.6%	(T)	(T)	(T)	0
Dandelion Greens	45	0.8	33	7	6 13.0%	(1) (2.8%)	(1) (2.2%)	(3) (6.7%)	0
Dock	28	0.5	20	5	2 9.0%	(T)	(T)	(1) (4.6%)	0
Eggplant 1 eggplant = 514 gms. 1 cup cooked = 257 gms.	25	0.4	20	3	2 6.7%	(T)	(T)	(1) (3.3%)	0
Endive Curly and escarole	20	0.3	15	4	1 4.2%	(T)	(T)	(T)	0
French or Belgian (See Chicory, witloof)									
Garbanzos (See **Chickpeas**)									
Garlic Cloves	137	2.3	118	17	2 1.2%	(T)	(T)	(1) (0.6%)	0
Ginger Root, Fresh	49	0.8	36	4	8 17.1%	(2) (3.5%)	(3) (5.9%)	(4) (8.5%)	0
Horseradish	87	1.4	76	9	3 2.8%	(T)	(T)	(1) (1.4%)	0
Kale Raw	53	0.9	32	15	7 12.6%	(2) (2.8%)	(1) (2.1%)	(4) (6.6%)	0
Frozen	32	0.5	20	8	4 13.1%	(1) (2.7%)	(1) (2.2%)	(2) (6.8%)	0
Kohlrabi	29	0.5	24	5	1 2.9%	(T)	(T)	(T)	0
Leeks	52	0.8	40	5	2 4.8%	(T)	(T)	(1) (2.4%)	0
Lentils, mature seed	340	5.7	245	86	9 2.7%	(1) (0.4%)	(2) (0.5%)	(5) (1.4%)	0
Lettuce Butterhead (Boston) 1 average head = 220 gms. (7 3/4 oz.)	14	0.2	9	3	2 11.4%	(T)	(T)	(1) (6.3%)	0
Cos (romaine), dark green and white parts 1 cup (broken pieces) = 43 gms. (1 1/2 oz.)	18	0.3	12	3	2 13.9%	(T)	(T)	(1) (7.2%)	0

TABLE XVI (continued)

	TC	*EE* *miles*	*C* *cal*	*P* *cal*	*F* *cal*	*S* *cal*	*M* *cal*	*PU* *cal*	*Chol.* *mg.*
Lettuce—continued									
Crisp head (iceberg), New York or Great Lakes									
1 head 4 3/4" dia. = 454 gms. (1 lb)									
1 cup broken pieces = 76 gms. (2 2/3 oz.)	13	0.2	10	2	1 6.1%	(T)	(T)	(T)	0
Mushrooms									
Raw									
1 cup trimmed = 72 gms. (2 1/2 oz.)	28	0.5	16	7	2 9.0%	(T)	(T)	(1) (4.5%)	0
Canned 1 cup = 244 gms. (8 1/2 oz.)	17	0.3	9	5	1 4.9%	(T)	(T)	(T)	0
Mustard Greens									
Raw	31	0.5	20	7	4 13.5%	(1) (2.6%)	(1) (2.2%)	(2) (6.3%)	0
Frozen, not thawed	20	0.3	11	6	3 16.8%	(1) (3.3%)	(1) (2.8%)	(2) (8.5%)	0
Mustard Spinach (Indian mustard)	22	0.4	14	5	2 11.4%	(1) (2.5%)	(T)	(1) (5.7%)	0
New Zealand Spinach	19	0.3	11	5	2 13.2%	(1) (2.9%)	(T)	(1) (6.6%)	0
Okra									
Raw	36	0.6	27	6	2 7.0%	(1) (1.5%)	(T)	(1) (3.5%)	0
Frozen	39	0.6	32	6	1 2.1%	(T)	(T)	(T)	0
Onions									
Mature									
2 1/2" onion = 110 gms. (3 3/4 oz.)									
1 cup chopped = 172 gms. (6 oz.)	38	0.6	33	4	1 2.2%	(T)	(T)	(T)	0
Young green									
Bulb and white portion 6 onions = 50 gms. (1 3/4 oz.)	45	0.8	40	3	2 3.7%	(T)	(T)	(1) (1.8%)	0
Tops only	27	0.5	19	4	3 12.2%	(1) (2.6%)	(T)	(2) (6.1%)	0
Welsh	34	0.6	25	5	3 9.8%	(1) (2.1%)	(1) (1.6%)	(2) (4.9%)	0
Parsley									
1/4 cup chopped = 16 gms. (1/2 oz.)	44	0.7	30	9	5 11.4%	(1) (2.5%)	(1) (1.9%)	(2) (5.7%)	0
Parsnips									
1 med. parsnip = 100 gms. (3 1/2 oz.)	76	1.3	67	5	4 5.5%	(1) (1.2%)	(1) (0.9%)	(2) (2.7%)	0
Peas									
Edible, podded	53	0.9	49	12	2 3.2%	(T)	(T)	(1) (2.6%)	0
Green immature, shelled 1 cup = 136 gms. (4 3/4 oz.)	84	1.4	59	22	3 4.0%	(1) (0.9%)	(T)	(2) (2.0%)	0

TABLE XVI (continued)

	TC	*EE miles*	*C cal*	*P cal*	*F cal*	*S cal*	*M cal*	*PU cal*	*Chol. mg.*
Peas–continued									
Canned (Alaska, early, and June)	66	1.1	51	12	2	(T)	(T)	(1)	0
1 cup = 249 gms. (8 3/4 oz.)					3.8%			(1.9%)	
Canned, sweet	57	1.0	42	12	2	(T)	(T)	(1)	0
1 cup = 249 gms. (8 3/4 oz.)					4.4%			(2.2%)	
Frozen	73	1.2	52	19	2	(T)	(T)	(1)	0
					3.4%			(1.7%)	
Peppers									
Hot chili									
Green	37	0.6	32	3	2	(T)	(T)	(1)	0
1 tbsp = 15 gms.					4.5%			(2.2%)	
Red	93	1.5	64	9	19	(4)	(3)	(10)	0
					20.8%	(4.3%)	(3.5%)	(10.4%)	
Sweet									
Green									
1 pod = 74 gms. (2 1/2 oz.)	22	0.4	17	3	2	(T)	(T)	(1)	0
or 1/2 cup chopped					7.6%			(3.8%)	
Red	31	0.5	25	3	2	(T)	(T)	(1)	0
1 pod = 74 gms. (2 1/2 oz.)					8.1%			(4.0%)	
Pickles, dill, cucumber									
	11	0.2	8	2	2	0	0	0	0
					15.4%				
Fresh, bread and butter	73	1.2	64	2	2	0	0	0	0
					2.7%				
Sour	10	0.2	7	1	2	0	0	0	0
					16.7%				
Sweet	146	2.4	130	2	3	0	0	0	0
1 cup chopped = 172 gms. (6 oz.)					2.3%				
Pimientos, canned	27	0.4	21	2	4	(1)	(1)	(2)	0
					15.5%	(2.9%)	(2.4%)	(7.3%)	
Potato Chips									
Prepared in cottonseed oil	568	9.5	192	15	361	90	76	180	0
					63.6%	15.9%	13.4%	31.8%	
Potatoes									
Raw	76	1.3	69	8	1	(T)	(T)	(T)	0
1 average = 150 gms. (5 1/4 oz.)					1.1%				
1 cup diced = 164 gms. (5 3/4 oz.)									
Dehydrated mashed, dry form	364	6.0	339	20	5	(1)	(1)	(2)	0
					1.4%	(0.3%)	(0.2%)	(0.7%)	
Frozen, not thawed	73	1.2	70	3	T	(T)	(T)	(T)	0
Pumpkin									
Raw	26	0.4	23	3	1	T	T	T	0
					3.2%				
Canned	33	0.6	28	3	2	T	T	T	0
1 cup = 228 gms. (8 oz.)					7.6%				
Radishes									
4 small radishes = 40 gms. (1 1/3 oz.)									
1 cup sliced = 129 gms. (4 1/2 oz.)	17	0.3	14	3	1	(T)	(T)	(T)	0
					4.9%				
Relish									
Sour, pickled	19	0.3	10	2	8	0	0	0	0
					(39.5%)				

TABLE XVI (continued)

	TC	*EE miles*	*C cal*	*P cal*	*F cal*	*S cal*	*M cal*	*PU cal*	*Chol. mg.*
Relish–continued									
Sweet	138	2.3	121	1	5 3.6%	0	0	0	0
Rutabaga	46	0.8	40	3	1 1.8%	(T)	(T)	(T)	0
Salsify	45	0.7	64	7	5 11.2%	(1) (2.6%)	(1) (1.9%)	(2) (5.6%)	0
Sauerkraut, canned, solids and liquid 1 cup = 235 gms. (8 1/4 oz.)	18	0.3	14	2	2 8.9%	0	0	0	0
Shallots	72	1.2	60	6	1 1.2%	(T)	(T)	(T)	0
Spinach									
Raw									
1 cup chopped = 50 gms. (1 3/4 oz.)	26	0.4	15	8	3 10.2%	(T)	(T)	(1) (5.1%)	0
Canned 1 cup = 180 gms. (6 1/3 oz.)	19	0.3	11	5	4 18.7%	(1) (3.6%)	(1) (3.1%)	(2) (9.3%)	0
Frozen, not thawed	24	0.4	14	7	3 11.1%	(T)	(T)	(1) (5.5%)	0
Squash									
Summer									
Crookneck, straightneck, yellow	20	0.3	15	3	2 8.8%	(T)	(T)	(1) (4.4%)	0
Scallop varieties, white and pale green	21	0.4	18	2	1 4.0%	(T)	(T)	(T)	0
Zucchini and cocozelle	17	0.3	13	3	1 4.9%	(T)	(T)	(T)	0
Frozen, not thawed	21	0.4	17	3	1 4.0%	(T)	(T)	(T)	0
Winter									
Acorn	44	0.7	40	4	1 1.9%	(T)	(T)	(T)	0
Butternut	54	0.9	50	3	1 1.5%	(T)	(T)	(T)	0
Hubbard	39	0.6	34	3	3 6.8%	(T)	(T)	(1) (3.4%)	0
Frozen	38	0.6	33	3	3 7.0%	(T)	(T)	(1) (3.5%)	0
Succotash (corn and lima beans)									
Frozen, not thawed	97	1.3	78	10	3 3.4%	(1) (0.7%)	(T)	(1) (1.7%)	0
Sweet Potatoes									
Raw	114	1.9	106	5	4 3.1%	(1) (0.6%)	(1) (0.5%)	(2) (1.5%)	0
Dehydrated	379	6.3	363	12	5 1.4%	(1) (0.3%)	(1) (0.2%)	(2) (0.7%)	0
Tomatoes									
Green	24	0.4	18	3	2 7.0%	(T)	(T)	(1) (3.5%)	0

TABLE XVI (continued)

	TC	*EE miles*	*C cal*	*P cal*	*F cal*	*S cal*	*M cal*	*PU cal*	*Chol. mg.*
Tomatoes–continued									
Ripe	22	0.4	17	3	2	(T)	(T)	(1)	0
1 3" tomato = 200 gms. (7 oz.)					7.6%			(3.8%)	
Ripe, canned	21	0.4	15	2	2	(T)	(T)	(1)	0
1 cup = 241 gms. (8 1/2 oz.)					8.0%			(4.0%)	
Tomato Catchup									
1 tbsp = 15 gms. (1/2 oz.)	106	1.8	91	5	3	(1)	(T)	(2)	0
					2.8%	(0.6%)		(1.4%)	
Tomato Chili Sauce									
1 cup = 286 gms. (10 oz.)	104	1.8	88	6	3	(T)	(T)	(1)	0
					2.4%			(1.7%)	
Tomato Paste, canned									
1 cup = 257 gms. (9 oz.)	82	1.4	66	8	3	(1)	(1)	(2)	0
					4.1%	(0.8%)	(0.6%)	(2.0%)	
Tomato Purée, canned									
1 cup = 257 gms. (9 oz.)	39	0.6	32	4	2	(T)	(T)	(1)	0
					4.3%			(2.1%)	
Tomato Juice, canned									
1 cup = 243 gms. (8 1/2 oz.)	19	0.3	15	2	1	(T)	(T)	(T)	0
					4.2%				
Turnips									
1 med. turnip = 100 gms.	30	0.5	25	3	2	(T)	(T)	(1)	0
(3 1/2 oz.)					5.6%			(2.3%)	
Turnip Greens									
Raw	28	0.5	18	7	2	(T)	(T)	(1)	0
					9.0%			(4.5%)	
Canned	18	0.3	11	4	2	(T)	(T)	(1)	0
					13.9%			(6.9%)	
Frozen, not thawed	23	0.4	14	6	2	(T)	(T)	(1)	0
					10.9%			(5.4%)	
Vegetables, mixed									
Frozen, not thawed	65	1.0	50	8	2	(T)	(T)	(1)	0
					3.8%			(1.9%)	
Watercress									
1 cup chopped = 36 gms.	19	0.3	11	5	2	(T)	(T)	(1)	0
(1 1/4 oz.)					13.2%			(7.6%)	
Yam, tuber	101	1.7	94	6	2	(T)	(T)	(1)	0
					1.7%			(0.8%)	
Yambean, tuber	55	0.9	52	4	2	(T)	(T)	(1)	0
					3.0%			(1.5%)	

*See page 283 for abbreviations and symbols.

#Imputed values for saturated fat, monounsaturated fat, monounsaturated fat, and polyunsaturated fat are calculated values in U.S.D.A. *Handbook No. 8* for soybeans (dry and immature seeds).

TABLE XVII: COMPOSITION OF BERRIES, FRUIT, AND MELONS
3 1/2 Ounces (100 Grams) Edible Portion*#

	TC	EE miles	C cal	P cal	F cal	S cal	M cal	PU cal	Chol. mg.
Apples									
1 cup diced = 150 gms. (5 1/4 oz.)									
1 apple = 163 gms. (5 3/4 oz.)									
Edible portion (92%) = 150 gms. (5 1/4 oz.)	58	1.0	52	1	5 8.6%	(T)	(T)	(T)	0
Frozen, sliced, sweetened	93	1.6	88	1	1 0.9%	(T)	(T)	(T)	0
Dehydrated	353	5.9	332	5	16.8 4.8%	(T)	(T)	(T)	0
Apple Butter									
1 cup = 180 gms. (6 1/3 oz.)	186	3.1	169	1	7 3.6%	(T)	(T)	(T)	0
Apple Juice									
1 cup = 248 gms. (8 3/4 oz.)	47	0.8	47	0	(T)	(T)	(T)	(T)	0
Applesauce, canned									
Sweetened 1 cup = 255 gms. (9 oz.)	91	1.3	90	0	1 0.9%	(T)	(T)	(T)	0
Unsweetened 1 cup = 244 gms. (8 1/2 oz.)	41	0.7	39	1	2 4.1%	(T)	(T)	(T)	0
Apricots									
1 cup (halves) = 142 gms. (5 oz.)	51	0.8	46	3	2 3.3%	(T)	(T)	(T)	0
Canned									
Water pack 1 cup = 250 gms. (8 3/4 oz.)	38	0.6	35	2	1 2.2%	(T)	(T)	(T)	0
Juice pack 1 cup = 250 gms. (8 3/4 oz.)	54	0.9	49	3	2 3.0%	(T)	(T)	(T)	0
Heavy sirup 1 cup = 259 gms. (9 oz.)	86	1.4	83	2	1 1.0%	(T)	(T)	(T)	0
Dehydrated	332	5.5	305	19	8 2.5%	(T)	(T)	(T)	0
Dried 1 cup = 150 gms. (5 1/4 oz.)	260	4.3	239	17	4 1.6%	(T)	(T)	(T)	0
Frozen, sweetened	98	1.6	90	0	1 0.8%	(T)	(T)	(T)	0
Apricot Nectar									
1 cup = 251 gms. (8 1/2 oz.)	57	1.0	57	1	1 1.5%	(T)	(T)	(T)	0
Avocados									
1 cup cubed = 150 gms. (5 1/4 oz.)									
Edible portion = 75% of whole avocado	167	2.3	23	7	137 82.0%	20 12.0%	58 35.0%	16 9.9%	0
Bananas									
1 banana = 150 gms. (5 1/4 oz.)									
1 cup sliced = 180 gms. (6 1/4 oz.)									
1 cup mashed = 268 gms. (9 3/8 oz.)	85	1.4	80	4	2 2.0%	(T)	(T)	(T)	0
Blackberries									
1 cup = 144 gms. (5 1/4 oz.)	58	1.0	46	4	7 12.1%	(T)	(T)	(T)	0
Canned									
Water pack 1 cup = 250 gms. (8 3/4 oz.)	40	0.7	32	3	5 12.5%	(T)	(T)	(T)	0

TABLE XVII (continued)

	TC	*EE miles*	*C cal*	*P cal*	*F cal*	*S cal*	*M cal*	*PU cal*	*Chol. mg.*
Blackberries—continued									
Juice pack	54	0.9	44	3	7	(T)	(T)	(T)	0
1 cup = 240 gms. (8 1/2 oz.)					12.4%				
Blackberry Juice									
Canned, unsweetened	37	0.6	31	1	5	(T)	(T)	(T)	0
1 cup = 246 gms. (8 1/2 oz.)					13.6%				
Blueberries									
1 cup = 144 gms. (5 1/4 oz.)	62	1.0	55	2	4	(T)	(T)	(T)	0
					6.8%				
Canned, water pack	39	0.6	35	2	2	(T)	(T)	(T)	0
1 cup = 250 gms. (8 3/4 oz.)					4.3%				
Frozen, not thawed, unsweetened	55	0.9	49	2	4	(T)	(T)	(T)	0
					7.6%				
Boysenberries									
Canned, water pack	36	0.4	33	2	1	(T)	(T)	(T)	0
1 cup = 250 gms. (8 3/4 oz.)					2.3%				
Frozen, not thawed, unsweetened	48	0.8	41	4	2	(T)	(T)	(T)	0
					5.2%				
Breadfruit	103	1.7	94	6	2	(T)	(T)	(T)	0
					2.4%				
Cherries									
Sour, red									
1 cup pitted = 160 gms.	58	1.0	52	6	2	(T)	(T)	(T)	0
(5 1/2 oz.)					4.3%				
Sweet									
1 cup pitted = 160 gms.	70	1.2	63	4	4	(T)	(T)	(T)	0
(5 1/2 oz.)					3.6%				
Canned pitted									
Sour red									
Water pack	43	0.7	38	3	2	(T)	(T)	(T)	0
1 cup = 207 gms. (7 1/4 oz.)					3.9%				
Heavy sirup	89	1.5	84	3	2	(T)	(T)	(T)	0
1 cup = 260 gms. (9 oz.)					1.9%				
Sweet									
Water pack	48	0.8	43	3	2	(T)	(T)	(T)	0
Edible portion with pits (95%)					3.5%				
Heavy sirup									
1 cup = 200 gms. (7 oz.)	81	1.3	76	3	2	(T)	(T)	(T)	0
Edible portion with pits (95%)					2.1%				
Frozen, not thawed	55	0.9	43	3	3	(T)	(T)	(T)	0
Sour red, unsweetened					6.1%				
Crabapple	68	1.0	64	1	2	(T)	(T)	(T)	0
					3.7%				
Cranberries									
Scant 1 cup = 100 gms.	46	0.8	39	1	6	(T)	(T)	(T)	0
(3 1/2 oz.)					12.7%				
Cranberry-Juice Cocktail (about 1/3 cranberry juice)									
1 cup = 250 gms. (8 3/4 oz.)	65	1.1	65	(T)	1	(T)	(T)	(T)	0
					1.3%				
Cranberry Sauce									
1 cup = 277 gms. (9 2/3 oz.)	146	2.4	135	(T)	2	(T)	(T)	(T)	0
					1.1%				

TABLE XVII (continued)

	TC	*EE miles*	*C cal*	*P cal*	*F cal*	*S cal*	*M cal*	*PU cal*	*Chol. mg.*
Cranberry-Orange Relish									
	178	3.0	164	1	3 1.9%	(T)	(T)	(T)	0
Currants	52	0.9	45	5	1 1.6%	(T)	(T)	(T)	0
Dates, natural									
1 cup pitted = 178 gms. (6 1/4 oz.)	274	4.6	262	7	4 1.5%	(T)	(T)	(T)	0
Elderberries									
	72	1.2	59	9	4 5.8%	(T)	(T)	(T)	0
Figs									
3 small figs = 112 gms. (4 oz.)	80	1.3	73	1	2 3.1%	(T)	(T)	(T)	0
Canned									
Water pack 1 cup = 250 gms. (8 3/4 oz.)	48	0.8	41	2	2 3.5%	(T)	(T)	(T)	0
Heavy sirup 1 cup = 258 gms. (9 oz.)	84	1.4	80	2	2 1.9%	(T)	(T)	(T)	0
Dried 1 cup = 170 gms. (6 oz.)	274	4.6	249	5	1 0.4%	(T)	(T)	(T)	0
Fruit Cocktail									
Canned									
Water pack 1 cup = 250 gms. (8 3/4 oz.)	37	0.6	35	1	1 2.3%	(T)	(T)	(T)	0
Heavy sirup 1 cup = 250 gms. (9 oz.)	76	1.3	71	1	1 1.1%	(T)	(T)	(T)	0
Gooseberries									
1 cup = 150 gms. (5 1/4 oz.)	39	0.7	35	3	2 4.3%	(T)	(T)	(T)	0
Canned									
Water pack	26	0.4	24	2	1 3.2%	(T)	(T)	(T)	0
Heavy sirup	90	1.5	87	2	1 0.8%	(T)	(T)	(T)	0
Grape Juice									
Canned or bottled 1 cup = 253 gms. (8 1/2 oz.)	66	1.1	65	(T)	(T)	(T)	(T)	(T)	0
Frozen concentrate, sweetened (diluted with 3 parts water by volume)	53	0.8	52	(T)	(T)	(T)	(T)	(T)	0
Grapefruit									
1 cup = 200 gms. (7 oz.)	41	0.7	38	2	1 2.0%	(T)	(T)	(T)	0
Canned segments, water pack 1 cup = 250 gms. (8 3/4 oz.)	30	0.5	27	2	1 2.8%	(T)	(T)	(T)	0
Grapefruit Juice									
Canned, unsweetened 1 cup = 247 gms. (8 3/4 oz.)	41	0.7	38	2	1 2.0%	(T)	(T)	(T)	0
Frozen concentrate, unsweetened (diluted with 3 parts water by volume) 1 cup = 247 gms. (8 3/4 oz.)	41	0.8	36	2	1 1.7%	(T)	(T)	(T)	0
Grapefruit and Orange Juice Blended									
Canned, unsweetened 1 cup = 250 gms. (8 3/4 oz.)	43	0.7	40	2	2 4.0%	(T)	(T)	(T)	0

TABLE XVII (continued)

	TC	*EE miles*	*C cal*	*P cal*	*F cal*	*S cal*	*M cal*	*PU cal*	*Chol. mg.*
Grapes									
American (slipskin) 1 cup = 153 gms. (5 1/4 oz.)	69	1.2	56	4	8 12.1%	(T)	(T)	(T)	0
European (adherent skin) 1 cup = 160 gms. (5 1/2 oz.)	67	1.1	62	2	2 3.8%	(T)	(T)	(T)	0
Kumquats									
5 or 6 kumquats (fresh only) 100 gms. (3 1/2 oz.)	65	1.1	62	3	1 1.3%	(T)	(T)	(T)	0
Lemons, peeled fruit									
1 lemon = 110 gms. (3 3/4 oz.)									
1 lemon (pulp only) = 73 gms. (2 1/2 oz.)	27	0.4	20	4	2 (9.6%)	(T)	(T)	(T)	0
Lemon Juice									
Fresh 1 cup = 244 gms. (8 1/2 oz.)	25	0.4	23	2	(T)	(T)	(T)	(T)	0
Canned or bottled 1 cup = 250 gms. (8 3/4 oz.)	23	0.4	21	1	(T)	(T)	(T)	(T)	0
Lemonade, frozen concentrate (diluted with 4 1/3 parts water by volume) 1 cup = 248 gms. (8 3/4 oz.)	44	0.7	43	(T)	(T)	(T)	(T)	(T)	0
Limes									
2 limes (edible portion) = 100 gms. (3 1/2 oz.)	28	0.5	24	2	2 6.0%	(T)	(T)	(T)	0
Lime Juice, fresh									
1 cup = 246 gms. (3 1/2 oz.)	26	0.4	25	1	(T)	(T)	(T)	(T)	0
Loganberries									
1 cup = 144 gms. (5 1/4 oz.)	62	1.0	54	3	5 8.1%	(T)	(T)	(T)	0
Canned									
Water pack	40	0.7	34	2	3 8.4%	(T)	(T)	(T)	0
Juice pack	54	0.9	51	2	4 7.4%	(T)	(T)	(T)	0
Heavy sirup	89	1.5	84	2	3 3.4%	(T)	(T)	(T)	0
Loquats	48	0.8	45	1	2 3.5%	(T)	(T)	(T)	0
Mangoes									
1 whole mango = 200 gms. (7 oz.)									
Edible portion = 133 gms. (4 2/3 oz.)	66	1.1	60	2	3 5.1%	(T)	(T)	(T)	0
Muskmelons (Cantaloupes)									
1 5" dia. whole = 750 gms. (26 oz.)									
Edible portion (50%) = 375 gms. (13 oz.)	30	0.5	26	3	2 5.6%	(T)	(T)	(T)	0
Nectarines									
Edible portion 92% of fresh-fruit weight	64	1.0	62	2	(T)	(T)	(T)	(T)	0

TABLE XVII (continued)

	TC	*EE miles*	*C cal*	*P cal*	*F cal*	*S cal*	*M cal*	*PU cal*	*Chol. mg.*
Olives, pickled									
Green									
9 to 12 olives (with pits) = 48 gms. (1 3/4 oz.) Edible portion = 40 gms. (1 1/3 oz.)	116	1.9	4	5	106 91.3%	17 14.5%	84 72.2%	8 7.2%	0
Ripe									
10 to 15 olives (with pits) = 50 gms. (1 3/4 oz.) Edible portion = 40 gms. (1 1/3 oz.)	129	2.2	10	4	116 89.9%	17 13.0%	84 64.9%	8 6.5%	0
Orange Juice									
Fresh 1 cup = 248 gms. (8 3/4 oz.)	45	0.8	41	2	2 3.7%	(T)	(T)	(T)	0
Canned, unsweetened 1 cup = 248 gms. (8 3/4 oz.)	48	0.8	44	2	2 3.5%	(T)	(T)	(T)	0
Frozen concentrate, unsweetened (diluted with 3 parts water by volume) 1 cup = 249 gms. (8 3/4 oz.)	45	0.8	42	2	1 1.9%	(T)	(T)	(T)	0
Oranges									
1 orange, whole = 180 gms. (6 1/4 oz.) Edible portion (73%) = 130 gms. (4 1/2 oz.)	50	0.8	45	3	2 3.4%	(T)	(T)	(T)	0
Papayas									
1 cup (cubes) = 182 gms. (6 3/8 oz.)	39	0.6	36	2	1 2.2%	(T)	(T)	(T)	0
Peach Nectar									
1 cup = 250 gms. (8 3/4 oz.)	48	0.8	44	1	(T)	(T)	(T)	(T)	0
Peaches									
1 peach whole = 114 gms. (4 oz.) Edible portion (76%) = 87 gms. (3 oz.)									
1 cup sliced = 168 gms. (6 oz.)	38	0.6	35	2	1 2.2%	(T)	(T)	(T)	0
Canned									
Water pack 1 cup = 245 gms. (8 1/2 oz.)	31	0.5	29	1	1 2.7%	(T)	(T)	(T)	0
Juice pack 1 cup = 250 gms. (8 3/4 oz.)	45	0.8	42	2	1 1.9%	(T)	(T)	(T)	0
Heavy sirup 1 cup = 250 gms. (9 oz.)	78	1.3	76	1	1 1.0%	(T)	(T)	(T)	0
Frozen, not thawed, sliced, sweetened	88	1.5	81	1	1 0.9%	(T)	(T)	(T)	0
Pear Nectar									
1 cup = 257 gms. (9 oz.)	52	0.9	52	1	2 3.2%	(T)	(T)	(T)	0
Pears									
1 pear whole = 182 gms. (6 1/4 oz.) Edible portion (91%) = 166 gms. (5 3/4 oz.)	61	1.0	55	2	3 5.5%	(T)	(T)	(T)	0
Canned									
Water pack 1 cup = 248 gms. (8 3/4 oz.)	32	0.5	30	1	1 5.2%	(T)	(T)	(T)	0
Juice pack 1 cup = 248 gms. (8 3/4 oz.)	46	0.8	43	1	2 5.4%	(T)	(T)	(T)	0
Heavy sirup 1 cup = 255 gms. (9 oz.)	76	1.3	74	1	1 2.2%	(T)	(T)	(T)	0

TABLE XVII (continued)

	TC	EE miles	C cal	P cal	F cal	S cal	M cal	PU cal	Chol. mg.
Persimmons									
Edible portion approximately 82%	127	2.1	121	3	3 2.6%	(T)	(T)	(T)	0
Pineapple									
1 cup diced = 140 gms. (5 oz.)	52	0.9	49	1	2 3.2%	(T)	(T)	(T)	0
Canned									
Juice pack 1 cup = 228 gms. (8 oz.)	58	1.0	56	1	1 1.4%	(T)	(T)	(T)	0
Heavy sirup 1 cup crushed = 260 gms. (9 oz.)									
2 small or 1 large slice with juice = 122 gms. (4 1/4 oz.)	74	1.2	72	1	1 1.1%	(T)	(T)	(T)	0
Pineapple Juice, canned, unsweetened									
1 cup = 249 gms. (8 3/4 oz.)	55	0.9	53	1	1 1.5%	(T)	(T)	(T)	0
Plums									
1 2" plum = 60 gms. (2 oz.) Edible portion (91%) = 55 gms. (2 oz.)	66	1.1	58	2	1 1.3%	(T)	(T)	(T)	0
Canned									
Heavy sirup 1 cup with pits = 256 gms. (9 oz.) Edible portion (96%) = 246 gms. (8 1/2 oz.)	83	1.4	81	1	1 1.0%	(T)	(T)	(T)	0
Prune Juice, canned or bottled									
1 cup = 256 gms. (9 oz.)	77	1.3	74	1	1 1.1%	(T)	(T)	(T)	0
Prunes, Dried									
16 med. prunes with pits = 114 gms. (4 oz.) Edible portion (85%) = 97 gms. (3 1/2 oz.)	255	4.2	242	7	5 2.0%	(T)	(T)	(T)	0
Quinces									
Edible portion about 60% of raw fruit	57	0.9	55	1	1 1.5%	(T)	(T)	(T)	0
Raisins									
1 cup = 165 gms. (5 3/4 oz.)	289	4.8	278	8	2 0.6%	(T)	(T)	(T)	0
Raspberries									
Black 1 cup = 127 gms. (4 1/2 oz.)	73	1.2	56	5	11 16.0%	(T)	(T)	(T)	0
Red 1 cup = 127 gms. (4 1/2 oz.)	57	1.0	49	4	4	(T)	(T)	(T)	0
Canned black, water pack	51	0.8	38	4	9 18.0%	(T)	(T)	(T)	0
Canned red, water pack	35	0.6	32	2	1 2.4%	(T)	(T)	(T)	0
Rhubarb									
1 cup diced = 157 gms. (4 1/2 oz.)	16	0.3	13	1	1 5.2%	(T)	(T)	(T)	0
Strawberries									
1 cup = 155 gms. (5 1/2 oz.)	37	0.6	30	2	4 11.3%	(T)	(T)	(T)	0
Canned, water pack	22	0.4	20	1	1 3.8%	(T)	(T)	(T)	0

TABLE XVII (continued)

	TC	*EE miles*	*C cal*	*P cal*	*F cal*	*S cal*	*M cal*	*PU cal*	*Chol. mg.*
Strawberries–continued									
Frozen, not thawed, sweetened, whole	92	1.5	89	1	2 1.8%	(T)	(T)	(T)	0
Tangerines									
1 tangerine whole = 116 gms. (4 oz.) Edible portion (74%) = 86 gms. (3 oz.)	46	0.8	42	3	2 3.6%	(T)	(T)	(T)	0
Watermelon	26	0.4	23	2	2 1.7%	(T)	(T)	(T)	0

*See page 283 for abbreviations and symbols.

#The amount of fat in a 100-gram portion is very small and the analytical data are not available. All saturated, monounsaturated, and polyunsaturated fats are considered to be present in trace (T) amounts.

TABLE XVIII: COMPOSITION OF FISH AND SHELLFISH
3 1/2 Ounces (100 Grams) Edible Portion*#

	TC	*EE miles*	*C cal*	*P cal*	*F cal*	*S cal*	*M cal*	*PU cal*	*Chol. mg.*
Bass									
Black sea	93	1.6	0	82	11	(3)	(4)	(4)	70
					11.6%	(3.4%)	(4.0%)	(3.8%)	
Small-mouth or large-mouth	104	1.7	0	81	24	(7)	(8)	(8)	70
					22.6%	(6.5%)	(7.7%)	(7.4%)	
Striped	105	1.7	0	81	25	(7)	(8)	(8)	70
					23.4%	(6.8%)	(8.0%)	(7.7%)	
White	98	1.6	0	77	21	(6)	(7)	(6)	40
					21.0%	(6.1%)	(7.2%)	(6.9%)	
Bluefish	117	2.0	0	88	30	(9)	(10)	(10)	70
					25.5%	(7.4%)	(8.7%)	(8.4%)	
Bonito	168	2.8	0	24	66	(19)	(23)	(22)	70
					39.2%	(11.3%)	(13.4%)	(12.9%)	
Buffalo Fish	113	1.9	0	75	38	(11)	(13)	(12)	70
					33.5%	(9.7%)	(11.5%)	(11.0%)	
Bullhead, black	84	1.4	0	70	14	(4)	(5)	(5)	70
					17.2%	(5.0%)	(5.9%)	(5.6%)	
Burbot	82	1.4	0	74	8	(2)	(3)	(3)	70
					9.9%	(2.9%)	(3.4%)	(3.3%)	
Butterfish									
Gulf	95	1.6	0	69	26	(8)	(9)	(9)	36
					27.6%	(8.0%)	(9.4%)	(9.1%)	
Northern	169	2.8	0	77	92	(27)	(31)	(30)	70
					54.5%	(15.8%)	(18.6%)	(17.9%)	
Carp	115	1.9	0	77	38	(11)	(13)	(12)	70
					32.9%	(9.5%)	(11.2%)	(10.8%)	
Catfish, fresh-water	103	1.7	0	75	28	(8)	(10)	(9)	70
					27.2%	(7.7%)	(9.3%)	(8.9%)	
Caviar	262	4.4	14	115	135	22[a]	–	27[a]	300
					51.5%	8.4%		10.3%	
Chub	145	2.4	0	65	79	(23)	(27)	(26)	70
					54.8%	(15.8%)	(18.7%)	(18.0%)	
Clams									
Soft meat only	82	1.4	5	60	17	6	4	6	(82)[b]
1 doz. = 250 gms.					20.9%	7.2%	5.5%	7.1%	
Hard meat only	80	1.3	24	47	8	3	2	3	82[b]
					10.1%	3.5%	2.7%	3.4%	
Canned, solids	98	1.6	8	67	23	8	6	8	82[b]
					23.1%	7.9%	6.1%	7.8%	
Cod	78	1.3	0	75	3	1	T	1	43[b]
					3.5%	1.4%		1.4%	
Crab									
Canned	101	1.7	4	74	23	6	7	5	52-98[b]
					22.8%	6.2%	7.3%	5.3%	
Steamed	93	1.6	2	74	17	5	5	4	52-98[b]
					18.4%	5.0%	5.9%	4.3%	
Crappie, white	79	1.3	0	72	7	(2)	(2)	(2)	70
					9.1%	(2.6%)	(3.1%)	(3.0%)	
Crayfish Lobster, spiny	72	1.2	4	62	4	(1)[a]	–	(T)[a]	200[b]
					6.3%	(1.3%)			

TABLE XVIII (continued)

	TC	EE miles	C cal	P cal	F cal	S cal	M cal	PU cal	Chol. mg.
Croaker									
Atlantic	96	1.6	0	76	20	(6)	(7)	(6)	70
					20.5%	(5.9%)	(7.0%)	(6.7%)	
White	84	1.4	0	77	7	(2)	(2)	(2)	70
					8.6%	(2.5%)	(2.9%)	(2.8%)	
Yellowfin	89	1.5	0	82	7	(2)	(2)	(2)	70
					8.1%	(2.3%)	(2.7%)	(2.6%)	
Dogfish, spiny (Grayfish)	156	2.6	0	75	81	(23)	(28)	(26)	70
					52.0%	(15.0%)	(17.8%)	(17.1%)	
Drum									
Fresh-water	121	2.0	0	74	47	(14)	(16)	(15)	70
					38.9%	(11.2%)	(13.3%)	(12.8%)	
Red (Redfish)	80	1.3	0	77	4	(1)	(1)	(1)	70
					4.5%	(1.3%)	(1.5%)	(1.5%)	
Eel, smoked	330	5.5	0	79	251	57[a]	–	45[a]	70
					76.0%	17.3%		13.6%	
Finnan Haddie (Smoked Haddock)	103	1.7	0	99	4	(1)[c]	(1)[c]	(2)[c]	25[b]
					3.5%	(1.1%)	(0.8%)	(1.5%)	
Fish Flakes, canned	111	1.8	0	105	5	(1)	(2)	(2)	70
					4.9%	(1.4%)	(1.7%)	(1.6%)	
Fish Flour									
From whole fish	336	5.6	0	93	T	T	T	T	(70)[k]
From filets	398	6.6	0	397	T	T	T	T	(70)[k]
Flatfish (Flounder, Sole, and Sand dab)	79	1.3	0	71	7	(2)	(2)	(2)	41[b]
					9.1%	(2.6%)	(3.1%)	(3.0%)	
Flounder (See **Flatfish**)									
Froglegs	79	1.3	0	78	1	T[a]	T[a]	T[a]	70[a]
					1.1%				
Haddock	79	1.3	0	78	1	T	T	T	25[b]
					1.1%				
Hake (Whiting)	74	1.2	0	70	4	(1)	(1)	(1)	70
					4.9%	(1.4%)	(1.7%)	(1.6%)	
Halibut									
Atlantic and Pacific	100	1.7	0	89	11	2	5	3	34[b]
					10.8%	2.4%	5.2%	2.9%	
Smoked	224	3.7	0	89	14	(4)	(5)	(4)	34[b]
					6.0%	(1.7%)	(2.0%)	(2.0%)	
California	97	1.6	0	85	13	(4)	(4)	(4)	34[b]
					13.0%	(3.8%)	(4.4%)	(4.3%)	
Greenland	146	2.4	0	70	76	(22)	(26)	(25)	34[b]
					51.9%	(15.0%)	(17.7%)	(17.0%)	
Herring									
Atlantic	176	2.9	0	24	102	(30)[d]	(47)[d]	(23)[d]	70
					58.0%	16.8%	26.7%	13.3%	
Pacific	98	1.6	0	75	24	7	11	6	25[b]
					24.0%	6.9%	11.0%	5.5%	
Pickled, Bismarck	223	3.7	0	8	136	(39)[d]	(63)[d]	(31)[d]	70
					61.0%	(17.7%)	(28.2%)	(14.0%)	
Smoked, kippered	211	3.5	0	95	116	(34)[d]	(54)[d]	(26)[d]	70
					55.0%	(16.0%)	(25.4%)	(12.6%)	
Jack Mackerel	143	2.4	0	92	50	(14)	(17)	(16)	48[b]
					35.3%	(10.2%)	(12.0%)	(11.6%)	

TABLE XVIII (continued)

	TC	EE miles	C cal	P cal	F cal	S cal	M cal	PU cal	Chol. mg.
Kingfish	105	1.8	0	78	27 25.8%	(8) (7.5%)	(9) (8.8%)	(9) (8.5%)	70
Lobster, Maine (Northern)	91	1.5	2	72	17 18.8%	4[a] 4.9%	–	2[a] 2.0%	200[b]
Rock or Spiny (See **Crayfish**)									
Mackerel									
Atlantic	191	3.2	0	81	110 57.6%	42 22.2%	34 17.6%	32 16.6%	70
Pacific	159	2.6	0	93	66 41.4%	(19) (12.0%)	(23) (14.2%)	(22) (13.6%)	70
Smoked	219	3.6	0	102	117 53.4%	(34) (15.4%)	(40) (18.3%)	(38) (17.5%)	70
Menhaden, Atlantic	172	2.9	0	80	92 53.5%	39 22.7%	22 12.8%	27 15.9%	70
Mullet	146	2.4	0	84	62 42.6%	21 14.5%	13 8.9%	22 14.9%	70
Mussels									
Canned solids	114	1.9	6	78	30 26.1%	10[a] 8.8%	–	5[a] 4.4%	(58)[b,e]
Raw meat only	95	1.6	14	61	20 21.0%	(7)[a,f] (7.0%)	–	(3)[a,f] (1.2%)	(58)[b,e]
Oysters									
Meat only, Eastern	66	1.1	14	36	16 24.9%	5 5.6%	2 3.9%	8 12.9%	58[b]
Pacific	91	1.5	26	45	20 22.0%	6[g] 6.7%	9[g] 10.3%	10[g] 11.4%	37[b]
Perch									
Fresh-water									
White	118	1.9	0	82	36 30.8%	(10) (8.9%)	(12) (10.5%)	(12) (10.1%)	70
Yellow	91	1.5	0	85	8 9.0%	(2) (2.6%)	(3) (3.1%)	(3) (3.0%)	70
Ocean	95	1.6	0	81	14 14.3%	3 3.2%	6 6.7%	4 3.8%	70
Pike									
Blue	90	1.5	0	82	8 9.1%	(2) (2.6%)	(3) (3.1%)	(3) (3.0%)	70
Northern	88	1.5	0	78	10 11.4%	(3) (3.3%)	(3) (3.9%)	(3) (3.7%)	70
Walleyed	93	1.6	0	82	11 11.7%	(3) (3.4%)	(4) (4.0%)	(4) (3.8%)	70
Pompano	166	2.8	0	80	87 52.1%	(25) (15.1%)	(30) (17.8%)	(28) (16.9%)	70
Raja (See **Skate**)									
Red and Gray Snapper	93	1.6	0	84	8 8.8%	(2) (2.5%)	(3) (3.0%)	(3) (2.9%)	33[b]
Rockfish	97	1.6	0	80	16 16.9%	5 5.2%	5 5.2%	6 6.5%	70
Redfish (See **Drum**)									
Sablefish	190	3.2	0	56	136 71.5%	38 20.1%	60 31.7%	37 19.6%	70

TABLE XVIII (continued)

	TC	*EE miles*	*C cal*	*P cal*	*F cal*	*S cal*	*M cal*	*PU cal*	*Chol. mg.*
Salmon									
Canned									
Atlantic	203	3.4	0	93	111	(32)	(38)	(36)	65[b]
					54.7%	(15.8%)	(18.7%)	(17.9%)	
Chinook (King)	210	3.5	0	84	127	35	59	26	70
					60.4%	16.7%	28.1%	12.4%	
Chum	139	2.3	0	92	42	10	17	13	42[b]
					30.4%	7.3%	12.2%	9.4%	
Caho (Silver)	153	2.6	0	89	64	13	25	21	70
					42.2%	8.4%	16.5%	14.1%	
Pink (Humpback)	141	2.4	0	87	54	11	16	23	70
1 cup = 140 gms.					38.1%	7.8%	11.5%	15.9%	
Sockeye (Blueback)	171	2.8	0	86	84	(24)	(29)	(28)	70
					49.4%	(14.3%)	(16.9%)	(16.2%)	
Raw									
Atlantic	217	3.6	0	96	122	(35)	(42)	(40)	65[b]
					56.3%	(16.3%)	(19.2%)	(18.5%)	
Chinook (King)	222	3.7	0	82	142	39	66	29	70
					64.0%	17.7%	29.8%	13.1%	
Pink (Humpback)	119	2.0	0	85	34	7	10	14	70
					28.3%	5.8%	8.5%	11.8%	
Smoked	176	2.9	0	92	84	(24)	(29)	(28)	70
					48.2%	(13.9%)	(16.5%)	(15.8%)	
Sand Dab (See **Flatfish**)									
Sardines									
Canned									
In mustard, solids and liquid	196	3.3	7	80	109	(32)	(37)	(36)	70
					55.6%	(16.1%)	(19.0%)	(18.2%)	
In oil, drained solids	203	2.4	0	102	101	(29)	(34)	(33)	70
					49.8%	(14.4%)	(17.0%)	(16.3%)	
In tomato sauce, solids and	197	3.3	7	80	111	(32)	(38)	(36)	70
liquid					56.4%	(16.3%)	(19.3%)	(18.5%)	
Raw	160	2.7	0	82	78	(22)	(27)	(26)	70
Pacific					48.9%	(14.1%)	(16.7%)	(16.0%)	
Scallops	81	1.4	14	64	2	T	T	1	60[b]
					2.2%			1.2%	
Sea Bass, white	96	1.6	0	91	4	(1)	(1)	(1)	44[b]
					4.7%	(1.4%)	(1.6%)	(1.5%)	
Shad	170	2.8	0	79	92	(26)	(31)	(30)	70
					54.1%	(15.6%)	(18.5%)	(17.7%)	
Shrimp, canned, drained solids									
1 cup = 114 gms.	116	1.9	3	103	10	(4)[a,h]	–	(2)[a,h]	150
					8.6%	(3.4%)		(1.7%)	
Skate	98	1.6	0	92	6	(2)	(2)	(2)	70
					6.4%	(1.8%)	(2.2%)	(2.1%)	
Spanish Mackerel	177	3.0	0	83	94	(27)	(32)	(31)	70
					53.0%	(15.3%)	(18.1%)	(17.3%)	
Sturgeon	94	1.6	0	77	17	(5)	(6)	(6)	70
					18.2%	(5.2%)	(6.2%)	(6.0%)	
Swordfish	118	2.0	0	82	36	(10)	(12)	(12)	70
					30.5%	(8.8%)	(10.4%)	(10.0%)	
Tautog (Blackfish)	89	1.5	0	79	9	(3)	(3)	(3)	70
					10.0%	(2.9%)	(3.4%)	(3.2%)	

TABLE XVIII (continued)

	TC	*EE miles*	*C cal*	*P cal*	*F cal*	*S cal*	*M cal*	*PU cal*	*Chol. mg.*
Trout									
Brook	101	1.7	0	82	19	(5)	(6)	(6)	70
					18.7%	(5.4%)	(6.4%)	(6.1%)	
Lake	168	2.8	0	78	92	(26)	(31)	(30)	70
					54.8%	(15.8%)	(18.7%)	(18.0%)	
Rainbow	195	3.2	0	92	103	21	33	41	70
					52.8%	10.8%	17.0%	21.2%	
Tuna									
Bluefin	145	2.4	0	107	37	13	13	10	52[b]
					25.5%	8.7%	9.2%	7.0%	
Yellowfin	133	2.2	0	105	27	11	6	9	52[b]
					20.2%	8.1%	4.7%	6.7%	
Canned									
In cottonseed oil, drained solids	197	3.3	0	123	74	20	16	30	52[b]
					37.5%	10.1%	8.1%	15.3%	
Water pack, solids and liquid	127	2.1	0	119	7	(2)	(2)	(2)	52[b]
					5.7%	(1.6%)	(1.9%)	(1.8%)	
Whitefish	155	2.6	0	80	74	14	30	24	70
					47.7%	9.4%	19.2%	15.5%	
Whiting (See **Hake**)									
Yellowtail, Pacific	138	2.3	0	90	48	(14)	(17)	(16)	70
					35.3%	(10.2%)	(12.1%)	(11.6%)	

*See page 283 for abbreviations and symbols.

#Values from *U.S.D.A. Handbook No. 8* with the percentage of saturated fat, monounsaturated fat, and polyunsaturated fat determined from reports of Stansby of the Bureau of Commercial Fisheries, unless otherwise noted.

[a]From Fetcher *et al.*

[b]From Thompson, U.S. Department of Commerce.

[c]Derived from values for haddock.

[d]Derived from herring, Pacific.

[e]Values for oysters used.

[f]Derived from clams.

[g]Derived from oysters, Eastern.

[h]Values for fresh shrimp used.

[k]U.S.D.A. values for fish are used.

( ) Derived values are either as indicated or based on the average of several different fishes reported by Stansby. The averages imputed here for our purposes are S, 29.9%; M, 34.2%; PU, 32.8%.

TABLE XIX: COMPOSITION OF POULTRY

3 1/2 Ounces (100 Grams) Edible Portion*#

	TC	*EE miles*	*C cal*	*P cal*	*F cal*	*S cal*	*M cal*	*PU cal*	*Chol. mg.*
Chicken, Fryer									
Flesh, skin, and giblets									
Ready-to-cook edible portion 68% of 147 gms. (5 1/4 oz.) = 100 gms. (3 1/2 oz.) edible portion	124	2.1	0	79	44 35.5%	(14) (11.2%)	(17) (13.4%)	(9) (6.9%)	60
Flesh and skin									
Ready-to-cook edible portion 68% of 685 gms. (24 oz.) = 466 gms. (16 1/4 oz.) edible portion	126	2.1	0	80	46 36.5%	(15) (11.6%)	(17) (14.0%)	(9) (7.1%)	60
Flesh only									
Edible portion 68% of 454 gms. (1 lb.) = 309 gms. (10 7/8 oz.) edible portion									
1/2 cup = 100 gms. (3 1/2 oz.)	107	1.8	0	82	24 24.3%	8 7.1%	9 8.4%	5 4.4%	60
Light meat without skin									
Edible portion 79% of 126 gms. (4 1/2 oz.) = 100 gms. (3 1/2 oz.) edible portion	101	1.7	0	88	14 13.4%	(4) (4.2%)	(5) (5.0%)	(3) (2.6%)	60
Dark meat without skin									
Edible portion 60% of 166 gms. (5 3/4 oz.) = 100 gms. (3 1/2 oz.) edible portion	112	1.9	0	77	34 30.5%	(11) (9.7%)	(13) (11.5%)	(7) (5.9%)	60
Light meat with skin									
Edible portion 79% of 126 gms. (4 1/2 oz.) = 100 gms. (3 1/2 oz.) edible portion	120	2.0	0	85	35 29.2%	(11) (9.3%)	(13) (11.0%)	(7) (5.7%)	60
Dark meat with skin									
Edible portion 60% of 166 gms. (5 3/4 oz.) = 100 gms. (3 1/2 oz.) edible portion	132	2.2	0	76	57 43.0%	(18) (13.6%)	(22) (16.2%)	(11) (8.4%)	60
Back									
Edible portion 54% of 185 gms. (6 1/2 oz.) = 100 gms. (3 1/2 oz.) edible portion	157	2.6	0	70	87 55.2%	(28) (17.5%)	(33) (20.8%)	(17) (10.8%)	60
Breast									
Edible portion 79% of 126 gms. (4 1/2 oz.) = 100 gms. (3 1/2 oz.) edible portion	110	1.8	0	88	22 19.6%	(7) (6.2%)	(8) (7.4%)	(4) (3.8%)	60
Drumstick									
Edible portion 60% of 166 gms. (5 3/4 oz.) = 100 gms. (3 1/2 oz.) edible portion	115	1.9	0	80	35 30.4%	(11) (9.6%)	(13) (11.5%)	(7) (5.9%)	60
Neck									
Edible portion 48% of 208 gms. (7 1/4 oz.) = 100 gms. (3 1/2 oz.) edible portion	151	1.9	0	66	85 56.3%	(27) (17.8%)	(32) (21.3%)	(17) (11.0%)	60
Rib									
Edible portion 51% of 196 gms. (6 3/4 oz.) = 100 gms. (3 1/2 oz.) edible portion	124	2.0	0	76	49 39.3%	(16) (12.4%)	(18) (14.8%)	(10) (7.6%)	60
Thigh									
Edible portion 75% of 133 gms. (4 3/4 oz.) = 100 gms. (3 1/2 oz.) edible portion	128	2.1	0	77	50 39.4%	(16) (12.5%)	(19) (14.9%)	(10) (7.7%)	60

TABLE XIX (continued)

	TC	EE miles	C cal	P cal	F cal	S cal	M cal	PU cal	Chol. mg.
Chicken, Fryer–continued									
Wing									
Edible portion 49% of 204 gms. (7 oz.) = 100 gms. (3 1/2 oz.) edible portion	146	2.5	0	79	67 45.7%	(21) (14.5%)	(25) (17.3%)	(13) (8.9%)	60
Chicken, Roaster									
Flesh and skin									
Edible portion 73% of 137 gms. (4 3/4 oz.) = 100 gms. (3 1/2 oz.) edible portion	197	3.3	0	83	114 57.4%	(36) (18.2%)	(43) (21.7%)	(22) (11.2%)	60
Flesh only									
Edible portion 73% of 137 gms. (4 3/4 oz.) = 100 gms. (3 1/2 oz.) edible portion	131	2.2	0	90	41 31.0%	(12) (9.0%)	(18) (13.2%)	(8) (6.4%)	60
Chicken, Hens and Cocks									
Flesh and skin									
Edible portion 73% of 137 gms. (4 3/4 oz.) = 100 gms. (3 1/2 oz.) edible portion	251	4.2	0	81	170 67.7%	(54) (21.5%)	(64) (25.6%)	(33) (13.2%)	60
Flesh only									
Edible portion 73% of 137 gms. (4 3/4 oz.) = 100 gms. (3 1/2 oz.) edible portion	155	2.6	0	92	63 40.6%	20 12.9%	76 15.3%	12 7.9%	60
Chicken, Capons									
Flesh and skin									
Edible portion 73% of 137 gms. (4 3/4 oz.) = 100 gms. (3 1/2 oz.) edible portion	291	4.9	0	91	191 65.6%	(60) (20.8%)	(72) (24.8%)	(37) (12.8%)	60
Duck									
Domestic									
Edible portion 82% of 122 gms. (4 1/4 oz.) = 100 gms. (3 1/2 oz.) edible portion	326	5.4	0	68	258 79.1%	(75) (23.1%)	(110) (33.8%)	(54) (16.4%)	60
Wild	233	3.9	0	90	142 61.0%	(41) (17.8%)	(61) (26.0%)	(29) (12.7%)	60
Goose									
Domestic									
Edible portion 73% of 137 gms. (4 3/4 oz.) = 100 gms. (3 1/2 oz.) edible portion	354	5.9	0	70	284 80.2%	(83) (23.4%)	(121) (34.2%)	(59) (16.7%)	60
Guinea Hen									
Edible portion 84% of 119 gms. (4 1/4 oz.) = 100 gms. (3 1/2 oz.) edible portion	156	2.6	0	98	58 37.0%	(17) (10.8%)	(25) (15.7%)	(12) (7.7%)	60
Pheasant									
Edible portion 87% of 115 gms. (4 oz.) = 100 gms. (3 1/2 oz.) edible portion	151	2.5	0	24	47 31.0%	(14) (9.0%)	(20) (13.2%)	(9) (6.4%)	60
Turkey									
Young (24 weeks or less)									
Flesh and skin									
Edible portion 73% of 137 gms. (4 3/4 oz.) = 100 gms. (3 1/2 oz.) edible portion	151	2.5	0	85	67 44.4%	(20) (13.0%)	(29) (19.0%)	(11) (9.2%)	60

TABLE XIX (continued)

	TC	EE miles	C cal	P cal	F cal	S cal	M cal	PU cal	Chol. mg.
Turkey, Young–continued									
Light meat	108	1.8	0	104	4 3.3%	(1) (1.0%)	(2) (1.4%)	(1) (0.7%)	60
Dark meat	111	1.9	0	88	23 21.1%	(7) (6.2%)	(10) (9.0%)	(5) (4.4%)	60
Medium fat (26-32 weeks)									
Flesh and skin									
Edible portion 73% of 137 gms. (4 3/4 oz.) = 100 gms. (3 1/2 oz.) edible portion	197	3.3	0	92	105 53.1%	(31) (15.5%)	(45) (22.7%)	(22) (11.0%)	60
Light meat	115	1.9	0	106	10 8.6%	(3) (2.5%)	(4) (3.7%)	(2) (1.8%)	60
Dark meat	127	2.1	0	89	38 29.8%	(11) (8.7%)	(16) (12.7%)	(8) (6.2%)	60
Fat (mature birds over 32 weeks)									
Total edible									
Ready-to-cook edible portion 73% of 137 gms. (4 3/4 oz.) = 100 gms. (3 1/2 oz.) edible portion	343	5.7	0	79	264 77.0%	(77) (22.5%)	(112) (32.9%)	(55) (16.0%)	60

*See page 283 for abbreviations and symbols.

#Values for composition of fat are computed from those given for chicken fat (S, 31.7%; M, 37.8%; PU, 19.5%) and turkey fat (S, 29.2%; M, 42.7%; PU, 20.8%) in the *U.S.D.A. Handbook No. 8.*

TABLE XX: COMPOSITION OF BEEF
3 1/2 Ounces (100 Grams) Edible Portion*#

	TC	EE miles	C cal	P cal	F cal	S cal	M cal	PU cal	Chol. mg.
Beef, fresh									
Chuck rib, 5th									
Choice									
Total edible	352	5.9	0	69	283 80.4%	137 38.9%	125 35.5%	6 1.7%	70
Separable lean	188	3.1	0	88	99 52.6%	48 25.5%	44 23.0%	2 0.9%	70
Good									
Total edible	303	5.0	0	74	228 75.3%	111 36.6%	101 33.4%	5 1.5%	70
Separable lean	163	2.7	0	90	72 44.2%	35 21.4%	32 19.6%	1 0.9%	70
Arm									
Choice									
Total edible	223	3.7	0	82	140 62.8%	68 30.4%	62 27.8%	3 1.3%	70
Separable lean	141	2.4	0	92	49 34.5%	24 16.7%	22 15.2%	1 0.7%	70
Good									
Total edible	191	3.2	0	87	105 55.5%	51 26.7%	46 24.3%	2 1.1%	70
Separable lean	129	2.2	0	93	36 27.9%	18 13.6%	16 12.4%	1 0.6%	70

TABLE XX (continued)

	TC	*EE miles*	*C cal*	*P cal*	*F cal*	*S cal*	*M cal*	*PU cal*	*Chol. mg.*
Beef, fresh–continued									
Flank steak									
Choice	144	2.4	0	92	51 35.7%	25 17.3%	23 15.8%	1 0.7%	70
Good	139	2.3	0	93	46 33.1%	22 16.1%	20 14.7%	1 0.6%	70
Hindshank									
Choice									
Total edible	289	4.8	0	78	211 73.0%	102 35.3%	94 32.4%	4 1.5%	70
Separable lean	134	2.2	0	92	42 31.0%	20 15.0%	18 13.7%	1 0.6%	70
Good									
Total edible	239	4.0	0	84	155 64.8%	75 31.4%	58 24.5%	3 1.3%	70
Separable lean	126	2.1	0	93	34 26.5%	16 12.9%	15 11.7%	1 0.5%	70
Porterhouse steak									
Choice									
Total edible	390	6.5	0	63	326 83.6%	158 40.5%	144 36.9%	6 1.7%	70
Separable lean	164	2.7	0	90	74 45.1%	36 21.9%	33 20.0%	1 0.9%	70
Good									
Total edible	370	6.2	0	65	305 82.5%	148 40.0%	135 36.5%	6 1.6%	70
Separable lean	141	2.4	0	92	50 35.1%	24 17.0%	22 15.5%	1 0.7%	70
T-bone steak									
Choice									
Total edible	397	6.6	0	63	334 89.2%	162 40.8%	148 37.3%	7 1.7%	70
Separable lean	164	2.7	0	90	73 44.5%	36 22.2%	32 19.7%	1 0.9%	70
Good									
Total edible	366	6.1	0	66	300 82.0%	146 40.0%	133 36.4%	6 1.6%	70
Separable lean	142	2.4	0	92	50 35.6%	24 17.3%	22 15.8%	1 0.7%	70
Club steak									
Choice									
Total edible	380	6.3	0	66	314 82.7%	152 40.0%	139 36.6%	6 1.6%	70
Separable lean	182	3.0	0	89	93 51.3%	45 24.8%	41 22.6%	2 1.0%	70
Good									
Total edible	324	5.4	0	72	251 77.5%	122 37.7%	111 34.3%	5 1.5%	70
Separable lean	158	2.6	0	90	67 42.8%	33 20.7%	30 18.9%	1 0.9%	70

TABLE XX (continued)

	TC	*EE miles*	*C cal*	*P cal*	*F cal*	*S cal*	*M cal*	*PU cal*	*Chol. mg.*
Beef, fresh – continued									
Sirloin steak, wedge or round bone									
Choice									
Total edible	313	5.2	0	72	241 77.0%	117 37.4%	107 34.2%	5 1.5%	70
Separable lean	143	2.4	0	92	51 35.9%	25 17.4%	23 15.9%	1 0.7%	70
Good									
Total edible	281	4.7	0	76	205 72.9%	100 35.4%	91 32.3%	4 1.5%	70
Separable lean	129	2.2	0	93	36 27.9%	18 13.6%	16 12.3%	1 0.6%	70
Sirloin steak, double-bone									
Choice									
Total edible	333	5.6	0	70	262 78.7%	127 38.1%	116 34.8%	5 1.6%	70
Separable lean	158	2.6	0	91	67 42.4%	32 20.2%	30 19.0%	1 0.8%	70
Good									
Total edible	293	4.9	0	75	217 74.0%	105 35.8%	96 32.8%	4 1.5%	70
Separable lean	135	2.3	0	92	42 31.4%	20 14.8%	19 13.9%	8 5.9%	70
Sirloin steak, hipbone									
Choice									
Total edible	412	6.9	0	62	350 85.0%	170 41.3%	155 37.6%	7 1.7%	70
Separable lean	179	3.0	0	89	89 49.8%	43 24.2%	40 22.1%	2 1.0%	70
Good									
Total edible	367	6.1	0	67	299 79.0%	145 39.5%	133 36.2%	6 1.6%	70
Separable lean	152	2.5	0	91	60 39.8%	29 19.4%	27 17.6%	1 0.8%	70
Short plate									
Choice									
Total edible	400	6.7	0	63	336 84.0%	163 40.7%	149 37.2%	7 1.7%	70
Separable lean	164	2.7	0	90	74 45.2%	36 21.9%	33 20.0%	1 0.9%	70
Good									
Total edible	356	5.9	0	69	288 81.0%	140 39.3%	128 35.9%	6 1.6%	70
Separable lean	146	2.4	0	92	54 37.1%	26 18.0%	24 16.4%	1 0.7%	70
Rib, 6th to 12th									
Choice									
Total edible	401	6.7	0	63	337 84.0%	164 40.9%	150 37.4%	7 1.7%	70
Separable lean	193	3.2	0	88	105 54.4%	51 26.4%	46 24.1%	2 1.1%	70

TABLE XX (continued)

	TC	EE miles	C cal	P cal	F cal	S cal	M cal	PU cal	Chol. mg.
Beef, fresh – continued									
Round									
Choice									
Total edible	197	3.3	0	86	111	54	49	2	70
					56.3%	27.3%	25.0%	1.1%	
Separable lean	135	2.2	0	92	42	21	19	1	70
					31.4%	15.3%	13.9%	0.6%	
Rump									
Choice									
Total edible	303	5.0	0	74	228	111	101	5	70
					75.3%	36.6%	33.4%	1.5%	
Separable lean	158	2.6	0	90	67	33	30	1	70
					42.8%	20.5%	18.9%	0.8%	
Good									
Total edible	271	4.5	0	78	193	94	86	3	70
					71.3%	34.6%	31.5%	1.1%	
Separable lean	141	2.3	0	92	49	24	22	1	70
					34.5%	16.5%	15.3%	0.7%	
Hamburger (Ground beef)									
Regular	268	4.5	0	76	191	93	84	4	70
					71.3%	34.6%	31.5%	1.4%	
Lean	179	3.0	0	88	92	45	41	2	70
					51.4%	24.9%	22.8%	1.0%	
Beef, canned									
Roast beef	224	3.7	0	107	117	57	52	2	70
					52.2%	24.9%	23.1%	1.0%	
Beef, corned									
Medium-fat									
Uncooked, boneless	293	4.9	0	68	225	109	100	4	70
					7.7%	37.2%	34.1%	1.5%	
Cooked	263	4.4	0	100	162	78	72	3	70
					61.5%	29.9%	27.3%	1.2%	
Canned, boneless									
Lean	185	3.1	0	113	72	35	32	1	70
					39.0%	18.9%	17.3%	0.8%	
Medium-fat	216	3.6	0	108	108	52	48	2	70
					50.0%	24.3%	22.1%	1.0%	
Beef, dried									
Chipped									
1/2 cup = 71 gms. (2 1/2 oz.)	203	3.4	0	146	57	28	25	1	70
					28.0%	13.6%	12.4%	0.6%	

*See page 283 for abbreviations and symbols.

#Composition of beef fat is computed from fat of a choice carcass (S, 48.5%; M, 44.3%; PU, 2%) given in the U.S.D.A. Handbook No. 8.

TABLE XXI: **COMPOSITION OF VEAL**
3 1/2 Ounces (100 Grams) Edible Portion*#

	TC	*EE miles*	*C cal*	*P cal*	*F cal*	*S cal*	*M cal*	*PU cal*	*Chol. mg.*
Chuck	173	2.9	0	83	90	42	40	3	90
					52.2%	24.5%	22.9%	1.6%	
Cutlet	185	3.0	0	98	81	38	36	2	90
1 cutlet = 100 gms. (3 1/2 oz.)					43.8%	20.5%	19.4%	1.1%	
Flank	314	5.2	0	70	244	115	107	7	90
					77.6%	36.6%	34.1%	2.3%	
Foreshank	156	2.6	0	84	72	34	32	2	90
					46.3%	21.7%	20.4%	1.4%	
Loin	181	3.0	0	82	99	46	44	3	90
					54.7%	25.7%	24.0%	1.6%	
Plate	231	3.8	0	78	153	72	62	5	90
					66.7%	31.2%	27.0%	2.0%	
Rib	207	3.4	0	80	126	59	56	4	90
					60.9%	28.6%	26.8%	1.8%	
Round with rump	164	2.7	0	83	81	38	36	2	90
					49.5%	23.3%	21.8%	1.5%	

*See page 283 for abbreviations and symbols.
#Composition of fat is from fat of medium carcass (S, 47%; M, 44%; PU, 3%) as given in *U.S.D.A. Handbook No. 8.*

TABLE XXII: **COMPOSITION OF PORK**
3 1/2 Ounces (100 Grams) Edible Portion*#

	TC	*EE miles*	*C cal*	*P cal*	*F cal*	*S cal*	*M cal*	*PU cal*	*Chol. mg.*
Uncured									
Boston butt									
Total edible	287	4.8	0	66	221	(80)	(93)	20	70
					77.0%	(27.5%)	(32.4%)	6.9%	
Separable lean	180	3.0	0	78	102	(37)	(43)	9	70
					56.7%	(20.4%)	(23.8%)	5.1%	
Ham									
Total edible	308	5.1	0	68	240	(86)	(101)	22	70
					77.9%	(28.0%)	(32.8%)	7.0%	
Separable lean	153	2.6	0	85	68	(24)	(28)	6	70
					44.2%	(15.9%)	(18.6%)	4.0%	
Loin									
Total edible	298	5.0	0	73	225	(81)	(94)	20	70
					75.5%	(27.2%)	(31.7%)	6.8%	
Separable lean	189	3.2	0	86	103	(37)	(43)	9	70
					54.5%	(19.6%)	(22.9%)	4.9%	
Picnic									
Total edible	290	4.8	0	67	223	(80)	(94)	20	70
					76.9%	(27.7%)	(32.3%)	6.9%	
Separable lean	150	2.5	0	83	67	24	28	6	70
					44.6%	16.0%	18.7%	4.0%	
Spareribs	361	6.0	0	62	300	(108)	(126)	27	70
					83.0%	(29.9%)	(34.9%)	7.5%	
Cured									
Bacon	665	11.1	0	36	625	(225)	(262)	(56)	70
					94.0%	(33.9%)	(39.4%)	(8.4%)	
Bacon, Canadian	216	3.6	0	85	130	(47)	(55)	(12)	70
					60.2%	(21.7%)	(25.3%)	(5.4%)	
Ham, canned	193	3.2	0	78	111	(40)	(47)	(10)	70
					57.5%	(20.5%)	(24.1%)	(5.2%)	
Salt pork	783	13.0	0	17	766	(276)	(322)	(69)	70
					97.9%	(35.3%)	(41.2%)	(8.8%)	
Light-Cured									
Boston butt									
Total edible	291	4.9	0	73	217	(78)	(91)	(20)	70
					74.6%	(26.9%)	(31.3%)	(6.7%)	
Separable lean	200	3.3	0	89	111	(40)	(47)	(10)	70
					55.5%	(20.0%)	(23.3%)	(5.0%)	
Ham									
Total edible	282	4.7	0	75	205	(74)	(86)	(18)	70
					72.7%	(26.2%)	(30.5%)	(6.6%)	
Separable lean	168	2.8	0	92	77	(28)	(32)	(7)	70
					45.6%	(16.4%)	(19.2%)	(4.1%)	
Picnic									
Total edible	285	4.8	0	72	213	(77)	(89)	(19)	70
					74.8%	(26.9%)	(31.4%)	(6.7%)	
Separable lean	167	2.8	0	91	76	(27)	(32)	(7)	70
					45.4%	(16.4%)	(19.0%)	(4.1%)	
Long-Cured, country-style									
Ham	389	6.5	0	72	316	(114)	(133)	(28)	70
					81.2%	(29.3%)	(34.2%)	(7.3%)	

*See page 283 for abbreviations and symbols.

#Composition of fat based on values for pork fat in *U.S.D.A. Handbook No. 8* as follows: S, 36%; M, 42%; PU, 9%. All values for pork are based on medium-fat class.

TABLE XXIII: **COMPOSITION OF LAMB**
3 1/2 Ounces (100 Grams) Edible Portion*#

	TC	EE miles	C cal	P cal	F cal	S cal	M cal	PU cal	Chol. mg.
Choice									
Leg									
Total edible	222	3.7	0	76	146 65.7%	(82) (36.8%)	(52) (23.7%)	(4) (2.0%)	70
Separable lean	130	2.2	0	85	45 34.7%	(25) (19.2%)	(16) (12.5%)	(1) (1.0%)	70
Loin									
Total edible	293	4.9	0	70	224 76.4%	(126) (43.0%)	(80) (27.6%)	(7) (2.3%)	70
Separable lean	138	2.3	0	85	53 38.6%	(30) (21.6%)	(19) (13.8%)	(2) (1.2%)	70
Rib									
Total edible	339	5.6	0	64	274 80.8%	(152) (44.9%)	(98) (29.1%)	(8) (2.4%)	70
Separable lean	158	2.6	0	82	76 48.0%	(42) (26.9%)	(27) (17.3%)	(2) (1.4%)	70
Shoulder									
Total edible	281	4.7	0	65	216 76.9%	(121) (43.1%)	(78) (27.7%)	(6) (2.3%)	70
Separable lean	148	2.5	0	79	70 47.0%	(39) (26.3%)	(25) (16.9%)	(2) (1.4%)	70

*See page 283 for abbreviations and symbols.

#Composition of fat based on values for fat in *U.S.D.A. Handbook No. 8* as follows: (S, 56%; M, 36%; PU, 3%). All values are for choice grade cuts.

TABLE XXIV: **COMPOSITION OF LUNCHEON MEATS AND SAUSAGES 3 1/2 Ounces (100 Grams)***

	TC	*EE miles*	*C cal*	*P cal*	*F cal*	*S cal*	*M cal*	*PU cal*	*Chol. mg.*
Luncheon Meats									
Blood sausage	394	6.6	1	60	333 84.5%	(120) (30.4%)	(150) (38.0%)	(23) (5.9%)	(100)
Bockwurst	264	4.4	2	48	224 89.9%	(81) (30.6%)	(101) (40.5%)	(16) (6.3%)	(100)
Bologna									
All samples	304	5.1	4	52	248 81.6%	(89) (29.4%)	(111) (36.7%)	(17) (5.7%)	(100)
All meat	277	4.6	14	57	206 74.3%	(74) (26.7%)	(93) (33.6%)	(14) (5.0%)	(100)
With cereal	248	4.4	15	60	186 75.0%	(67) (27.0%)	(84) (33.9%)	(13) (5.2%)	(100)
Frankfurters									
All samples	309	5.2	7	53	249 80.5%	(90) (29.0%)	(112) (36.2%)	(17) (5.6%)	(100)
All meat	296	4.9	10	56	230 77.7%	(83) (28.0%)	(103) (34.9%)	(16) (5.4%)	(100)
Nonfat dry milk	300	5.0	13	56	231 77.0%	(83) (27.7%)	(104) (34.6%)	(16) (5.4%)	(100)
With cereal	248	4.1	1	61	186 75.0%	(67) (27.0%)	(84) (33.8%)	(13) (5.3%)	(100)
Liverwurst	307	4.1	0	75	173 56.3%	(62) (20.2%)	(78) (25.4%)	(12) (3.9%)	(100)
Meat, Potted	248	4.1	0	75	173 69.7%	(62) (25.1%)	(78) (31.4%)	(12) (4.5%)	(100)
Salami	450	7.5	5	102	344 76.5%	(124) (27.5%)	(155) (34.4%)	(24) (5.3%)	(100)
Sausage									
Country-style	345	5.8	0	64	281 81.5%	(99) (28.7%)	(117) (33.9%)	(27) (7.8%)	(100)
Polish-style	304	5.1	5	67	233 76.6%	(84) (27.6%)	(105) (34.5%)	(16) (5.4%)	(100)
Pork, link or bulk	498	8.3	0	40	458 92.0%	162 32.6%	189 37.9%	45 9.0%	(100)
Vienna, canned	240	4.0	1	60	179 74.6%	(64) (26.8%)	(79) (33.6%)	(12) (5.2%)	(100)

*See page 283 for abbreviations and symbols.

TABLE XXV: **COMPOSITION OF ORGAN MEATS**
3 1/2 Ounces (100 Grams)*

	TC	*EE miles*	*C cal*	*P cal*	*F cal*	*S cal*	*M cal*	*PU cal*	*Chol. mg.*
Brains	125	2.1	3	44	78	(34)	(38)	(1)	2,000
					62.0%	(27.6%)	(30.0%)	(1.2%)	
Heart									
With visible fat	253	4.2	T	66	187	(83)	(91)	(4)	150
					73.8%	(32.7%)	(35.8%)	(1.5%)	
Lean	108	1.8	3	73	32	(14)	(16)	(1)	150
					30.0%	(13.3%)	(14.6%)	(0.6%)	
Calf	124	2.1	7	64	53	(24)	(26)	(1)	150
					42.9%	(19.0%)	(20.8%)	(0.8%)	
Hog	113	1.9	2	72	40	(14)	(17)	(4)	150
					35.0%	(12.6%)	(14.7%)	(3.2%)	
Lamb	162	2.7	4	72	86	(38)	(42)	(2)	150
					53.5%	(23.5%)	(25.9%)	(1.1%)	
Kidney									
Beef	130	2.2	3.5	66	60	(26)	(29)	(1)	375
					45.5%	(20.2%)	(22.1%)	(0.9%)	
Calf	113	1.9	T	71	42	(19)	(20)	(1)	375
					36.6%	(16.2%)	(17.7%)	(0.7%)	
Hog	106	1.8	4	67	32	(12)	(13)	(3)	375
					30.6%	(11.0%)	(12.9%)	(2.8%)	
Liver									
Beef	140	2.3	20	85	34	(15)	(16)	(1)	300
					24.4%	(10.8%)	(11.8%)	(0.5%)	
Calf	140	2.3	16	82	42	(19)	(20)	(1)	7
					30.3%	(13.4%)	(15.0%)	(0.6%)	
Chicken	129	2.2	11	84	33	(10)	(12)	(6)	300
					25.6%	(8.1%)	(9.6%)	(5.0%)	
Hog	131	2.2	10	88	33	(12)	(14)	(3)	300
					25.5%	(9.2%)	(10.7%)	(2.3%)	
Lamb	136	2.3	11	90	35	(20)	(13)	(1)	300
					25.9%	(14.5%)	(9.3%)	(0.8%)	
Sweetbreads									
Pancreas									
Beef									
Lean only	141	2.4	0	75	66	(29)	(32)	(1)	(250)
					46.7%	(20.7%)	(22.6%)	(0.9%)	
Medium-fat	283	4.7	0	58	226	(100)	(110)	(4)	(250)
					79.9%	(35.4%)	(38.8%)	(1.6%)	
Calf	161	2.7	0	19	144	64	70	3	(250)
					69.6%	39.8%	33.8%	1.4%	
Hog	242	4.0	0	63	180	(65)	(76)	(16)	(250)
					74.4%	(26.8%)	(31.2%)	(6.7%)	
Thymus									
Beef, yearling	207	2.4	0	62	144	(64)	(70)	(3)	250
					69.6%	(30.8%)	(33.8%)	(1.4%)	
Calf	94	1.6	0	76	18	(8)	(9)	(T)	250
					19.2%	(8.5%)	(9.3%)		
Lamb	94	1.6	0	60	34	(19)	(12)	(1)	250
					36.4%	(20.4%)	(13.1%)	(1.1%)	
Spleen									
Beef or calf	104	1.7	0	77	27	(12)	(13)	(T)	(250)
					26.1%	(11.6%)	(12.6%)		

*See page 283 for abbreviations and symbols.

TABLE XXV (continued)

	TC	*EE miles*	*C cal*	*P cal*	*F cal*	*S cal*	*M cal*	*PU cal*	*Chol. mg.*
Spleen–continued									
Hog	107	1.8	0	73	34 32.0%	(12) (11.5%)	(14) (13.4%)	(3) (2.9%)	(250)
Lamb	115	1.9	0	80	35 30.6%	(20) (17.1%)	(13) (11.0%)	(1) (0.9%)	(250)
Tongue									
Beef, medium-fat	207	3.4	2	70	135 65.2%	(60) (28.9%)	(65) (31.6%)	(3) (1.3%)	(120)
Calf	130	2.2	4	79	48 36.8%	(21) (16.3%)	(23) (17.8%)	(1) (0.7%)	(120)
Hog	215	3.6	2	72	141 65.5%	(51) (23.4%)	(59) (27.5%)	(13) (5.9%)	(120)
Lamb	199	3.3	2	59	138 69.3%	(77) (38.8%)	(50) (24.9%)	(4) (2.1%)	(120)
Canned or cured, all types	267	4.4	1	82	183 68.5%	(81) (30.3%)	(89) (33.2%)	(4) (1.4%)	(120)

TABLE XXVI: **COMPOSITION OF DESSERTS**
3 1/2 Ounces (100 Grams)*

	TC	EE miles	C cal	P cal	F cal	S cal	M cal	PU cal	Chol. mg.
Cake									
Angel food	269	4.5	222	25	2 0.7%	–	–	–	0
Boston cream pie 3-inch wedge = 80 gms. (2 3/4 oz.)	302	5.0	185	18	85 28.1%	27 8.9%	–	7 2.3%	48
Cheese	262	4.4	–	–	132 50.4%	75 28.6%	–	3 1.1%	68
Chiffon	381	6.4	–	–	136 35.7%	32 8.4%	–	56 14.7%	195
Chocolate devil's food	366	6.1	192	17	155 42.3%	81 22.1%	–	9 2.5%	76
Commercial devil's food	380	6.3	206	16	158 41.6%	81 21.3%	–	9 2.4%	63
Fruit	379	6.3	221	17	138 36.4%	36 9.5%	–	18 4.7%	63
Plain	364	6.1	207	16	125 34.3%	36 9.9%	–	9 2.5%	45
Pound	411	6.9	202	22	168 40.9%	45 10.9%	–	9 2.2%	99
Sponge	297	5.0	200	27	51 17.2%	18 6.1%	–	0	220
Yellow	363	6.1	215	16	114 31.4%	36 9.9%	–	9 2.5%	45
Cookies									
Coconut macaroons	475	7.9	245	19	209 44.0%	144 30.3%	–	9 1.9%	10
Medium-fat grocery	444	7.4	252	21	151 34.0%	36 8.1%	–	9 2.0%	50
Pillsbury fresh-dough products									
Butterscotch nut	451	7.5	228	17	219 48.6%	66 14.6%	131 29.0%	22 4.9%	48
Chocolate chip 3-4 dozen = 454 gms. (16 oz.)	425	7.1	238	16	190 44.7%	57 13.4%	113 26.6%	19 4.5%	51
Fudge brownies	389	6.5	245	18	144 37.0%	43 11.1%	86 22.1%	14 3.6%	49
Fudge nut	429	7.1	232	16	200 46.6%	59 13.8%	120 28.0%	20 4.7%	29
Oatmeal raisin	413	6.9	240	18	167 40.4%	50 12.1%	100 24.2%	17 4.1%	29

*See page 283 for abbreviations.

TABLE XXVI (continued)

	TC	*EE miles*	*C cal*	*P cal*	*F cal*	*S cal*	*M cal*	*PU cal*	*Chol. mg.*
Cookies, Pillsbury fresh-dough products–continued									
Peanut butter	451	7.5	218	28	221 49.0%	67 14.9%	132 29.3%	22 4.9%	58
Sugar 3 1/2 dozen = 511 gms. (18 oz.)	442	7.4	225	16	203 45.9%	60 13.6%	122 27.6%	21 4.8%	36
Frosting									
Caramel or white cream	360	6.0	283	5	60 16.7%	36 10.0%	–	0	22
Coconut	364	6.1	277	7	69 19.0%	63 17.3%	–	0	22
Ice cream 1 cup = 133 gms. (4 5/8 oz.)	207	3.5	76	14	112 54.1%	63 30.4%	36 17.4%	0	60
Ice milk 1 cup = 131 gms. (4 5/8 oz.)	152	2.5	83	17	46 30.3%	27 17.8%	18 11.8%	0	5
Pie, baked									
Cream or chiffon	255	4.3	139	13	92 36.1%	31 12.2%	–	7 2.7%	64
Custard	218	3.6	87	21	100 45.9%	36 16.5%	–	9 4.1%	66
Fruit	256	4.3	141	8	100 39.1%	27 10.5%	–	9 3.5%	8
Pecan	418	6.7	190	18	206 49.3%	27 6.5%	–	36 8.6%	48
Pumpkin	211	3.5	91	14	101 47.9%	42 19.9%	–	8 3.8%	66
Pastries, Pillsbury fresh-dough products									
Apple Coffeetime	366	6.1	266	13	136 37.2%	41 11.2%	81 22.1%	14 3.8%	13
Apple turnover 8 = 400 gms. (14 oz.)	372	6.2	196	11	172 46.2%	51 13.7%	104 28.0%	17 4.6%	12
Blueberry turnover 8 = 400 gms. (14 oz.)	344	5.7	154	12	181 52.6%	54 15.7%	109 31.7%	18 5.2%	13
Cherry Coffeetime	323	5.4	180	13	133 41.2%	40 12.4%	80 24.8%	13 4.0%	13

TABLE XXVI (continued)

	TC	*EE miles*	*C cal*	*P cal*	*F cal*	*S cal*	*M cal*	*PU cal*	*Chol. mg.*
Pastries, Pillsbury fresh-dough products									
Cherry turn-over 8 = 400 gms. (14 oz.)	339	5.7	160	12	171 50.4%	51 15.0%	103 30.4%	17 5.0%	12
Puddings									
Made with whole eggs 1 cup = 240 gms. (8 3/8 oz.)	115	1.9	–	–	50 43.4%	27 23.5%	–	0	100
Cornstarch, no eggs 1 cup = 240 gms. (8 3/8 oz.)	111	1.9	59	12	35 31.5%	18 16.2%	–	0	10

TABLE XXVII: COMPOSITION OF NUT PRODUCTS
3 1/2 Ounces (100 Grams)*

	TC	*EE* *miles*	*C* *cal*	*P* *cal*	*F* *cal*	*S* *cal*	*M* *cal*	*PU* *cal*	*Chol.* *mg.*
Almonds									
Roasted or salted	627	10.5	79	64	483 77.0%	42 6.7%	326 52.0%	100 16.0%	0
Shelled 1 cup whole = 142 gms. (5 oz.)	598	10.0	79	64	454 75.9%	34 5.6%	301 50.3%	92 15.4%	0
Beechnuts	568	9.5	82	67	418 73.5%	34 5.9%	226 39.8%	134 23.6%	0
Brazil nuts	654	10.9	44	50	560 85.7%	109 16.7%	268 41.0%	142 21.7%	0
Cashew nuts	386	6.4	119	60	383 68.2%	67 17.3%	268 69.4%	25 6.4%	0
Coconut									
Dried									
Sweetened, shredded	548	9.1	217	12	327 59.7%	285 52.0%	25 4.6%	T	0
Unsweetened, dried	662	11.0	94	25	543 82.0%	469 70.8%	42 6.3%	T	0
Fresh	346	5.8	38	12	296 85.5%	251 72.5%	17 4.8%	T	0
Filberts (Hazelnuts)	634	10.6	68	44	522 82.3%	25 4.0%	285 45.0%	84 13.2%	0
Hickory nuts	673	11.2	52	46	575 85.5%	50 7.4%	394 58.5%	100 14.9%	0
Peanut butter, with small amounts of added fat, sweetener, and salt 1 tbsp = 16 gms. (1/2 oz.)	582	6.7	79	88	414 71.1%	76 13.0%	202 34.6%	112 19.2%	0
Peanuts 1 cup = 144 gms. (5 oz.)	564	9.4	76	90	398 70.5%	84 14.9%	167 29.6%	117 20.8%	0
Pecans 1 cup chopped = 126 gms. (4 1/2 oz.)	687	11.4	59	32	596 86.9%	42 6.1%	376 54.7%	117 17.0%	0
Pistachio nuts	594	9.9	77	67	450 75.9%	42 7.0%	293 49.3%	84 14.1%	0
Sunflower seed	560	9.3	81	83	396 70.7%	50 8.9%	75 13.5%	251 44.8%	0

*See page 283 for abbreviations and symbols.

TABLE XXVII (continued)

	TC	*EE miles*	*C cal*	*P cal*	*F cal*	*S cal*	*M cal*	*PU cal*	*Chol. mg.*
Walnuts									
Black									
1 cup chopped = 126 gms. (4 1/2 oz.)	628	10.5	60	71	496 79.0%	34 5.3%	176 28.0%	236 37.6%	0
English									
1 cup chopped = 126 gms. (4 1/2 oz.)	651	10.8	64	51	535 82.1%	34 5.1%	84 12.9%	335 51.4%	0

TABLE XXVIII: COMPOSITION OF BEVERAGES
3 1/2 Ounces (100 Grams)*

	TC	*EE miles*	*C cal*	*P cal*	*F cal*	*S cal*	*M cal*	*PU cal*	*Chol. mg.*
Beer									
Alcohol 4.5% by volume (3.6% by weight) 12 fl. oz. = 360 gms. (12 5/8 oz.)	42	0.7	16	1	0	0	0	0	0
Carbonated, nonalcoholic									
Club soda, unsweetened	0	0	0	0	0	0	0	0	0
Cola type 12 fl. oz. = 369 gms. (13 oz.)	39	0.7	39	0	0	0	0	0	0
Cream sodas 12 fl. oz. = 370 gms. (13 oz.)	43	0.7	43	0	0	0	0	0	0
Fruit-flavored (including Tom Collins) 12 fl. oz. = 372 gms. (13 oz.)	46	0.8	46	0	0	0	0	0	0
Ginger ale 12 fl. oz. = 366 gms. (13 oz.)	31	0.5	31	0	0	0	0	0	0
Quinine sodas, sweetened 12 fl. oz. = 366 gms. (13 oz.)	31	0.5	31	0	0	0	0	0	0
Root beer 12 fl. oz. = 370 gms. (13 oz.)	41	0.7	41	0	0	0	0	0	0
Gin, Rum, Vodka, Whisky									
80-proof 1 1/2 fl. oz. jigger = 42 gms. (1 1/2 oz.)	231	3.8	T	0	0	0	0	0	0
86-proof 1 1/2 fl. oz. jigger = 42 gms. (1 1/2 oz.)	249	4.2	T	0	0	0	0	0	0
90-proof 1 1/2 fl. oz. jigger = 42 gms. (1 1/2 oz.)	263	4.4	T	0	0	0	0	0	0
94-proof 1 1/2 fl. oz. jigger = 42 gms. (1 1/2 oz.)	275	4.6	T	0	0	0	0	0	0
100-proof 1 1/2 fl. oz. jigger = 42 gms. (1 1/2 oz.)	295	5.0	T	0	0	0	0	0	0
Wines									
Dessert, alcohol 18.8% by volume 3 1/2 fl. oz. = 103 gms.	137	2.3	28	T	0	0	0	0	0
Table, alcohol 12.2% by volume 3 1/2 fl. oz. = 102 gms.	85	1.4	15	T	0	0	0	0	0

*See page 283 for abbreviations and symbols.

TABLE XXIX: MASTER FOOD-EXCHANGE LIST

White- and Green-Point Foods
(Calories 35% Fat or Less and 10% Saturated Fat or Less)

	TC	*White Points*	*Green Points*	*Blue Points*	*Gold Points*	*Choles-terol Milli-grams*
No-Cholesterol Foods						
Sugars and sirups						
Honey						
1 tbsp = 21 gms. (3/4 oz.)	64	22	6	0	0	0
1 tsp = 7 gms. (1/4 oz.)	21	7	2	0	0	0
Jams and preserves						
1 tbsp = 20 gms. (3/4 oz.)	54	19	5	0	0	0
1 tsp = 7 gms. (1/4 oz.)	18	6	2	0	0	0
Jellies						
1 tbsp = 20 gms. (3/4 oz.)	55	19	5	0	0	0
1 tsp = 7 gms. (1/4 oz.)	18	6	2	0	0	0
Molasses, cane						
Light						
1 tbsp = 20 gms. (3/4 oz.)	50	18	5	0	0	0
1 tsp = 7 gms. (1/4 oz.)	17	6	2	0	0	0
Medium						
1 tbsp = 20 gms. (3/4 oz.)	46	16	5	0	0	0
1 tsp = 7 gms. (1/4 oz.)	15	5	2	0	0	0
Blackstrap						
1 tbsp = 20 gms. (3/4 oz.)	43	15	4	0	0	0
1 tsp = 7 gms. (1/4 oz.)	14	5	1	0	0	0
Sirups						
Cane						
1 tbsp = 21 gms. (3/4 oz.)	55	19	5	0	0	0
1 tsp = 7 gms. (1/4 oz.)	18	6	2	0	0	0
Corn						
1 tbsp = 21 gms. (3/4 oz.)	61	21	6	0	0	0
1 tsp = 7 gms. (1/4 oz.)	20	7	2	0	0	0
Maple						
1 tbsp = 20 gms. (3/4 oz.)	50	18	5	0	0	0
1 tsp = 7 gms. (1/4 oz.)	17	6	2	0	0	0
Sorgum						
1 tbsp = 21 gms. (3/4 oz.)	54	19	5	0	0	0
1 tsp = 7 gms. (1/4 oz.)	18	6	2	0	0	0
Table, cane or maple						
1 tbsp = 21 gms. (3/4 oz.)	53	18	6	0	0	0
1 tsp = 7 gms. (1/4 oz.)	18	6	2	0	0	0
Sugars						
Brown						
1 cup = 220 gms. (7 3/4 oz.)	820	288	81	0	0	0
1 tbsp = 14 gms. (1/2 oz.)	52	18	5	0	0	0
1 tsp = 5 gms. (1/6 oz.)	17	6	2	0	0	0
Maple						
1 cup = 220 gms. (7 1/4 oz.)	765	268	77	0	0	0
1 tbsp = 14 gms. (1/2 oz.)	49	17	5	0	0	0
1 tsp = 5 gms. (1/6 oz.)	16	6	2	0	0	0
White, granulated						
1 cup = 200 gms. (7 oz.)	770	270	76	0	0	0
1 tbsp = 12.5 gms. (4/10 oz.)	48	34	5	0	0	0
1 tsp = 4 gms. (1/8 oz.)	16	11	2	0	0	0

TABLE XXIX (continued)

	TC	*White Points*	*Green Points*	*Blue Points*	*Gold Points*	*Cholesterol Milligrams*
No-Cholesterol Foods, Sugar and sirups, sugar—continued						
White, powdered						
1 cup = 120 gms. (4 1/4 oz.)	462	162	46	0	0	0
1 tbsp = 8 gms. (1/4 oz.)	29	10	3	0	0	0
1 tsp = 2.5 gms. (1/12 oz.)	10	3	1	0	0	0
Miscellaneous						
Baking powder						
Sodium aluminum sulfate						
With monocalcium phosphate monohydrate						
1 tbsp = 14 gms. (1/2 oz.)	18	6	2	0	0	0
1 tsp = 4.5 gms. (1/6 oz.)	6	2	1	0	0	0
With monocalcium phosphate monohydrate and calcium carbonate						
100 gms. (3 1/2 oz.)	78	27	8	0	0	0
With monocalcium phosphate monohydrate and calcium sulfate						
100 gms. (3 1/2 oz.)	104	36	10	0	0	0
Straight phosphate						
100 gms. (3 1/2 oz.)	121	42	12	0	0	0
Cream of tartar						
100 gms. (3 1/2 oz.)	78	27	8	0	0	0
Chocolate-flavored sirup, thin						
1 cup = 300 gms. (10 1/2 oz.)	735	207	48	24	0	0
Gelatin, Knox						
1 envelope	28	10	3	0	0	0
Cereals						
Barley						
Pearled						
1 cup = 200 gms. (7 oz.)	698	228	70	0	8	0
Pat or Scotch						
100 gms. (3 1/2 oz.)	348	112	35	0	4	0
Buckwheat flour						
Dark						
1 cup = 100 gms. (3 1/2 oz.)	333	96	33	0	0	0
Light						
1 cup = 100 gms. (3 1/2 oz.)	347	111	35	0	0	0
Corn grits						
1 cup = 245 gms. (8 1/2 oz.)	887	294	86	2	5	0
Cornmeal						
Whole, ground, unbolted, dry						
1 cup = 122 gms. (4 1/2 oz.)	433	112	43	0	21	0
Bolted, nearly dry						
1 cup = 122 gms. (4 1/2 oz.)	442	120	44	0	21	0
Degermed, enriched						
1 cup = 138 gms. (4 3/4 oz.)	502	161	50	0	23	0
Cornstarch						
1 cup = 125 gms. (4 1/2 oz.)	452	159	45	0	0	0
1 tbsp = 8 gms. (1/4 oz.)	28	10	3	0	0	0
1 tsp = 2.5 gms. (1/12 oz.)	9	3	1	0	0	0
Farina, enriched, regular						
1 cup = 245 gms. (8 1/2 oz.)	909	299	88	2	10	0

TABLE XXIX (continued)

	TC	*White Points*	*Green Points*	*Blue Points*	*Gold Points*	*Cholesterol Milligrams*
No-Cholesterol Foods, Cereals–continued						
Oatmeal, rolled oats						
1 cup = 82 gms. (2 3/4 oz.)	320	61	25	7	14	0
Popcorn						
Unpopped 100 gms. (3 1/2 oz.)	362	87	28	8	25	0
Popped, plain						
1 quart = 24 gms. (5/6 oz.)	93	22	7	2	6	0
Rice						
Brown						
1 cup = 185 gms. (6 1/2 oz.)	666	203	61	6	18	0
Instant dry						
1 cup = 86 gms. (3 oz.)	322	111	32	0	0	0
White, enriched						
1 cup = 185 gms. (6 1/2 oz.)	672	229	67	0	0	0
Rye flour						
Light						
1 cup = 100 gms. (3 1/2 oz.)	357	123	36	0	0	0
Medium						
1 cup = 100 gms. (3 1/2 oz.)	350	108	32	3	9	0
Dark						
1 cup = 128 gms. (4 1/2 oz.)	419	119	37	5	15	0
Wheat flour						
All-purpose, enriched						
1 cup = 120 gms. (4 1/4 oz.)	437	143	34	2	5	0
1 tbsp = 7.5 gms. (1/4 oz.)	27	9	2	0	0	0
1 tsp = 2.5 gms. (1/12 oz.)	9	3	1	0	0	0
Cake or pastry						
1 cup = 100 gms. (3 1/2 oz.)	364	121	35	1	3	0
Gluten						
1 cup = 125 gms. (4 1/4 oz.)	472	145	42	4	10	0
Self-rising, enriched						
1 cup = 125 gms. (4 1/4 oz.)	440	144	41	2	5	0
Whole wheat						
1 cup = 120 gms. (4 1/4 oz.)	400	120	36	4	10	0
Wheat germ						
1 cup = 114 gms. (4 oz.)	414	41	22	19	48	0
Wheat, whole meal						
100 gms. (3 1/2 oz.)	338	115	30	3	8	0
Wild rice						
1 cup = 160 gms. (5 1/2 oz.)	565	189	56	0	0	0
Prepared cereals						
Bran flakes						
40% bran						
1 cup = 35 gms. (1 1/4 oz.)	106	32	10	0	0	0
With raisins						
1 cup = 50 gms. (1 3/4 oz.)	144	49	14	0	0	0
Corn flakes						
1 cup = 24 gms. (7/8 oz.)	93	32	9	0	0	0
Corn, puffed, added nutrients						
100 gms. (3 1/2 oz.)	399	104	36	4	18	0
Oats, puffed, with added nutrients						
1 cup = 25 gms. (7/8 oz.)	99	23	8	1	2	0

TABLE XXIX (continued)

	TC	*White Points*	*Green Points*	*Blue Points*	*Gold Points*	*Choles-terol Milli-grams*
No-Cholesterol Foods, Cereals–continued						
Rice flakes, added nutrients						
100 gms. (3 1/2 oz.)	390	134	37	0	0	0
Rice, puffed, added nutrients						
1 cup = 15 gms. (1/2 oz.)	60	20	6	0	0	0
Wheat flakes, added nutrients						
1 cup = 30 gms. (1 oz.)	106	33	10	1	2	0
Wheat, puffed, added nutrients						
1 cup = 15 gms. (1/2 oz.)	54	17	5	0	1	0
Wheat, shredded						
1 biscuit = 25 gms. (5/6 oz.)	88	30	8	1	2	0
1 cup = 30 gms. (1 oz.)	106	36	10	1	2	0
Dairy products						
Eggs, whites only						
1 white = 33 gms. (1 1/6 oz.)	17	6	2	0	0	0
Sauces and dressings						
Horseradish, prepared						
1 cup = 258 gms. (9 oz.)	98	29	10	0	0	0
Salad dressing, commercial, French						
Low-fat						
1 tbsp = 15 gms. (1/2 oz.)	2	0	0	0	0	0
Vinegar						
1 tbsp = 15 gms. (1/2 oz.)	2	1	0	0	0	0
Worcestershire sauce, French's						
1 tbsp = 15 gms. (1/2 oz.)	6	2	1	0	0	0
Vegetables						
Artichokes 100 gms. (3 1/2 oz.)	28	8	2	0	1	0
Asparagus						
Raw 100 gms. (3 1/2 oz.)	26	7	2	0	1	0
Canned						
1 cup = 145 gms. (5 oz.)	30	6	1	1	3	0
Frozen						
100 gms. (3 1/2 oz.)	24	7	2	0	1	0
Bamboo shoots						
100 gms. (3 1/2 oz.)	27	7	2	0	1	0
Beans						
Lima						
Immature seeds, raw 100 gms. (3 1/2 oz.)	123	39	11	1	2	0
Immature seeds, canned, drained solids						
1 cup = 170 gms. (6 oz.)	163	53	15	2	2	0
Immature seeds, baby lima, frozen						
100 gms. (3 1/2 oz.)	122	41	12	0	1	0
Mature seeds						
1/2 cup = 79 gms. (2 3/4 oz.)	273	92	25	2	5	0
Mung, mature seeds						
100 gms. (3 1/2 oz.)	340	108	32	2	6	0
Pinto (calico or red Mexican), mature seeds						
1 cup = 100 gms. (3 1/2 oz.)	349	112	34	1	5	0

TABLE XXIX (continued)

	TC	*White Points*	*Green Points*	*Blue Points*	*Gold Points*	*Choles-terol Milli-grams*
No-Cholesterol Foods, Vegetables, beans–continued						
Red,						
raw mature seeds						
1/2 cup = 100 gms. (3 1/2 oz.)	343	107	32	2	7	0
Canned						
1 cup = 255 gms. (9 oz.)	230	71	23	0	5	0
Snap, green						
Raw						
1 cup = 100 gms. (3 1/2 oz.)	32	10	3	0	1	0
Canned, drained solids						
1 cup = 125 gms. (4 3/8 oz.)	30	9	2	0	1	0
Frozen 100 gms. (3 1/2 oz.)	26	8	3	0	0	0
Snap, yellow or wax						
Raw						
1 cup = 100 gms. (3 1/2 oz.)	27	8	3	0	1	0
Canned, drained solids						
1 cup = 125 gms. (4 3/8 oz.)	30	8	2	0	2	0
Frozen 100 gms. = (3 1/2 oz.)	28	9	3	0	0	0
White						
Mature seeds						
1/2 cup = 100 gms. (3 1/2 oz.)	340	106	32	2	7	0
Mature seeds canned with pork and tomato sauce						
1 cup = 255 gms. (9 oz.)	311	54	10	20	0	T
Mature seeds canned without pork						
1 cup = 190 gms. (6 2/3 oz.)	228	72	21	2	4	0
Beet greens 100 gms. (3 1/2 oz.)	24	6	2	0	1	0
Beets, common red						
Raw 1 2-inch beet = 50 gms. (1 3/4 oz.)	21	7	2	0	0	0
Cooked, drained. peeled, diced or sliced						
1 cup = 170 gms. (6 oz.)	63	20	7	0	0	0
Canned						
1 cup = 246 gms. (8 1/2 oz.)	84	27	7	0	0	0
Blackeye peas (See Cowpeas)						
Broad beans						
Immature seeds						
100 gms. (3 1/2 oz.)	105	34	10	0	2	0
Mature seeds						
100 gms. (3 1/2 oz.)	338	104	32	2	7	0
Broccoli						
Raw						
100 gms. (3 1/2 oz.)	32	9	3	1	1	0
Cooked spears, boiled and drained						
1 cup = 155 gms.	40	11	5	0	2	0
Frozen spears						
100 gms. (3 1/2 oz.)	28	8	3	0	1	0
Brussels sprouts						
Raw						
100 gms. (3 1/2 oz.)	45	12	4	1	2	0

TABLE XXIX (continued)

	TC	*White Points*	*Green Points*	*Blue Points*	*Gold Points*	*Cholesterol Milligrams*
No-Cholesterol Foods, Vegetables, brussels sprouts–continued						
Frozen						
100 gms. (3 1/2 oz.)	36	11	4	0	1	0
Cabbage						
Common						
1 cup shredded = 80 gms. (2 3/4 oz.)	19	6	2	0	1	0
Cooked						
1 cup = 145 gms. (5 oz.)	30	7	3	0	1	0
Chinese						
1 cup cut = 75 gms. (2 2/3 oz.)	10	3	1	0	0	0
Spoon						
100 gms. (3 1/2 oz.)	16	4	2	0	1	0
Carrots						
Raw						
2 carrots = 100 gms. (3 1/2 oz.)	42	13	4	0	1	0
Canned						
1 cup diced = 145 gms. (5 oz.)	40	12	4	0	1	0
Cauliflower						
Raw						
100 gms. (3 1/2 oz.)	27	8	3	0	1	0
Cooked						
1 cup = 120 gms. (4 1/4 oz.)	25	7	2	0	1	0
Frozen						
100 gms. (3 1/2 oz.)	22	6	2	0	1	0
Celeriac root						
100 gms. (3 1/2 oz.)	40	12	4	0	1	0
Celery						
1 stalk = 40 gms. (1 1/2 oz.)	7	2	1	0	0	0
Chard, Swiss						
100 gms. (3 1/2 oz.)	25	6	2	0	1	0
Chickpeas, mature seeds						
100 gms. (3 1/2 oz.)	360	86	36	0	17	0
Chicory						
Witloof						
100 gms. (3 1/2 oz.)	15	4	2	0	0	0
Greens						
100 gms. (3 1/2 oz.)	20	4	2	0	1	0
Chives						
100 gms. (3 1/2 oz.)	28	7	3	0	1	0
Collards						
Leaves, raw						
100 gms. (3 1/2 oz.)	45	9	3	2	3	0
Frozen						
100 gms. (3 1/2 oz.)	32	8	2	1	2	0
Corn						
Field, whole-grain, mature						
100 gms. (3 1/2 oz.)	348	89	35	0	17	0

	TC	White Points	Green Points	Blue Points	Gold Points	Choles-terol Milli-grams
No-Cholesterol Foods, Vegetables, corn—continued						
Sweet						
Raw						
100 gms. (3 1/2 oz.)	96	25	9	1	4	0
Cooked, drained						
1 cup = 168 gms. (5 9/10 oz.)	139	25	13	2	7	0
Canned, cream-style						
100 gms. (3 1/2 oz.)	82	24	8	0	3	0
Canned, whole-kernel						
1 cup = 170 gms. (6 oz.)	112	31	12	0	3	0
Frozen						
100 gms. (3 1/2 oz.)	82	24	8	0	2	0
Cowpeas						
Mature seeds						
100 gms. (3 1/2 oz.)	343	108	33	2	6	0
Canned						
100 gms. (3 1/2 oz.)	70	22	7	0	1	0
Frozen						
100 gms. (3 1/2 oz.)	131	42	13	0	2	0
Cress, garden						
100 gms. (3 1/2 oz.)	32	5	2	1	3	0
Cucumbers						
1 7 1/2-inch by 2-inch cucumber (pared) = 207 gms. (7 oz.)	31	8	4	0	0	0
Dandelion greens						
100 gms. (3 1/2 oz.)	45	10	3	1	3	0
Dock						
100 gms. (3 1/2 oz.)	28	7	3	0	1	0
Eggplant						
100 gms. (3 1/2 oz.)	25	7	2	0	1	0
Endive						
Curly or escarole						
100 gms. (3 1/2 oz.)	20	6	2	0	0	0
French or Belgian (See Chicory, witloof)						
Garbanzos (See Chickpeas)						
Garlic cloves						
100 gms. (3 1/2 oz.)	137	46	14	0	1	0
Ginger root, fresh						
100 gms. (3 1/2 oz.)	49	9	3	2	4	0
Hominy grits (See Cereals, Corn grits)						
Horseradish						
100 gms. (3 1/2 oz.)	87	28	9	0	1	0
Kale						
Raw						
100 gms. (3 1/2 oz.)	53	12	4	1	3	0
Frozen						
100 gms. (3 1/2 oz.)	32	7	2	1	2	0
Kohlrabi						
100 gms. (3 1/2 oz.)	29	9	3	0	0	0

TABLE XXIX (continued)

	TC	*White Points*	*Green Points*	*Blue Points*	*Gold Points*	*Choles-terol Milli-grams*
No-Cholesterol Foods, Vegetables –continued						
Leeks						
100 gms. (3 1/2 oz.)	52	16	5	0	1	0
Lentils, mature seed						
100 gms. (3 1/2 oz.)	340	110	33	1	5	0
Lettuce						
Butterhead (Boston)						
1 average head = 220 gms. (7 3/4 oz.)	31	6	2	0	2	0
Cos (romaine), dark green, and white parts						
1 cup (broken pieces) = 43 gms. (1 1/2 oz.)	8	2	1	0	0	0
Crisp head (Iceberg), New York, and Great Lakes						
1 cup (broken pieces) = 76 gms. (2 2/3 oz.)	9	3	1	0	0	0
Mushrooms						
Raw						
1 cup (trimmed) = 72 gms. (2 1/2 oz.)	20	5	2	0	1	0
Canned						
1 cup = 244 gms. (8 1/2 oz.)	41	12	5	0	0	0
Mustard greens						
Raw						
100 gms. (3 1/2 oz.)	31	7	2	1	2	0
Frozen						
100 gms. (3 1/2 oz.)	20	4	1	1	2	0
Mustard spinach (Indian mustard)						
100 gms. (3 1/2 oz.)	22	5	2	1	1	0
New Zealand spinach						
100 gms. (3 1/2 oz.)	19	4	1	1	1	0
Okra						
Raw						
100 gms. (3 1/2 oz.)	36	10	3	1	1	0
Frozen						
100 gms. (3 1/2 oz.)	39	13	4	0	0	0
Onions						
Mature						
1 cup chopped = 172 gms. (6 oz.)	65	21	7	0	0	0
Young green						
Bulb and white portion						
6 onions = 50 gms. (1 3/4 oz.)	22	7	2	0	0	0
Tops only						
100 gms. (3 1/2 oz.)	27	6	2	1	2	0
Welsh						
100 gms. (3 1/2 oz.)	34	9	3	1	2	0
Parsley						
1/4 cup chopped = 16 gms. (1/2 oz.)	44	2	0	0	0	0

TABLE XXIX (continued)

	TC	*White Points*	*Green Points*	*Blue Points*	*Gold Points*	*Cholesterol Milligrams*
No-Cholesterol Foods, Vegetables —continued						
Parsnips						
1 medium parsnip = 100 gms. (3 1/2 oz.)	76	22	7	1	2	0
Peas, edible podded						
100 gms. (3 1/2 oz.)	53	17	5	0	1	0
Peas, green immature						
Shelled						
1 cup = 136 gms. (4 3/4 oz.)	114	35	11	1	3	0
Canned (Alaska, early, or June)						
1 cup = 249 gms. (8 3/4 oz.)	164	52	17	0	2	0
Canned, sweet						
1 cup = 249 gms. (8 3/4 oz.)	142	42	15	0	2	0
Frozen						
100 gms. (3 1/2 oz.)	73	23	7	0	1	0
Peppers, hot chili						
Green						
1 tbsp = 15 gms. (1/2 oz.)	5	2	1	0	0	0
Red						
100 gms. (3 1/2 oz.)	93	13	5	4	10	0
Peppers, sweet						
Green						
1 pod (1/2 cup chopped) = 74 gms. (2 1/2 oz.)	16	4	1	0	1	0
Red						
1 pod (1/2 cup chopped) = 74 gms. (2 1/2 oz.)	23	6	2	0	1	0
Pickles, cucumber						
Sweet						
1 cup chopped = 172 gms. (6 oz.)	251	82	25	0	0	0
Dill						
100 gms. (3 1/2 oz.)	11	2	1	0	0	0
Fresh (bread and butter)						
100 gms. (3 1/2 oz.)	73	24	7	0	0	0
Sour						
100 gms. (3 1/2 oz.)	10	0	1	0	0	0
Pimientos, canned						
100 gms. (3 1/2 oz.)	27	5	2	1	2	0
Potatoes						
Raw						
1 average potato = 150 gms. (5 1/4 oz.)	114	39	12	0	0	0
Dehydrated, mashed, dry form						
100 gms. (3 1/2 oz.)	364	122	35	1	2	0
Frozen						
100 gms. (3 1/2 oz.)	73	26	7	0	0	0
Pumpkin						
Raw						
100 gms. (3 1/2 oz.)	26	8	3	0	0	0
Canned						
1 cup = 228 gms. (8 oz.)	75	20	7	0	0	0

TABLE XXIX (continued)

	TC	*White Points*	*Green Points*	*Blue Points*	*Gold Points*	*Cholesterol Milligrams*
No-Cholesterol Foods, Vegetables –continued						
Radishes						
4 small radishes = 40 gms. (1 1/3 oz.)	7	2	1	0	0	0
Relish, pickled sweet						
100 gms. (3 1/2 oz.)	138	43	14	0	0	0
Rutabaga						
100 gms. (3 1/2 oz.)	46	15	5	0	0	0
Salsify						
100 gms. (3 1/2 oz.)	45	11	3	1	2	0
Sauerkraut, canned, solids and liquid						
1 cup = 235 gms. (8 1/4 oz.)	18	5	2	0	0	0
Shallot						
100 gms. (3 1/2 oz.)	72	24	7	0	0	0
Spinach						
Raw						
1 cup chopped = 50 gms. (1 3/4 oz.)	13	3	1	0	0	0
Canned						
1 cup = 180 gms. (6 1/3 oz.)	34	5	2	2	4	0
Frozen						
100 gms. (3 1/2 oz.)	24	6	2	0	1	0
Squash, summer						
Crookneck, Straightneck, Yellow						
100 gms. (3 1/2 oz.)	20	5	2	0	1	0
Scallop varieties, white and pale green						
100 gms. (3 1/2 oz.)	21	6	2	0	0	0
Zucchini and cocozelle						
100 gms. (3 1/2 oz.)	17	5	2	0	0	0
Frozen						
100 gms. (3 1/2 oz.)	21	6	2	0	0	0
Squash, winter						
Acorn						
100 gms. (3 1/2 oz.)	44	15	4	0	0	0
Butternut						
100 gms. (3 1/2 oz.)	54	18	5	0	0	0
Hubbard						
100 gms. (3 1/2 oz.)	39	11	4	0	1	0
Frozen						
100 gms. (3 1/2 oz.)	38	11	4	0	1	0
Succotash (corn and Lima beans)						
Frozen						
100 gms. (3 1/2 oz.)	97	31	10	1	2	0
Sweet potatoes						
Raw						
100 gms. (3 1/2 oz.)	114	36	11	1	2	0
Dehydrated, powder form						
100 gms. (3 1/2 oz.)	379	127	37	1	3	0
Tomatoes						
Green						
100 gms. (3 1/2 oz.)	24	7	2	0	1	0

TABLE XXIX (continued)

	TC	*White Points*	*Green Points*	*Blue Points*	*Gold Points*	*Choles-terol Milli-grams*
No-Cholesterol Foods, Vegetables, tomatoes–continued						
Ripe						
1 3-inch tomato = 200 gms. (7 oz.)	44	12	4	0	2	0
Ripe, canned						
1 cup = 241 gms. (8 1/2 oz.)	51	14	5	0	2	0
Tomato catchup						
1 tbsp = 15 gms. (1/2 oz.)	16	5	2	2	2	0
Tomato chili sauce						
1 cup = 286 gms. (10 oz.)	297	101	30	0	6	0
Tomato juice, canned						
1 cup = 243 gms. (8 1/2 oz.)	46	15	5	0	0	0
Tomato paste, canned						
1 cup = 257 gms. (9 oz.)	211	65	21	3	5	0
Tomato purée, canned						
1 cup = 257 gms. (9 oz.)	100	31	10	0	3	0
Turnip greens						
Raw						
100 gms. (3 1/2 oz.)	28	7	3	0	1	0
Canned						
100 gms. (3 1/2 oz.)	18	4	2	0	1	0
Frozen						
100 gms. (3 1/2 oz.)	23	6	2	0	1	0
Turnips						
1 medium turnip = 100 gms. (3 1/2 oz.)	30	9	3	0	1	0
Vegetables, mixed, frozen						
100 gms. (3 1/2 oz.)	65	20	6	0	1	0
Water cress						
1 cup chopped = 36 gms. (1 1/4 oz.)	7	1	1	0	0	0
Yam tuber						
100 gms. (3 1/2 oz.)	101	33	10	0	1	0
Yam bean, tuber						
100 gms. (3 1/2 oz.)	55	18	6	0	1	0
Berries, fruits, and melons						
Apples						
Raw						
edible portion of 1 apple = 163 gms. (5 3/4 oz.)	94	25	9	0	0	0
1 cup diced = 150 gms. (5 1/4 oz.)	87	23	9	0	0	0
Dehydrated						
100 gms. (3 1/2 oz.)	353	107	35	0	0	0
Frozen						
100 gms. (3 1/2 oz.)	93	32	9	0	0	0
Apple butter						
1 cup = 180 gms. (6 1/3 oz.)	335	104	34	0	0	0
Apple juice						
1 cup = 248 gms. (8 3/4 oz.)	116	40	12	0	0	0
Applesauce						
Canned, sweetened						
1 cup = 255 gms. (9 oz.)	232	76	23	0	0	0

TABLE XXIX (continued)

	TC	*White Points*	*Green Points*	*Blue Points*	*Gold Points*	*Cholesterol Milligrams*
No-Cholesterol Foods, Berries, fruits, and melons, applesauce–continued						
Canned, unsweetened						
1 cup = 244 gms. (8 1/2 oz.)	100	32	10	0	0	0
Apricot nectar						
1 cup = 251 gms. (8 3/4 oz.)	143	48	15	0	0	0
Apricots						
Raw						
1 cup halves = 142 gms. (5 oz.)	72	23	7	0	0	0
Canned						
Water pack						
1 cup = 250 gms. (8 3/4 oz.)	95	30	10	0	0	0
Juice pack						
1 cup = 250 gms. (8 3/4 oz.)	135	42	12	0	0	0
Heavy sirup						
1 cup = 259 gms. (9 oz.)	223	75	23	0	0	0
Dehydrated						
100 gms. (3 1/2 oz.)	332	108	33	0	0	0
Dried						
1 cup = 150 gms. (5 1/4 oz.)	390	130	39	0	0	0
Frozen, sweetened						
100 gms. (3 1/2 oz.)	98	34	10	0	0	0
Bananas						
1 banana = 150 gms. (5 1/4 oz.)	128	42	12	0	0	0
1 cup sliced = 180 gms. (6 1/4 oz.)	153	50	14	0	0	0
Blackberries						
Raw						
1 cup = 144 gms. (5 1/4 oz.)	84	19	9	0	0	0
Canned						
Water pack						
1 cup = 250 gms. (8 3/4 oz.)	100	22	10	0	0	0
Juice pack						
1 cup = 240 gms. (8 1/2 oz.)	130	29	12	0	0	0
Blackberry juice						
1 cup = 246 gms. (8 1/2 oz.)	91	20	10	0	0	0
Blueberries						
Raw						
1 cup = 144 gms. (5 1/4 oz.)	89	24	9	0	0	0
Canned, water pack						
1 cup = 250 gms. (8 3/4 oz.)	98	30	10	0	0	0
Frozen, unsweetened						
100 gms. (3 1/2 oz.)	55	15	5	0	0	0
Boysenberries						
Canned, water pack						
1 cup = 250 gms. (8 3/4 oz.)	90	30	10	0	0	0
Frozen, unsweetened						
100 gms. (3 1/2 oz.)	48	14	5	0	0	0
Breadfruit						
100 gms. (3 1/2 oz.)	103	34	10	0	0	0
Cantaloupe (See Muskmelon)						

TABLE XXIX (continued)

	TC	*White Points*	*Green Points*	*Blue Points*	*Gold Points*	*Cholesterol Milligrams*
No-Cholesterol Foods, Berries, fruits, and melons, boysenberries —continued						
Cherries						
Raw						
Sour red						
1 cup pitted = 160 gms. (5 1/2 oz.)	93	29	10	0	0	0
Sweet						
1 cup pitted = 160 gms. (5 1/2 oz.)	112	35	11	0	0	0
Canned						
Sour red, pitted, water pack						
1 cup = 207 gms. (7 1/4 oz.)	89	27	8	0	0	0
Sour red, pitted, heavy sirup						
1 cup = 260 gms. (9 oz.)	231	75	23	0	0	0
Sweet, pitted, water pack						
100 gms. (3 1/2 oz.)	48	15	5	0	0	0
Sweet, pitted, heavy sirup						
1 cup = 200 gms. (7 oz.)	162	54	16	0	0	0
Frozen, sour red, unsweetened						
100 gms. (3 1/2 oz.)	55	16	6	0	0	0
Crabapple						
100 gms. (3 1/2 oz.)	68	21	7	0	0	0
Cranberries						
Scant 1 cup = 100 gms. (3 1/2 oz.)	46	10	5	0	0	0
Cranberry-juice cocktail (about 1/3 cranberry juice)						
1 cup = 250 gms. (8 3/4 oz.)	162	55	5	0	0	0
Cranberry sauce						
1 cup = 277 gms. (9 2/3 oz.)	404	138	42	0	0	0
Cranberry-orange relish						
100 gms. (3 1/2 oz.)	178	59	18	0	0	0
Currants						
100 gms. (3 1/2 oz.)	52	17	5	0	0	0
Dates, natural						
1 cup pitted = 178 gms. (6 1/4 oz.)	488	164	48	0	0	0
Elderberries						
100 gms. (3 1/2 oz.)	72	21	7	0	0	0
Figs						
Raw						
3 small figs = 112 gms. (4 oz.)	90	29	9	0	0	0
Canned						
Water pack						
1 cup = 250 gms. (8 3/4 oz.)	48	15	5	0	0	0
Heavy sirup						
1 cup = 258 gms. (9 oz.)	217	72	21	0	0	0
Dried						
1 cup = 170 gms. (6 oz.)	466	162	46	0	0	0
Fruit cocktail, canned						
Water pack						
1 cup = 250 gms. (8 3/4 oz.)	92	30	10	0	0	0

TABLE XXIX (continued)

	TC	White Points	Green Points	Blue Points	Gold Points	Cholesterol Milligrams
No-Cholesterol Foods, Berries, fruits, and melons, fruit cocktail, canned–continued						
Heavy sirup						
1 cup = 260 gms. (9 oz.)	198	68	21	0	0	0
Gooseberries						
Raw						
1 cup = 150 gms. (5 1/4 oz.)	58	18	6	0	0	0
Canned						
Water pack						
100 gms. (3 1/2 oz.)	26	8	3	0	0	0
Heavy sirup						
100 gms. (3 1/2 oz.)	90	31	9	0	0	0
Grape juice						
Canned or bottled						
1 cup = 253 gms. (8 1/2 oz.)	167	58	18	0	0	0
Frozen concentrate, diluted 3 parts water by volume						
100 gms. (3 1/2 oz.)	53	18	5	0	0	0
Grapes						
American (slipskin)						
1 cup = 153 gms. (5 1/4 oz.)	106	24	11	0	0	0
European (adherent skin)						
1 cup = 160 gms. (5 1/2 oz.)	107	34	11	0	0	0
Grapefruit						
Raw						
1 cup = 200 gms. (7 oz.)	82	28	8	0	0	0
Canned segments, water pack						
1 cup = 250 gms. (8 3/4 oz.)	75	25	8	0	0	0
Grapefruit juice						
Canned, unsweetened						
1 cup = 247 gms. (8 3/4 oz.)	101	35	10	0	0	0
Frozen concentrate, unsweetened, diluted with 3 parts water by volume						
1 cup = 247 gms. (8 3/4 oz.)	101	35	10	0	0	0
Grapefruit and orange juice blended						
Canned, unsweetened						
1 cup = 250 gms. (8 3/4 oz.)	108	32	10	0	0	0
Kumquats						
5 or 6 kumquats (fresh only) = 100 gms. (3 1/2 oz.)	65	22	6	0	0	0
Lemon						
1 (pulp only) = 73 gms. (2 1/2 oz.)	20	5	2	0	0	0
Lemon juice						
Fresh						
1 cup = 244 gms. (8 1/2 oz.)	61	22	5	0	0	0
Canned or bottled, unsweetened						
1 cup = 250 gms. (8 3/4 oz.)	58	20	5	0	0	0
Lemonade, concentrate, frozen diluted with 4 1/3 parts water by volume						
1 cup = 248 gms. (8 3/4 oz.)	109	37	10	0	0	0

	TC	White Points	Green Points	Blue Points	Gold Points	Cholesterol Milligrams
No-Cholesterol Foods, Berries, fruits, and melons, lemonade –continued						
Lime juice, fresh						
1 cup = 246 gms. (8 1/2 oz.)	64	22	7	0	0	0
Limes						
2 limes (edible portion) = 100 gms. (3 1/2 oz.)	28	8	3	0	0	0
Loganberries						
Raw						
1 cup = 144 gms. (5 1/4 oz.)	89	24	9	0	0	0
Canned						
Water pack						
100 gms. (3 1/2 oz.)	40	11	4	0	0	0
Juice pack						
100 gms. (3 1/2 oz.)	54	15	5	0	0	0
Heavy sirup						
100 gms. (3 1/2 oz.)	89	28	9	0	0	0
Loquats						
100 gms. (3 1/2 oz.)	48	15	5	0	0	0
Mangoes						
1 mango, edible portion = 133 gms. (4 2/3 oz.)	88	27	9	0	0	0
Muskmelon (Cantaloupe)						
1 muskmelon, edible portion = 375 gms. (13 oz.)	112	34	11	0	0	0
Nectarines						
100 gms. (3 1/2 oz.)	64	22	6	0	0	0
Orange juice						
Fresh						
1 cup = 248 gms. (8 3/4 oz.)	112	35	10	0	0	0
Canned, unsweetened						
1 cup = 248 gms. (8 3/4 oz.)	119	37	12	0	0	0
Frozen concentrate, unsweetened, diluted with 3 parts water by volume						
1 cup = 249 gms. (8 3/4 oz.)	112	37	10	0	0	0
Oranges						
1 orange, edible portion = 130 gms. (4 1/2 oz.)	65	21	6	0	0	0
Papayas						
1 cup (cubes) = 182 gms. (6 3/8 oz.)	71	24	7	0	0	0
Peach nectar						
1 cup = 250 gms. (8 3/4 oz.)	120	42	12	0	0	0
Peaches						
Raw						
1 peach, edible portion = 87 gms. (3 oz.)	33	10	3	0	0	0
1 cup sliced = 168 gms. (6 oz.)	64	20	7	0	0	0
Canned						
Water pack						
1 cup = 245 gms. (8 1/2 oz.)	76	24	7	0	0	0

TABLE XXIX (continued)

	TC	White Points	Green Points	Blue Points	Gold Points	Cholesterol Milligrams
No-Cholesterol Foods, Berries, fruits, and melons, peaches, raw –continued						
Juice pack						
1 cup = 250 gms. (8 3/4 oz.)	112	38	10	0	0	0
Heavy sirup						
1 cup = 257 gms. (9 oz.)	200	67	21	0	0	0
Frozen, sliced, sweetened						
100 gms. (3 1/2 oz.)	88	30	9	0	0	0
Pear nectar						
1 cup = 257 gms. (9 oz.)	134	41	13	0	0	0
Pears						
Raw						
1 pear, edible portion = 166 gms. (5 3/4 oz.)	101	30	10	0	0	0
Canned						
Water pack						
1 cup = 248 gms. (8 3/4 oz.)	79	25	7	0	0	0
Juice pack						
1 cup = 248 gms. (8 3/4 oz.)	114	35	12	0	0	0
Heavy sirup						
1 cup = 255 gms. (9 oz.)	194	64	20	0	0	0
Persimmons						
100 gms. (3 1/2 oz.)	127	41	13	0	0	0
Pineapple						
Raw						
1 cup diced = 140 gms. (5 oz.)	73	22	7	0	0	0
Canned						
Juice pack						
1 cup = 228 gms. (8 oz.)	132	46	14	0	0	0
Heavy sirup						
1 cup crushed = 260 gms. (9 oz.)	192	65	18	0	0	0
2 small or 1 large slice with juice = 122 gms. (4 1/4 oz.)	90	30	8	0	0	0
Pineapple juice, canned, unsweetened						
1 cup = 249 gms. (8 3/4 oz.)	137	45	15	0	0	0
Plums						
Raw						
Edible portion 1 2-inch plum = 55 gms. (2 oz.)	36	12	4	0	0	0
Canned, heavy sirup						
Edible portion 1 cup with pits = 246 gms. (8 1/2 oz.)	204	69	20	0	0	0
Prune juice, canned or bottled						
1 cup = 256 gms. (9 oz.)	197	67	20	0	0	0
Prunes, dried						
Edible portion 16 medium prunes = 97 gms. (3 1/2 oz.)	247	81	64	0	0	0
Quinces						
100 gms. (3 1/2 oz.)	57	19	6	0	0	0
Raisins						
1 cup = 165 gms. (5 3/4 oz.)	477	163	48	0	0	0

TABLE XXIX (continued)

	TC	*White Points*	*Green Points*	*Blue Points*	*Gold Points*	*Cholesterol Milligrams*
No-Cholesterol Foods, Berries, fruits, and melons–continued						
Raspberries						
Raw						
Black						
1 cup = 127 gms. (4 1/2 oz.)	93	18	9	0	0	0
Red						
1 cup = 127 gms. (4 1/2 oz.)	72	20	8	0	0	0
Canned						
Black, water pack						
100 gms. (3 1/2 oz.)	51	17	5	0	0	0
Red, water pack						
100 gms. (3 1/2 oz.)	35	11	4	0	0	0
Rhubarb						
1 cup diced = 157 gms. (4 1/2 oz.)	25	8	3	0	0	0
Strawberries						
Raw						
1 cup = 155 gms. (5 1/2 oz.)	57	14	6	0	0	0
Canned, water pack						
100 gms. (3 1/2 oz.)	22	7	2	0	0	0
Frozen, sweetened, whole						
100 gms. (3 1/2 oz.)	92	30	9	0	0	0
Tangerines						
Edible portion: 1 tangerine = 86 gms. (3 oz.)	40	12	4	0	0	0
Watermelon						
100 gms. (3 1/2 oz.)	26	9	3	0	0	0
Beverages						
Beer (alcohol 4.5% by volume or 3.6% by weight)						
12 fl. oz. = 360 gms. (12 5/8 oz.)	151	53	15	0	0	0
Carbonated, nonalcoholic						
Club soda, unsweetened						
100 gms. (3 1/2 oz.)	0	0	0	0	0	0
Cola-type						
12 fl. oz. = 369 gms. (13 oz.)	144	50	14	0	0	0
Cream soda						
12 fl. oz. = 370 gms. (13 oz.)	159	56	16	0	0	0
Fruit-flavored (including Tom Collins)						
12 fl. oz. = 372 gms. (13 oz.)	171	60	17	0	0	0
Ginger ale						
12 fl. oz. = 360 gms. (13 oz.)	112	39	11	0	0	0
Quinine soda, sweetened						
12 fl. oz. = 366 gms. (13 oz.)	113	40	11	0	0	0
Root beer						
12 fl. oz. = 370 gms. (13 oz.)	152	53	15	0	0	0
Coffee						
1 cup	2	0	0	0	0	0
Gin, Rum, Vodka, Whisky						
80-Proof 1 1/2 fl. oz. jigger = 42 gms. (1 1/2 oz.)	97	34	10	0	0	0

TABLE XXIX (continued)

	TC	*White Points*	*Green Points*	*Blue Points*	*Gold Points*	*Cholesterol Milligrams*
No-Cholesterol Foods, Beverages, gin, rum, vodka, whisky–continued						
86-Proof 1 1/2 fl. oz. jigger = 42 gms. (1 1/2 oz.)	105	37	10	0	0	0
90-Proof 1 1/2 fl. oz. jigger = 42 gms. (1 1/2 oz.)	110	38	11	0	0	0
94-Proof 1 1/2 fl. oz. jigger = 42 gms. (1 1/2 oz.)	116	40	12	0	0	0
100-Proof 1 1/2 fl. oz. jigger = 42 gms. (1 1/2 oz.)	124	43	12	0	0	0
Wines						
Dessert, 18.8% by volume 3 1/2 fl. oz. = 103 gms. (3 1/2 oz.)	141	49	14	0	0	0
Table, 12.2% by volume 3 1/2 fl. oz. = 102 gms. (3 1/2 oz.)	87	30	9	0	0	0
Candies						
Tootsie Roll Midgees 100 gms. (3 1/2 oz.)	400	72	31	9	3	0
Tootsie Roll Pops 100 gms. (3 1/2 oz.)	388	118	37	2	1	0
Tootsie Roll Pop Drops 100 gms. (3 1/2 oz.)	388	118	37	2	1	0
Desserts						
Angle-food cake 100 gms. (3 1/2 oz.)	269	92	27	0	0	0
Low-Cholesterol Foods (100 milligrams or less for 100 gms. (3 1/2 oz.)						
Miscellaneous						
Bouillon cubes (Wyler's) 1 cube = 7 calories	7	2	1	0	0	T
Dairy products						
Cheese, natural						
Cottage, uncreamed 100 gms. (3 1/2 oz.)	86	27	9	0	0	15
Eggstra (Tillie Lewis) 1 large egg = 50 gms. (1 3/4 oz.)	43	4	1	4	1	57
Milk, cow's						
Buttermilk, cultured from skim milk 1 cup = 245 gms. (8 1/2 oz.)	88	29	10	0	0	(7)
Nonfat milk powder, diluted (1 1/3 cup per quart) 1 cup = 245 gms. (8 1/2 oz.)	88	29	7	0	0	(7)
Nonfat milk powder, dry 1 cup = 68 gms. (2 1/3 oz.)	247	82	89	0	0	(22)
Partially skimmed (1%) with 2% nonfat milk solids added 1 cup = 246 gms. (8 1/2 oz.)	125	20	0	12	0	(12)
Skimmed 1 cup = 245 gms. (8 1/2 oz.)	88	29	10	0	0	7

TABLE XXIX (continued)

	TC	*White Points*	*Green Points*	*Blue Points*	*Gold Points*	*Cholesterol Milligrams*
Low-Cholesterol Foods, Dairy products, milk cow's—continued						
Skimmed with 2% nonfat milk solids added						
1 cup = 246 gms. (8 1/2 oz.)	103	34	10	0	0	(7)
Breads, rolls, and pastas						
Bread						
French or Vienna, enriched						
1 slice (18 per loaf) = 25 gms. (7/8 oz.)	72	18	6	2	1	(1)
Italian, enriched						
1 slice (18 per loaf) = 25 gms. (7/8 oz.)	69	24	7	0	1	(1)
Raisin						
1 slice (18 per loaf) = 25 gms. (7/8 oz.)	65	17	5	2	1	(1)
Rye, American						
1 slice (18 per loaf) = 25 gms. (7/8 oz.)	61	19	6	0	0	(1)
Rye, pumpernickel						
1 slice (18 per loaf) = 25 gms. (7/8 oz.)	62	19	6	0	0	(1)
White enriched, firm-crumb type						
1 slice (20 per loaf) = 23 gms. (4/5 oz.)	65	15	5	2	1	(1)
1 slice (34 per 2-pound loaf) = 27 gms. (1 oz.)	75	18	5	2	1	(1)
White enriched, soft-crumb type						
1 slice (24 1 1/2 pound loaf) = 28 gms. (1 oz.)	75	18	3	2	1	(1)
1 slice (28 per 1 1/2 pound loaf) = 24 gms. (7/8 oz.)	65	16	3	2	1	(1)
1 slice (18 per 1 pound loaf) = 25 gms. (7/8 oz.)	65	16	3	2	1	(1)
1 slice (22 per 1 pound loaf) = 20 gms. (3/4 oz.)	55	13	2	1	1	(1)
Whole-wheat						
1 slice (16 per 1 pound loaf) = 28 gms. (1 oz.)	67	17	6	1	1	(1)
Bread crumbs, dry, grated						
1 cup = 100 gms. (3 1/2 oz.)	390	92	30	9	9	(3)
Biscuits (Pillsbury fresh-dough products)						
Buttermilk						
1 biscuit = 23 gms. (4/5 oz.)	58	12	3	3	1	1
Country-style						
1 biscuit = 23 gms. (4/5 oz.)	58	12	3	3	1	T
Extra-light buttermilk						
1 biscuit = 23 gms. (4/5 oz.)	58	9	3	3	1	1
Hungry Jack buttermilk						
1 biscuit = 27 gms. (1 oz.)	72	9	2	5	2	1
Oven-ready 100 gms. (3 1/2 oz.)	251	51	14	11	4	2
Crackers						
Graham						
4 (2 1/2 inch square) crackers = 28 gms. (1 oz.)	108	14	6	5	2	(1)

TABLE XXIX (continued)

	TC	White Points	Green Points	Blue Points	Gold Points	Choles-terol Milli-grams
Low-Cholesterol Foods,						
Crackers–continued						
Saltine						
4 crackers = 11 gms. (1/3 oz.)	48	5	2	3	1	(T)
Macaroni						
100 gms. (3 1/2 oz.)	369	118	37	0	0	(T)
Pizza dough with sauce (Pillsbury fresh-dough products)						
100 gms. (3 1/2 oz.)	173	38	10	7	2	1
Pretzels						
100 gms. (3 1/2 oz.)	390	97	30	9	4	(3)
Rolls and buns, commercial						
Partially baked (brown and serve)						
1 roll = 28 gms. (1 oz.)	84	12	4	4	2	(1)
Ready-to-serve						
Hard rolls						
1 roll = 50 gms. (1 3/4 oz.)	155	40	12	4	2	(1)
Plain or cloverleaf						
1 roll = 28 gms. (1 oz.)	85	15	5	3	2	(1)
Dinner rolls						
Butterflake						
1 roll = 19 gms. (3/5 oz.)	54	3	1	4	2	6
Hungry Jack, hot						
100 gms. (3 1/2 oz.)	296	9	1	29	9	16
Parkerhouse						
100 gms. (3 1/2 oz.)	265	39	11	16	5	22
Snowflake						
100 gms. (3 1/2 oz.)	296	9	1	29	9	2-8
Rolls, sweet						
Packaged sweet roll						
100 gms. (3 1/2 oz.)	316	29	14	18	9	70
Swirls (Pillsbury fresh-dough products)						
Caramel						
100 gms. (3 1/2 oz.)	364	16	3	33	11	4-7
Cinnamon						
100 gms. (3 1/2 oz.)	364	16	3	33	11	4-7
Orange						
100 gms. (3 1/2 oz.)	364	16	3	33	11	4-7
Spaghetti						
100 gms. (3 1/2 oz.)	369	118	37	0	0	T
Soup (Campbell soup company products)						
Heat-processed						
Bean with bacon						
100 gms. (3 1/2 oz.)	133	9	3	10	10	(1-6)
Beef						
100 gms. (3 1/2 oz.)	87	12	2	7	0	(1-6)
Beef broth						
100 gms. (3 1/2 oz.)	22	8	2	0	0	(1-6)
Black bean						
100 gms. (3 1/2 oz.)	80	15	7	1	6	(1-6)
Chicken broth						
100 gms. (3 1/2 oz.)	36	4	1	3	3	(1-6)
Chicken gumbo						
100 gms. (3 1/2 oz.)	49	7	3	2	3	(1-6)

TABLE XXIX (continued)

	TC	*White Points*	*Green Points*	*Blue Points*	*Gold Points*	*Choles-terol Milli-grams*
Low-Cholesterol Foods, Soup (Campbell soup company products) –continued						
Heat-processed						
Chicken noodle						
100 gms. (3 1/2 oz.)	55	5	2	3	3	5
Chicken Noodle-O's						
100 gms. (3 1/2 oz.)	59	6	2	4	4	5
Chicken with rice						
100 gms. (3 1/2 oz.)	43	3	1	3	3	(1-6)
Chicken & Stars						
100 gms. (3 1/2 oz.)	50	6	2	3	3	(1-6)
Chicken vegetable						
100 gms. (3 1/2 oz.)	60	5	3	3	4	(1-6)
Clam chowder						
100 gms. (3 1/2 oz.)	63	3	4	2	9	(1-6)
Consommé						
100 gms. (3 1/2 oz.)	28	10	3	0	0	(1-6)
Green pea						
100 gms. (3 1/2 oz.)	116	27	3	9	1	(1-6)
Hot-dog bean						
100 gms. (3 1/2 oz.)	153	6	0	15	9	(1-6)
Minestrone						
100 gms. (3 1/2 oz.)	72	3	3	4	10	(1-6)
Split pea with ham						
100 gms. (3 1/2 oz.)	141	26	4	10	2	(1-6)
Tomato						
100 gms. (3 1/2 oz.)	69	10	5	2	6	3
Tomato rice, old-fashioned						
100 gms. (3 1/2 oz.)	87	7	4	5	10	(1-6)
Vegetable						
100 gms. (3 1/2 oz.)	68	9	3	3	5	3
Vegetable beef						
100 gms. (3 1/2 oz.)	66	2	2	5	0	5
Vegetable, old-fashioned						
100 gms. (3 1/2 oz.)	53	4	0	5	5	(1-6)
Vegetarian vegetable						
100 gms. (3 1/2 oz.)	62	8	4	2	6	6
Frozen						
Green Pea with ham						
100 gms. (3 1/2 oz.)	109	17	4	7	2	(1-6)
Fish and shellfish						
Bass						
Black sea						
100 gms. (3 1/2 oz.)	93	22	6	3	4	70
Small-mouth or large-mouth						
100 gms. (3 1/2 oz.)	104	13	4	7	8	70
Striped						
100 gms. (3 1/2 oz.)	105	12	3	7	8	70
White						
100 gms. (3 1/2 oz.)	98	14	3	6	7	70
Bluefish						
100 gms. (3 1/2 oz.)	117	11	3	9	10	70
Buffalo fish						
100 gms. (3 1/2 oz.)	113	2	0	11	12	70

TABLE XXIX (continued)

	TC	*White Points*	*Green Points*	*Blue Points*	*Gold Points*	*Cholesterol Milligrams*
Low-Cholesterol Foods, fish and shellfish—continued						
Bullhead, black						
100 gms. (3 1/2 oz.)	84	15	4	4	5	70
Burbot						
100 gms. (3 1/2 oz.)	82	20	6	2	3	70
Butterfish, Gulf						
100 gms. (3 1/2 oz.)	95	7	2	8	9	36
Carp	115	2	0	11	12	70
Catfish, fresh-water						
100 gms. (3 1/2 oz.)	103	8	2	8	9	70
Clams						
Soft meat only						
100 gms. (3 1/2 oz.)	82	12	3	6	6	82
Hard meat only						
100 gms. (3 1/2 oz.)	80	20	6	3	3	82
Canned, solids						
100 gms. (3 1/2 oz.)	98	12	2	8	8	82
Cod						
100 gms. (3 1/2 oz.)	78	26	7	1	1	43
Crab						
Canned						
100 gms. (3 1/2 oz.)	101	12	4	6	5	52-98
Steamed						
100 gms. (3 1/2 oz.)	93	15	5	5	4	52-98
Crappie, white						
100 gms. (3 1/2 oz.)	79	20	6	2	2	70
Croaker						
Atlantic						
100 gms. (3 1/2 oz.)	96	14	4	6	6	70
White						
100 gms. (3 1/2 oz.)	84	22	6	2	2	70
Yellowfin						
100 gms. (3 1/2 oz.)	89	24	7	2	2	70
Drum, red (Redfish)						
100 gms. (3 1/2 oz.)	80	24	7	1	1	70
Finnan Haddie (Smoked Haddock)						
100 gms. (3 1/2 oz.)	103	32	9	1	2	25
Fish flakes, canned						
100 gms. (3 1/2 oz.)	111	33	10	1	2	70
Fish flour						
From whole fish						
100 gms. (3 1/2 oz.)	336	118	34	0	0	70
From filets						
100 gms. (3 1/2 oz.)	398	139	40	0	0	70
Flatfish (Flounder, Sole, and Sand dabs)						
100 gms. (3 1/2 oz.)	79	20	6	2	2	41
Flounder (See Flatfish)						
Frog Legs						
100 gms. (3 1/2 oz.)	79	27	8	0	0	70
Haddock						
100 gms. (3 1/2 oz.)	79	27	8	0	0	25

TABLE XXIX (continued)

	TC	White Points	Green Points	Blue Points	Gold Points	Choles-terol Milli-grams
Low-Cholesterol Foods, fish and shellfish–continued						
Hake (Whiting)						
100 gms. (3 1/2 oz.)	74	22	6	1	1	70
Halibut						
Atlantic and Pacific						
100 gms. (3 1/2 oz.)	100	24	10	2	3	34
California						
100 gms. (3 1/2 oz.)	97	21	6	4	4	34
Smoked						
100 gms. (3 1/2 oz.)	224	65	19	4	4	34
Herring, Pacific						
100 gms. (3 1/2 oz.)	98	11	3	7	5	25
Jack mackerel						
100 gms. (3 1/2 oz.)	143	0	0	50	17	48
Kingfish						
100 gms. (3 1/2 oz.)	105	10	3	8	9	70
Mussels						
Canned solids						
100 gms. (3 1/2 oz.)	114	10	1	10	5	58
Meat only						
100 gms. (3 1/2 oz.)	95	13	3	7	1	58
Oysters, meat only						
Eastern						
100 gms. (3 1/2 oz.)	66	6	2	5	8	58
Pacific						
100 gms. (3 1/2 oz.)	91	12	3	6	10	37
Perch, fresh-water						
White						
100 gms. (3 1/2 oz.)	118	5	1	10	12	70
Yellow						
100 gms. (3 1/2 oz.)	91	24	7	2	3	70
Perch, ocean						
100 gms. (3 1/2 oz.)	95	20	6	3	4	70
Pike						
Blue						
100 gms. (3 1/2 oz.)	90	23	7	2	3	70
Northern						
100 gms. (3 1/2 oz.)	88	21	6	3	3	70
Walleyed						
100 gms. (3 1/2 oz.)	93	22	6	3	4	70
Raja (See Skate)						
Redfish (See Drum)						
Red and gray snapper						
100 gms. (3 1/2 oz.)	93	24	7	2	3	33
Rockfish						
100 gms. (3 1/2 oz.)	97	18	5	5	6	70
Salmon						
Canned, chum						
100 gms. (3 1/2 oz.)	139	6	4	10	13	42
Raw, pink (Humpback)						
100 gms. (3 1/2 oz.)	119	8	5	7	14	70
Sand dabs (See Flatfish)						
Sea bass, white						
100 gms. (3 1/2 oz.)	96	29	8	1	1	44

TABLE XXIX (continued)

	TC	White Points	Green Points	Blue Points	Gold Points	Choles-terol Milli-grams
Low-Cholesterol Foods, fish and shellfish–continued						
Scallops						
100 gms. (3 1/2 oz.)	81	26	8	0	1	60
Skate						
100 gms. (3 1/2 oz.)	98	28	8	2	2	70
Sole (See Flatfish)						
Sturgeon						
100 gms. (3 1/2 oz.)	94	16	4	5	6	70
Swordfish						
100 gms. (3 1/2 oz.)	118	5	0	10	12	70
Tautog (Blackfish)						
100 gms. (3 1/2 oz.)	89	22	6	3	3	70
Trout, brook						
100 gms. (3 1/2 oz.)	101	16	5	5	6	70
Tuna						
Bluefin						
100 gms. (3 1/2 oz.)	145	14	2	13	10	52
Yellowfin						
100 gms. (3 1/2 oz.)	133	20	2	11	9	52
Packed in water, solids and liquid						
100 gms. (3 1/2 oz.)	127	37	10	2	2	52
Whiting (See Hake)						
Yellowtail, Pacific						
100 gms. (3 1/2 oz.)	138	0	0	14	16	70
Poultry						
Chicken, fryer						
Whole, flesh only						
1/2 cup = 100 gms. (3 1/2 oz.)	107	11	3	8	5	60
Without skin						
Light meat						
Edible portion 100 gms. (3 1/2 oz.)	101	22	6	4	3	60
Dark meat						
Edible portion 100 gms. (3 1/2 oz.)	112	5	0	11	7	60
With skin, light meat						
Edible portion 100 gms. (3 1/2 oz.)	120	7	1	11	7	60
Breast						
Edible portion 100 gms. (3 1/2 oz.)	110	17	4	7	4	60
Drumstick						
Edible portion 100 gms. (3 1/2 oz.)	115	5	0	11	7	60
Chicken, roaster, flesh only						
Edible portion 100 gms. (3 1/2 oz.)	131	5	1	12	8	60
Pheasant						
Edible portion 100 gms. (3 1/2 oz.)	151	6	2	14	10	60
Turkey						
Young (24 weeks or less)						
Light meat						
Edible portion 100 gms. (3 1/2 oz.)	108	34	10	1	1	60

TABLE XXIX (continued)

	TC	*White Points*	*Green Points*	*Blue Points*	*Gold Points*	*Choles-terol Milli-grams*
Low-Cholesterol Foods, poultry, young turkey (24 weeks or less) –continued						
Dark meat						
Edible portion 100 gms. (3 1/2 oz.)	111	15	4	7	5	60
Medium-fat (26-32 weeks)						
Light meat						
Edible portion 100 gms. (3 1/2 oz.)	115	30	9	3	2	60
Dark meat						
Edible portion 100 gms. (3 1/2 oz.)	127	7	2	11	8	60
Desserts						
Cake						
Boston cream pie						
1 3-in. wedge = 80 gms. (2 3/4 oz.)	242	17	3	22	6	38
Plain						
100 gms. (3 1/2 oz.)	364	2	0	36	9	45
Yellow						
100 gms. (3 1/2 oz.)	363	13	0	36	9	45
Cookies, medium-fat grocery						
100 gms. (3 1/2 oz.)	444	4	8	36	9	50
Frosting, caramel or white cream						
100 gms. (3 1/2 oz.)	360	66	0	36	0	22
Moderate Cholesterol Foods (over 100 to 300 milligrams for 100 gms. (3 1/2 oz.)						
Fish and shellfish						
Crayfish (Spiny lobster)						
100 gms. (3 1/2 oz.)	72	21	6	1	0	200
Lobster						
Maine (Northern)						
100 gms. (3 1/2 oz.)	91	15	5	4	2	200
Rock or spiny (See Crayfish)						
Shrimp						
Raw						
100 gms. (3 1/2 oz.)	91	25	4	4	2	150
Canned, drained solids						
1 cup = 114 gms. (4 oz.)	132	35	9	4	2	171
Organ meats						
Liver						
Chicken						
100 gms. (3 1/2 oz.)	129	12	2	10	6	300
Hog						
100 gms. (3 1/2 oz.)	131	12	1	12	3	300
Sweetbread, thymus						
Calf	94	15	1	8	0	250
Desserts						
Sponge cake						
100 gms. (3 1/2 oz.)	297	53	12	18	0	220
Recipes						
Dairy products						
Recipe #2 Sweet-Cream Substitute	267	89	27	0	0	11

TABLE XXIX (continued)

	TC	*White Points*	*Green Points*	*Blue Points*	*Gold Points*	*Cholesterol Milligrams*
Recipes, dairy products–continued						
Recipe #3 Whipped-Cream Substitute	632	217	63	0	0	22
Recipe #4 Sour-Cream Substitute	256	83	26	0	0	40
Breads						
Recipe #5 Low-Fat White Bread	2965	972	285	12	30	22
Recipe #6 High-Protein Low-Fat White Bread	3016	992	289	12	30	22
Recipe #7 Sugar-Free White Bread	2869	941	275	11	29	22
Recipe #8 Whole-Wheat Bread	2847	871	205	80	60	22
Recipe #9 Rye Bread	3085	1033	302	6	15	22
Recipe #10 High-Protein Gluten Bread	2173	676	202	15	39	22
Recipe #11 Kneaded Gluten Bread	1070	333	100	7	20	11
Recipe #15 English Muffins	1985	653	190	8	20	11
Recipe #16 Cinnamon Rolls	3350	1109	322	13	30	22
Recipe #17 Brown-Sugar Rolls	3761	1252	365	11	30	22
Recipe #18 Banana Bread	1937	653	190	4	10	0
Recipe #19 Banana-Nut Bread	2737	263	227	47	433	0
Recipe #20 Banana-Date Bread	2425	817	238	4	10	0
Recipe #22 Date Bread	2292	766	225	5	11	11
Recipe #23 Date-Nut Bread	3158	319	259	57	158	11
Recipe #24 Corn Bread	1250	368	123	2	36	11
Recipe #25 Baking-Powder Biscuits	1460	6	93	53	269	7
Recipe #26 Drop Biscuits	1460	6	93	53	269	7
Recipe #27 Orange Biscuits	1508	21	98	53	268	7
Recipe #29 Nonfat Baking-Powder Biscuits	986	325	95	4	10	7
Recipe #30 Nonfat Drop Biscuits	986	325	95	4	10	7
Recipe #31 Nonfat Orange Biscuits	1034	342	99	4	10	7
Recipe #32 Maple-Sugar Biscuits	1843	140	131	53	267	7
Recipe #33 Nonfat Maple-Sugar Biscuits	1369	459	133	4	10	7
Recipe #34 Nonfat Whole-Wheat Biscuits	912	278	83	8	20	7
Recipe #35 Plain Muffins	1717	93	118	53	268	11
Recipe #36 Blueberry Muffins	1806	117	128	52	267	11
Recipe #37 Nonfat Muffins	1237	411	120	4	10	11
Recipe #38 Nonfat Blueberry Muffins	1326	436	129	4	11	11
Recipe #39 Nonfat Pecan Muffins	1526	262	131	21	60	11
Recipe #40 Raisin Muffins (using Recipe #35)	1876	148	135	53	268	11
Recipe #40 Raisin Muffins (using Recipe #37)	1396	466	135	4	10	11
Recipe #41 Whole-Wheat Muffins (using Recipe #35)	1680	71	112	55	272	11
Recipe #41 Whole-Wheat Muffins (using Recipe #37)	1200	388	114	6	14	11
Recipe #42 Plain Wheat Cakes	547	180	53	2	5	7

TABLE XXIX (continued)

	TC	*White Points*	*Green Points*	*Blue Points*	*Gold Points*	*Cholesterol Milligrams*
Recipes, breads–continued						
Recipe #43 Blueberry Griddle Cakes	638	208	62	2	5	7
Recipe #44 Banana Griddle Cakes	707	233	68	2	5	7
Recipe #45 Apple Griddle Cakes	674	217	65	2	5	7
Recipe #46 Buckwheat Cakes	1038	323	103	1	2	22
Recipe #47 Plain Waffles	547	180	52	2	5	7
Recipe #48 Cinnamon Toast	721	188	56	16	8	8
Recipe #51 Milk Toast	618	113	40	22	16	26
Sauces, gravies and salad dressings						
Recipe #55 Milk Gravy	355	118	36	0	2	22
Recipe #57 Newburg Sauce	290	88	25	4	0	72
Recipe #58 White Sauce	178	59	18	0	1	11
Recipe #59 Cheese Sauce	264	86	26	0	1	26
Recipe #60 Tomato Cream Sauce	278	88	28	0	3	11
Recipe #61 Tomato Cheese Sauce	364	115	36	0	3	26
Recipe #62 Soubise Sauce	346	114	35	0	1	11
Recipe #63 Oyster Sauce	524	104	29	23	39	152
Recipe #64 Mushroom Sauce	188	62	19	0	2	11
Recipe #65 Shrimp Sauce	222	71	20	2	2	68
Recipe #66 Lobster Sauce	232	68	21	2	2	125
Recipe #67 Celery Sauce	190	62	19	0	1	11
Recipe #68 Asparagus Cheese Sauce	306	95	29	2	5	26
Recipe #69 Curry Sauce	179	60	18	0	1	11
Recipe #70 Spanish Creole Sauce	168	49	17	0	3	0
Recipe #71 Barbecue Sauce	491	160	47	2	5	0
Recipe #72 Spaghetti Sauce	1647	202	7	156	22	492
Recipe #77 Nonfat French Dressing	16	6	2	0	0	0
Recipe #79 French Dressing with Cheese	59	19	6	0	0	8
Recipe #80 French Dressing with Horseradish	18	6	2	0	0	0
Recipe #81 French Dressing with Mustard	23	5	1	1	1	0
Recipe #82 French Dressing with Lemon	31	11	3	0	0	0
Recipe #83 Nonfat Mayonnaise	395	134	40	0	0	22
Recipe #84 Russian Dressing	150	40	15	0	4	6
Recipe #85 Shrimp Salad Dressing	305	102	30	0	1	6
Recipe #86 Chiffonade Salad Dressing	413	135	40	1	0	22
Recipe #87 Sherry Mayonnaise	416	141	42	0	0	0
Recipe #88 Thousand Island Salad Dressing	572	191	56	1	2	22
Recipe #89 Tartare Sauce	165	52	16	1	0	8
Recipe #90 Horseradish Creamy Dressing	286	94	29	0	0	22
Recipe #91 Seafood Cocktail Sauce	89	29	8	1	1	0
Recipe #93 Maple Sauce	3884	684	346	43	423	0
Recipe #94 Cornstarch Sauce	410	139	41	0	0	22
Recipe #96 Caramel Sauce	770	270	77	0	0	0

TABLE XXIX (continued)

	TC	*White Points*	*Green Points*	*Blue Points*	*Gold Points*	*Cholesterol Milligrams*
Recipes–continued						
Bouillon, consommé, chowder, and soup						
Recipe #103 Jellied Bouillon, Consommé, Stock	84	29	8	0	0	0
Recipe #104 Vegetable Variety Soup	178	57	17	1	4	0
Recipe #105 Green Pea Soup	581	184	54	4	13	0
Recipe #106 Tomato Chowder	963	310	96	0	6	44
Recipe #106 Tomato Chowder Variation	1093	316	90	20	6	94
Recipe #107 Corn Chowder	790	257	79	0	3	22
Recipe #107 Corn-Chowder Variation	1088	321	89	20	4	72
Recipe #108 Corn and Tomato Chowder	958	295	96	0	10	22
Recipe #108 Corn and Tomato Chowder Variation	1088	300	89	20	11	72
Recipe #109 Corn and Potato Chowder	625	182	58	5	15	0
Recipe #110 Mixed Vegetable Chowder	949	304	95	0	8	22
Recipe #110 Mixed Vegetable Chowder Variation	1079	308	88	19	9	72
Recipe #111 Fish and Potato Chowder	1025	342	102	0	0	136
Recipe #112 Oyster Stew	1289	191	62	67	94	326
Recipe #113 Salmon and Pea Chowder	1344	281	94	40	70	243
Recipe #114 Cream of Salmon Soup	750	178	59	16	19	45
Recipe #115 Creamed Vegetable Soup	650	209	65	0	5	44
Recipe #116 Cheese Variation of Vegetable Soup	693	222	69	0	5	52
Recipe #117 Cream of Chicken Soup	359	119	36	0	1	22
Recipe #118 Navy- or Black-Bean Soup	1368	425	128	8	29	0
Recipe #119 Lima-Bean Soup	1098	350	104	6	23	0
Vegetables						
Recipe #122 Asparagus Casserole	587	161	50	8	11	28
Recipe #123 Lima-Bean Casserole	817	250	73	9	11	28
Recipe #124 Boston Baked Beans	2997	944	285	15	57	0
Recipe #125 Harvard Beets	859	293	86	0	0	0
Recipe #126 Beets in Orange Sauce	422	136	42	0	0	0
Recipe #127 Spiced Beets	460	152	46	0	0	0
Recipe #128 Broccoli Casserole	677	188	61	7	14	28
Recipe #129 Cabbage Casserole Variation	616	164	55	7	13	13

TABLE XXIX (continued)

	TC	*White Points*	*Green Points*	*Blue Points*	*Gold Points*	*Cholesterol Milligrams*
Recipes, Vegetables–continued						
Recipe #129 Cauliflower Casserole Variation	635	177	56	7	11	28
Recipe #128 Eggplant Casserole Variation	749	207	68	7	17	28
Recipe #129 Stuffed Eggplant	971	239	80	17	23	12
Recipe #130 Broiled Eggplant	146	41	15	0	5	0
Recipe #131 Mushrooms au gratin	274	86	27	0	4	11
Recipe #132 Okra and Tomatoes	174	47	15	2	6	0
Recipe #133 Baked Stuffed Onions	430	141	43	0	1	11
Recipe #137 Sweet Potatoes in Honey	1306	419	125	5	18	0
Recipe #139 Mashed Sweet Potatoes	1132	358	107	6	18	11
Recipe #140 Baked Tomatoes	567	146	52	5	20	3
Berries, fruits, and melons						
Recipe #142 Applesauce	475	134	48	0	0	0
Recipe #143 Baked Apples	612	166	61	0	0	0
Recipe #144 Baked Stuffed Apples	2450	49	191	54	147	0
Recipe #146 Maple Bananas	1463	452	143	3	26	0
Recipe #148 Stewed Rhubarb	458	155	46	0	0	0
Recipe #149 Baked Rhubarb	651	223	65	0	0	0
Recipe #153 Strawberry Gelatin Supreme	394	132	39	0	0	0
Recipe #154 Black-Cherry Wine Gelatin	656	226	66	0	0	0
Salads						
Recipe #157 Salmon Salad	247	9	9	16	32	98
Recipe #159 Seafood Pineapple Salad	213	62	16	5	2	171
Recipe #161 Potato Salad	656	220	66	0	0	11
Recipe #162 Tomato Aspic	240	76	24	0	0	0
Recipe #163 Cole Slaw	317	107	32	0	2	10
Recipe #164 Chicken Salad	509	81	19	32	20	240
Recipe #164 Chicken Salad Pineapple Variation	781	170	46	32	21	243
Recipe #165 Chicken and Asparagus Salad	455	80	24	21	16	233
Fish and shellfish						
Recipe #183 Tuna Roll	1081	304	91	17	17	222
Recipe #183 Salmon Roll Variation	1137	135	60	53	101	294
Recipe #184 Scalloped Tuna and Peas	779	215	65	13	16	214
Recipe #185 Salmon Stew	1089	124	59	50	106	340
Recipe #186 Clam Chowder	650	127	35	30	34	410
Recipe #187 Clam-Corn-Pimento Casserole	532	114	34	19	22	171
Recipe #188 Broiled Oysters	370	60	16	21	35	130
Recipe #189 Oysters à la King	722	169	49	23	42	163
Recipe #190 Shrimp à la King	1172	333	90	27	18	1051
Recipe #191 Shrimp Curry	1154	329	89	27	16	1051

TABLE XXIX (continued)

	TC	*White Points*	*Green Points*	*Blue Points*	*Gold Points*	*Cholesterol Milli grams*
Recipes, Fish and shellfish—continued						
Recipe #192 Shrimp Creole	698	188	52	18	12	686
Recipe #193 Broiled Breaded Shrimp	1077	304	81	27	14	1051
Recipe #194 Pan-Broiled Scallops	762	223	70	9	14	275
Recipe #195 Broiled Scallops	758	211	67	9	14	275
Poultry						
Recipe #199 Smothered Chicken	1707	225	46	125	78	927
Recipe #200 Smothered Chicken with Sweet Potatoes	4295	1039	283	146	124	927
Recipe #201 Chicken Casserole	1788	422	80	98	62	758
Recipe #203 Boiled Chicken Dinner	2134	476	136	77	58	565
Recipe #204 Chicken Espagnole	2090	343	86	123	88	927
Recipe #205 Chicken with Rice	1854	412	111	74	48	556
Recipe #206 Chicken and Spaghetti	1189	352	110	8	10	60
Recipe #207 Baked Chicken Orleans	465	80	23	24	19	180
Recipe #208 Chicken in Wine	760	118	27	49	31	371
Recipe #209 Chicken Newburg	504	114	30	20	10	192
Recipe #210 Chicken and Sauce	333	67	17	16	11	27
Recipe #210 Chicken and Sauce Variation	298	51	14	16	12	20
Recipe #211 Chicken à la King	372	80	21	16	10	31
Recipe #212 Chicken Pot Pie	1793	72	111	68	280	34
Recipe #213 Quick Chicken Curry	469	67	15	32	20	240
Recipe #213 Chicken Curry Variation	392	86	23	16	11	31
Recipe #214 Wild-Rice Stuffing	302	100	30	0	0	0
Meat						
Beef						
Recipe #221 Corned Beef Boil	4777	769	76	401	38	1271
Recipe #223 Chili con Carne	1236	219	28	95	18	318
Recipe #226 Arroz con Carne Español	2476	624	154	94	20	318
Recipe #227 Stuffed Green Peppers	443	101	20	24	5	80
Recipe #228 Beef Curry Deluxe	959	223	47	49	8	170
Pork						
Recipe #241 Spicy Sauce for Roast Pork	186	63	19	0	0	0
Recipe #243 Glazed Pork and Sweet Potatoes	3029	421	82	221	64	636
Organ meat						
Recipe #251 Baked Heart	1315	151	6	125	14	699
Desserts						
Recipe #260 Maple Pudding	1586	425	146	13	68	6
Recipe #261 Maple-Walnut Pudding	1844	308	162	22	210	0
Recipe #262 Rice Pudding	1454	496	145	0	0	44
Recipe #263 Rice Pudding Caramel Variation	1480	505	148	0	0	44

TABLE XXIX (continued)

	TC	*White Points*	*Green Points*	*Blue Points*	*Gold Points*	*Choles-terol Milli-grams*
Recipes, Desserts—continued						
Recipe #264 English Pudding	3648	270	263	102	533	7
Recipe #265 Molasses-Fruit Pudding	1516	153	114	38	198	6
Recipe #266 Blancmange	1021	349	102	0	0	44
Recipe #266 Blancmange Chocolate Variation	1077	332	88	19	0	44
Recipe #266 Blancmange Caramel Variation	1047	358	105	0	0	44
Recipe #268 Apple Pie	3274	98	226	101	524	0
Recipe #269 Fresh Peach Pie	2899	14	188	101	525	0
Recipe #271 Fresh Cherry Pie	3248	130	224	101	526	0
Recipe #273 Blackberry Pie	3014	51	199	102	527	0
Recipe #274 Blueberry Pie	3086	62	207	102	528	0
Recipe #275 Uncooked Blackberry Pie	2113	194	160	51	262	0
Recipe #275 Uncooked Blueberry Pie Variation	2138	222	162	51	263	0
Recipe #275 Uncooked Peach Pie Variation	2013	199	151	50	264	0
Recipe #275 Uncooked Strawberry Pie Variation	1978	166	146	51	263	0
Recipe #276 Uncooked Banana Pie	2205	265	170	51	262	0
Recipe #277 Pumpkin Pie	1844	138	133	52	264	16
Recipe #278 Cream Flour Filling For Pies	768	262	77	0	2	16
Recipe #279 Chocolate Devils Food Cake	3409	75	167	174	525	0
Recipe #280 Silver Cake	2612	251	193	68	353	11
Recipe #281 Angel Ginger Cake	1911	168	140	52	266	4
Recipe #282 Orange Cake	2097	71	145	65	350	0
Recipe #283 Orange Tea Cake	2432	104	168	75	396	0
Recipe #284 Corn-Sirup Spice Cake	2478	124	171	77	396	6
Recipe #285 Honey Cake	2558	153	179	77	394	4
Recipe #286 White Cake	3202	371	243	77	400	11
Recipe #287 Gingerbread Cake	2469	118	170	76	392	8
Recipe #288 Marble Cake	2027	330	164	39	202	7
Recipe #289 Angel-Food Cake	729	248	72	1	4	0
Recipe #290 Chocolate Angel-Food Cake	1517	476	124	27	3	0
Recipe #291 Baked Meringue Frosting	855	299	86	0	0	0
Recipe #292 Peppermint Icing	2002	701	200	0	0	6
Recipe #293 White Icing	841	294	84	0	0	0
Recipe #295 Applesauce Spice Cookies	2418	181	174	68	353	0
Recipe #296 Basic Drop Cookies	1901	165	139	51	266	3
Recipe #299 Banana-Nut Cookies	2938	24	206	88	564	0
Recipe #300 Vanilla Wafers	2061	220	154	51	266	3
Recipe #301 Molasses Cookies	2694	275	202	67	353	4
Recipe #303 Gingersnaps	2210	108	152	68	354	0
Recipe #304 Chocolate Nut Kisses	3212	71	71	250	421	0

TABLE XXIX (continued)

	TC	*White Points*	*Green Points*	*Blue Points*	*Gold Points*	*Choles-terol Milli-grams*
Recipes, Desserts–continued						
Recipe #305 Simple Meringue Cookies	2447	856	245	0	0	0
Recipe #306 Vanilla Ice Cream Variation	738	258	74	0	0	4
Recipe #307 Nonfat Vanilla Ice Cream I	1099	375	110	0	0	30
Recipe #308 Nonfat Vanilla Ice Cream II	1708	582	171	0	0	88
Recipe #320 Hot Cocoa	972	270	63	34	0	44

White- and Red-Point Foods
(Calories 35% Fat or Less and over 10% Saturated Fat)

	TC	*White Points*	*Red Points*	*Blue Points*	*Gold Points*	*Choles-terol Milli-grams*
No-Cholesterol Foods						
Miscellaneous						
Chocolate, semisweet, small pieces 1 cup = 170 gms. (6 oz.)	860	17	70	156	0	0
Chocolate-flavored sirup, fudge type 1 cup = 285 gms. (10 oz.)	940	20	71	165	0	0
Low-Cholesterol Food (100 or less milligrams)						
Dairy products						
Cheese, natural						
Cottage, creamed 100 gms. (3 1/2 oz.)	106	0	7	18	0	15
Milk, cow's						
Partially skimmed (2% fat) with 2% Nonfat milk solids added 1 cup = 246 gms. (8 1/2 oz.)	143	2	12	25	0	(17)
Canned, condensed, sweetened 1 cup = 306 gms. (10 1/2 oz.)	982	110	22	119	0	(67)
Vegetables						
Beans, white, mature seeds						
Canned with pork and sweet sauce 1 cup = 255 gms. (9 oz.)	382	33	5	43	0	T
Soup (Campbell soup company products)						
Heat-processed						
Beef noodle 100 gms. (3 1/2 oz.)	58	3	0	6	2	6
Chili beef 100 gms. (3 1/2 oz.)	131	13	2	15	1	(1-6)
Pepper pot 100 gms. (3 1/2 oz.)	83	0	3	11	2	(1-6)
Potato, cream of 100 gms. (3 1/2 oz.)	59	4	1	7	4	(1-6)

TABLE XXIX (continued)

	TC	*White Points*	*Red Points*	*Blue Points*	*Gold Points*	*Choles-terol Milli-grams*
Low-Cholesterol Food, Soup (Campbell soup company products),						
Heat-processed–continued						
Scotch broth						
100 gms. (3 1/2 oz.)	74	4	4	11	3	(1-6)
Tomato, bisque of						
100 gms. (3 1/2 oz.)	101	17	1	11	1	(1-6)
Frozen						
Vegetable with beef, old-fashioned						
100 gms. (3 1/2 oz.)	68	3	2	9	3	(1-6)
Beef						
Arm						
Choice, separable lean						
100 gms. (3 1/2 oz.)	141	1	9	24	1	70
Good, separable lean						
100 gms. (3 1/2 oz.)	129	9	5	18	1	70
Flank Steak						
Good						
100 gms. (3 1/2 oz.)	139	3	8	22	1	70
Hindshank						
Choice, separable lean						
100 gms. (3 1/2 oz.)	134	5	7	20	1	70
Good, separable lean						
100 gms. (3 1/2 oz.)	126	11	4	16	1	70
Porterhouse						
Good, separable lean						
100 gms. (3 1/2 oz.)	141	0	10	24	1	70
Sirloin steak, wedge or roundbone						
Good, separable lean						
100 gms. (3 1/2 oz.)	129	9	5	18	1	70
Sirloin steak, double bone						
Good, separable lean						
100 gms. (3 1/2 oz.)	135	5	6	20	8	70
Round						
Choice, separable lean						
100 gms. (3 1/2 oz.)	135	5	7	21	1	70
Rump						
Good, separable lean						
100 gms. (3 1/2 oz.)	141	1	9	23	1	70
Lamb						
Leg						
Choice, separable lean						
100 gms. (3 1/2 oz.)	130	0	12	25	1	70
Desserts						
Frosting, coconut						
100 gms. (3 1/2 oz.)	364	58	27	63	0	22
Ice milk						
1 cup = 131 gms. (4 5/8 oz.)	199	9	16	35	0	6
Pudding, cornstarch (no eggs)						
1 cup = 240 gms. (8 3/8 oz.)	266	9	16	43	0	24
Candy						
Chocolate-covered nougat caramel bar						
100 gms. (3 1/2 oz.)	416	24	2	44	9	74

TABLE XXIX (continued)

	TC	*White Points*	*Red Points*	*Blue Points*	*Gold Points*	*Choles-terol Milli-grams*
Low-Cholesterol Foods, Candy—continued						
Chocolate-coated fudge 100 gms. (3 1/2 oz.)	430	9	10	53	9	74
Chocolate vanilla creams 100 gms. (3 1/2 oz.)	435	2	10	53	9	74
Vanilla fudge 100 gms. (3 1/2 oz.)	398	41	4	44	9	74
Moderate-Cholesterol Foods (over 100 to 300 milligrams for 100 gms. [3 1/2 oz.])						
Organ meats						
Heart						
Beef, lean 100 gms. (3 1/2 oz.)	108	5	4	14	1	150
Hog 100 gms. (3 1/2 oz.)	113	0	3	14	4	150
Liver						
Beef 100 gms. (3 1/2 oz.)	140	15	1	15	1	300
Calf 100 gms. (3 1/2 oz.)	140	7	5	19	1	300
Lamb 100 gms. (3 1/2 oz.)	136	12	6	20	1	300
Spleen						
Beef or calf 100 gms. (3 1/2 oz.)	104	9	2	12	0	(250)
Hog 100 gms. (3 1/2 oz.)	107	3	2	12	3	(250)
Lamb 100 gms. (3 1/2 oz.)	115	5	8	20	1	(250)
High-Cholesterol Foods (over 300 milligrams for 100 gms. [3 1/2 oz.])						
Organ meats						
Kidney, hog 100 gms. (3 1/2 oz.)	106	5	1	12	3	375
Recipes						
Salads						
Recipe #166 Ham and Chicken Salad	598	1	13	73	24	126
Meat						
Beef						
Recipe #217 Swiss Steak	1276	147	16	144	11	477
Recipe #219 Beef Stew with Red Wine	1408	194	1	142	11	477
Recipe #222 Corned Beef and Cabbage	3236	272	78	401	32	1271
Recipe #225 Beef Meat Loaf	1402	156	11	151	17	480
Recipe #229 Steak and Green Peppers	661	38	29	95	8	318
Recipe #231 Beef Shish Kebab	871	99	8	95	11	318
Veal						
Recipe #238 Veal Scallopine Napoli	2282	46	119	347	27	828

TABLE XXIX (continued)

	TC	*White Points*	*Red Points*	*Blue Points*	*Gold Points*	*Cholesterol Milligrams*
Recipes, meat—continued						
Pork						
Recipe #239 Pork Steaks with Grape Apples	1893	47	28	218	55	636
Recipe #242 Roast Pork and Sweet Potatoes	1893	28	32	221	62	636
Recipe #245 Ham and Green Beans	3100	16	71	381	99	953
Desserts						
Recipe #294 Chocolate Frosting	817	34	58	140	4	22

Black- and Green-Point Foods
(Calories over 35% Fat and 10% Saturated Fat or Less)

	TC	*Black Points*	*Green Points*	*Blue Points*	*Gold Points*	*Cholesterol Milligrams*
No-Cholesterol Foods						
Fats and oils						
Corn oil						
1 cup = 220 gms. (7 3/4 oz.)	1945	1265	0	194	1032	0
1 tbsp = 14 gms. (1/2 oz.)	124	80	0	12	66	0
Safflower oil						
1 cup = 220 gms. (7 3/4 oz.)	1945	1265	40	156	1401	0
1 tbsp = 14 gms. (1/2 oz.)	124	80	2	10	89	0
Sauces and dressings						
Barbecue sauce						
1 cup = 250 gms. (8 3/4 oz.)	228	73	82	15	82	0
1 tbsp = 15 gms. (1/2 oz.)	14	4	0	1	5	0
Mustard						
1 tbsp = 15 gms. (1/2 oz.)	11	12	3	1	2	0
Salad dressings, commercial						
Blue cheese and Roquefort, low-fat						
1 tbsp = 15 gms. (1/2 oz.)	3	0	0	0	0	0
French, low-fat						
1 tbsp = 15 gms. (1/2 oz.)	14	1	0	1	3	0
Thousand Island, low-calorie						
1 tbsp = 16 gms. (1/2 oz.)	27	9	0	3	9	0
Vegetables						
Relish, pickled, sour	19	1	0	0	0	0
Nut products						
Almonds						
Roasted and salted						
100 gms. (3 1/2 oz.)	627	263	19	42	100	0
Shelled, dried						
100 gms. (3 1/2 oz.)	598	244	26	33	92	0
Beech nuts						
100 gms. (3 1/2 oz.)	568	219	23	34	134	0
Filberts						
100 gms. (3 1/2 oz.)	634	300	38	25	84	0

TABLE XXIX (continued)

	TC	*Black Points*	*Green Points*	*Blue Points*	*Gold Points*	*Cholesterol Milligrams*
No-Cholesterol Foods, nut products–continued						
Hickory nuts						
100 gms. (3 1/2 oz.)	673	340	17	50	100	0
Pecans						
1 cup chopped = 126 gms. (4 1/2 oz.)	866	536	34	53	147	0
Pistachio nuts						
100 gms. (3 1/2 oz.)	594	243	18	42	84	0
Sunflower seed						
100 gms. (3 1/2 oz.)	560	200	6	50	251	0
Walnuts						
Black						
1 cup chopped = 126 gms. (4 1/2 oz.)	791	348	37	43	297	0
English						
1 cup chopped = 126 gms. (4 1/2 oz.)	820	386	40	43	422	0
Low-Cholesterol Foods (100 or less milligrams for 100 gms. [3 1/2 oz.])						
Breads, rolls and pastas						
Doughnuts, cake-type						
1 doughnut = 32 gms. (1 1/6 oz.)	125	10	3	12	4	(1)
Soup (Campbell soup company products)						
Heat-processed						
Turkey noodle						
100 gms. (3 1/2 oz.)	63	1	0	6	6	(1-6)
Turkey vegetable						
100 gms. (3 1/2 oz.)	64	3	0	6	6	(1-6)
Vegetable and beef stockpot						
100 gms. (3 1/2 oz.)	79	3	1	7	11	(1-6)
Fish and shellfish						
Pompano						
100 gms. (3 1/2 oz.)	166	28	8	25	28	70
Salmon, canned						
Coho (Silver)						
100 gms. (3 1/2 oz.)	153	11	2	13	21	70
Pink (Humpback)						
100 gms. (3 1/2 oz.)	141	4	3	11	22	70
Tuna, canned						
In cottonseed oil, drained solids						
100 gms. (3 1/2 oz.)	197	5	0	20	30	52
Whitefish						
100 gms. (3 1/2 oz.)	155	20	1	15	24	70
Desserts						
Cake, fruit						
100 gms. (3 1/2 oz.)	379	5	2	36	18	63
Pie, pecan						
100 gms. (3 1/2 oz.)	418	60	15	27	36	48
Moderate-Cholesterol Foods (over 100 to 300 milligrams for 100 gms. 3 1/2 oz.)						
Desserts						
Cake, chiffon						
100 gms. (3 1/2 oz.)	381	3	6	32	56	195

TABLE XXIX (continued)

	TC	*Black Points*	*Green Points*	*Blue Points*	*Gold Points*	*Cholesterol Milligrams*
High-Cholesterol Foods (over 300 milligrams for 100 gms. [3 1/2 oz.])						
Fish and shellfish						
Caviar						
100 gms. (3 1/2 oz.)	262	43	4	22	27	300
Recipes						
Breads						
Recipe #28 Whole-Wheat Biscuits	1386	42	82	57	277	7
Recipe #39 Pecan Muffins	2006	56	130	70	317	11
Sauces, gravies, and salad dressings						
Recipe #78 Polyunsaturated-Fat French Dressing	259	152	2	24	129	0
Salads						
Recipe #156 Apple-Nut Salad	1147	139	82	32	316	8
Desserts						
Recipe #263 Steamed Apple Pudding	1889	344	89	100	521	0
Recipe #267 Pie Crust	1846	345	83	102	526	0
Recipe #270 Peach Pie	2437	149	141	102	526	0
Recipe #272 Cherry Pie	2332	184	130	103	527	0
Recipe #297 Cocoa Drops	4760	157	248	228	952	11
Recipe #298 Chocolate-Chip Cookies	3241	236	26	298	560	0
Recipe #302 Brownies	2776	444	44	233	688	0
Recipe #306 Polyunsaturated Vanilla Ice Cream	1234	65	84	39	355	4
Recipe #311 Peach Ice Cream	1407	10	101	39	356	4
Recipe #312 Black Walnut Ice Cream	2025	413	119	83	652	4

Black- and Red-Point Foods
(Calories over 35% Fat and over 10% Saturated Fat)

	TC	*Black Points*	*Red Points*	*Blue Points*	*Gold Points*	*Cholesterol Milligrams*
No-Cholesterol Foods						
Fats and oils						
Margarine						
Bluebonnet, regular						
Stick = 1/2 cup = 113 gms. (4 oz.)	814	520	90	172	141	0
1 tbsp = 14 gms. (1/2 oz.)	101	64	11	21	18	0
Bluebonnet, soft						
1 tbsp = 14 gms. (1/2 oz.)	101	64	6	16	26	0
Fleischmann's diet						
1 tbsp = 14 gms. (1/2 oz.)	50	32	4	9	20	0
Fleischmann's salted						
1 tbsp = 14 gms. (1/2 oz.)	101	64	6	16	26	0
Fleischmann's unsalted						
1 tbsp = 14 gms. (1/2 oz.)	101	64	6	16	26	0

TABLE XXIX (continued)

	TC	*Black Points*	*Red Points*	*Blue Points*	*Gold Points*	*Cholesterol Milligrams*
No-Cholesterol Foods, fats and oils, margarine—continued						
Fleischmann's soft						
1 tbsp = 14 gms. (1/2 oz.)	101	64	7	18	39	0
Mazola, diet						
1 tbsp = 14 gms. (1/2 oz.)	49	36	2	7	20	0
Mazola, salted or unsalted						
1 tbsp = 14 gms. (1/2 oz.)	101	64	6	16	29	0
Nucoa, regular						
1 tbsp = 14 gms. (1/2 oz.)	101	64	8	18	27	0
Nucoa, soft						
1 tbsp = 14 gms. (1/2 oz.)	101	64	9	19	43	0
Oils and fats						
Coconut						
1 cup = 220 gms. (7 3/4 oz.)	1945	1265	1478	1672	4	0
Cottonseed						
1 cup = 220 gms. (7 3/4 oz.)	1945	1265	293	486	972	0
1 tbsp = 14 gms. (1/2 oz.)	124	80	19	31	62	0
Olive						
1 cup = 220 gms. (7 3/4 oz.)	1945	1265	20	213	136	0
1 tbsp = 14 gms. (1/2 oz.)	124	80	1	14	9	0
Peanut						
1 cup = 220 gms. (7 3/4 oz.)	1924	1265	156	350	563	0
1 tbsp = 14 gms. (1/2 oz.)	124	80	10	22	36	0
Sesame						
1 cup = 220 gms. (7 3/4 oz.)	1945	1265	77	273	816	0
1 tbsp = 14 gms. (1/2 oz.)	124	80	5	17	52	0
Soy oil						
1 cup = 220 gms. (7 3/4 oz.)	1945	1265	97	293	1012	0
1 tbsp = 14 gms. (1/2 oz.)	124	80	6	19	64	0
Miscellaneous						
Chocolate						
Bitter or baking						
1 sq. = 28 gms. (1 oz.)	141	75	56	40	2	0
Cocoa, dry powder						
High-fat (breakfast)						
1 cup = 100 gms. (3 1/2 oz.)	299	93	79	109	0	0
1 tbsp = 6 gms. (2/10 oz.)	19	6	5	7	0	0
1 tsp = 2 gms. (.07 oz.)	6	2	2	2	0	0
Medium-fat						
100 gms. (3 1/2 oz.)	265	66	65	92	0	0
Medium-low-fat						
100 gms. (3 1/2 oz.)	220	29	36	58	0	0
Low-fat						
100 gms. (3 1/2 oz.)	187	1	15	34	0	0
Dairy products						
Cream, imitation						
Powdered, from vegetable fat						
1 cup = 94 gms. (3 1/3 oz.)	477	123	225	273	0	0
Whipped topping						
1 cup = 70 gms. (2 1/2 oz.)	190	83	113	132	0	0
Sauces and dressings						
Salad dressing, commercial						
French, regular						
1 tbsp = 16 gms. (1/2 oz.)	62	30	3	9	27	0

TABLE XXIX (continued)

	TC	*Black Points*	*Red Points*	*Blue Points*	*Gold Points*	*Choles-terol Milli-grams*
No-Cholesterol Foods, sauces and dressings, salad dressing, commercial—continued						
Italian, regular						
1 tbsp = 15 gms. (1/2 oz.)	83	50	0	13	41	0
Italian, low-calorie						
1 tbsp = 15 gms. (1/2 oz.)	8	4	1	1	3	0
Russian						
1 tbsp = 15 gms. (1/2 oz.)	74	41	5	12	34	0
Thousand Island						
1 tbsp = 16 gms. (1/2 oz.)	80	28	4	12	33	0
Tartare sauce						
1 tbsp = 15 gms. (1/2 oz.)	78	48	4	12	34	0
Vegetables						
Potato chips						
100 gms. (3 1/2 oz.)	568	162	34	90	181	0
Berries, fruits, and melons						
Avocado						
1 cup cubed = 150 gms. (5 1/4 oz.)	250	117	4	30	24	0
Olives, pickled						
Green						
Edible portion of 9 to 12 olives = 40 gms. (1 1/3 oz.)	46	26	2	7	3	0
Ripe						
Edible portion of 10 to 15 olives = 40 gms. (1 1/3 oz.)	52	28	2	7	3	0
Nut products						
Brazil nuts						
100 gms. (3 1/2 oz.)	654	332	44	109	142	0
Cashew nuts						
100 gms. (3 1/2 oz.)	386	128	7	67	17	0
Coconut						
Dried, sweetened, shredded						
100 gms. (3 1/2 oz.)	548	135	230	285	0	0
Dried, unsweetened						
100 gms. (3 1/2 oz.)	662	311	402	469	0	0
Fresh						
100 gms. (3 1/2 oz.)	346	175	216	251	0	0
Peanuts						
1 cup = 144 gms. (5 oz.)	812	288	40	121	168	0
Peanut butter						
with small amount of added fat, sweetener, salt						
1 tbsp = 16 gms. (1/2 oz.)	93	34	3	12	18	0
Candy						
Semisweet chocolate bar						
100 gms. (3 1/2 oz.)	520	112	130	182	9	0
Low-Cholesterol Foods (100 or less milligrams for 100 gms. [3 1/2 oz.])						
Fats and oils						
Lard						
1 cup = 205 gms. (7 oz.)	1849	1201	517	701	184	195
1 tbsp = 13 gms. (1/2 oz.)	117	76	33	44	12	12

TABLE XXIX (continued)

	TC	*Black Points*	*Red Points*	*Blue Points*	*Gold Points*	*Choles-terol Milli-grams*
Low-Cholesterol Foods–continued						
Dairy products						
Cheese, natural						
Blue or Roquefort						
100 gms. (3 1/2 oz.)	368	139	120	157	9	100
Brick						
100 gms. (3 1/2 oz.)	370	139	117	158	9	100
Camembert						
100 gms. (3 1/2 oz.)	299	112	102	132	9	100
Cheddar (American domestic)						
100 gms. (3 1/2 oz.)	398	143	118	158	9	100
Limburger						
100 gms. (3 1/2 oz.)	345	126	98	132	9	100
Parmesan						
100 gms. (3 1/2 oz.)	393	92	93	132	9	100
Swiss						
100 gms. (3 1/2 oz.)	370	117	95	132	9	100
Cheese, pasteurized						
American						
100 gms. (3 1/2 oz.)	370	134	95	132	9	100
Swiss						
100 gms. (3 1/2 oz.)	355	112	96	132	9	100
Cheese spread, American						
100 gms. (3 1/2 oz.)	288	87	103	132	9	100
Cream						
Half cream and half milk						
1 cup = 242 gms. (8 1/2 oz.)	363	111	56	128	7	97
Imitation sour						
from nonfat dry milk and						
vegetable oil						
1 cup = 235 gms. (8 1/4 oz.)	439	179	263	308	0	(14)
Light (coffee or table)						
1 cup = 240 gms. (8 1/2 oz.)	506	254	187	238	10	168
Sour						
1 cup = 230 gms. (8 oz.)	485	244	179	228	9	(218)
Whipped, in pressurized container						
1 cup = 60 gms. (2 oz.)	135	2	4	28	0	(25)
Whipping, light						
1 cup = 239 gms. (8 1/2 oz.)	717	406	289	361	17	(167)
Milk						
Cow's						
Whole (3.7%) fat						
1 cup = 244 gms. (8 1/2 oz.)	161	22	27	41	0	27
Canned, evaporated,						
unsweetened						
1 cup = 252 gms. (9 3/4 oz.)	345	53	55	88	0	(55)
Goat's						
Whole						
1 cup = 244 gms. (8 1/2 oz.)	164	29	27	44	0	(27)
Breads, rolls, and pastas						
Biscuits (Pillsbury fresh-dough						
products)						
Butter Tastin'						
100 gms. (3 1/2 oz.)	338	36	13	46	15	2
Flaky baking powder						
100 gms. (3 1/2 oz.)	331	33	11	44	14	3

TABLE XXIX (continued)

	TC	*Black Points*	*Red Points*	*Blue Points*	*Gold Points*	*Choles-terol Milli-grams*
Low-Cholesterol Foods, breads, rolls and pastas, biscuits (Pillsbury fresh-dough products)–continued						
Flaky buttermilk						
100 gms. (3 1/2 oz.)	347	45	15	50	16	4
Kentucky-style, light buttermilk						
100 gms. (3 1/2 oz.)	337	31	11	45	14	4
Rolls, dinner (Pillsbury fresh-dough products)						
Crescent						
1 roll = 28.6 gms. (1 oz.)	94	9	3	12	4	4
Rolls, sweet (Pillsbury fresh-dough products)						
Almond Danish						
100 gms. (3 1/2 oz.)	362	24	9	45	15	10
Caramel Danish						
1 roll = 43 gms. (1 1/2 oz.)	162	15	1	17	7	5
Cinnamon Danish						
100 gms. (3 1/2 oz.)	353	10	5	40	14	10
Cinnamon with icing						
1 roll = 34 gms. (1.2 oz.)	120	5	2	14	5	1
Orange Danish						
100 gms. (3 1/2 oz.)	354	16	6	41	14	10
Rolls, sweet bakery						
100 gms. (3 1/2 oz.)	422	64	21	63	18	70
Sauces and dressings						
Mayonnaise, Hellman's						
1 tbsp = 15 gms. (1/2 oz.)	108	67	6	16	48	8
Salad dressings, commercial						
Blue and Roquefort cheese						
Regular						
1 tbsp = 15 gms. (1/2 oz.)	76	43	7	15	33	4
Low-fat						
1 tbsp = 15 gms. (1/2 oz.)	11	4	3	4	0	(T)
Soup (Campbell soup company products)						
Heat-processed						
Asparagus, cream of						
100 gms. (3 1/2 oz.)	70	0	7	14	5	(1-6)
Celery, cream of						
100 gms. (3 1/2 oz.)	66	12	4	11	12	(1-6)
Cheddar cheese						
100 gms. (3 1/2 oz.)	125	25	17	29	17	(1-6)
Chicken, cream of						
100 gms. (3 1/2 oz.)	76	13	3	11	9	(1-6)
Chicken 'n Dumplings						
100 gms. (3 1/2 oz.)	83	14	2	10	12	(1-6)
Golden mushroom						
100 gms. (3 1/2 oz.)	70	7	4	11	5	(1-6)
Mushroom, cream of						
100 gms. (3 1/2 oz.)	115	38	14	26	30	1
Noodles and ground beef						
100 gms. (3 1/2 oz.)	80	5	6	14	1	(1-6)
Onion						
100 gms. (3 1/2 oz.)	37	0	1	5	0	(1-6)

TABLE XXIX (continued)

	TC	*Black Points*	*Red Points*	*Blue Points*	*Gold Points*	*Cholesterol Milligrams*
Low-Cholesterol Foods, soup (Campbell soup company products)						
Heat-processed–continued						
Oyster stew						
100 gms. (3 1/2 oz.)	57	9	11	17	0	(1-6)
Frozen						
Clam chowder (New England style)						
100 gms. (3 1/2 oz.)	108	20	15	26	11	(1-6)
Oyster stew						
100 gms. (3 1/2 oz.)	102	21	22	32	3	(1-6)
Potato, cream of						
100 gms. (3 1/2 oz.)	90	7	13	22	4	(1-6)
Shrimp, cream of						
100 gms. (3 1/2 oz.)	132	44	23	36	34	(1-6)
Fish and shellfish						
Bonito						
100 gms. (3 1/2 oz.)	168	7	2	19	22	70
Butterfish, Northern						
100 gms. (3 1/2 oz.)	169	33	10	27	30	70
Chub						
100 gms. (3 1/2 oz.)	145	29	8	23	26	70
Dogfish						
100 gms. (3 1/2 oz.)	156	26	8	23	26	70
Drum, fresh-water						
100 gms. (3 1/2 oz.)	121	5	14	14	15	70
Eel, smoked						
100 gms. (3 1/2 oz.)	330	135	24	57	45	70
Halibut, Greenland						
100 gms. (3 1/2 oz.)	146	25	7	22	25	34
Herring						
Atlantic						
100 gms. (3 1/2 oz.)	176	40	12	30	33	70
Pickled, Bismarck						
100 gms. (3 1/2 oz.)	223	58	17	39	31	70
Smoked, kippered						
100 gms. (3 1/2 oz.)	211	42	13	34	26	70
Mackerel						
Atlantic						
100 gms. (3 1/2 oz.)	191	43	23	42	32	70
Pacific						
100 gms. (3 1/2 oz.)	159	10	3	19	22	70
Smoked						
100 gms. (3 1/2 oz.)	219	40	12	34	38	70
Menhaden, Atlantic						
100 gms. (3 1/2 oz.)	172	32	20	39	27	70
Mullet						
100 gms. (3 1/2 oz.)	147	11	7	21	22	70
Sablefish						
100 gms. (3 1/2 oz.)	190	69	19	38	37	70
Salmon						
Canned						
Atlantic						
100 gms. (3 1/2 oz.)	203	40	12	32	36	65
Chinook (King)						
100 gms. (3 1/2 oz.)	210	53	14	35	26	70

TABLE XXIX (continued)

	TC	*Black Points*	*Red Points*	*Blue Points*	*Gold Points*	*Choles-terol Milli-grams*
Low-Cholesterol Foods, fish and shellfish, salmon, canned–continued						
Sockeye						
100 gms. (3 1/2 oz.)	171	24	7	24	28	70
Salmon						
Raw						
Atlantic						
100 gms. (3 1/2 oz.)	217	46	14	35	40	65
Chinook (King)						
100 gms. (3 1/2 oz.)	222	64	17	39	29	70
Smoked						
100 gms. (3 1/2 oz.)	176	23	7	24	28	70
Sardines						
In mustard, solids and liquid						
100 gms. (3 1/2 oz.)	196	40	12	32	36	70
In oil, drained solids						
100 gms. (3 1/2 oz.)	203	10	9	29	33	70
In tomato sauce, solids and liquid						
100 gms. (3 1/2 oz.)	197	42	12	32	36	70
Raw, Pacific						
100 gms. (3 1/2 oz.)	160	22	6	22	26	70
Shad						
100 gms. (3 1/2 oz.)	170	32	10	27	30	70
Spanish mackerel						
100 gms. (3 1/2 oz.)	177	32	9	27	31	70
Trout						
Lake						
100 gms. (3 1/2 oz.)	168	33	10	26	30	70
Rainbow						
100 gms. (3 1/2 oz.)	195	35	2	21	41	70
Poultry						
Chicken, fryer						
Flesh, skin, and giblets						
100 gms. (3 1/2 oz.)	124	1	2	14	9	60
Flesh and skin						
100 gms. (3 1/2 oz.)	126	2	2	15	9	60
Dark meat with skin						
100 gms. (3 1/2 oz.)	132	11	5	18	11	60
Back						
100 gms. (3 1/2 oz.)	157	32	12	27	17	60
Neck						
100 gms. (3 1/2 oz.)	151	32	12	27	17	60
Rib						
100 gms. (3 1/2 oz.)	124	5	3	15	9	60
Thigh						
100 gms. (3 1/2 oz.)	128	6	3	16	10	60
Wing						
100 gms. (3 1/2 oz.)	146	16	7	21	13	60
Chicken, roaster						
Flesh and skin						
100 gms. (3 1/2 oz.)	197	44	16	36	22	60
Chicken, hens and cocks						
Flesh and skin						
100 gms. (3 1/2 oz.)	251	82	29	54	33	60

TABLE XXIX (continued)

	TC	*Black Points*	*Red Points*	*Blue Points*	*Gold Points*	*Cholesterol Milligrams*
Low-Cholesterol Foods, poultry, chicken, hens and cocks—continued						
Flesh only						
100 gms. (3 1/2 oz.)	155	9	4	20	12	60
Chicken, capon						
Flesh and skin						
100 gms. (3 1/2 oz.)	291	89	31	61	37	60
Duck						
Domestic						
100 gms. (3 1/2 oz.)	326	144	43	75	53	60
Wild						
100 gms. (3 1/2 oz.)	233	61	18	41	30	60
Goose, domestic						
100 gms. (3 1/2 oz.)	354	160	47	83	59	60
Guinea hen						
100 gms. (3 1/2 oz.)	156	3	1	17	12	60
Turkey						
Young (24 weeks and under)						
Flesh and skin						
100 gms. (3 1/2 oz.)	151	14	4	20	14	60
Medium-fat (24 to 32 weeks)						
Flesh and skin						
100 gms. (3 1/2 oz.)	197	36	11	31	22	60
Fat (mature birds over 32 weeks)						
Total edible						
100 gms. (3 1/2 oz.)	343	144	43	77	55	60
Beef						
Chuck rib, 5th						
Choice						
Total edible						
100 gms. (3 1/2 oz.)	352	160	102	137	6	70
Separable lean						
100 gms. (3 1/2 oz.)	188	33	29	48	2	70
Good						
Total edible						
100 gms. (3 1/2 oz.)	303	122	81	111	5	70
Separable lean						
100 gms. (3 1/2 oz.)	163	15	18	35	1	70
Arm						
Choice						
Total edible						
100 gms. (3 1/2 oz.)	223	62	45	68	3	70
Good						
Total edible						
100 gms. (3 1/2 oz.)	191	38	32	51	2	70
Flank steak						
Choice						
100 gms. (3 1/2 oz.)	144	1	10	25	1	70
Hindshank						
Choice						
Total edible						
100 gms. (3 1/2 oz.)	289	110	73	102	4	70
Good						
Total edible						
100 gms. (3 1/2 oz.)	239	71	51	75	3	70

TABLE XXIX (continued)

	TC	*Black Points*	*Red Points*	*Blue Points*	*Gold Points*	*Cholesterol Milli-grams*
Low-Cholesterol Foods, beef–continued						
Porterhouse steak						
Choice						
Total edible						
100 gms. (3 1/2 oz.)	390	189	119	158	7	70
Separable lean						
100 gms. (3 1/2 oz.)	164	17	20	36	1	70
Good						
Total edible						
100 gms. (3 1/2 oz.)	370	176	111	148	6	70
T-bone steak						
Choice						
Total edible						
100 gms. (3 1/2 oz.)	397	215	122	162	7	70
Separable lean						
100 gms. (3 1/2 oz.)	164	16	20	36	1	70
Good						
Total edible						
100 gms. (3 1/2 oz.)	366	172	110	146	6	70
Separable lean						
100 gms. (3 1/2 oz.)	142	8	10	25	1	70
Club steak						
Choice						
Total edible						
100 gms. (3 1/2 oz.)	380	181	114	152	6	70
Separable lean						
100 gms. (3 1/2 oz.)	182	30	27	45	2	70
Good						
Total edible						
100 gms. (3 1/2 oz.)	324	138	90	122	5	70
Separable lean						
100 gms. (3 1/2 oz.)	158	12	17	33	1	70
Sirloin steak						
Wedge and round-bone						
Choice						
Total edible						
100 gms. (3 1/2 oz.)	313	131	86	117	5	70
Separable lean						
100 gms. (3 1/2 oz.)	143	1	11	25	1	70
Good						
Total edible						
100 gms. (3 1/2 oz.)	281	106	71	99	4	70
Double-bone						
Choice						
Total edible						
100 gms. (3 1/2 oz.)	333	146	94	127	5	70
Separable lean						
100 gms. (3 1/2 oz.)	158	12	16	32	1	70
Good						
Total edible						
100 gms. (3 1/2 oz.)	293	114	76	105	4	70
Hipbone						
Choice						
Total edible						
100 gms. (3 1/2 oz.)	412	206	129	170	7	70

TABLE XXIX (continued)

	TC	*Black Points*	*Red Points*	*Blue Points*	*Gold Points*	*Cholesterol Milligrams*
Low-Cholesterol Foods, beef, sirloin steak, hipbone, choice –continued						
Separable lean						
100 gms. (3 1/2 oz.)	179	26	25	43	2	70
Good						
Total edible						
100 gms. (3 1/2 oz.)	367	161	108	145	6	70
Separable lean						
100 gms. (3 1/2 oz.)	152	7	14	29	1	70
Short plate						
Choice						
Total edible						
100 gms. (3 1/2 oz.)	400	196	123	163	7	70
Separable lean						
100 gms. (3 1/2 oz.)	164	17	20	36	1	70
Good						
Total edible						
100 gms. (3 1/2 oz.)	356	164	104	140	6	70
Separable lean						
100 gms. (3 1/2 oz.)	146	3	12	26	1	70
Rib, 6th to 12th						
Choice						
Total edible						
100 gms. (3 1/2 oz.)	401	196	124	164	7	70
Separable lean						
100 gms. (3 1/2 oz.)	193	37	32	51	2	70
Round						
Choice						
Total edible						
100 gms. (3 1/2 oz.)	197	42	34	54	2	70
Rump						
Choice						
Total edible						
100 gms. (3 1/2 oz.)	303	122	81	111	5	70
Separable lean						
100 gms. (3 1/2 oz.)	158	12	17	32	1	70
Good						
Total edible						
100 gms. (3 1/2 oz.)	271	98	67	94	3	70
Hamburger (ground beef)						
Regular						
100 gms. (3 1/2 oz.)	268	97	66	93	4	70
Lean						
100 gms. (3 1/2 oz.)	179	29	27	45	2	70
Canned roast beef						
100 gms. (3 1/2 oz.)	224	38	33	56	2	70
Corned, boneless						
Uncooked medium-fat						
100 gms. (3 1/2 oz.)	293	123	80	109	4	70
Cooked medium-fat						
100 gms. (3 1/2 oz.)	263	70	52	79	3	70
Canned, lean						
100 gms. (3 1/2 oz.)	185	7	16	35	1	70
Canned, medium-fat						
100 gms. (3 1/2 oz.)	216	32	31	52	2	70

TABLE XXIX (continued)

	TC	Black Points	Red Points	Blue Points	Gold Points	Cholesterol Milligrams
Low-Cholesterol Foods, beef–continued						
Dried, chipped						
1/2 cup = 71 gms. (2 1/2 oz.)	144	10	5	20	1	50
Veal						
Chuck						
100 gms. (3 1/2 oz.)	173	30	25	42	3	90
Cutlet						
100 gms. (3 1/2 oz.)	185	33	17	38	2	90
Flank						
100 gms. (3 1/2 oz.)	314	134	84	115	7	90
Foreshank						
100 gms. (3 1/2 oz.)	156	18	18	34	2	90
Loin						
100 gms. (3 1/2 oz.)	181	36	28	46	3	90
Plate						
100 gms. (3 1/2 oz.)	231	73	49	72	5	90
Rib						
100 gms. (3 1/2 oz.)	207	54	38	59	4	90
Round with rump						
100 gms. (3 1/2 oz.)	164	24	22	38	2	90
Pork						
Uncured						
Boston butt						
Total edible						
100 gms. (3 1/2 oz.)	287	120	50	79	20	70
Separable lean						
100 gms. (3 1/2 oz.)	180	39	19	37	9	70
Ham						
Total edible						
100 gms. (3 1/2 oz.)	308	132	55	86	22	70
Separable lean						
100 gms. (3 1/2 oz.)	153	14	9	24	6	70
Loin						
Total edible						
100 gms. (3 1/2 oz.)	298	121	51	81	20	70
Separable lean						
100 gms. (3 1/2 oz.)	189	37	18	37	9	70
Picnic						
Total edible						
100 gms. (3 1/2 oz.)	290	122	51	223	20	70
Separable lean						
100 gms. (3 1/2 oz.)	150	14	9	24	6	70
Spareribs						
100 gms. (3 1/2 oz.)	361	173	72	108	27	70
Cured						
Bacon						
100 gms. (3 1/2 oz.)	665	392	159	225	56	70
Canadian						
100 gms. (3 1/2 oz.)	216	54	25	47	12	70
Canned						
100 gms. (3 1/2 oz.)	193	43	20	40	10	70
Salt pork						
100 gms. (3 1/2 oz.)	783	492	198	276	69	70

TABLE XXIX (continued)

	TC	*Black Points*	*Red Points*	*Blue Points*	*Gold Points*	*Cholesterol Milligrams*
Low-Cholesterol Foods, pork–continued						
Light-cured						
Boston butt						
Total edible						
100 gms. (3 1/2 oz.)	291	115	20	78	19	70
Separable lean						
100 gms. (3 1/2 oz.)	200	41	20	40	10	10
Ham						
Total edible						
100 gms. (3 1/2 oz.)	282	106	46	74	19	70
Separable lean						
100 gms. (3 1/2 oz.)	168	18	11	28	7	70
Picnic						
Total edible						
100 gms. (3 1/2 oz.)	285	113	48	77	19	70
Separable lean						
100 gms. (3 1/2 oz.)	167	17	11	27	7	70
Long-cured, country-style						
Ham						
100 gms. (3 1/2 oz.)	389	180	75	114	28	70
Lamb						
Choice						
Leg, total edible						
100 gms. (3 1/2 oz.)	222	68	37	82	4	70
Loin						
Total edible						
100 gms. (3 1/2 oz.)	293	121	97	126	7	70
Separable lean						
100 gms. (3 1/2 oz.)	138	5	16	30	2	70
Rib						
Total edible						
100 gms. (3 1/2 oz.)	339	155	118	152	8	70
Separable lean						
100 gms. (3 1/2 oz.)	158	20	27	43	2	70
Shoulder						
Total edible						
100 gms. (3 1/2 oz.)	281	118	93	121	6	70
Separable lean						
100 gms. (3 1/2 oz.)	148	18	24	39	2	70
Luncheon meats						
Blood sausage						
100 gms. (3 1/2 oz.)	394	195	80	120	23	(100)
Bockwurst						
100 gms. (3 1/2 oz.)	264	145	54	81	17	(100)
Bologna						
All samples						
100 gms. (3 1/2 oz.)	304	142	59	89	17	(100)
All-meat						
100 gms. (3 1/2 oz.)	277	109	46	74	14	(100)
With cereal						
100 gms. (3 1/2 oz.)	248	99	42	67	13	(100)
Frankfurters						
All samples						
100 gms. (3 1/2 oz.)	309	141	59	90	17	(100)

TABLE XXIX (continued)

	TC	*Black Points*	*Red Points*	*Blue Points*	*Gold Points*	*Choles-terol Milli-grams*
Low-Cholesterol Foods, luncheon meats, frankfurters–continued						
All-meat						
100 gms. (3 1/2 oz.)	296	126	53	83	16	(100)
With nonfat dry milk						
100 gms. (3 1/2 oz.)	300	126	53	86	16	(100)
With cereal						
100 gms. (3 1/2 oz.)	248	99	42	67	13	(100)
Liverwurst						
100 gms. (3 1/2 oz.)	307	65	31	62	12	(100)
Meat, potted						
100 gms. (3 1/2 oz.)	248	86	37	62	11	(100)
Salami						
100 gms. (3 1/2 oz.)	450	187	79	124	24	(100)
Sausage						
Country-style						
100 gms. (3 1/2 oz.)	345	160	64	99	27	(100)
Polish-style						
100 gms. (3 1/2 oz.)	304	126	54	84	16	(100)
Pork, links or bulk						
100 gms. (3 1/2 oz.)	498	284	112	162	45	(100)
Vienna, canned						
100 gms. (3 1/2 oz.)	240	95	40	64	12	(100)
Desserts						
Cake						
Cheese						
100 gms. (3 1/2 oz.)	262	41	49	75	3	68
Chocolate devil's food						
100 gms. (3 1/2 oz.)	366	27	44	81	9	76
Commercial devil's food with chocolate icing						
100 gms. (3 1/2 oz.)	380	25	43	81	9	63
Pound						
100 gms. (3 1/2 oz.)	411	24	4	45	9	99
Cookies						
Coconut macaroons						
100 gms. (3 1/2 oz.)	475	43	96	144	9	10
Pillsbury fresh-dough products						
Butterscotch nut						
100 gms. (3 1/2 oz.)	451	61	21	66	22	48
Chocolate chip						
1 cookie = 11 gms. (4/10 oz.)	47	4	2	6	2	6
Fudge brownies						
100 gms. (3 1/2 oz.)	389	8	4	43	14	49
Fudge nut						
100 gms. (3 1/2 oz.)	429	50	16	59	20	29
Oatmeal-raisin						
100 gms. (3 1/2 oz.)	413	22	9	50	17	29
Peanut butter						
100 gms. (3 1/2 oz.)	451	63	22	67	22	58
Sugar						
1 cookie = 12 gms. (4/10 oz.)	53	6	2	7	3	4
Ice cream						
1 cup = 133 gms. (4 5/8 oz.)	275	52	56	84	0	80

TABLE XXIX (continued)

	TC	*Black Points*	*Red Points*	*Blue Points*	*Gold Points*	*Choles-terol Milli-grams*
Low-Cholesterol Foods, desserts–continued						
Pie, baked						
Cream or chiffon						
100 gms. (3 1/2 oz.)	255	3	6	31	7	64
Custard						
100 gms. (3 1/2 oz.)	218	24	14	36	9	66
Fruit						
100 gms. (3 1/2 oz.)	256	11	1	27	9	8
Pumpkin						
100 gms. (3 1/2 oz.)	211	27	21	42	8	66
Pastries (Pillsbury fresh-dough products)						
Apple Coffeetime						
100 gms. (3 1/2 oz.)	366	8	4	41	14	13
Apple turnover						
1 = 50 gms. (1 3/4 oz.)	186	21	7	26	8	6
Blueberry turnover						
1 = 50 gms. (1 3/4 oz.)	172	30	10	27	9	6
Cherry Coffeetime						
100 gms. (3 1/2 oz.)	323	20	8	40	13	13
Cherry turnover						
1 = 50 gms. (3 1/2 oz.)	170	26	8	26	8	6
Puddings made with eggs						
1 cup = 240 gms. (8 3/8 oz.)	276	23	27	65	0	240
Candy						
Chocolate-coated						
Coconut bar						
100 gms. (3 1/2 oz.)	438	2	44	88	0	74
Peanuts						
100 gms. (3 1/2 oz.)	561	167	41	97	62	74
Raisins						
100 gms. (3 1/2 oz.)	425	1	45	88	0	74
Fudge with nuts						
100 gms. (3 1/2 oz.)	426	4	10	53	53	74
Peanut-butter hard candy						
100 gms. (3 1/2 oz.)	463	10	6	53	18	74
Sweet milk, plain						
100 gms. (3 1/2 oz.)	520	102	124	176	9	74
Hershey's						
Milk-chocolate bar						
100 gms. (3 1/2 oz.)	536	107	117	171	9	18
Milk-chocolate bar with almonds						
100 gms. (3 1/2 oz.)	543	133	112	166	10	16
Mr. Goodbar						
100 gms. (3 1/2 oz.)	539	135	86	140	45	10
Reese peanut-butter cup						
100 gms. (3 1/2 oz.)	503	92	58	108	43	9
Moderate-Cholesterol Foods (over 100 to 300 milligrams for 100 gms. [3 1/2 oz.])						
Dairy products						
Butter						
Stick = 1/2 cup = 113 gms. (4 oz.)	809	520	375	456	20	282

TABLE XXIX (continued)

	TC	*Black Points*	*Red Points*	*Blue Points*	*Gold Points*	*Choles-terol Milli-grams*
Moderate-Cholesterol Foods, dairy products, butter–continued						
1 tbsp = 14 gms. (1/2 oz.)	100	64	46	57	2	35
Cheese, natural						
Cream						
100 gms. (3 1/2 oz.)	374	200	147	185	9	120
Cream						
Whipping, heavy						
1 cup = 238 gms. (8 1/2 oz.)	838	493	357	440	26	(286)
Organ meats						
Heart						
Beef with visible fat						
100 gms. (3 1/2 oz.)	253	98	57	83	4	150
Beef, calf						
100 gms. (3 1/2 oz.)	124	10	11	24	1	150
Lamb						
100 gms. (3 1/2 oz.)	162	30	22	38	2	150
Sweetbreads						
Pancreas						
Beef, lean only						
100 gms. (3 1/2 oz.)	141	16	15	29	1	(250)
Beef, medium-fat						
100 gms. (3 1/2 oz.)	283	127	72	100	4	(250)
Calf						
100 gms. (3 1/2 oz.)	161	56	34	64	2	(250)
Hog						
100 gms. (3 1/2 oz.)	242	95	41	65	16	(250)
Thymus						
Beef, yearling						
100 gms. (3 1/2 oz.)	207	72	43	64	3	250
Lamb						
100 gms. (3 1/2 oz.)	94	1	10	19	1	250
Tongue						
Beef, medium-fat						
100 gms. (3 1/2 oz.)	207	62	39	60	3	(120)
Calf						
100 gms. (3 1/2 oz.)	130	2	8	21	1	(120)
Hog						
100 gms. (3 1/2 oz.)	215	66	38	50	13	(120)
Lamb						
100 gms. (3 1/2 oz.)	199	68	57	77	4	(120)
Canned or cured, all types						
100 gms. (3 1/2 oz.)	267	89	54	81	4	(120)
High-Cholesterol Foods (over 300 milligrams for 100 gms. [3 1/2 oz.])						
Dairy products						
Eggs, whole						
1 egg = 50 gms. (1 3/4 oz.)	81	23	10	18	4	275
Eggs, yolks						
1 yolk = 17 gms. (6/10 oz.)	59	26	9	15	3	255
Organ meats						
Brains						
100 gms. (3 1/2 oz.)	125	34	22	34	1	2000
Kidney						
Beef						
100 gms. (3 1/2 oz.)	130	20	46	26	1	375

TABLE XXIX (continued)

	TC	*Black Points*	*Red Points*	*Blue Points*	*Gold Points*	*Choles-terol Milli-grams*
High-Cholesterol Foods, organ meats, kidney–continued						
Calf						
100 gms. (3 1/2 oz.)	113	2	7	18	1	375
Recipes						
Meat						
Veal						
Recipe #232 Wiener Schnitzel	1178	74	110	228	12	540
Recipe #233 Braised Veal Steak with Mushrooms	1728	133	173	346	17	817
Recipe #234 Veal Fricassee Jardinière	1644	166	181	345	20	817
Recipe #235 Veal Birds	1613	172	184	345	18	828
Recipe #237 Veal Steak with Wine Sauce	2737	153	244	517	27	1225
Organ meats						
Recipe #259 Creamed Sweetbreads	1118	266	179	291	15	1146
Desserts						
Recipe #309 Chocolate Ice Cream	1657	288	84	250	361	4

A P P E N D I X

I N D E X

APPENDIX

How to Calculate Points

The point system used in this book was devised to provide an exchange list that could be used to meet the recommended objectives of the Inter-Society Commission for Heart Disease. If you know the food values of other foods you can calculate their point values. The method for calculation is as follows:

WHITE POINTS (for foods with 35.0 per cent or less of their calories as fat):

$$\frac{\text{Calorie value of food}}{100} \times (35.0\% - \text{percentage of calories as fat in the food item}) = \text{White Points.}$$

Note that a food item with exactly 35.0 per cent of its calories as fat will have zero white points. Foods high in calories and low in fat have the greatest number of white points. A low-calorie food, low in fat, will also have a low white-point value.

BLACK POINTS (for foods with more than 35.0 per cent of their calories as fat):

$$\frac{\text{Caloric value of food}}{100} \times (\text{percentage of calories as fat in the food item} - 35.0\%) = \text{Black Points.}$$

GREEN POINTS (for foods with 10.0 per cent or less of their calories as saturated fat):

$$\frac{\text{Caloric value of food}}{100} \times (10.0\% - \text{percentage of calories as saturated fat in the food item}) = \text{Green Points.}$$

RED POINTS (for foods with more than 10.0 per cent of their calories as saturated fat):

$$\frac{\text{Caloric value of food}}{100} \times (\text{percentage of calories as saturated fat in the food item} - 10.0\%) = \text{Red Points.}$$

BLUE POINTS: the calories in the food from saturated fat.
GOLD POINTS: the calories in the food from polyunsaturated fat.

How to Devise a New Food-Exchange List

If you need to reduce the percentage of calories from fat in your diet below the recommendations of the Inter-Society Commission for Heart Disease, you can use a formula similar to the one described above. Let us assume you wish to construct an exchange list limiting the fat intake to 25 per cent of the total calories. All you need to do to calculate white and black points is to substitute 25.0 for 35.0 in the two formulas. It is of course necessary to know the values of fat in calories. The formula for white points would be as follows:

$$\frac{\text{Calories in food}}{100} \times (25.0\% - \text{percentage of calories as fat in food item}) = \text{White Points.}$$

In a similar fashion you can calculate a new point system for saturated fat if you wish. The new value should be substituted for 10.0 to calculate green and red points.

How to Calculate Values for Recipes

Using the food-value tables in this book, you can calculate the values for any new recipe you wish to use. Unfortunately, not all foods have been analyzed for values, and recipes that contain such foods cannot be calculated. If you have values for a similar item you can sometimes estimate the values. To calculate the values for a recipe, proceed as follows:

1. List the amounts of all the ingredients in table form at the left side of your calculation sheet. The table should provide a space for the values of each item—TC, P, C, F, S, M, PU, and Chol.

2. Since your tables of values, except for the master exchange list (which is not used to calculate the values for recipes) are for 100-gram (3½-ounce) portions you may need to convert the values in the table. In the example recipe below for plain wheat cakes, Recipe #42, one cup of all-purpose wheat flour is used. Look at Table X and you will see that one cup of flour weighs 120 grams (listed in the left-hand margin). To convert the values in the table to the amount used in the recipe, multiply the values in the table by

$$\frac{\text{weight in grams of the amount of the ingredient used}}{\text{100 grams}}$$

In this instance the values are multiplied by 120/100. Table X shows that 100 grams of flour has 364 calories. The calories in one cup of flour are

$$364 \times 120/100, \text{ or } 437 \text{ calories.}$$

In a similar fashion the other values are calculated:
P = 40 × 120/100 = 48 calories.
C = 301 × 120/100 = 361 calories.
F = 8 × 120/100 = 10 calories.
S = 2 × 120/100 = 2 calories (to nearest whole number).
M = 3 × 120/100 = 3 calories.
PU = 4 × 120/100 = 5 calories.
Chol = 0 × 120/100 = 0 milligrams.
Salt has no caloric value and can be ignored.

For sugar look at Table III. A cup of sugar weighs 200 grams. Since a cup contains 48 teaspoons, one teaspoon of sugar weighs 200/48 grams, or 4.16 grams.

As Table III shows, 100 grams of sugar contains 385 calories (all carbohydrate), hence

$$4.16/100 \times 385 = 16 \text{ calories of carbohydrate.}$$

The values for the other ingredients are calculated and tabulated in the same way.

3. All the tabulated columns are then added to give the values for the entire recipe.

4. To determine the percentage of calories as fat, divide the total calories of fat by the total calories for the recipe and multiply by 100. In this example

$$\%F = 11/547 \times 100 = 2.0\%.$$

5. In a similar fashion

$$\%S = 2/547 \times 100 = 0.4\%$$
$$\%M = 3/547 \times 100 = 0.5\%$$
$$\%PU = 5/547 \times 100 = 0.9\%.$$

6. Now you have the total calories for the recipe and the percentage of calories from fat and saturated fat. This information enables you to calculate the white- and green-point values for the entire recipe, as follows:

$$547/100 \times (35.0 - 2.0) = 180 \text{ white points}$$
$$547/100 \times (10.0 - 0.4) = 53 \text{ green points.}$$

7. There are two blue points, or calories of saturated fat, and five gold points, or calories of polyunsaturated fat. The total cholesterol in the recipe is seven milligrams.

8. The tabulation of the recipe is as follows:

RECIPE #42 PLAIN WHEAT CAKES

	TC	P	C	F	S	M	PU	Chol
1 cup flour	437	48	361	10	2	3	5	0
½ tsp salt	0	0	0	0	0	0	0	0
1 tsp sugar	16	0	16	0	0	0	0	0
2 tsp baking powder	12	0	10	0	0	0	0	0
⅓ cup nonfat milk powder	82	35	46	1	0	0	0	7
TOTAL	547	83	433	11	2	3	5	7
Percentage				2.0	0.4	0.5	0.9	

White points	180
Green points	53
Blue points	2
Gold points	5

ACKNOWLEDGMENTS

No one can prepare a book of this nature without help, and I had a lot. The suggestion that I should prepare a book on food and its preparation for healthful living was first made to me by Beatrice Rosenfeld, Consulting Editor of The Viking Press, and I greatly appreciate her suggestions and encouragement during the project.

Finding facts supported with actual numbers concerning what food contains is not easy. There is lots of information but it is hard to compile it in a comprehensive, usable form. The best and most widely used source of actual numbers that I was able to find was Merrill, A. L., and Watt, B. K.: *Composition of Foods, Raw, Processed, Prepared, Agriculture Handbook No. 8,* Washington, D.C., 1963, from the U.S. Department of Agriculture. This book is used widely by the food industry and many companies provide samples of their products for analysis to provide the data.

Of the large number of bulletins on general food products provided by different governmental agencies two others were particularly useful; Goddard, V. R., and Goodall, L.: *Fatty Acids in Food Fats, Home Economics Research Report No. 7,* U.S. Department of Agriculture, and *Nutritional Value of Foods, Home and Garden Bulletin No. 72,* Revised 1971, U.S. Department of Agriculture.

Among the numerous values published in articles on nutrition, the one I used most often for general information, particularly for cholesterol content of foods, was, Fetcher, E. S.; Foster, N.; Anderson, J. T.; Grande, Francisco; and Keys, A.: "Quantitative Estimates of Diets to Control Serum Cholesterol," *The American Journal of Clinical Nutrition,* Volume 20, May 1967. Two other reports were helpful in providing information on meat: Kiernat, B. H.; Johnson, J. A.; and Siedler, A. J.: *A Summary of Nutrient Content of Meat, American Meat Institute Foundation Bulletin No. 57,* July 1964; and Tu, C.; Powrie, W. D.; and Fennema, O.: "Free and Esterified Cholesterol Content of Animal Muscles and Meat Products," *Journal of Food Science,* 1967.

After a long trail through the Department of Interior and the Department of Commerce my search was rewarded by the most recently available information on the composition of fish. In addition to the *U.S. Department of Agriculture Handbook No. 8,* for this information I relied most heavily upon the following publications:

Gruger, E. H., Jr.; Nelson, R. W.; and Stansby, M. E.: "Fatty Acid Composition of Oils from 21 Species of Marine Fish, Fresh-Water Fish and Shellfish," *Journal of the American Oil Chemists' Society,* Volume 41, No. 10, October 1964.

Stansby, M. E.: "Nutritional Properties of Fish Oils," *World Review of Nutrition and Dietetics,* Volume 11, 1969.

Stansby, M. E., and Hall, A. S.: *Chemical Composition of Commercially Important Fish of the United States, FIR Reprint 47,* from *Fishery Industrial Research,* Volume 3, No. 4, March 1967.

Thompson, M. H.: *Cholesterol Content of Various Species of Shellfish 1. Method of Analysis and Preliminary Survey of Variables,* reprint from U.S. Fish and Wildlife Service, Bureau of Commercial Fisheries, *Industrial Research,* Volume 2, No. 3, and personal communication.

Although numerous cookbooks were used in reviewing cooking methods and searching for different recipes that could be modified for diets to restrict fat and cholesterol, three were used as basic source books. These or similar books can be used in conjunction with the methods described here to meet dietary objectives and still enjoy a wide variety of different foods adequate for the most discriminating palate. The three sound basic books which I recommend to anyone are

Berolzheimer, Ruth: *The American Woman's Cook Book,* Garden City Publishing Co. Inc., Garden City, New York, 1967.

Berolzheimer, Ruth: *Culinary Arts Institute Encyclopedic Cookbook,* Culinary Arts Institute, Chicago, distributed by Grosset and Dunlap, New York, 1968.

Heseltine, Marjorie, and Dow, Ula M.: *The Revised Basic Cookbook,* Houghton Mifflin Company, Boston, 1967.

There are several publications that provide information on the history of food. The most recent and most helpful one in preparing this book was Trager, James: *The Food Book,* Grossman, New York, 1970. This book is delightfully written as well as a storehouse of interesting and important information.

Books to help people better understand food and how to prepare diets for health are not new. Particularly helpful in providing information on methods of preparation was one of the earliest and best by Dobbin, E. Virginia; Gofman, Helen F.; Jones, Helen C.; Lyon, Lenore; and Young, Clara-Beth: *The Low-Fat Low-Cholesterol Diet,* Doubleday and Company, Inc., New York, 1951.

I am appreciative of the response from many segments of the food industry. I wrote to most of the major companies and most of them were helpful in providing specific analysis of their products and enthusiastic about the concept of preparing such a book. This information was correlated and checked against the *Agriculture Handbook No. 8* and other material. When the products' values were found to agree well with the sources, the *Handbook* values were used. For products that were distinctly different or unique brand-name identification has been used. Various government agencies and associations also were most helpful in providing information for the project. Among these I would like particularly to thank

American Bakeries Company
American Heart Association
American Meat Institute Foundation
Campbell Soup Company
Carnation Company
Chicago Dietetic Supply, Inc.
CPC International Inc. Best Foods
Del Monte Corporation
Dr. Pepper Company
Dole Company
The R. T. French Company
Frito-Lay, Inc.
General Foods Kitchens
General Mills, Inc.
Green Giant Company
Hershey Foods Corporation
Hunt-Wesson Foods, Inc.
Kellogg Company
Libby, McNeill and Libby
National Fisheries Institute, Inc.
National Live Stock and Meat Board
The Pillsbury Company
The Quaker Oats Company
Royal Crown Cola Co.
The Seven Up Company
Shasta Beverages of Consolidated Foods Corporation
The J. M. Smucker Co.
Standard Brands Inc.
Standard Fruit and Steamship Company
Tillie Lewis Foods, Inc.
Tootsie Roll Industries, Inc.
United Fruit Company
U.S. Department of Agriculture, Agricultural Research Service, Consumer and Food Economics Research Division
U.S. Department of Commerce, National Oceanic and Atmospheric Administration, National Marine Fisheries Service
U.S. Department of Health, Education and Welfare, Public Health Service, Food and Drug Administration
U.S. Department of the Interior, Bureau of Commercial Fisheries

Other organizations provided help in locating information or the source of information. Some portions of the food industry were unable to help at this time for a variety of reasons, the most commonly stated being the lack of sufficiently detailed information needed for this book.

Mr. Ralph M. Jackson, for many years a superb technician in my laboratories and now at the Texas Children's Hospital in Houston, Texas, sketched Figure 1 for the book.

While no special testing was needed for many items, such as a green salad or standard pie recipe after the pie-crust recipe was proved to be satisfactory, many others did require testing. Many of these were tested by Mrs. Lee Ann Werner, then processed by the little Werners and her husband, Robert. I would like to thank Robert Werner also for helping with part of the calculations.

Last, but by no means least, I want to express my thanks to Mr. Russell Oppenheim and Joyce Boston, as well as the staff of the San Antonio office of Manpower, Inc., for a major assist on calculations necessary for the tables and recipes, as well as the typing and preparation of the manuscript. The detailed tables and typing presented a major task and they did it admirably.

INDEX

A

Abbreviations, used in food-value tables, 283
Adrenal gland, 27
Adrenalin, 274
Alcohol, 25, 26, 252–54
American Diabetic Association, 23*n.*
American Heart Association, 23*n.*, 27, 208
Amino acids, 20, 262; essential, 20, 21, 262
Anchovies, 137
Anemia, 43
Angel-food cake, 221, 227; chocolate, 227–228
Angel ginger cake, 222
Appetizers, 241, 244, 245, 246, 247
Apple griddle cakes, 74–75
Apple meringue pudding, 129
Apple-nut salad, 133
Apple pie, 214–15
Apple pudding, steamed, 211
Apples, 126; baked, 127–28; baked stuffed, 128
Applesauce, 127
Applesauce-spice cookies, 230
Arroz con carne español, 187
Arteries, fatty deposits in, 4, 5, 6, 7, 10, 264, 271, 272, 273, 277
Artificial sweetener, 208, 258
Ascorbic acid, *see* Vitamin C
Asparagus, protein in, 21
Asparagus casserole, 116–17
Asparagus cheese sauce, 85
Asparagus salad and chicken, 143
Atherosclerosis, 4, 5, 7, 21, 25, 26, 37, 253
Avocados, 126, 136, 245

B

Bacon, 195, 245; calories in, 10, 11, 16, 195; Canadian, 195, 273; water content of, 11
Baked apples, 127–28
Baked beans, Boston, 117
Baked chicken Orleans, 171
Baked fish fillets, 149
Baked fish steaks with sauce, 148
Baked heart, 202
Baked meringue frosting, 228
Baked onions, stuffed, 121–22
Baked rhubarb, 130
Baked smoked ham, 199
Baked stuffed apples, 128
Baked tomatoes, 124
Baked whole fish, 147; with sauce, 148
Baking, at high altitude, 41
Baking-powder biscuits, 66; nonfat, 68
Banana bread, 63–64
Banana-date bread, 64
Banana griddle cakes, 74
Banana-nut bread, 64
Banana-nut cookies, 232–33
Banana pie, uncooked, 219
Bananas, 126, 127; maple, 129
Barbecue sauce, 86–87
Barbecued lamb, 200
Barbecued poultry, 165
Barley, 42, 45
Basal metabolism, 14
Bass, 145
Basting, defined, 39
Beans, 117; Boston baked, 117; calories in, 113; cooked dried, 124–25; iron in, 33, 34, 262; lima, 112, 117; protein in, 21, 113, 262
Beef, 177–79; boiled, 183–85; calories in, 178, 179; consumption of, in United States, 177–78; corned, 178, 184; iron in, 34; protein in, 44; roast, 181–83
Beef bouillon, 101
Beef brisket with sauerkraut, 185
Beef burger, 186, 249
Beef curry deluxe, 188
Beef meat loaf, 186
Beef sandwiches, 249

Beef shish kebab, 189
Beef stew with red wine, 182–83
Beef stroganoff, 189
Beets, 137; Harvard, 118; in orange sauce, 118; spiced, 119
Beriberi, 30
Berries, 126, 127
Bile, 26
Biscuits, 66–69
Black-bean soup, 112
Blackberry pie, 217; uncooked, 218
Black-cherry wine gelatin, 132
Black-walnut ice cream, 240
Black walnuts, 243
Blancmange, 209, 213
Blood pressure, high, 5, 7, 13, 276
Blood sugar, 274, 275
Blueberry griddle cakes, 74
Blueberry muffins, 70; nonfat, 71
Blueberry pie, 217–18
Boiled beef and vegetables, 183–84
Boiled chicken, 168–69
Boiled pork, 198
Boiled tongue, 204
Boiled vegetables, 114–25
Boiling, as low-fat cooking method, 40
Bologna, 201
Boston baked beans, 117
Boston brown bread, 64–65
Bouillon, 38, 99, 100, 101, 116, 257; beef or ham, 101
Brain, as organ meat, 27, 201, 202, 270
Brain disease, 5
Braised veal steak with mushrooms, 191–92
Braising, defined, 40
Brandy sauce, 98
Bread sticks, 241
Bread stuffing, all-purpose, 175
Breading, 39
Breads, 55–60, 241; quick, 63–66
Breakfast, 271–73
Brisket, beef, with sauerkraut, 185
Broccoli, protein in, 21
Broccoli casserole, 119–20
Broiled chicken legs, 247
Broiled eggplant, 120
Broiled fish, 149
Broiled fish fillets, 150
Broiled oysters, 156
Broiled poultry, 164
Broiled round steak, 180
Broiled scallops, 159
Broiled shrimp, breaded, 158
Broiled sweetbreads, 205
Broiling, as low-fat cooking method, 40
Brownies, 234
Browning, 39
Brown-sugar rolls, 63
Buckwheat, 45
Buckwheat cakes, 75
Bulgar wheat, 45
Butter, 23, 37, 47, 48, 147; calories in, 48; cholesterol in, 48; vitamin A in, 28
Buttermilk, 51

C

Cabbage: red, 137; vitamin K in, 29
Caffein, 254, 255, 256, 257, 258
Cakes, 220–28
Calcium, 32, 56, 262; daily requirement of, 32; in milk, 32, 49, 50
Calf heart, 202; baked, 202; sautéed, 202–203
Calories, 12; in alcohol, 25, 252–53; in bacon, 10, 11, 16, 195; in beans, 113; in beef, 178, 179; in butter, 48; and carbohydrates, daily requirement of, 20; in cereals, 43–44; counting, 263–64; defined, 11; and EE unit, 15; in eggs, 47; in fats, 10, 22, 48; in fish, 145; in fruits, 126; in ice cream, 236–37; in lard, 11, 195; in milk, whole, 50; number of, for basal metabolism, 14; in nuts, 243; in pork, 194; in poultry, 161; used in walking, 14–15
Cancer: of colon, 4, 8; of lung, 8; of rectum, 4, 8; of skin, 8
Cantaloupes, 126
Caramel ice cream, 240
Caramel sauce, 97
Carbohydrates, 17–20, 275; limitation of, 277–78; processed, 18; *see also* Starch; Sugar
Carbonated beverages, 257–58
Carrots, 137; vitamin A in, 28
Casabas, 126
Casseroles, 116–17, 119–20, 155, 167
Celery sauce, 85
Cellulose, 11
Cereals, calories in, 43–44
Cheddar cheese, 20–21
Cheese, 49, 53–54; calcium in, 54; cheddar, 20–21; chive, 242; cottage, creamed, 54; cottage, uncreamed, 11, 21, 30, 38, 50, 54, 242, 250, 262; cream, 250; French dressing with, 90; protein in, 54; vitamin A in, 28

Cheese dips, 242, 245
Cheese sauce, 82; asparagus, 85; tomato, 83
Cheese spreads, 242, 243
Cheese variation of vegetable soup, 111
Cherry pie, 216–17; fresh, 216
Chicken, 160, 161, 270; à la king, 173; and asparagus salad, 143; baked, 171; boiled, 168–69; broiled, 164; espagnole, 169; fryer, 21, 31, 161, 163, 167, 247, 249; and ham salad, 144; Newburg, 172; with rice, 170; and sauce, 172–73; sautéed, 165; smothered, 166; smothered with sweet potatoes, 166–67; and sphaghetti, 170–71; stewed, 167–74; in wine, 171–172
Chicken appetizers, 247
Chicken curry, quick, 174
Chicken liver, 247
Chicken-mushroom casserole, 167
Chicken pot pie, 173–74
Chicken salad, 143
Chicken-salad ham roll, 247
Chicken sandwiches, 249
Chicken soup, cream of, 111–12
Chicken stock, 101–102
Chiffonade salad dressing, 93
Chili con carne, 185
Chips, potato, 241, 242
Chive cheese, 242
Chives, 38, 54
Chocolate, 208, 256
Chocolate angel-food cake, 227–28
Chocolate-chip cookies, 232
Chocolate devil's-food cake, 221
Chocolate frosting, 229
Chocolate ice cream, 239–40
Chocolate nut kisses, 235
Cholesterol, 4, 7, 26–27; in common foods, 27; and Food-Exchange Table, 261; levels of, types of, 277, 278; limitation of, 27, 270, 277
Chowders, 104–109, 154–55
Cigarettes, 6, 25; *see also* Smoking
Cinnamon rolls, 62–63
Cinnamon toast, 76; creamed, 76
Clam chowder, 154–55
Clam-corn-pimiento casserole, 155
Clams, 147
Clearing stock, 102–103
Coagulation, blood, 29
Coca-Cola, 257
Cocaine, 257
Cocktail sauce: fruit, 96; seafood, 95
Cocoa, 255–56; hot, 256
Cocoa drop cookies, 231
Coconut: saturated fat in, 243; shredded, 208
Coconut oil, 23, 52, 89, 208
Codfish, 145, 249
Coffee, 254–55
Cold cuts, 201, 245, 250
Cole slaw, 142–43
Commercial dehydrated salad dressing, low-calorie, 89
Compote, hot fruit, 130–31
Consommé, 99
Constipation, 4, 8
Cookies, 230–36
Cooking: double-boiler, 114; of grains, 45; at high altitude, 41; low-fat, *see* Low-fat cooking; waterless, 114
Copper, 32
Corn, 113, 116, 262
Corn and potato chowder, 107
Corn and tomato chowder, 106
Corn bread, 65–66
Corn chowder, 105–106
Corn oil, 23, 78, 89, 136, 207
Corned beef, 178, 184
Corned beef and cabbage, 184
Corned-beef boil, 184
Corn-sirup spicecake, 224
Cornstarch sauce, 96–97
Cottage cheese: creamed, 54; uncreamed, 11, 21, 30, 38, 50, 54, 242, 250, 262
Cottage-cheese salads, 134–35
Cottage-cheese sandwiches, 250
Council on Foods and Nutrition of American Medical Association, 23*n*.
Crab-flake salad, 140
Crabs, 146, 244
Crayfish, 146
Cream, 51
Cream cheese, 250
Cream of chicken soup, 111–12
Cream of salmon soup, 110
Creamed cinnamon toast, 76
Creamed cottage cheese, 54
Creamed sweetbreads, 205
Creamed vegetable soup, 110–11
Creole sauce, Spanish, 86
Crescents, 61
Croquettes, fish, 151
Croutons, 76
Curry powder, 116, 277
Curry sauce, 86
Cypriots, longevity of, 49

D

Date bread, 65
Date-nut bread, 65
Dehydrated salad dressing, low-calorie commercial, 89
Department of Agriculture Handbook No. 8, 27, 283
Dessert sauces, 95–98
Deviled eggs, 244
Devil's-food cake, chocolate, 221
Dextrine, 37
Diabetes, 6, 7, 13, 27, 273, 274, 275, 282
Diarrhea, 28, 49
Diet: balanced, when to begin, 278; and Food-Exchange Table, 260–61; foods for balanced, 262–63; and improvement of polyunsaturated-to-saturated fat ratio, 266; planning, 259–78; and salt restriction, 274, 276, 277; special medical considerations in, 273–78; *see also* Cholesterol
Dips, 242, 244, 245; do's and don'ts of, 242
Double-boiler cooking, 114
"Dredging," 39
Dressings, salad, 78, 89–95
Dried beans, cooked, 124–25
Drop biscuits, 67; nonfat, 68
Drop cookies: basic, 230–31; cocoa, 231
Drumfish, 145, 147
Dry-roasted poultry, 161–64
Ducks, 160

E

EE (exercise equivalent), 15, 16, 18, 25
Egg sandwiches, 250
Egg white: in appetizers, 244; in cakes, 220; in nonfat cooking, 36; protein in, 21, 47; in puddings, 209; riboflavin in, 30; as thickening agent, 37; in tossed salad, 137
Egg yolk: calories in, 47; cholesterol in, 27, 46, 47, 208, 244, 270; iron in, 34; vitamin A in, 28
Eggplant: broiled, 120; stuffed, 120
Eggstra, 81*n.*, 270
English muffins, 61–62
English pudding, 211–12
English walnuts, 243
Enzymes, 32
Essential amino acids, 20, 21, 262
Exercise, 15, 16
Exercise equivalent (EE), 15, 16, 18, 19, 25

F

Fats, 21–25, 262, 275; calories in, 10, 22, 48; daily requirement for, 22; limiting intake of, 264–65; metabolism of, 277, 278; monounsaturated, 23, 25, 179; polyunsaturated, 23, 25, 42, 48, 136, 139, 146, 262; saturated, *see* Saturated fats; unsaturated, 22, 23; vitamins soluble in, 22
Filet mignon, 179
Fillets, fish, *see* Fish fillets
Fish, 21, 28, 145–54, 244, 276; baked, 147–48; broiled, 149; calcium in, 33; calories in, 145; pan-broiled, 150; in parchment, 152; polyunsaturated fats in, 139, 146; protein in, 138, 146; sautéed, 152; scalloped, 152–53; steamed, 151–152; vitamins in, 29, 30, 31; *see also* Seafood; Shellfish
Fish and potato chowder, 108
Fish croquettes, 151
Fish fillets: baked, 149; broiled, 150; Florentine, 148; poached in white-wine sauce, 151
Fish flour, 33
Fish loaf, 149
Fish oil, 146
Fish relish, 79
Fish salads, 138–40
Fish sandwiches, 249
Fish sauce, 79
Fish steaks, 150
Fish stock, 102
Flank steak, 178, 179
Flavoring agents, 37, 38
Flounder, 249, 270
Food and Drug Administration, 23*n.*
Food-Exchange Table, 260–61, 267, 271, 282
Food-value tables, use of, 281–84
Freezer, home, 237
French dressing: with cheese, 90; with horseradish, 90–91; with lemon, 91; with mustard, 91; nonfat, 89–90; polyunsaturated-fat, 90
Fricasseeing, defined, 40
Frostings, 228, 229
Fruit cocktail sauce, 96

Fruit compote, hot, 130–31
Fruit salads, 137, 138; fruits used in, 138
Fruit sauce, 98
Fruit snow, 128–29
Fruit sponge, 133
Fruits, 126–27; calories in, 126
Fryer chickens, 21, 31, 161, 163, 167, 247, 249
Frying, in low-fat cooking, 40

G

Galactose, 49, 54
Gangrene, 5
Garlic, 38
Gelatin, 21, 36, 37, 209, 213, 257; black-cherry wine, 132
Gelatin supreme, strawberry, 132
Gingerbread cake, 225–26
Gingersnaps, 234–35
Glazed pork and sweet potatoes, 197–98
Glazes, 88–89
Glucose, 17, 27, 49, 54
Gluten bread: high-protein, 59; kneaded, 59–60
Goose, 161
Gravies, 78–81
Green beans, ham with, 198
Green pea soup, 104
Green peppers: and steak, 188; stuffed, 187
Griddle cakes, 74–75
Grilled sweet potatoes, 123
Guinea hens, 163

H

Haddock, 145, 270
Ham, 194, 195, 198, 246; baked smoked, 199; and chicken salad, 144; with green beans, 198
Ham-and-cheese roll, 246–47
Ham-and-chicken salad, 144
Ham bouillon, 101
Ham glaze, 88
Ham loaf, 199
Ham sandwiches, 250
Hamburger, 178, 245, 249
Harvard beets, 118
Heart, as organ meat, 202–203
Heart attack, 4, 5, 6, 7, 25, 26, 37, 254
Heart disease, 4, 5, 6, 8, 18, 21, 25, 26, 30, 43, 49, 52, 253, 255, 276
Herbs, 37, 38
Heredity, 6
Herring, pickled, 244
High blood pressure, 5, 7, 13, 276
Honey, 19; sweet potatoes in, 123
Honey cake, 224–25
Honeydews, 126
Hopkins, Frederick, 43
Hormones, 27; female, 4, 26, 177
Hors d'oeuvres, 241, 243, 247
Horseradish creamy dressing, 94–95
Hydrogenation, 23, 48
Hyperlipidemia, 278
Hypoglycemia, 274, 275, 276

I

Ice cream, 36, 236–40; calories in, 236–37
Ice milk, 237
Icings, 228, 229
Insulin, 273, 274, 275
Intelligence, influenced by food, 8
Inter-Society Commission for Heart Disease, 22, 25, 27, 47, 146–47, 202, 265, 269, 270, 277
Iodine, 274
Iron, 32, 33, 43; daily requirement of, 33; food sources of, 33–34

J

Jam sandwiches, 251
Jellied stock, 103
Jello, 209
Jelly sandwiches, 251

K

Kidney, as organ meat, 206
Kidney disease, 276
Kitchen timer, 36

L

Lactase, 49
Lactose, 49, 50, 54, 262
Lamb, 199–201; barbecued, 200; roast leg of, 201
Lamb glaze, 88
Lamb stew, 200–201

Lard, calories in, 11, 195
Lecithin, as coating for cooking utensils, 39
Lima-bean casserole, 117
Lima-bean soup, 112
Linoleic acid, 23
Lipoproteins, 4
Liquor sauce, 98
Liver: bile formed by, 26; as organ meat, 27, 30, 34, 203, 270; riboflavin in, 30; vitamin A stored in, 28
Liver disease, 29, 33, 253, 276
Lobster sauce, 85
Lobsters, 146, 147, 243–44
Longevity, 8, 9; of Cypriots, 49
Low blood sugar, 274, 275, 276
Low-fat cooking, 35–41; methods of, 39–41; utensils for, 38–39
Low-fat white bread, 57; high-protein, 58
Luncheon meats, 201
Lung cancer, 8

M

Magee, Sylvester, 8
Magnesium, 32
Maple bananas, 129
Maple pudding, 209
Maple sauce, 96
Maple-sugar biscuits, 69; nonfat, 69
Maple-walnut pudding, 209–10
Marble cake, 226
Margarine, 23, 47, 48, 73, 116, 147, 248, 270; calories in, 48
Marshmallow sauce, 97
Marshmallow sweet potatoes, 123
Mashed potatoes, 122
Mashed sweet potatoes, 124
Master Food-Exchange List, 260–61, 267, 271, 282
Mayonnaise: nonfat, 36, 38, 78, 91–92, 116, 138, 248, 249, 250; sherry, 93
Mayonnaise salads, 135
Measurements, household, 281–82
Meat loaf, beef, 186
Melons, 126, 127
Menu-planning, daily, 267–69
Meringue cookies, 236
Meringue frosting, 228
Meringue pudding, apple, 129
Metabolism, basal, 14
Mile-equivalent factor, and body weight, 15
Milk, 18, 49; butterfat in, 49, 50; calcium in, 32, 49, 50; calories in whole, 50; enriched, 43; protein in, 49; reconstituted, 51; riboflavin in, 30; skim, 21, 54, 237, 262, 264, 270, 272; whole, 20, 44, 49–50
Milk gravy, 80
Milk powder, nonfat, 33, 36, 45, 50–51, 56, 237, 262, 272
Milk-simmered vegetables, 116
Milk toast, 77
Millet, 45
Milligram, defined, 26
Minerals, 32–34
Molasses, blackstrap, 19, 34
Molasses cookies, 233–34
Molasses-fruit pudding, 212
Muffins, 61–62, 69–72; nonfat, 71
Muscle atrophy, 30
Mushroom sauce, 84
Mushrooms: au gratin, 121; braised veal steak with, 191–92
Mustard, 91, 248, 249

N

Navy soup, 112
Neuritis, 30
Newburg, chicken, 172
Newburg sauce, 81, 147
Niacin (nicotinic acid), 31; daily requirement of, 31; deficiency of, 31
Nuts, 243

O

Oatmeal, 44
Obesity, 6, 7, 10, 13, 14, 21, 276; childhood, 14; prevention of, 15, 16, 265; and sugar, 19
Okra and tomatoes, 121
Old age, 5, 8
Oleic acid, 23
Olive oil, 89
Olives, 126, 136–37, 245
Onions: baked stuffed, 121–22; and liver, 203
Orange biscuits, 67; nonfat, 68
Orange cake, 223
Orange sauce, beets in, 118
Orange tea cake, 223–24

Oranges, 126
Organ meats, 27, 30, 34, 201–206
Osteoporosis, 32
Oyster sauce, 84
Oyster stew, 109
Oysters, 146, 244; à la king, 156; broiled, 156

P

Pan-broiled fish, 150
Pan-broiled poultry, 165
Pan-broiled scallops, 158
Pan-broiling, as low-fat cooking method, 40
Pan gravy, 79–80
Pancakes, 72–73; toppings for, 73
Pancreas, 274
Paprika, 39
Parboiled sweetbreads, 204
Pea and salmon chowder, 109
Pea soup, green, 104
Peach ice cream, 240
Peach pie, 215–16; fresh, 215
Peach pineapple pyramid, 131
Peaches, 126; in meringue, 131
Peanut-butter sandwiches, 250
Pears, 127
Pecan muffins, 71
Pectin, 37
Pellagra, 31
Peppermint icing, 228
Peppers, green, *see* Green peppers
Peptic ulcer, 254, 255
Pheasants, 163
Pie crust, 213, 214
Pies, 213–20; cream filling for, 220
Pimiento-cheese spread, 242
Pimientos, 137, 139
Pineapple-peach pyramid, 131
Pineapple-seafood salad, 140
Polyunsaturated-fat French dressing, 90
Popcorn, 243
Pork, 194–99; boiled, 198; calories in, 194; glazed, and sweet potatoes, 197–98; roast, *see* Roast pork
Pork fat: calories in, 10; water content of, 11
Pork steaks with grape apples, 195–96
Pork tenderloin, 195
Porterhouse steak, 179
Pot roast, 182
Potassium, 32, 126, 276
Potato and corn chowder, 107
Potato and fish chowder, 108
Potato chips, 241, 242
Potato salad, 141
Potatoes: mashed, 122; scalloped, 122; sweet, *see* Sweet potatoes
Poultry, 160–76; barbecued, 165; broiled, 164; calories in, 161; dry-roasted, 161–164; pan-broiled, 165; sautéed, 165–67; *see also* Chicken; Turkey
Poultry breast, roasted, 164
Proteins, 20–21, 262, 275, 276; sources of, 20–21, 44, 54, 55
Prunes, 126
Puddings, 129, 208–13
Pumpkin pie, 219–20
Pyridoxine (vitamin B_6), 31

Q

Quail, 163
Quick breads, 63–66
Quick chicken curry, 174

R

Radishes, 137
Raisin muffins, 72
Raisins, 126
Red cabbage, 137
Redfish, 145, 147
Rennet, 53, 54
Rhubarb: baked, 130; stewed, 130
Riboflavin, *see* Vitamin B_2
Rice, 18, 30, 42, 44, 45; brown, 45; chicken with, 170; converted, 45; enriched, 43, 44; puffed, 44, 45
Rice pudding, 210
Rickets, 29, 50
Roast beef, 181–83
Roast leg of lamb, 201
Roast pork, 196; spicy sauce for, 196; and sweet potatoes, 197
Roast veal, 192
Roasting, as low-fat cooking method, 40
Roll glaze, 60
Rolls: dinner, 60–62; sweet, 62–63
Round steak, 178, 179, 245, 249, 263; broiled, 180
Russian dressing, 92
Rye bread, 55, 58

S

Saccharometer, 41
Safflower oil, 23, 78, 89, 136, 207
Salad dressings, 78, 89–95
Salad fillings for sandwiches, 249
Salads: cottage-cheese, 134–35; fish, 138–140; fruit, *see* Fruit salads; mayonnaise, 135; melon, 137, 138; potato, 141; tossed, *see* Tossed salads; vegetable, non-leafy, 140–43
Salmon, 139, 146, 244, 276
Salmon and pea chowder, 109
Salmon salad, 139
Salmon soup, cream of, 110
Salmon stew, 154
Salt: iodized, 274; restriction of, 274, 276, 277; substitutes for, 276
Sandwiches, 248–51
Sardines, 244
Saturated fats, 22, 23, 25, 26, 32, 48; limiting intake of, 265–66
Sauces, 36, 37, 38, 78, 81–87; dessert, 95–98
Sauerkraut, beef brisket with, 185
Sausage, 201, 245
Sautéed chicken, 165
Sautéed fish, 152
Sautéed heart, 202–203
Sautéed liver, 203
Sautéed poultry, 165–67
Sautéed sweetbreads, 205
Sautéing, defined, 40
Scalloped fish, 152–53
Scalloped potatoes, 122
Scalloped tuna and peas, 153–54
Scallops, 146, 244; broiled, 159; pan-broiled, 158
Scurvy, 31, 43
Seafood, 25, 145; *see also* Fish; Shellfish
Seafood cocktail sauce, 95
Seafood-pineapple salad, 140
Seeds, sunflower, 243
Senility, 4, 5, 8
Shellfish, 18, 27, 138, 139, 145, 146, 147, 244; cholesterol in, 146–47, 243–44; protein in, 244; *see also* Fish; Seafood
Sherry mayonnaise, 93
Shish kebab, 189; miniature, 246
Shrimp, 145, 146, 243; à la king, 157; broiled breaded, 158; Creole, 157; curry, 157
Shrimp-salad dressing, 92–93
Shrimp sauce, 84
Silver cake, 221–22
Sirloin steak, 178, 179
Sirup, 19, 73, 257
Skim milk, 21, 54, 237, 262, 264, 270, 272
Skin cancer, 8
Smoking, 6, 8, 25
Smörgåsbord, 241, 247
Snapper, 270
Soda-pop, 257
Sodium, 32, 126, 274, 276
Sole, 270
Sole amandine, 150
Soubise sauce, 83
Soups, 99, 100, 103, 104–12
Sour-cream substitute, 53
Soybean oil, 89
Soybeans, 21
Spaghetti and chicken, 170–71
Spaghetti sauce, 87
Spanish Creole sauce, 86
Spicecake, corn-sirup, 224
Spices, 37, 38, 47, 137, 277
Spinach: iron in, 34; protein in, 21; vitamin A in, 28; vitamin K in, 29
Spleen, as organ meat, 206
Spread: pimiento-cheese, 242; tomato-cheese, 243
Squash, vitamin A in, 28
Starch, 17, 18, 36–37; composition of, 17; *see also* Carbohydrates
Steak, 179; fat in, 20; flank, 178, 179; and green peppers, 188; niacin in, 31; porter-house, 179; round, *see* Round steak; sirloin, 178, 179; Swiss, 180; T-bone, 179, 264, 266; veal, with wine sauce, 193; water content of, 11
Steak tidbits, 245–46
Steamed apple pudding, 211
Steamed fish, 151–52
Steaming, as low-fat cooking method, 40
Stew: beef, with red wine, 182–83; lamb, 200–201; oyster, 109; salmon, 154
Stewed chicken, 167–74
Stewed rhubarb, 130
Stewing, as low-fat cooking method, 40–41
Stock: chicken, 101–102; clearing, 102–103; fish, 102; jellied, 103
Strawberry gelatin supreme, 132
Stress, 6, 26
Stroganoff, beef, 189
Stroke, 4, 5, 6, 7, 21
Stuffings, 175–76; ingredients and seasonings for, 176

Sugar, 18; calories in, 11, 15, 18; composition of, 17; increased consumption of, 18; and obesity, 19; as possible factor in heart and vascular disease, 18; refined, 18; substitutes for, 19; *see also* Carbohydrates
Sugar-tolerance test, 275
Sunflower seeds, 243
Sweet-cream substitute, 52
Sweet potatoes: chicken smothered with, 166–67; and glazed pork, 197–98; grilled, 123; in honey, 123; marshmallow, 123; mashed, 124; and roast pork, 197; vitamin A in, 28
Sweetbreads, 204–205
Sweetener, artificial, 208, 258
Swiss steak, 180
Symbols, used in food-value tables, 283

T

Tartare sauce, 38, 94, 248
T-bone steak, 179, 264, 266
Tea, 255
Tea cake, orange, 223–24
Teflon, 38, 39
Theophylline, 255
Thiamine, *see* Vitamin B_1
Thousand Island dressing, 93–94
Timer, kitchen, 36
Toast, 76–77
Toast sticks, 76
Tomato and corn chowder, 106
Tomato aspic, 142
Tomato-boat salad, 141
Tomato-cheese sauce, 83
Tomato-cheese spread, 243
Tomato chowder, 104–105
Tomato cream sauce, 83
Tomatoes: baked, 124; and okra, 121; vitamins in, 29, 262
Tongue, boiled, 204
Toppings for pancakes and waffles, 73
Tossed salads, 135–37; ingredients of, 136
Transparent glaze, 88–89
Triglycerides, 4, 146
Trout, 145
Tuna, 139, 244; scalloped, and peas, 153–154
Tuna roll, 153
Turkey, 160, 161, 163, 270; broiled, 164; sautéed, 165

U

Ulcer, peptic, 254, 255

V

Vanilla, 38, 73
Vanilla ice cream, 238–39; polyunsaturated, 238
Vanilla wafers, 233
Vascular disease, 6, 8, 18, 26, 49, 52
Veal, 190–94; roast, 192
Veal birds, 192
Veal fricassee jardinière, 191–92
Veal scallopine Napoli, 193–94
Veal steak: braised, with mushrooms, 191–192; with wine sauce, 193
Vegetable chowder, mixed, 110–11
Vegetable salads, non-leafy, 140–43
Vegetable soup: cheese variation of, 111; creamed, 110–11; variety, 103
Vegetables: for appetizers, 245; boiled, 114–25; and boiled beef, 183–84; free from cholesterol, 113; list of, and approximate cooking time, 115; milk-simmered, 116
Vitamin A, 28, 50, 262; daily requirement of, 28; deficiency of, 28; functions of, 28; soluble in fat, 22, 28; toxicity of, 28
Vitamin B_1 (thiamine), 30, 43; daily requirement of, 30
Vitamin B_2 (riboflavin), 30; daily requirement of, 30
Vitamin B_6 (pyridoxine), 31
Vitamin C (ascorbic acid), 31–32, 257, 262; daily requirement of, 31
Vitamin D, 29, 50; daily requirement of, 29; soluble in fat, 22
Vitamin E, 29, 262; soluble in fat, 22
Vitamin K, 29

W

Wafers, vanilla, 233
Waffles, 72–73, 75; toppings for, 73
Walnuts, 243
Water content in food, 11
Watermelons, 126
Weight, 13, 14; EE converted to values for, 15
Wheat, 42
Wheat cakes, plain, 73–74

Wheat germ, 30, 45
Whipped-cream substitute, 52
White bread, 55; enriched, 31, 43; low-fat, *see* Low-fat white bread; sugar-free, 58
White cake, 225
White fish, 139
White icing, 229
White sauce, 82
Whole-wheat biscuits, 67; nonfat, 69
Whole-wheat bread, 55, 58
Whole-wheat muffins, 72
Wiener schnitzel, 190
Wild rice, 45
Wild-rice stuffing, 175
Wine, 25, 55, 95, 252, 253; beef stew with, 182–83; chicken in, 171–72
Wine gravy, 80–81
Worcestershire sauce, 116, 179, 245

Y

Yeast, 55, 56
Yogurt, 54

Z

Zinc, 32